The Hidden Adult

The Hidden Adult

Defining Children's Literature

PERRY NODELMAN

The Johns Hopkins University Press
Baltimore

© 2008 The Johns Hopkins University Press
All rights reserved. Published 2008
Printed in the United States of America on acid-free paper

2 4 6 8 9 7 5 3

The Johns Hopkins University Press
2715 North Charles Street
Baltimore, Maryland 21218-4363
www.press.jhu.edu

Library of Congress Cataloging-in-Publication Data
Nodelman, Perry.
The hidden adult : defining children's literature / Perry Nodelman.
p. cm.
Includes bibliographical references and index.
ISBN-13: 978-0-8018-8979-0 (hardcover : alk. paper)
ISBN-13: 978-0-8018-8980-6 (pbk. : alk. paper)
ISBN-10: 0-8018-8979-0 (hardcover : alk. paper)
ISBN-10: 0-8018-8980-4 (pbk. : alk. paper)
1. Children's literature—History and criticism. 2. Children—Books and reading.
I. Title.
Z1037.A1N625 2008
028.5'5—dc22   2007049673

A catalog record for this book is available from the British Library.

*Special discounts are available for bulk purchases of this book. For more information,
please contact Special Sales at 410-516-6936 or specialsales@press.jhu.edu.*

The Johns Hopkins University Press uses environmentally friendly book
materials, including recycled text paper that is composed of at least 30 percent
post-consumer waste, whenever possible. All of our book papers are acid-free,
and our jackets and covers are printed on paper with recycled content.

The little child is supposed to be pure and innocent. . . . The children alone take no part in this convention; they assert their animal nature naively enough and demonstrate persistently that they have yet to learn their "purity."

—*Sigmund Freud*, A General Introduction to Psychoanalysis

In reality, childhood is deep and rich. It's vital, mysterious, and profound. I remember my *own* childhood vividly. . . . I knew terrible things . . . but I knew I mustn't let adults *know* I knew. . . . It would scare them.

—*Maurice Sendak, in Art Spiegelman's* In the Dumps

CONTENTS

Nationality 287 / The Genre in the Field 305 / Distinctive Texts in the Genre 315 / Conclusion: Children's Literature as Nonadult? 338

I thank Jayne Hildebrand for her careful work on the manuscript of this book. Jayne's work was funded by Mavis Reimer, Canada Research Chair in the Culture of Childhood, and the Centre for Research in Young People's Texts and Culture at the University of Winnipeg. The University of Winnipeg also supported my own work on the book by means of a number of study leaves. Leslie McGrath, head of the Osborne Collection of Early Children's Books at the Toronto Public Library, provided me with information. My thanks also to Joe Abbott for his careful work as manuscript editor.

I have been thinking about the matters I discuss in this book for some decades and have presented earlier versions of aspects of them in *Children's Literature Association Quarterly, Children's Literature, The Lion and the Unicorn, CCL/LCJ: Canadian Children's Literature/Littérature canadienne pour la jeunesse, CREArTA, Studies in the Literary Imagination, Children's Literature in Education,* and the *Journal of Children's Literature;* in my earlier books, *Words about Pictures: The Narrative Art of Children's Picture Books* and, in collaboration with Mavis Reimer, the third edition of *The Pleasure of Children's Literature;* in papers presented at conferences of the Children's Literature Association, the Modern Language Association, the National Centre for Research in Children's Literature at Reading University, and the Linguistic Circle of Manitoba and North Dakota; and in keynote addresses at conferences of the International Research Society for Children's Literature in Stockholm, the Children's Book Council of Australia in Canberra, the Australasian Children's Literature Association for Research in Sydney, the Center for the Study of Children's Literature at Simmons College in Boston, the conference on Modern Critical Approaches to Children's Literature in Nashville, the Center for Børnelitteratur in Copenhagen, and the Minnesota Conference on Cultural Emblematics at the University of Minnesota in Minneapolis. My thanks to the editors of these journals, the publishers of the books, and the sponsors of the conferences for the opportunity to test my ideas and converse with others about them.

I learned a great deal about the field of children's literature and the publishing industry from my agents and editors, Shelley Tanaka, David Gale, George Nicholson, Peter Atwood, and David Bennett and, especially, from my collaborator in writing children's fiction, Carol Matas. I learned much about literature generally from my teachers, particularly Walter Swayze, Gerry Bedford, Alice Hamilton, William Clyde DeVane, and Dwight Culler; from my colleagues in the University of Winnipeg English department; and from the students I taught at the university between 1968 and 2005. I learned (and am still learning) about children's literature criticism through conversations with many friends and colleagues in the field, among them Margaret Esmonde, Patricia Dooley, Joan Blos, Susan Gannon, Anita Moss, Virginia Wolf, Lois Kuznets, Jon Stott, Jon Cech, Rod McGillis, Mike Steig, Adrienne Kertzer, Eliza Dresang, Mary Rubio, Marie Davis, Ben Lefebvre, Peter Hunt, Lissa Pauls, Torben Weinreich, Maria Nikolajeva, John Stephens, Pam McIntyre, Alice Mills, Rosemary Johnston, Clare Bradford, Thomas Travisano, Margaret Higonnet, Elizabeth Keyser, Gillian Adams, June Cummins, Karen Coats, Mike Cadden, Anne Rusnak, Charlie Peters, and Rebecca Rabinowitz. I have also learned much from conversation on Childlit, the listserv devoted to questions of children's literature and literary theory, and from my interactions with contributors to the journals I have edited: *Children's Literature Association Quarterly* and *CCL/LCJ: Canadian Children's Literature/Littérature canadienne pour la jeunesse.* I have especially benefited from lengthy conversations over many years about all aspects of literature and education with my friends and collaborators Kay Unruh DesRoches, Jill May, and Mavis Reimer, and with my wife, Billie, and my children, Josh, Asa, and Alice.

The Hidden Adult

CHAPTER ONE

Six Texts

Different Texts, Same Genre

Consider the following narratives:

• In Maria Edgeworth's "The Purple Jar," which first appeared in 1801, young Rosamond, out walking with her mother, sees a beautiful purple jar in a chemist's window. Given the choice by her mother, Rosamond buys the jar instead of the new pair of shoes she needs. She quickly discovers that the purple color disappears once the jar is empty, and her slipshod shoes cause her to suffer from sore feet and missed expeditions for some weeks.

• In Lewis Carroll's *Alice's Adventures in Wonderland*, first published in 1865, a young girl having a boring summer day falls down a rabbit hole, finds herself growing larger and smaller as she ingests various substances, and has a series of encounters with various talking animals, insects, and people.

• In Hugh Lofting's 1920 novel *Dr. Dolittle* a bachelor doctor who likes animals more than people gives up his human medical practice, fills his house with animals, and learns their language. His medical abilities become known to animals worldwide, and he is called to Africa to deal with a group of sick monkeys. After a series of adventures in which various kinds of animals help him to escape from serious troubles caused by bad human beings, Dr. Dolittle returns home happy and wealthy.

• In the first chapter of Beverly Cleary's *Henry Huggins*, first published in 1950, a boy finds a dog he names Ribsy and then tries to bring Ribsy home on the bus, with unsettling results. In later episodes Henry has to deal with rapidly multiplying guppies, earn enough money to pay a friend for the loss of his football, cope with an embarrassing appearance in a school play, prepare Ribsy for a dog show, and undergo the reappearance of Ribsy's original owner. In all these stories Ribsy complicates Henry's life but also makes it more interesting.

• In Ezra Jack Keats's 1962 picture book *The Snowy Day* young Peter awakes to find that snow has fallen, discovers a variety of ways to play in the snow, then tries to bring a snowball indoors. After it melts, he feels sad, but he awakes next morning to find newly fallen snow that he and a friend can enjoy.

• In Virginia Hamilton's 1993 novel *Plain City* twelve-year-old Buhlaire feels alone in her community because of her unusual appearance—her skin is golden orange rather than brown like her schoolmates—and the oddity of her family, which includes a mother who sings and strips in nightclubs and a number of aunts and uncles who all live with her and apart from everyone else, in houses on stilts in the river valley. She fights with a boy who teases her at school but follows her on her wandering expeditions without ever actually letting himself be seen. After wandering out of town during a whiteout, Buhlaire is rescued by a homeless man who turns out to be the father she had been told was dead. He is mentally ill and erratic. Buhlaire comes to accept him, plans to run off with him, and then realizes that she cannot. In realizing this, she comes to a new understanding and acceptance of herself and the rest of the family.

This diverse group of texts was published in two different countries over a period spanning almost two centuries. *Alice's Adventures in Wonderland* is a fantasy in which animals talk, and so is *The Story of Dr. Dolittle;* but *Plain City* is a realistic portrayal of fairly ordinary human life, as is *Henry Huggins*. Edgeworth, Carroll, and Lofting were writers from the British Isles, and their books have English settings and protagonists. The settings and protagonists of American writers Keats, Cleary, and Hamilton are American. But despite their many differences, all six texts do have one thing in common: most people would identify them as "children's literature."

Their provenance as such is clear. *Early Lessons,* the name of the book in which "The Purple Jar" first appeared, clearly identifies its audience as young children in need of education. As Mitzi Myers suggests in her own discussion of the story, "If my readers know any of Edgeworth's tales for youngsters, it is surely 'The Purple Jar.' Famous, or notorious, as an example of the Georgian didactic tale, this story is the only one of Edgeworth's discussed in any depth in the standard histories of children's literature."[1] Lewis Carroll first made up the story of *Alice's Adventures in Wonderland* for a group of three young sisters, and the published book was then marketed for a general audience of children. *The Story of Dr. Dolittle* is dedicated "To all children / Children in years and children in heart," and my copy of it is a paperback in the Dell Yearling series—a series marketed to those purchasing books for child readers.[2] My copy of *Henry Huggins* is also a Dell Yearling; its back cover quotes reviews from *Parents' Magazine* and *Elementary English* and specifies a reading level of 4.9, presumably that of children in the fourth grade. As a short, brightly colored book with pictures filling almost every page and very few words, *The Snowy Day* clearly announces its intended audience of young children to anyone even moderately familiar with children's literature. Finally, *Plain City* is published by Scholastic, a company that focuses exclusively on books for child and adolescent readers, and its author is widely known and respected as a writer of fiction for those readers. Not surprisingly, the names of all six writers appear in Peter Hunt's *Children's Literature: An Illustrated History* and in the *International Companion Encyclopedia of Children's Literature,* edited by Hunt; all but Edgeworth appear in two reference volumes focused on more contemporary writing, *Twentieth Century Children's Writers,* edited by D. L. Kirkpatrick, and *Children's Books and Their Creators,* edited by Anita Silvey; and all but the currently neglected Lofting are mentioned in the recent *Norton Anthology of Children's Literature,* edited by Jack Zipes and other prominent scholars of children's literature, which actually includes a picture from *The Snowy Day,* a later story about Rosamond by Edgeworth, and a later story about Henry Huggins's friend Ramona by Cleary. Anyone with much knowledge of children's literature would recognize these writers as significant contributors to writing for the young and these texts as fairly representative examples of that writing.

It might seem surprising that texts so diverse could so easily share the same label or fit into the same category. Do they have anything in common?

They do. Each of them—and most of the other texts identified as "children's literature"—is included in this category by virtue of what the category implies, not so much about the text itself as about its intended audience. This in itself makes the term highly unusual as a category of literature. *Victorian literature* or *women's literature,* for instance, are terms that refer to the writers of the texts more than to their audiences—and while Victorian literature was all written by Victorians, and most women's literature is written by women, few children write the literature published professionally as "children's literature." This is not to say that children do not write fiction and poetry, and I will have more to say about the relationship between that writing and the texts that adults produce for children later. But generally, throughout this book, I use the phrase "children's literature" to refer to the body of texts, like these six, produced by professional publishing houses: writing for young people by adults.

The only other literary category identifier I can think of that defines an audience rather than a time or a place or a specific type of writing like romance or tragedy is what is often called "popular literature"—texts like the novels of Stephen King and Danielle Steel. Such texts can be conceived of as "popular" primarily because they are, or at least are intended to be, widely and popularly read. Not surprisingly, there are scholars of children's literature who wish to perceive it in the same way, to say that children's literature is not defined by specific literary characteristics. Just as popular literature is whatever is popular with a lot of readers, children's literature is whatever literature children happen to read. From this point of view, the identification of the six texts I listed above as children's literature does not necessarily mean they have anything in common with each other. It merely means that certain groups of children do or did once read them. Any differences among the texts can be accounted for by differences in the children.

But for someone who hopes, as I do, to develop useful knowledge of how literature does or might operate as an adult practice with intentions toward child readers, claiming that anything any child ever reads is children's literature is a seriously counterproductive move. It means simply that all texts, from Milton's *Paradise Lost* to the Marquis de Sade's *Justine,* are or might be children's literature. It prevents any development of understanding of what adults most often mean— what has most cultural power—when they use the phrase "children's literature." It is that sort of understanding I propose to try to develop here.

There is, however, some logic to the idea that children's literature consists of what children actually read—at least in terms of the intention of its producers. As workers in a field of economic production, writers and publishers are unlikely ever to produce texts of children's literature without wishing for audiences of children to read them or, at least, have them available to read—and presumably, the more children, the better. From this point of view, children's literature is much like popular literature or like the books that Pierre Bourdieu identifies as "middle-brow literature": "these works are entirely defined by their public. Thus, the very ambiguity of any definition of the 'average public' or the 'average viewer' very realistically designates the field of potential action which producers of this type of art and culture *explicitly* assign themselves, and which determines their technical and aesthetic choices."[3] Just as "middlebrow literature" might be defined as those texts produced in the hope of appealing to a middlebrow audience, children's literature might be defined as those texts produced in the hope of attracting an audience of children. Children's literature is not so much what children read as what producers hope children will read.

This is not exactly true, however. The actual purchasers of children's books are and always have been, overwhelmingly, not children but parents, teachers, librarians: adults. That this is the case seems part of the same cultural phenomenon that leads adults to write and publish the books to begin with—the conviction that children need things done for them by adults. In terms of success in production, what children actually want to read or do end up reading is of less significance than what adult teachers, librarians, and parents will be willing to purchase for them to read.

Nevertheless, these adults make their purchases on the basis of their ideas about what the children they purchase for like to and need to read—so it is those ideas that writers must appeal to in order to be successful. This makes the production of children's literature a more complex variation of the situation of "middlebrow literature" as Bourdieu outlines it. Its producers must make judgments about what to produce based not on what they believe will appeal to children but rather on what they believe adult consumers believe they know will appeal to children (or perhaps, what should appeal to them, or what they need to be taught).

With both popular literature and children's literature, however, success (popularity with the group in question) confirms the rightness of the producer's judgments about what the audience likes or needs and will purchase. Whether or not the texts satisfy existing taste or shape those tastes, it is the judgments of the producers that engender the texts, not the actual characteristics of the audiences. In other words, the characteristics of both popular literature and children's literature relate most centrally not to the actual characteristics of their intended audiences but to the ideas that producers and consumers have about those audiences: what constitutes and satisfies popular or middlebrow taste in one case, what children might like to read or be able to read or need to read—what children are—in the other. Whether or not child readers do match how adults think about them, the children in the phrase "children's literature" are most usefully understood as the child readers that writers, responding to the assumptions of adult purchasers, imagine and imply in their works.

Similarly, I believe, the "young adults" in the phrase "literature for young adults" are most usefully seen as the adolescent readers that writers, responding to the assumptions of adult purchasers, imagine and imply in their works. In both cases the intended audiences of the texts are defined by their presumed inability to produce such books or make such decisions about purchases of books for themselves—an inability accounted for in both cases by their being younger and therefore less experienced or capable than those who do these things for them. The six texts I have described were all written or published with the idea that their main readers would be children or teenagers and the conviction that the youthfulness of these readers would influence what they might like to or be able to or need to read. The texts all address young readers in terms that make their youth a matter of significance. For this reason literature for young adults (*Plain City*, for instance) can usefully be considered alongside literature for younger children in a book like this one. When I refer to "children's literature" in this book, consequently, I include both children's literature and literature for young adults. I will say more later about how legitimate this conjoining might be and about how these two kinds of texts for young people might be similar to and different from each other.

For, of course, they are different. As I suggested above, the foundational assumptions about youthfulness that all texts of children's and young-adult literature share also account for their differences from each other. While each has an audience defined as younger than its writer, the audiences do differ from each other. The shape and format of *The Snowy Day* tells anyone familiar with books that it is intended primarily to be read to very young nonreaders by adults or read by only slightly less young beginning readers. Meanwhile, the shape and format of the edition of *Plain City* I discuss here—the typical size, shape, and shiny cover of a mass-market paperback—suggests an audience of older children and young adults. Assuming that three- or four-year-old readers have little in common with twelve- and thirteen-year-olds, no one should find anything surprising about how different *Plain City* is from *The Snowy Day*.

Nor should it be surprising that *The Snowy Day* is so different from "The Purple Jar." They were published 162 years apart, in different countries; one is about a white English girl, the other about an African American boy. If nation or time or assumptions about gender have any influence on people's views of such matters, then the ideas about what children are and how they should be addressed that helped to shape these texts are bound to vary. They have certainly varied in the years between the publication of "The Purple Jar" and the publication of *The Snowy Day*. The "children" implied as the audience for these texts of "children's literature" are not necessarily the same or even similar children. The fact that "children's literature" is defined primarily by its adult purchasers' ideas about its child audience implies that the literature will change as conceptions of the audience change. And, of course, conceptions do change, not just from century to century, or from one country to another, but also as the "children" being implied vary in age or gender. The uniformity implied by the shared label is, apparently, illusory.

For this reason most recent scholarly discussion of children's literature focuses on the specific characteristics of texts produced in specific times or places or by specific groups of people. As their titles suggest, texts like Andrew O'Malley's *The Making of the Modern Child: Children's Literature and Childhood in the Late Eighteenth Century* or Beverly Clark's *Kiddie Lit: The Cultural Construction of Children's Literature in America* or Clare Bradford's *Reading Race: Aboriginality in Aus-*

tralian Children's Literature focus on how cultural and ideological forces at work in specific milieus interweave to produce for children texts with distinct characteristics, characteristics they tend to share with others produced in the same time or place or by the same group of people but not necessarily with other texts for children.

As the critical works I have mentioned also make clear, such a focus can be intensely revealing, and I can only echo what Fredric Jameson urges at the beginning of *The Political Unconscious*: "Always historicize!"[4] Readers can develop the most specific and detailed understandings of texts and their significance by being aware of the historic forces that produced them. But paying attention exclusively to the distinguishing details of a particular time or place and neglecting to notice more broadly based forces that might still be operating may well lead readers to miss important aspects of the history they wish to understand. Underlying the differences in ideas about young people that produce different texts in different times and places and for different specific audiences, there might be a current of sameness, a consistent sense of how young human beings differ from older ones, that underlies even apparently quite different texts. There might be something worth noticing and thinking about shared by a large proportion of the texts produced specifically for children in the times and places such literature has been produced—perhaps something that emerges from the very idea that such texts ought to exist. It is that possibility I intend to explore here.

I want to do so because, as I first read each of the six texts listed above, I found myself in what felt like familiar territory. Almost immediately, I identified them as texts intended for young readers. I did so, I believe, not just because I approached them from contexts that gave them that label and provided them with that provenance. There was something about the texts themselves, some feeling or quality, that not only told me that each of them was children's literature but that also made them seem somehow similar to each other. What follows is a report of my explorations of these six texts and my responses to them as I reread them in order to try to define what I was sensing. Why did such diverse texts seem to me to have so much in common? What were the common qualities?

To try to learn these things, my plan was to read and think about the six texts as intensively as I could, trying to pay close attention to any and all of the details I noticed in my reading. In doing this, of course, I was operating in terms of the reading and interpretive practices I have learned as a reader and scholar. For instance, I began my thinking about the texts by considering what I could discover of their qualities in terms of specific categories of texts that I have been encouraged to pay attention to: style, plot, character, and so on. Since my choosing to approach the texts in this way obviously influenced what I experienced of them, I will explore the implications and the potential benefits and limitations of my reading practices in the next chapter.

Language: The Text and Its Shadows

The first thing that struck me as I began to reread "The Purple Jar" was the simplicity of its diction and the straightforward nature of its style. There is minimal description of people or places and a fairly consistent focus on actions—on what people say and do rather than on detailed descriptions of where they do it or of what they feel or think about as they do it. The first sentence signals what follows: "Rosamond, a little girl about seven years old, was walking with her mother in the streets of London."[5] Beyond the fact of Rosamond's age, which, I assume, readers need to know because it implies some characteristic aspects of her behavior, there is no information here about what she looks like or acts like—and later, readers can know what she thinks mainly through her conversation and what she does in terms of quick general summations of her actions. This simplicity of style and focus on action is the first and most obvious marker that a text might be intended for an audience of children. C. S. Lewis, author of the Narnia series, once famously wrote that he was attracted to writing children's books because "this form permits, or compels, one to leave out things I wanted to leave out. It compels one to throw all the force of the book into what was done and said."[6]

Much less is said in the opening sentence of "The Purple Jar" than might be said. To me, the few simple words seem to hint at an unspoken complexity that I might notice were I an actual observer of the scene being so minimally described, so I understand their simple directness as a clever way of suggesting that I ought as a reader to think past the straightforward view of things they describe. The simple text implies an unspoken and much more complex repertoire that amounts to a second, hidden text—what I will call a "shadow text."

I have to wonder, of course, if a child reader would be equally aware of this shadow text. The obvious answer to that question seems to be "No." The reason for the simplicity is the author's assumption about the limited abilities of the implied audience. Wouldn't that mean that child readers see no more than the simple words actually say?

But perhaps agreeing that this is so is just accepting a stereotypical view of children's limited abilities—and in any case logic suggests that to some degree, at least, they must see more than the few words say. That Rosamond is seven or that she walks in a street with her mother is uselessly indigestible information unless, as response theorists like Wolfgang Iser suggest, a reader can extrapolate more complex information by referring to a "repertoire" of knowledge already possessed: what it means for someone to be seven, what it is like to be in a street and walking, what behavior may typically be expected of such a person in such a situation.[7] Without that knowledge, the simplicity of Edgeworth's prose becomes merely opaque and confusing. It seems that the simple mechanics of comprehension, including the requisite context of knowledge required to make meaning of the necessarily limited and always knowledge-evoking information of any text, make every text simpler than the complex world of the shadow text it evokes. In the pronounced simplicity of its diction, writing for children is merely a pronounced case of an inevitable situation.

It is quite possible that a reader younger or less experienced than I might not be so consciously aware of how the text says less than needs to be known or as prone as I am to enjoy that awareness and see it as a main reason for the pleasure I take in a story like "The Purple Jar." But the simplicity of such a story does require that a reader have more knowledge than it actually contains within itself in order to make something like the implied sense out of it. I have to suspect that this is a facet of all writing for children. The simpler it is, then the more obviously will it say less than it hints at, demand an implied reader who knows more—and therefore, the more likely it will be that child readers who can make sense of it will understand more than is actually said.

Henry Huggins is equally straightforward and short on detail—and equally inviting of a reader with more knowledge than it actually does itself provide. Its first paragraph offers some specific and relatively complicated details about Henry: "His hair looked like a scrubbing brush and most of his grown-up front teeth were in. He lived with his mother and father in a square white house on Klickitat Street."[8] These details tell me something larger and more abstract than they actually say. As I approach them in terms of my repertoire of previous reading and TV viewing, they seem to have been carefully chosen to make Henry representative rather than unique—a "typical" boy of his age and time. A reader who knows how to make sense of the presence of a brush cut, an incomplete set of teeth, and a square white house will understand that Henry is a sort of stereotype of a 1950s middle-class suburban Everyboy—a version of TV's Beaver Cleaver. Such a reader will be ready to think about Henry's behavior as described in the story that follows in terms of a conventional set of assumptions about normalcy and boyishness and what about them is to be expected and allowable or even delightful.

Once more, however, I have to ask if a child reader would be likely to generalize Henry's typical boyishness from the few specific details actually provided. Whether or not any particular child would, it is clear that the text implies and invites a reader capable of making this move into its shadow text. It says much less than it implies.

A somewhat different sort of repertoire demands an even more complex response from knowledgeable readers of the simple opening words of *The Story of Doctor Dolittle:* "Once upon a time." These familiar words suggest that the story will be a certain kind of story, a kind that makes specific demands on readers. It will be a fairy tale—the kind of story that, in the popular imagination, always begins with exactly these words. In such a story things will happen that do not usually happen in the world that we recognize as real. For a knowledgeable reader—and surely most European and North American children in Lofting's time and many still now would possess this particular bit of repertoire—the shadow accompanying this text will include a set of realizations about ways in which the events the text describes as happening do and do not mirror the actual possibilities of reality.

As in traditional fairy tales, meanwhile—and as in "The Purple Jar" and *Henry Huggins*—description in *The Story of Dr. Dolittle* is minimal. The text often contains passages that quickly sum up a series of complex actions in fairly vague terms. For instance, it skims over the details of a series of encounters the doctor has with a variety of different kinds of animals in one quick phrase: "After a while, with the parrot's help, the Doctor got to learn the language of the animals. . . . Then he gave up being a people's doctor altogether" (10). It also tends to sum up a series of similar occasions in just one general statement, for instance, "soon it became a common sight" (13). The focus is on what happened and what it then led to, not on what it looked like or felt like as it was happening—on actions and consequences rather than on the detailed textures of felt experience.

The very short text of *The Snowy Day* is even simpler and more focused on the broad outlines of actions. It begins, "One winter morning Peter woke up and looked out the window. Snow had fallen during the night."[9] These sentences suggest no detail about and no emotional response to the actions they describe, and they make no attempt to describe the snow on which they focus. Here, however, the situation is complicated by the presence of the pictures. While the text does not say what the snow looked like, the accompanying illustration shows it, which not only fills in the information but also provides the mood lacking in the text on its own. Readers know, for instance, what sort of bed Peter sleeps in and what he looks like as he awakes even though the text is silent on these matters. Later, Peter finds something in the snow: "It was a stick—a stick that was just right for smacking a snow-covered tree." This says nothing about his realizing it was a stick, then thinking, "Hey, I can hit a tree with it," and so on; but viewers can determine these things from the information provided in the illustration. The pictures here operate as a visual equivalent of the shadow text provided by a reader's repertoire of additional knowledge that I discussed earlier. They fill in details, offering both factual information about how objects and people look and emotional information (conveyed by the connotations of specific styles, colors, textures, shapes, and so on) about what it feels like to be in the presence of those people and objects.

Most of the books adults provide for younger children are, like *The Snowy Day*, picture books (something I so much take for granted that I neglected to mention it), and it was the overall appearance of *The Snowy Day*—its few words and large picture on each double-page spread—that first informed me it was a text of children's literature. As in many if not most picture books produced for children, the pictures in *The Snowy Day* are more complex than the text. For one thing, the details of visual information they provide have implications that go well beyond the simple story implied by the text. As I describe in my book *Words about Pictures*, pictures operate as a complex system of signifiers conveying information about who characters are and what they do. Consider, for example, the one detail that attracted the most attention when *The Snowy Day* appeared in 1962: Peter's dark complexion. The color that represents his (and his mother's) skin tone implies that he is an African American—a possibility the text never confirms or denies, indeed, never mentions at all. In 1962 this was viewed as a daring innovation. For many adult readers it implied a wonderful degree of tolerance. Peter could be black without his blackness being the focus of attention or a feature of any obvious significance to the story being told. This is a story about being a child, told specifically about a child who just happens to be black, so that his being black doesn't matter, which, of course, is something that matters a lot.

But it doesn't matter because the text doesn't mention it; what is most meaningful is what the text doesn't say. A visual detail provided by the pictures makes the text's apparent simplicity itself a source of great complexity, fraught with a political and cultural import it would not have had if it had simply named what its pictures showed. The complexity increases at the end of the book, as Peter and his friend head out "into the deep, deep snow"; as my colleague at the University of Winnipeg, Debra Schnitzer, once pointed out to me, the picture shows them from behind, facing into a shape that looks a lot like an outline map of the continent of Africa. This peculiar visual detail turns an apparently straightforward visit outside into something rich, strange, and hard to comprehend. While I am not sure I understand all that it means, I do know that these pictures make the story told by words and pictures together far more complicated than the one implied by the words on their own.

The complexity is stylistic as well as intellectual. Viewing the story's illustrations in the context of my own repertoire of visual art, I find their appearance reminiscent of an elegantly tasteful sort of expressionist art that, when found in gallery painting, is assumed to be understandable only by refined viewers. If Keats's illustrations for this book were separated from the text and hung in a gallery, viewers without much knowledge of the history of art might respond to them with bafflement and wonder why artists don't show things the way they actually look. Yet I find it hard to imagine anyone responding to the pictures that way in the context of the book.

Is that contradictory? Perhaps not: the language usually used to describe this particular kind of sophisticated art implies that it is childlike. Ruskin once famously suggested that taking sensuous pleasure in pictures—and especially pictures of this sort—requires adults to regain an "innocence of the eye" he described as "childish."[10] The implication is that children, not having yet learned the supposedly counterproductive sophistication that leads adults to view pictures only in terms of their potential to convey information, are automatically in possession of innocent eyes, automatically capable of taking spontaneous delight in the colors and textures of pictures.

But according to W. J. T. Mitchell, "This sort of 'pure' visual perception, freed from concerns with function, use, and labels, is perhaps the most highly sophisticated sort of seeing that we do; it is not the 'natural' thing that the eye does (whatever that would be). The 'innocent eye' is a metaphor for a highly experienced and cultivated sort of vision."[11] Similarly, Arthur Danto asserts that "to see something as art requires something the eye cannot descry—an atmosphere of artistic theory, a knowledge of the history of art: an artworld."[12] Children who are unaware of the ethical value of an "innocent eye" and who are untutored in the "artworld" might somehow be unconsciously emulating the behavior of more knowledgeable adults. Their innocent eyes might actually be perceiving as those adults do, despite the children's lack of experience and cultivation. But somehow this seems doubtful.

I suspect that the opposite is true—that because adults feel free to give children access to sophisticated pictures like those in *The Snowy Day* because of the rhetoric of the "innocent eye" traditionally associated with such pictures, many children do learn how to make sense of them—become exactly the knowledgeable viewers these pictures imply and demand. With enough experience of picture books of this sort, and with adults talking with them about the pictures and helping them to see the meanings in them that the adults see, they learn to understand visual language such as that used in *The Snowy Day* as representative of innocence and childishness—and perhaps even, to some extent, understand the book as I and many other adults do, as intending to be a celebration of the joys of the childlike. They develop the knowledge of what one particular adult philosophy understands to be the meaning of their own existence as young human beings, and possibly they even learn to view themselves and their own actions as this philosophy understands them. They learn childlikeness from children's books.

Meanwhile, however, a different set of assumptions popularly held about language tends to limit the access children have to equivalently complex written texts. The result is the development of a form such as the picture book, which combines the simplest of written texts with surprisingly complex visual images. The existence of such a form suggests something about the logic of children's literature in general. That these books for the youngest of readers contain sophisticated pictures that fill in the bare outlines of their simple texts with complex information suggests the belief that such texts are inadequate, unable to convey the required information on their own. They need the pictures to shadow them, to show and tell all that the written words cannot say.

Although texts intended for older readers often contain pictures (*Henry Huggins* and *Dr. Dolittle* both include line drawings, for example), there are proportionately fewer than are found in *The Snowy Day*. *Plain City*, intended for young-adult readers, contains no visual images but the one on its cover. There is a progression here. The older and more experienced the intended audience, the less visual information is offered by pictures. Readers of these three novels are expected to fill in on their own the sort of information that the pictures in *The Snowy Day* actually provide, suggesting that the more experienced readers become, the less they need in the way of pictorial information. The assumption seems to be that the reader's increasingly expanding repertoire can substitute for the actual presence of pictures. The presence of pictures in *The Snowy Day* and other picture books makes clear, then, how much texts like *Henry Huggins* and *Dr. Dolittle* do imply a shadow text, how much they imply readers who know and are capable of filling in much more than the relatively few simple things they actually say.

Even so, the most significant feature of the style of all these books is how much they leave unsaid and require a reader to fill in—how much they do imply a shadow text. *Plain City*, which strikes me as the most complex verbal text of my group of six, does offer detailed information both about the characters' physical appearance and about their emotions and thoughts. The protagonist, Buhlaire, for instance, playfully thinks of the history of her past as "back time"[13] and of her family as "pieces on a chain, not even touching. Mom is the chain's big center piece of gold" (41). Virginia Hamilton has a reputation for complexity, for writing tough books that are hard for many young readers to understand. But this novel, which consists mainly of clear simple sentences with little in the way of "poetic" or complex language, is noticeably simpler in style than most characteristic literary fiction intended for adult readers. Buhlaire's playfulness with language connects her to characters in novels by authors such as Toni Morrison, an African American writer like Hamilton with a strong interest in the textures of language but one who usually writes for and about adults rather than young people. But compared to the subtle intricacies of Morrison's prose, *Plain City* is assertively straightforward. A *Booklist* review quoted at the front of my paper edition says, "Hamilton's style gets plainer, but her words lose none of their music or their depth."

I share that opinion. This is a text that resonates, one in which apparently simple things—descriptions of places like Buhlaire's isolated home on stilts above the water, for instance, or of events like a whiteout in the midst of which Buhlaire finds her homeless father—come to have complex meanings. The text seems continually to be inviting readers to consider those meanings, to think about what water or snow might stand for. It tells of Buhlaire's thinking, "It felt as if the white was tracking her down" (104) and that "You can't stop running water. . . . You can't stop, me" (193). This relatively more complex text implies an even more complex shadow text; the actual words on the page clearly leave much for a reader to fill in and are most remarkable, therefore, for their comparative simplicity. That quality, I think, helps to identify *Plain City* as a text for young readers. While fictional texts for adult audiences often have shadow texts more complex than the texts are themselves, there's rarely such an obvious disjunction between their texts and their shadow texts.

Near the beginning of *Alice's Adventures in Wonderland,* Alice expresses a sentiment that explains much about this entire group of texts: " 'What is the use of a book,' thought Alice, 'without pictures or conversations?' "[14] For a moment let me assume, incorrectly, that Alice is actually asking a question, that instead of simply meaning that she herself has no use for such books, she genuinely does not know what the use of them might be. If she meant that, she would be expressing a state of mind shared by the implied readers of all six of these books—an inability to make sense of texts that communicate by means other than pictures and conversations. All the texts but *The Snowy Day* include quite a lot of conversation. All except *Plain City* and "The Purple Jar" were originally published with pictures.[15] All focus on actions and leave descriptive subtleties and meaningful resonances either to illustrations or to the operations of the readers' repertoires they evoke and imply. *Alice's Adventures in Wonderland* is no exception. It reports the strange things that happen to Alice as she moves through Wonderland in simple language and in a decidedly straightforward fashion, using much conversation and very little verbal description, leaving descriptive information to be provided in its illustrations. It has a style that I clearly and quickly recognize as characteristic of texts written for children.

My response to *Alice* is complicated, however, by my knowledge of the history of its reception. It is certainly the most widely known of these six books—the one that adults without a special knowledge of writing for children would most likely readily recognize as a text of children's literature. It is also the only one of the six texts that has received any amount of interpretive attention of the sort critics usually provide for adult texts of literature, attention we often tend to believe children's texts, in their simplicity, do not require. Critics have analyzed *Alice* from a spectrum of perspectives, including Freudian, Jungian, and Lacanian approaches and a variety of historical frameworks. In doing so, furthermore, they rarely take into account that the intended audience is meant to be childlike. An online search of the MLA International Bibliography conducted on July 24, 2006, returned 778 citations to discussions of Carroll, surprisingly few of which discuss the *Alice* books specifically as literature for children or in relation to other texts of children's literature. These commentators find decidedly unchildlike and deeply complex meanings lurking under the apparently simple and childlike surface of the text, and they tend not to deal with the fact of the implied child reader, except perhaps, to dismiss it as a screen Carroll used, a pretense at being merely whimsical that would allow him his conscious or unconscious exploration of dangerously illicit adult concerns. All that might suggest that *Alice* is not simple at all and that it therefore differs significantly from the other five texts.

More likely, however, it suggests that *Alice* shares the main defining quality of the other five texts. It is a decidedly simple text that not only allows but demands that readers approach it in the context of a wider and more complex knowledge than it actually offers. Its simplicity evokes the complex shadow text that critics describe in their analyses of it. Seen from this point of view, *Alice* differs from the other five texts only by degree. The gulf between the apparent simplicity of its surface and the complexity of the shadow texts it evokes for many readers is startlingly wide. Uncovering Jungian archetypes or postmodern conceptions of schizophrenia or arcane references to Victorian politics is not just a matter of filling in the text's references to rabbits or gardens with one's knowledge of what rabbits or gardens are and what they look like.

I see no reason why I could not search for Jungian archetypes in *The Snowy Day* or contemporary political references in *Henry Huggins*. I could identify the long stick Peter finds, and the firm but all-too-meltable snowball he tries to bring indoors, with his search for manhood; or I could consider Henry Huggins's rescue of the dog Ribsy in terms of the American effort to help England win World War II. But I suspect most people would not be persuaded by these interpretations and conclude that I was bringing more invention than the text actually seemed to call for, using parts of my own personal repertoire that the text was not necessarily working to evoke. I could make the same arguments about *Alice*, but I would do so with some degree of unease. While I may not necessarily accept any particular one of the many complex interpretations of *Alice*, I have to admit that the text does seem in some way to invite or at least allow this kind of response to it. What is there about *Alice* that differs from the other texts in so generously opening up a space for complex interpretations?

It might be Tenniel's illustrations that create this opening. Their sly references to political figures of the time, pointed out in Michael Hancher's *The Tenniel Illustrations to the "Alice" Books* and elsewhere, clearly suggest a relevance to the world outside Wonderland that readers might well transfer to the text. But I suspect that Tenniel, too, was merely responding as a reader to a quality already present in the text before he created his pictures for it.

That quality might be simply that, unlike *The Snowy Day* or *Henry Huggins*, *Alice's Adventures in Wonderland* is a fantasy. Fantasy situations and characters like those in *Alice* are clearly not intended to mirror things actually existing in reality; but there are long-standing traditions of interpretation that allow readers to connect them to reality by reading them as allegoric or symbolic versions of real things. I suspect most readers feel less comfortable with assuming that people or events that actually do already mirror reality, like those in *The Snowy Day* and *Henry Huggins*, might somehow also be representing other aspects of reality. Even so, *Dr. Dolittle* is a fantasy, and I find myself resisting the idea that it, like *Alice*, leaves room for unexpectedly complex interpretations. This is partly because of the nature of the fantasy. *Dr. Dolittle* allows a few strange elements into an otherwise ordinary reality that seems therefore resistant to allegorical interpretations, whereas *Alice* constantly changes its settings and characters in a disconcertingly dreamlike way that seems to diverge greatly from the ordinarily understandable and, if only to make readers feel more comfortable, demands some explanation that grounds it in ordinary understandings.

Alice makes the need for explanation particularly clear by focusing on it so obsessively as a subject of the text. In *Dr. Dolittle,* as in many fairy tales and other children's fantasies based on them, strange events tend to be taken for granted. Part of the pleasure offered by such stories is the delightful pretense that nothing strange is going on at all, that this is the way things are. I once wrote, "Only by ignoring the fact that it is fantastic, by pretending to be a true story about a real world shared by the characters in the story, the storyteller, and the people who hear the story, can a fantasy establish its credibility and work its magic on those who actually hear it."[16] If that is in any way true, then *Alice's Adventures in Wonderland,* possibly the most famous of children's fantasies, is a huge exception.

Or is it? *Alice* is central to Eric Rabkin's alternative view of fantasy as a kind of literature that works by unsettling the worlds it creates rather than confirming them. In *The Fantastic in Literature* Rabkin defines "the fantastic" as "a quality of astonishment that we feel when the ground rules of a narrative world are suddenly made to turn about 180°."[17] Such astonishing turns do appear in many whimsical fantasies for children. But their presence in texts like Chris Raschkas's *Arlene Sardine* or Thomas King's *Coyote Columbus Story* or Shaun Tan's *The Lost Thing*—or, for that matter, in *Alice's Adventures in Wonderland*—does tend to distress adult readers of children's books often enough to suggest the extent to which they defy conventional expectations of children's literature. World-establishing texts like Tolkien's *The Hobbit* or Rowling's only minimally anarchic Harry Potter series are more typical.

At any rate, Alice constantly questions the reality around her and demands explanations of themselves from the various creatures she meets, who are also constantly demanding explanations of herself from her; and whenever she feels comfortable enough with the creatures to accept them as they are, she takes the opportunity to ask them questions about other things, to interrogate the explanations they offer, and to offer her own explanations. Readers, invited to view Wonderland from the viewpoint of Alice's inquisitive questioning of it, are primed to be in a mood that asks questions about the meanings of things and engenders explanations of them. It seems logical, then, that there are so many interpretations of Carroll's book.

In a sense *Alice's Adventures in Wonderland* operates as a metafictional account of any reader's encounter with any fictional world. The first paragraph, which includes Alice's dismissal of books without pictures and conversations placed just under a picture and inside quotation marks that signal a conversation she is having with herself, announces its metafictional bent. Within the book Alice's questioning and explaining response to the strange new world she encounters replicates a reader's encounter with the mystery of a fictional text. Alice operates in Wonderland as readers of fiction often must. She assumes that there is more than meets the eye, that what is being taken for granted as simple and obvious by the characters she encounters is not simple at all. She assumes, in a sense, that she is in a story, that her experiences are meaningful in a larger context of a unified plot, recurring themes, and so on, and that, despite its mysterious incompleteness, what she encounters is explicable and understandable if only she can fill in the knowledge that explains it. She operates, in other words, with the assumption that there is a more complete shadow text that fills in the gaps and disjunctions of the actual text she is encountering.

Alice's Adventures in Wonderland offers within itself a replication of the activity that it demands of readers, that all other fictional texts demand, and that, apparently, fictional texts written for children demand in a particularly intense way that defines them as a distinctive kind of text. It depicts someone exploring a shadow text larger and more complex than the actual words of the text itself.

Focalization: Who Sees and What They Know

I have suggested that readers, asked to view Wonderland as Alice herself responds to it, are primed to adopt her questioning mode and seek explanations for what she encounters just as she does. I am assuming, obviously, that readers tend to identify with the characters through whose perspective they view the action—those through whom Gérard Genette would say the events are focalized. This is a popular assumption of adults thinking about children's literature and the way children read it (as well as the way they are encouraged by adults to read it). It is an assumption that clearly operates in the minds of many writers of fictional texts intended for children, many of which not only have child protagonists but also focalize the action through those child protagonists and ask readers to think of themselves in terms of what happens to the child protagonists. I suspect that focalization through a central child character is another quality that marks a text for me as one intended for child readers.

Five of the texts I am exploring here have child protagonists and tend to tell about the action as those protagonists understand and experience it. While "The Purple Jar" is told by a third-person narrator, it describes events from Rosamond's point of view and frequently reports her interior responses—matters readers know about but that she does not share with her mother or anyone else in the story: "[she] saw a great variety of different sorts of things of which she did not know the use, or even the names. . . . She was afraid to let go her mother's hand. . . . Rosamond was very sorry that her mother wanted nothing" (141–142). *Alice* works in much the same way, and so do *Henry Huggins, Plain City,* and the text of *The Snowy Day*. All four follow their protagonists through the events described, rarely if ever reporting on what other characters think or on what they do when the protagonist is not present. Also, Carroll frequently describes what Alice thinks, such as her opinions about books without pictures. Cleary says, "I wish something exciting would happen, Henry often thought" (7). Keats reports that Peter "thought it would be fun to join the big boys." And while the third sentence of *Plain City* and most of what follows it is told by a third-person narrator who often describes Buhlaire's responses to events, the first two sentences actually report a thought of Buhlaire's in direct quotation: "*You all don't scare me. Snap!*" (1). So all these texts not only center on events in the life of a child but also report those events as the child feels and thinks about them.

The *Story of Dr. Dolittle* is a notable exception. Its protagonist is not a child. Like many of the traditional fairy tales on which it seems in some ways (its opening phrase, the inclusion of talking animals) to be modeled, *Dr. Dolittle* is about an adult. But like the central characters in those fairy tales (the passively innocent but marriageable girls of tales like Perrault's "Cinderella" and "Sleeping Beauty," for instance, or the ingenuous young men who figure in tales like Perrault's "Puss in Boots" or the Grimm Brothers' "The Golden Bird"), Dr. Dolittle is a childlike adult—at least in terms of the qualities usually considered to be childlike. He is a bachelor, and he appears not only uninterested in sexuality (as adults often assume children are) but in contacts with human beings altogether (with the interesting exception of one child he meets on his journeys, a boy whom he helps). As he says, "I like animals better than the 'best people'" (4). Like the protagonists of "Puss in Boots" and "The Golden Bird," he can communicate with animals and gets help in his endeavors from them. He even tends to be somewhat animal-like. As the Cat's-meat-Man tells him, "You might have been a cat yourself. You know the way they think" (7). The many texts of children's literature centering on animals who talk suggest the degree to which childlike behavior is conventionally identified with that of animals, childlike thinking with what is assumed to be the nature of animal thinking. In his empathy with animals, Dr. Dolittle becomes childlike—a protagonist as childlike as the actual children who appear in our other five texts.

Dr. Dolittle is unlike the other five texts in another way: it is not in any obvious way focalized through its protagonist. The narrator reports few of his thoughts. While readers do find out at one point that "he was happy and liked his life very much" (16), the text usually reveals only the thoughts he tells other characters about in direct conversation. He does that quite often, however, and there is no sense he is being dishonest in his reporting of his feelings when he says, for instance, "O, bother it! Money again. . . . Goodness! I shall be glad to get to Africa where we don't have to have any" (31). The general effect is that readers do tend to know what the doctor feels and thinks about most of the events the text describes. There is a sense that the text conveys interpretations of events as he experiences them even though there is little actual evidence to support that sense.

So all six texts do have childlike protagonists; and all six do focalize the events through the responses of those characters. Interestingly, however, none of them are first-person narratives. There are, of course, many texts written for children in which characters do tell their own story—from Ellen Raskin's picture book *Nothing Ever Happens on My Block* to Judy Blume's young-adult novel *Are You There, God? It's Me, Margaret*—but by far the greater proportion of texts for children operate like these six and tell of the main characters' response through the medium of a third-person narrator.

There is one particularly significant result of this, and it suggests another quality that causes me to identify a text as possibly being intended for child readers: a sense that there is a second point of view, that of the narrator. These texts all seem to offer hints that the focalized child character is not seeing everything there is to see or possibly not understanding events in the various ways they might be understood. The narrator seems to see more and know more.

Consider, for instance, the sentence in "The Purple Jar" that I quoted above: "[she] saw a great variety of different sorts of things of which she did not know the use, or even the names" (141). Is this Rosamond's perspective, as she thinks about how many fascinating things there are that she has never seen before? Or is someone else who knows better implying some criticism of her ignorance? The presence of the more knowledgeable observer becomes obvious a few paragraphs later, as readers learn something of which Rosamond herself is unaware: "It was a chemist's shop, but she did not know that" (142). And by the end of the story, Rosamond has come to see beyond her former ignorance, and say, "I hope I shall be wiser another time" (145). The first of the three sentences implies, and the second makes obvious, the presence of a point of view at odds with Rosamond's. The third sentence removes the opposition and dissipates the sense of a double perspective, as Rosamond moves away from her own previous perception and adopts that of the second voice.

I can imagine a number of ways in which different readers might make sense of this movement. A reader who identified with Rosamond's ignorance (as the text seems to invite and perhaps many adults generally assume children would) might not even hear the hint of criticism in the first sentence, be warned of the limitations of adopting a perspective like Rosamond's only by the second sentence, and confirm a lesson learned by accepting the wisdom Rosamond enunciates in the third sentence. A reader with some sophistication (an adult?) might catch the hint of the danger in Rosamond's ignorance in the first sentence, find it confirmed by the second, and rejoice in knowing from the third sentence that Rosamond is now as wise as the reader was from the beginning. It is even possible that a reader committed to the sort of celebration of childlike innocence affirmed by texts like *Dr. Dolittle* (this would be a different sort of adult reader) might be delighted by Rosamond's superior vision as affirmed by the first sentence and implied by her lack of knowledge of the mundane reality of the chemist's in the second, and read Rosamond's proclamation in the third sentence as a signal of a terrible defeat. Whichever of these paths a reader follows, all involve an acknowledgment of the possibility of two points of view, one innocent or ignorant and the other healthily or dangerously knowing. Also, all three involve a perception of a conflict between the two and some sort of resolution of that conflict.

What I find most interesting here is the degree to which Edgeworth, despite her reputation as a profoundly didactic writer who sees children's lack of knowledge as a dangerous ignorance and works to move readers past it, leaves room for these different sorts of readings. Throughout Rosamond's conversations with her mother, readers know only what they say to each other, with neither point of view being supported by any obvious agreement or disagreement on the part of the narrator. While it might seem obvious to a reader committed to adult knowledge that the mother is making excellent sense and Rosamond is being foolishly wrongheaded, it would seem equally obvious to a reader committed to the wisdom of innocence that the mother is being egregiously devoid of imagination and Rosamond delightfully engaged in the pleasures of the sensuous world. Many readers respond in just that way—and get angry at Edgeworth for being so militantly opposed to the delights of childlike thinking. Harvey Darton asserts, "You hate the mother. . . . You know she is right, and you loathe rectitude accordingly."[18] And Gillian Avery says, "Rosamond's mother chills."[19] But while it is not hard to realize that Edgeworth clearly (and perhaps foolishly) agrees with the mother, she never allows her narrator to say so. She merely lets events develop in a way that leads Rosamond to teach herself what Edgeworth wants her to know— just as Rosamond's mother merely lets events develop in a way that leads Rosamond to teach herself—and leaves readers room to interpret the story. The simultaneous presence of two different focalizations implying two opposite points of view opens a dispute between alternative views of the relative merits of innocence and knowledge that seems quite able to survive the author's attempt at a one-sided closure of it.

Even more obviously than in "The Purple Jar," the text of *Alice* implies a narrator who sees more and differently than does its focalized child protagonist, so that readers simultaneously see as Alice sees and also stand back from her and observe the narrator's different reading of her situation. "In another moment," the text says near the beginning, "down went Alice after it [the white rabbit], never once considering how in the world she was to get out again" (10). If the text is being focalized through Alice's thoughts and she didn't consider it, then how can readers know about it? They can because the narrator is clearly there as well as Alice, and can report not just what Alice does think but also what she doesn't. A few sentences later, Alice praises herself on being so brave that she "wouldn't say anything about it, even if I fell off the top of the house!" The narrator then intrudes once more, adding, "which was very likely true"—an implied reference to the consequences of such a fall that nicely undercuts Alice's bravura. Not only are two different points of view being expressed here, but as in "The Purple Jar," they are distinguished from each other by the amount of knowledge they imply. The narrator knows more and apparently uses the knowledge to undercut the validity of the child protagonist's innocence.

As a result, I think, an awareness of that innocence becomes a significant focus of a reader's attention here, just as it does in "The Purple Jar." Consider, for instance, the comment that follows Alice's thoughts about what latitude and longitude she has gotten to: "Alice had not the slightest idea what Latitude was, nor Longitude either, but she thought they were nice grand words to say" (11). As in "The Purple Jar," a reader who also doesn't know their meaning can agree that they are nice grand words to say, no matter what they mean; and a reader who does know the meaning can stand at some distance from Alice's ignorance and either be delighted by it or wish she knew better and hope she learns to do so. The text allows a variety of responses, but the responses tend to revolve around the relative merits of two different and opposing points of view and concern the relative value of knowledge and lack of it. Not only are these texts centrally about children, but they are constructed in ways that work to encourage readers to consider what it means to see or think in ways usually considered to be childlike— ways defined by their relative lack of knowledge or complexity. They open a discourse about what children are, about how they are different from adults, and about the relative merits of the different qualities. And in doing so, they invite their readers, not just adults but also children, to think about what it means to be a child and what it means, therefore, to know less than older people do. In a sense they replicate the foundational situation of their writing—an adult knowing more writing for children because children know less and need to understand the implications of knowing less.

Plain City offers the same invitation in an even more obvious way. The story is focalized through Buhlaire's perception, even outside of the passages in italics directly quoting Buhlaire's thoughts that occur throughout the book. But as in "The Purple Jar" and *Alice*, there is another mind present, seeing things differently. At the bottom of the first page, for instance, there is a paragraph about what Buhlaire looks like—a description of her as someone else might see her that could not possibly be in her own thoughts, for as the text reports a few pages later, Buhlaire "had no idea what she looked like outside herself, to people" (5). After the original description of Buhlaire establishes a second point of view, it is hard not to find it in other places also. Is it Buhlaire herself who thinks, "At first glance, Buhlaire was invisible from the neck down" (2) or "Buhlaire could startle. It took a few seconds to see all of her in her snowy getup" (3) or "Easy to see in the classroom how young she was" (3)? Or are these the reports of an outside observer? As in the sentences I have just quoted, the narration often summarizes Buhlaire's thoughts rather than reporting the details of them as she herself would think them. This implies a narrator detached enough to abstract the general patterns from the specifics on which they are based.

Meanwhile there are hints, possibly in Buhlaire's thoughts or possibly not, that there may be more going on than she is allowing herself to acknowledge. For instance, "She knew about the war. Her daddy was missing from it, wasn't he?" (6). Is it Buhlaire who feels the uncertainty expressed in that last phrase, or is it a narrator pointing out to readers that she may be being too certain? One way or the other, the narration keeps focusing on that uncertainty, suggesting that what Buhlaire thinks and knows is not the whole picture and thus inviting readers to distrust her point of view. Buhlaire herself constantly thinks about what she might look like to other people, as opposed to what she sees and assumes to be true herself, or about how other people may be seeing events differently than she does and thus undermining the validity of her perceptions. And her school principal forces her into the realization that what any one person sees at any given moment is never the whole truth:

> "When you start growing up, things don't look the same each day."
> "It's like that!" she said. "It's like, I wake up now, and I see things that were always there, only I see them more, or something." (27)

With these words Buhlaire summarizes the main action of the novel and one of its major thematic concerns: her growing perception of the limitations of the youthful lack of knowledge she is in the process of moving beyond. The action constantly places Buhlaire in situations in which she finds out things she did not know—about herself, about who her father is, about her friend Grady and who his father is, about her family history, about her mother's relationship with her uncle —and then confronts their implications and grows beyond her ignorance.

As happens in "The Purple Jar," Buhlaire rejects the ways of seeing that she began with for being limited and inaccurate, and she adopts the views implied by the outside perspective of the other focalization. Also as in "The Purple Jar," the thrust of the action clearly supports the wisdom of her doing so. By the end of the novel, Buhlaire's own perceptions are at one with the narrative point of view she so clearly diverged from at the beginning, and she totally rejects the truth of what she once saw: "It was like I was asleep," she thinks. "Just hibernated, way deep down under" (193). I have suggested that "The Purple Jar," a text produced in an era noted for the didacticism of its children's books, left a space for readers to entertain either of its focalized points of view—retain some regard for the wisdom of the childlike instead of for what adults like Rosamond's mother hope to teach them. Paradoxically, *Plain City*, the product of an era in which most people involved professionally with children's books look down on obvious didacticism, is far more aggressively assertive and one-sided about the dangers of a youthful perspective and the wisdom of an adult one. Readers are invited to question the validity of Buhlaire's perceptions throughout and to be aware of the dangers of her innocence continually. And once Buhlaire finds out what the adults in her life have been keeping from her, she is wise enough to use the knowledge to solve her own problems and conflicts. I find it much more difficult to assert that like "The Purple Jar," this novel leaves room for readers to feel some ambivalence about the possible loss involved in the gaining of maturity.

That one-sidedness suggests something interesting about the reader *Plain City* implies. That reader, invited from the start to see past Buhlaire and know more than she does, is never as innocent as Buhlaire is. It seems that such a reader must already have undergone—or at the very least is being encouraged to imagine him- or herself as having already undergone—the process that the novel describes Buhlaire herself as going through. Nevertheless, it is clear that a young reader is being invited to identify with Buhlaire, to see him- or herself as being something like her. So the reader who accepts the identification perceives himself or herself as sharing Buhlaire's ignorance and learning the value of growing beyond it. At the same time, the reader implied by the doubleness of the focalization already knows more. If texts work to construct the subjectivity of their readers—make them think of themselves in certain ways—then the subjects constructed by *Plain City* are somehow both innocent and not innocent and are therefore deeply divided. So, too, are the ones constructed by "The Purple Jar" and *Alice*, for as I have suggested, all three texts invite readers both to see with the eyes of innocence and to see beyond that innocence at almost exactly the same time.

In *Henry Huggins* the third-person narrator is less willing to assert a view at odds with Henry's than Edgeworth, Carroll, and Hamilton are—or, perhaps, just less willing to be obvious about it. The narrator rarely, if ever, makes direct comments that are noticeably different from the focalized child protagonist's reading of his own situation. I still contend, however, that most readers will find it hard to read very far into this text without developing the sense that Henry's view of his situation is often incomplete or otherwise inadequate—certainly different from the view of him that the reader is encouraged to develop. Just as I found myself imagining a more complex shadow to the characteristically simple language of texts written for children, I also find myself here providing a second and more complex point of view.

For instance, the text says, "Except for having his tonsils out when he was six and breaking his arm falling out of a cherry tree when he was seven, nothing much happened to Henry" (7). I understand that this is Henry's own reading of the situation because the next sentence tells me so: "I wish something exciting would happen, Henry often thought." But I also cannot help thinking that there is some irony implied by the weird disjunction between the idea of nothing happening and the hugeness of the serious exceptions provided. I also find myself standing back from and being amused by Henry's apparent desire to suffer. He seems to conflate excitement with the experience of pain. My repertoire of previous reading of texts of children's fiction suggests to me that the most likely development of this plot is for Henry to get what he wants and then realize how wrong he was to want it. (Consider, for instance, "The Purple Jar.") All of these considerations push me away from identification with Henry and into a way of seeing and understanding more than he does that amounts to a second point of view.

As I did with the shadow text, I have to ask if child readers are likely to be aware of this shadowy second focalization—if it is a quality of the text available to its intended audience. Does the child reader this text implies see more than Henry does, as the child reader of *Plain City* sees more than Buhlaire does?

Later in the first chapter, after something exciting does happen and Henry finds himself in conversation with a policeman, he asks if he is going to be arrested, and the policeman asks him if he thinks he ought to be. The text then says, "He thought the policeman was joking, but he wasn't sure. It was hard to tell about grownups sometimes" (26–27). As a grown-up, I know that the policeman is joking. Children simply do not get arrested for bringing dogs on buses. But if Cleary is accurately capturing childlike thinking in her report of Henry's uncertainty about when grown-ups mean what they say, then presumably child readers would be less sure—would share Henry's reading of the situation, and not see the shadow focalization I find here.

But if they did so, they would surely have to feel some alarm. If arrest is, as Henry believes, a real possibility, then Henry's situation would have to seem serious and painful indeed. For Henry it seems just that way and the fitting end of a series of frightening events. Not only has he failed to find a viable solution to his problem of getting his new dog home, but he has been publicly humiliated and attracted the attention of a number of adults, who have ended up laughing up-roariously at him for reasons he does not and cannot possibly understand. For readers who see nothing but what Henry sees, this text would have to be frighten-ing—a juvenile version of a Kafkaesque horror story.

My own response, however, is quite different. For me the situation is clearly humorous, and I find it hard not to imagine that it was meant to engender laughter in readers. Furthermore, the back cover of my Yearling edition asserts that the book is about "Henry's hilarious adventures" and quotes reviews calling it "a genuinely humorous story" and "very funny." The adults who wrote these comments share my reading.

They seem to believe that child readers will share it also. The *San Francisco Chronicle* reviewer asserts that "Henry and his dog will delight any child," but a child genuinely worried about Henry's potential arrest would hardly be delighted. I am able to laugh at Henry's situation because I see it differently from the way he does and can assess it more accurately than he does. The same must be true for the other adult readers whose opinions I have just cited. It becomes possible to laugh at the events being described here only if one realizes the limitations of Henry's understanding because one knows more. A child reader delighted by the humor of what happens to Henry must then know more than Henry does—perceive him at least to some extent in terms of something like the shadow focalization I myself postulate as I make my way through the text. I have to conclude that the child reader implied by the text—one who gets the comic tone and can read the ironies, see past Henry's own reading of his situation, and find it possible therefore to laugh at Henry's predicaments as the reviewers assume children will—must be conscious of its two different focalizations, just as the reader implied by *Plain City* would be.

And as in *Plain City*, such a child is being invited to have a peculiarly ambiva-lent understanding of what it means to be a child. On the one hand, Henry's misapprehension of his situation is clearly identified with his being a child and not yet comprehending the ways of adults or knowing better; and as the comment about the policeman's joking suggests, the text clearly invites child readers to identify with Henry because they, too, lack such knowledge and are bewildered by the behavior of adults. On the other hand, however, one is expected to know more than Henry and to laugh at his ignorance—see through and beyond his childlike vision and laugh at what he doesn't know and what happens to him as a result of it just as the adult passengers on the bus do.

In *Plain City*, I have suggested, the second focalization has the obvious purpose of putting readers in a position to be able to dismiss the value of the first. But that is not so in *Henry Huggins*. In the world of *Henry Huggins*, it seems, adults like children to know less than they do (or, perhaps more accurately, like to be able to believe that children know less than they do?) and reward them for being so or seeming to be so. This is certainly what happens to Henry. His lack of knowledge not only leads him into the interesting situations for which he had wished, but the apparent danger in those situations conveniently disappears. Far from being arrested, Henry gets a ride home in a police car and finds his parents not angry with him even though he is late. It is clear (to me as an adult reader, at least) that they have counted on his being ignorant (or childish) enough to get into trouble and have worked behind the scenes to save him from it. Furthermore, Henry himself remains, even at the end, resolutely ignorant of what readers who laugh have come to understand about his situation. He never does learn how one is supposed to carry a dog on a bus and cannot even understand why people are so upset: "Golly, Mom," he says, "I didn't do anything. I just brought my dog home on the bus like you said" (29). If he does not learn, then clearly readers who have identified with him are not being invited to learn either. Above all, Henry's childlike ignorance has given both the adults on the bus in the story and child readers pleasure—the pleasure of knowing more than he does and finding his ignorance comical. For those who know better, childish ignorance is pleasing.

Assuming there is a message here—that the story is, as children's literature characteristically is, somehow didactic—the message is this: Be childish, like Henry, and you will please other people, especially adults and children with an adult degree of knowledge. But since you can receive the message only by possessing that adult degree of knowledge yourself, the message is transformed. To please adults, you must pretend to a childish innocence you no longer possess. You must, in effect, enact childhood for an audience of adults who, the story has suggested, expect and want you to do so.

As in *Henry Huggins*, the text of *The Snowy Day* seems to present its child protagonist's point of view without question or comment. It does not even attempt to explain to readers why the snowball Peter put into his pocket outside has disappeared since he came inside. I can imagine child readers who don't know why. But I suspect most either do know or are told by the adults who share the story with them—it is a common temptation of adults to use children's stories as a means of making child audiences wiser than child protagonists. Once more by merely describing the innocent thoughts of a person without knowledge, the text seems inevitably to evoke a shadowy second focalization that represents more knowledge than the first and therefore attracts attention to the limitations of the first.

In the picture accompanying Peter's discovery that his snowball is gone, a dark patch at the bottom of his coat pocket shows readers what the text does not say— that the snowball has melted. The picture actually does contain explanatory infor- mation that Peter does not understand and that therefore the text, focalized purely through his point of view, remains silent on. It actually does offer the information that I provided for myself from my repertoire of knowledge about what happens to snow in warm places. And in doing so, it provides a second focalization quite different from that of the text. The text reports how Peter experiences things; the picture shows him experiencing them as they would be seen by someone else standing far enough away from him to observe him. As Andrea Wyile suggests is true of most picture books, "the third-person perspective of the pictures is a constant reminder to readers that they are merely spectators."[20]

Wyile goes on to suggest that the distancing of pictures makes first-person fo- calized texts with pictures different from those without them and that purely verbal texts for children and young adults often invite engagement with their narrator characters rather than distance from them. I agree that they do, but the engage- ment represents an acceptance of an identification with an adult-engendered childlikeness that emerges from and implies an awareness of a less engaging shadow text. The pictures thus invite viewers to take a second, more detached point of view in addition to the one the text invites readers to identify with, to be outside observers as well as interior empathizers—to think about what it means for the focalized child protagonist to be a child. Like the verbal descriptions of Buhlaire as seen from outside in *Plain City*, these and many other visual images in picture books pull readers away from an identification with a focalized protagonist by showing more than what the protagonist sees. They operate as visible and unavoid- able shadows that imply the subjective nature and therefore the limitations of the focalized characters' innocent perceptions.

In *The Snowy Day* Keats makes his intention of doing just that clear by provid- ing specific information in the pictures that actively invite viewers to see through and beyond Peter's understanding of things. For instance, the text does not mention the key bit of information underlying his conclusion that, despite his wish to do so, he isn't old enough to join the older boys in their snowball fight: that he has been hit hard enough by one of their snowballs to be thrown to the ground by it. Once I know this, and therefore notice that Peter seems to be avoiding thinking about it or about how his decision to leave the game after being hit like that might imply some lack of machismo, I have no choice but to read his thoughts about not being old enough yet as self-protective rationalization. That interpretation probably wouldn't have occurred to me without the information provided in the picture.

Like *Henry Huggins, The Snowy Day* does not seem to have provided this second, more knowing, focalization in order to undermine the value of the innocent first one. Quite the opposite. "In this book sparkling with atmosphere," says the *Horn Book* review quoted on its back cover, "a small boy experiences the joys of a snowy day." The implication is that readers will experience the events as purely joyful—value Peter's innocence for the pleasure it allows him. As I suggested earlier, it seems that adult readers and child readers are being invited to do that in two different ways. The adults are clearly being encouraged to feel some nostalgic delight in the childlike, perhaps even admire the ways in which Peter can avoid or ignore the self-deflating aspects of his experience and view it as superior to adult experience. To do this, the adults need to see and dismiss the undermining significance of the information provided by the more knowing focalization—see Peter's innocent view as preferable to the more knowing one, as Wordsworth does in his "Intimations" ode when he sees a child's developing knowledge as "shades of the prison-house" that dissipate the childlike "clouds of glory."[21] For this sort of reader, the two focalizations allow the innocent one to triumph as a distinct and meaningful way of being, something that would not be obvious if the more knowing perspective were not there. The presence of the outsider's perspective reveals and allows the philosophic implications of the first.

This is particularly true because the second focalization is provided in great part by pictures that, paradoxically, represent an outsider's view of Peter's childlikeness in a style viewers tend to identify as childlike. As I suggested earlier, the actual sophistication of these theoretically childlike pictures implies an interpretation of childhood and a reading of its significance that enforces its value. The pictures offer information that undermines Peter's view of himself only in order to replace that view with a more knowing adult vision of the wonderfulness of the childlike.

As for child readers, they must either share Peter's ignorance and be quite unaware of the perspective provided by the second focalization, or, more likely, they must make sense of that second focalization exactly as adults might and, as I suggested earlier, learn to see Peter's (and therefore their own) innocence through the filter of the significance adults want to place on it. For such an inexperienced reader, the book might operate as a set of instructions not only for what to do on a snowy day but also for how to feel about it and understand it—a primer in being appropriately childlike in terms of one common adult conception of desirable and rewardable childlikeness.

Once more, and like the other five texts, *The Snowy Day* offers or implies two focalizations that allow or enforce a consideration of the meanings of childhood and specifically of the relative value of knowledge and innocence. It does not merely contain a child protagonist's perceptions. It is a book about the nature and meaning of childlike perception.

In focalization, as in other matters, *The Story of Dr. Dolittle* seems to be an exception. I can find no clear evidence of any disjunction between how Dr. Dolittle sees and understands himself and how the narrator sees and understands him. Because I am offered no way of seeing through or beyond Dr. Dolittle's childlike view of what his life means, I have no choice but to conclude that his view is the only possible correct one.

This is not to say that the text precludes the possibility of an alternative—and less childlike—point of view. Indeed, it insists on admitting one: Dr. Dolittle's sister tells him, "You are ridiculous" (4). His parrot calls people "silly" and says, "People make me sick" (16), clearly excepting the good doctor himself as the only non-silly person. The Chief Chimpanzee makes a similar exception later on when he says, "Surely these Men be strange creatures!" (73). Comments like these throughout the text clearly imply that animals and the doctor who can think like an animal are wiser than humans and that their wisdom consists exactly in ways their values directly oppose those of adult civilized human beings. And since the doctor's animal-like views are identified as childlike (the text says, for instance, that the doctor is followed through the town by "the dogs and the cats and the children" [5], a phrase that seems to equate the three), this text follows the familiar trajectory of differentiating between childlike and adult perceptions and values and, like *Henry Huggins* and *The Snowy Day*, clearly invites readers to come down on the side of the childlike.

Even so, it is interesting that it does not do so in terms of offering or implying a second focalization. I suspect this happens because *Dr. Dolittle* invites and implies a quite different relationship between its protagonists and its readers than the ones the other five texts invite their readers to develop. All five ask readers to identify with their protagonists in order to learn from their experiences and to change as the protagonists change. Because Dr. Dolittle is already an adult, and unlikely to change, it is more difficult for child readers to identify with him. Because such readers would be outside and detached from him already, there is no reason to qualify his "childlikeness" or offer a means of comparing it with something else inside the text itself.

This difference spotlights a quality the other five texts share: their assumption that children can, indeed must, change and become adults. For that reason they all offer a second focalization precisely to make readers consider the implications of the first and therefore determine their understanding of their own process of maturing. "The Purple Jar" and *Plain City* offer the second focalization in order to encourage readers to move from the first. *Henry Huggins* and *The Snowy Day* offer the second focalization in order to encourage readers to see the value of the first by moving from an unqualified experience of it to a more knowing appreciation of it. The end of *Alice's Adventures in Wonderland* implies a similar conclusion extravagantly extended into adult life, as Alice's sister "pictured to herself how this same little sister of hers would, in the after-time, be herself a grownup woman, and how she would keep, through all her riper years, the simple and loving heart of her childhood; and how she would gather about her other little children . . . and find a pleasure in all their simple joys, remembering her own child-life" (111). As her sister imagines it, the adult Alice somehow both remains childlike and develops an adult appreciation of what it means to be childlike. Much like Rosamond and Buhlaire, Alice, as described here by her sister, moves from her original innocent perceptions of herself to the view of herself taken from the beginning by the narrator of her story, who, like the narrators of *The Snowy Day* and *Henry Huggins,* possesses an adult knowledge of the value of childlike innocence. Although Henry and Peter do not move past their innocence toward the narrator's more knowledgeable perception of themselves, all five of these texts work to encourage some version of that movement in their reader's self-percep-tions. All five assume not only that child readers can change but that they must— that the ability and inevitability of change is part of what defines them as children. Childhood is a time when people change. All five texts therefore work to change their child readers in the proper way.

Dr. Dolittle seems to imply an opposite view of the childlike. Dr. Dolittle does not change, apparently never did change. Childhood can, it seems, be permanent, so permanent that Dolittle doesn't even have to think about its meaning or value. Unlike the adult Alice or the readers of *The Snowy Day,* Dr. Dolittle seems to have no consciousness of the value of his childlikeness. There is no reason to think about it or to view it from another perspective. It simply is the way he is, always was, and always will be.

But that, of course, is impossible. No human being is immune from change, and that makes *The Story of Dr. Dolittle* something of a utopian dream, a wish-fulfillment fantasy of a world in which one can be innocent forever yet still survive and triumph. This places *Dr. Dolittle* firmly in one specific line of children's books—those primarily British books produced early in the twentieth century (such as *Peter Pan* or *The Wind in the Willows* or *Winnie the Pooh* or *Mary Poppins*) that equate adulthood with a fall from utopian perfection and work to confirm that the supposed childlikeness of certain adults is a state for all human beings, children and adults, to admire and aspire to. It is interesting how often these are the children's books widely read by audiences of adults when no children are around.

In this sort of utopia one's inability to share adult values allows one to talk with animals and have adventures. Someone without any money can easily find a sailor willing to lend a boat for a trip to Africa and then later find another boat simply by trusting that "perhaps we'll find one lying about on the beach that nobody is using" (*Dr. Dolittle*, 86). Dr. Dolittle and his animal friends can travel easily through the uninhabited jungle because "no matter what it was they asked for, Chee-Chee and Polynesia always seemed to be able to get it for them—or something like it" (54). Dr. Dolittle's world is what I have called elsewhere a "progressive utopia," a story in which things start well and get better all the time.[22] His reputation, at first local, becomes international; his fortune, at first moderate, becomes immense. Such a world can exist only if there is no greater wisdom to question its possibility or establish that childhood innocence does end simply by suggesting a more knowing and therefore nonchildlike perspective. The lack of a second focalization in *Dr. Dolittle* represents the triumph of desire over knowledge—a way of getting what one wants by ignoring the facts that make it impossible.

If *Dr. Dolittle* does vary from the other five books in this significant way, should it still be considered a text of children's literature? Clearly, I think it should—I chose to include it in my group of six because I intuited its likeness to the other five. It does lack a second focalization that undercuts desire with knowledge, the presumably childlike with the presumably adult. But as an adult who has and rejects adult knowledge in order to enact the childlike, its protagonist shares the ambivalent mixing of childhood and adulthood found in the protagonists of the other books. As a result, and like the other five texts, *Dr. Dolittle* does offer a childlike point of view, does so in a way that focuses attention on what it means to be childlike, and does that particularly in terms of questions of knowledge and desire. Along with its simplicity, and the talking animal characters it shares with many other texts for children, these features make it recognizable as a text of children's literature.

Desire Confronts Knowledge

My considerations of focalization have continually led me to questions about how desire confronts knowledge—about what the characters in these six texts want and what they know or learn and about what readers are expected to want and invited to know. A concern with desire, knowledge, and the ways they affect each other is obviously central to my identification of these narratives as texts for children.

"The Purple Jar" hinges on Rosamond's desire for the jar and her discovery of the implications of getting what she wants. Because her desire for the jar is based on her ignorance about its true nature, the plot hinges equally on her lack of knowledge and her gaining of it. The knowledge she gains then reveals the bad consequences of acting on the original desire.

This movement mirrors Rosamond's surrender of her own point of view and her adoption of that of the implied adult narrator. But throughout the story Rosamond's mother is a far more obvious voice of adult values than the narrator. Conscious both of the innocence of the child in her charge and of her own adult duty to share her wisdom with her, she frequently offers Rosamond information in a clearly didactic manner. When Rosamond suggests she might use the pretty jar to keep flowers in, her mother says, "You have a flower-pot . . . and that is not a flower-pot" (142). When Rosamond expresses dislike for the smell of the shoe shop, her mother tells her, "That smell is the smell of new leather" (143). Her most revealing comment is a response to Rosamond's conviction that the pair of shoes she sees in the shop will fit her: "Perhaps they might; but you cannot be sure till you have tried them on, anymore than you can be quite sure that you should like the purple vase *exceedingly,* till you have examined it more attentively" (143). Her ironic quotation of Rosamond's overenthusiastic language makes clear how greatly she distances herself from and feels superior to her daughter's impulsive and childlike thoughtlessness. She directly states her conviction that having knowledge—gained through careful examination of the world—is a corrective to the dangers of impulse and childishness.

Despite the mother's willingness to give Rosamond information, however, she does not use her knowledge to protect Rosamond from the consequences of her impulsiveness. It would be a simple matter for her to tell Rosamond why the jar she desires is purple. If she did, of course, the knowledge would dissipate the desire, and there would be even less to the story than there already is. Nevertheless, it seems strangely illogical that Rosamond's mother both understands the limitations and dangers of her daughter's innocence and allows her to act on it. Her justification is, "I want you to think for yourself" (143). And this accords with a view of childhood learning espoused by Edgeworth and others in her time that invests a great deal in the ability of children to learn through experience. According to Mitzi Myers, " 'The Purple Jar' rewrites cultural stereotypes of females as passive victims at the mercy of external circumstances and their own undisciplined emotions by granting girlhood the potentiality for rational agency and self-command."[23] But for all its apparent respect for children, the mother's declared attitude is at least a little deceptive. Since she knows about Rosamond's ignorance of the information that would actually allow her to make a valid choice, she also knows exactly what the outcome of Rosamond's "thinking for herself" will be. She is very much thinking for Rosamond, keeping her ignorant enough to make the wrong choice in order to get her to perceive the wrongness of the choice and thus end up thinking like her mother.

Rosamond's mother needs her daughter's childlike ignorance—needs it so much she refuses to dissipate it. But she needs it in order to get Rosamond to move herself past it—which means her childishness does eventually get dissipated anyway. Or does it? Having been manipulated into sharing her mother's view of the world, but believing it is something she has figured out for herself, Rosamond either remains ignorant of the manipulation and of the degree to which her fate is being controlled by the adult in charge of her, or else she simply accepts it as the way things are and should be. Either way, the adult retains power over the child. The main thing Rosamond learns here is not the obvious lesson that appearances are deceiving—the knowledge that might help her move past the ignorance of childhood. When she expresses something like that conclusion, saying, "If I had known that it was not really purple, I should not have wished to have it so much," her mother reminds her that she told her she should have examined it more closely, and Rosamond arrives at the truly important lesson, the learning of which preserves her childhood: "I wish I had believed you at once" (144). Paradoxically, in learning to be more thoughtful herself, Rosamond has merely confirmed the validity of her mother's knowledge and how it justifies her mother's authority over her and manipulation of her.

In a sense, then, the story undermines its own apparent message about the value of children moving past the urge to act on their desires by developing adult levels of knowledge. It does so by keeping Rosamond in a childlike position in relation to her parent—and it justifies doing so by keeping Rosamond childlike despite her apparent growth in adult forms of knowledge. She is still, it seems, prone to act on desire: note that she wishes she had believed her mother and, at the end, hopes she will be wiser in the future. It hasn't happened yet.

By inviting child readers to adopt the views it espouses, and thus implying that Rosamond's story is applicable to other children, the story seems to evoke two opposing views of childhood. First, childhood is defined by its ignorance and consequent willingness to act on desire, and it therefore ends when the development of adult forms of knowledge dissipates foolish desire. But second, childhood's ignorance and willingness to act on desire are ongoing and survive specific bits of adult knowledge learned and specific desires undermined. Seen from this second point of view, children inevitably continue to be childlike until, presumably, they reach the age of adults or otherwise leave the security that adult authority offers them. They therefore continually need adult control of the sort Rosamond's mother wields in her supposed efforts to teach her daughter independence. The issue is, exactly, control: whatever one is or does, one is defined as needing control as long as one is being controlled.

Child readers who identify with Rosamond or learn from what happens to her might learn two interconnected but different lessons. The most obvious one is that giving in to your desires gets you into trouble, and you should try to know as much as adults do in order to protect yourself from danger. A less obvious one is that you are doomed as a child to keep on being childlike, which means that you will continue to try to act on your desires because you will always have less knowledge than the adults around you. Therefore, you must accept your dependence on wiser and more careful adults and their right to control your environment and manipulate your thinking for your own good.

In discussing focalization earlier, I suggested that "The Purple Jar" left a space for readers to deny the superiority of adult wisdom over Rosamond's childlike point of view. It might be its ambivalent and contradictory views of childhood, and particularly of the degree to which children can absorb and act on adult forms of knowledge, that allow that space. Readers may feel free to object to the apparent triumph of the mother's and the narrator's adult vision over Rosamond's original trust in her childlike desires exactly to the extent that they accept the hidden message about the triumphant continuing of Rosamond's childlikeness, despite or even as evidenced by her willingness to agree with her mother. If all Rosamond has learned is the danger of acting on impulses she actually can't control, then all that has happened is the development of her guilt over her own essential nature, a guilt that the mother obviously views as a triumph of good parenting. Now that her daughter feels suitably unhappy about her own bad tendencies, the mother feels justified in keeping power over her. And, in any case, if Rosamond were innocent enough to require manipulation by her mother and to be successfully manipulated by her, is it anything but sadistic of the mother to knowingly put Rosamond in a situation in which her innocence causes her such suffering? Or is the story trying to persuade readers that such sadism is both necessary and unavoidable when it comes to dealing with dangerously ignorant creatures such as children? The very aspects of the mother's ideas about childhood that govern her behavior toward her daughter also suggest what might be wrong with that behavior and leave a space for readers to disagree with the value of her accomplishments.

What most interests me about these contradictions is the degree to which they might be an inherent foundational quality of children's literature as a genre. "The Purple Jar," a text from fairly early on in the history of children's literature, clearly reveals the assumptions that might have led adults to begin producing such a literature. While its object—and the mother's object within it also—is to educate, it refuses to do so directly. It acts on the faith that learning occurs best when it sneaks up on the learner in the context of events with the ostensible purpose of providing pleasure—such as the pleasure of having a purple jar or of reading a story about the delights of purple jars. For many centuries and until not many decades before "The Purple Jar" was first printed, writers who wanted to educate children simply and obviously asserted what they wanted the children to learn. Meanwhile, there were texts—broadsheet ballads and such—that children read or heard read for pure pleasure, with no particularly explicit didactic purpose. "The Purple Jar" represents a combination of the pleasurable and didactic that puts the pleasure in the service of the didactic—and does so as its main adult character does, by disguising the didactic in the mask of allowing the pleasurable.

The implication is that disguise is necessary—that children must be led to arrive at the conclusion adults want them to reach without the adult insisting on it or asserting it. It appears that pleasure is being offered and also the freedom to make one's own choices. But the pleasure is a mask for something else—often, as in the case of "The Purple Jar," a statement against pleasure and an invitation to feel guilty about it—and the freedom is deceptive, highly qualified by the manipulation that encourages one to arrive at the desired conclusion. As I think about the children's texts published since "The Purple Jar" that I have read, I sense that these remain central characteristics of texts of children's literature. They tend still to disguise their didactic intentions inside pleasurable stories, often wish-fulfillment fantasies of pleasure desired and gained. And they often offer readers an illusory freedom to think about what the events they describe mean, all the while manipulating the readers toward a conclusion about who and what they are that their adult authors want readers to share.

If this is true, then my conclusions about "The Purple Jar" and the complex contradictions at its heart might well apply to a vast range of texts—perhaps even be the central marker of children's literature. That would be logical. The exact same contradictions seem to underpin the ideas about children and childhood that have been current in the years in which texts that most adults now would recognize as being intended for children have been produced.

Like "The Purple Jar," *Alice's Adventures in Wonderland* is built around a child getting what she wants and discovering the implications of wanting it. It begins by implying Alice's wish to do something other than sit on the riverbank, a wish soon fulfilled as the white rabbit appears. The entire trip to Wonderland that follows spells out the sometimes pleasurable and often frightening implications of her wish being granted. During that trip, meanwhile, Alice constantly wishes and must face the consequences of the wishes being fulfilled. Desperate to get into the garden that she can see through a small door, she wishes she could shut up like a telescope, and then must face the consequences of being exactly as small as she wanted to be—which leads her to want to be larger, and then face the consequences of that wish being fulfilled. And so it goes. Alice continues for some time to grow smaller and larger as she wishes and to suffer from it in some way each time it happens.

It seems fairly clear that part of Carroll's agenda in *Alice's Adventures in Wonderland* was to send up the strenuously didactic texts of children's literature common in his time. For instance, Carroll's replacement of Isaac Watts's diligent "little busy bee," who "improve[s] each shining hour,"[24] with an equally diligent crocodile, who "improve[s] his shining tail" and "welcomes little fishes in, / With gently smiling jaws" (19), nicely deflates the earnestness of Watts's poem, earnestly titled "Against Idleness and Mischief." Similarly, Alice's experiences of having her wishes fulfilled in the bizarre ways they are in Wonderland operates as a parody of stories like "The Purple Jar," in which the consequences of getting what you want are equally uncomfortable but far less bizarre or interesting. It seems odd that Carroll would make the consequences for Alice so uncomfortable, and thus confirm what the didactic stories like "The Purple Jar" want to teach: getting what you want always has bad consequences, and therefore wanting is not a wise thing to do. He even has Alice appear to affirm this didactic message, just as Rosamond ends up confirming the foolishness of her original desire: " 'It was much pleasanter at home,' thought poor Alice, 'when one wasn't always growing larger and smaller, and being ordered about by mice and rabbits' " (33).

But then, Alice adds a sentence with an interesting "almost" in it: "I almost wish I hadn't gone down that rabbit-hole." Apparently she is not sure her wish was a bad one even despite the discomfort it resulted in, and her next thought confirms her resistance to the idea that getting what you want is a bad thing: "and yet—and yet—it's rather curious, you know, this sort of life!" The newness and weirdness of the experience balance off the danger. Childhood desire has actually led to good things as much or even more than it has led to bad ones.

The good things are, exactly, things to know—things one can be curious about. Unlike "The Purple Jar," *Alice* does not oppose knowledge and desire so much as conflate them: far from undermining or denying the desirability of what one desires, knowledge is what one desires. If I followed the logic that seems to be emerging from my considerations of these matters—that according to these texts, the possession of a true and certain knowledge that controls one's urge to act on desire is what makes one adult and gives one the power adults have, especially over those who have less knowledge and therefore are more subject to desire—then I would have to conclude that what Alice wants most fervently is to stop being a child.

If she does, then this text is just as much about the thwarting of her desire as "The Purple Jar" is, although in quite different terms. Whereas the mother's superior and certain knowledge of the ways things always unquestionably are reveals the inadequacy of Rosamond's desires for things to be as they seem, the shifting uncertainties of Wonderland constantly undermine what Alice already thinks she knows and make it almost impossible for her to fulfill her desire to know more.

Even worse, it undermines her sense of trust in what she knows already. She is constantly trying to apply her knowledge about normal reality to the abnormal world of Wonderland. When she falls into the pool of tears, for instance, she decides she can get back home by railway, for, as Carroll helpfully explains, she "had been to the seaside once in her life" (20) and has concluded that all bodies of saltwater will, like the one she visited before, have railway stations. A few paragraphs later, she says "O Mouse" to a creature floating in the water because she has seen that phrase in her brother's Latin grammar and hopes it will be the right way to address a mouse and based on "her knowledge of history" (21), wonders if it was a French mouse who came over with William the Conqueror. In all these instances, of course, Alice's knowledge fails her—as it does when she assumes, not much later, that birds and mice will share her view of cats or that it will be harmless fun to play with the cute puppy that towers over her, and as it does again and again throughout the book. Almost every sequence in the book involves Alice confronting a situation that transcends the expectation she has built on her previous knowledge and teaches her again and again how untrustworthy that knowledge is.

Many of these sequences directly involve the discussion of what Alice does and does not know and how she uses her knowledge. The Duchess directly tells her, "You don't know much . . . and that's a fact" (53), and later responds to her statement "I've a right to think" by saying, "Just about as much right . . . as pigs have to fly" (81); and the Mad Hatter interrupts Alice beginning to say, "I don't think—" by telling her, "Then you shouldn't talk" (67).

The most significant aspect of Alice's knowledge undermined by her experience of Wonderland is her sense of who she is. If everything around her is different, she wonders, then how can she be the same person herself: "If I'm not the same, the next question is, 'Who in the world am I?' Ah, *that's* the great puzzle!" (18). Alice's method of figuring out the puzzle is instructive: "I'll try if I know all the things I used to know" (19), she thinks, apparently on the theory that who she is equates with the sum of the knowledge she has. When she discovers she no longer can remember what she once knew, she becomes distressed and uncertain enough to start crying. She returns to the question later when she talks to the caterpillar, telling him that she hardly knows herself and that she cannot explain herself "because I'm not myself, you see" (41); and when the pigeon asks her what she is if not the serpent he accuses her of being, she says "rather doubtfully" (48) that she's a little girl. Much later, she retains this uncertainty as she offers to tell the Gryphon and the Mock Turtle of her adventures that day but adds, "but it's no use going back to yesterday, because I was a different person then" (92).

The odd thing about all this is how little Alice is disturbed by it. Like Henry Huggins's abortive bus trip, the events of Alice's trip to a place she does not know and cannot be certain of ought to be a nightmare; but they aren't—neither for the fictional child at the center of them nor for the reader implied by the text, who, despite the fearful adult readers I mentioned earlier, is clearly meant to be entertained rather than horrified. Even Alice's moment of deep unhappiness as she realizes she no longer knows who she is is surprisingly short-lived. It comes to an end as soon as something unexpected and curious happens that gives her something more to be confused by or to try to figure out—in this case, that she has begun to shrink again. And again and again throughout the novel, her response to strange new things happening is to be delighted by them exactly because she does not understand them and can work at doing so—can think about them, try to develop knowledge of them. Paradoxically, *Alice* is a wish-fulfillment fantasy exactly because Alice's wish to know for sure is never fulfilled and never can be fulfilled in a place so uncertain, where what one needs to understand is always changing. That leaves Alice in the state of always being in the process of having to figure things out, of always having less knowledge than she needs in order to feel certain about anything. Both the responses of Alice herself and the tone the novel takes toward what happens to her imply that this state of being in uncertainty and therefore being able to try to be certain is more utopian than nightmarish.

Alice's one moment of certain knowledge about the Wonderland creatures is the assertion that ends her stay in this utopian land: "You're nothing but a pack of cards!" (109). The certainty of this assertion of the way things really are is the exact equivalent of Rosamond's mother's certainty that her daughter's purple jar is nothing but a perfectly ordinary clear one. The point at which the two children accept the certainty of the assertion—adopt the knowledge commonly accepted by most adults as true—is the point at which their fantasy worlds of desire must and do end.

This implies that the state of being in uncertainty, of not knowing a world that keeps changing and not understanding a self that keeps changing, is the opposite of what adulthood is—that it is the essence of what it means to be a child and that it is utopian. Finally, *Alice* comes down on the exact opposite side of the dispute between childlike and adult forms of knowledge from that which "The Purple Jar" did. In making the uncertainty of not knowing everything for sure a utopian state, *Alice* confirms a desire for a world in which anything might be possible—not just because of the wonderfulness of some of the possibilities (such as, say, the existence of purple jars) but also because of the wonderfully frightening and frighteningly wonderful state of being in flux, uncertain, not finished yet.

To admire such a state, and to privilege it over the stable "reality" perceived through the filter of adult forms of knowledge and certainty, is to fly in the face of conventional wisdom. Not only does it reverse the conventional hierarchy and privilege childhood openness to possibility over the limited certainties of adult knowledge, but it does so by denying the simplicity and lack of complexity of childhood experience. In Wonderland Alice constantly experiences more than her knowledge—the knowledge communicated to her as true and complete by adults —will contain. Furthermore, many adult readers have interpreted Alice's responses to the Wonderland creatures as accurate portraits of common existential dilemmas for both children and adults in the real world. Wonderland may be merely where people usually are—the complex, confusing, unsettling, and interesting reality that always surrounds human beings but that most people manage to suppress their consciousness of as they grow up through a cleavage to conventional knowledge that blinds them to the oddities. If Wonderland is the world, then the fact that Alice, a mere child, experiences it in all its unsettling and dangerous uncertainty flies in the face of conventional wisdom about the simplicity, safety, and delight of childhood. It is for this reason that many adults now think of *Alice* as a children's book unsuitable for children.

In this context it is especially interesting to remember how the novel ends, with Alice's sister thinking pleasant thoughts about "the simple joys" of Alice's child-life. After the many pages describing Alice's often horrific and always complicated and unsettling adventures, her sister's view of childhood seems decidedly inadequate—as inadequate as Alice has been discovering much adult knowledge to be. Why does the end of the novel reassert and apparently reinstate a conventional view of childhood that the story itself has undermined? Is Carroll being ironic here, allowing readers' previous knowledge of the Wonderland experiences to deflate the sister's inadequate views? Was he unaware of the unsettling implications of his story? Or was he simply not willing to admit them?

If the latter, then there is something happening in this text akin to what Eve Kosofsky Sedgwick calls "the epistemology of the closet" in relation to attitudes toward homosexuality common both in Carroll's time and now. The metaphoric closet, in which gay men and women and those who know them have traditionally hidden the fact of their forbidden sexuality, has an open door. The secret hidden knowledge is an open secret, the knowledge not hidden at all. Something that is not supposed to be happening is happening, and everyone knows it is happening, but nobody acknowledges it; and as long as nobody acknowledges it or draws attention to it or speaks about it, then it can go on happening in full view of everybody. In such a situation, the really dangerous person is not the one who indulges in illicit behavior but the one who insists on noticing it and drawing attention to it—he or she who actually dares to speak about "the love which dare not speak its name." Something similar seems to be happening in *Alice's Adventures in Wonderland* in regard to the uncertainties and complexities of childhood. As long as everyone who knows that childhood experience is always uncertain and often complex ignores that knowledge and speaks instead of "simple joys," the uncertain, complex experiences most children actually have can continue in full sight.

Even Alice herself takes part in the effort to disguise the import of her experiences and the nature of her true responses to them. Throughout the novel, as I said earlier, she almost always enjoys the complexities and uncertainties of her situation because they give her things to think about and develop knowledge of. She loves to learn and she tends to see the situations she finds herself in as opportunities both to learn and to teach others. But at one point, she asks, "Shall I *never* get any older than I am now? That'll be a comfort, one way—never to be an old woman—but then—always to have lessons to learn! Oh, I shouldn't like *that!*" (33). Alice's explicit expression here of an antieducational attitude conventionally assumed to be typical of children, who in their simple ignorance and commitment to thoughtless desire cannot see the value of knowledge, allows her to go on being educated and enjoying it. The text once more allows its radical view of childhood knowledge and childhood desire by a public announcement of the opposite, more conventional view.

I suggested earlier that "The Purple Jar" seems unwilling to acknowledge the presence within it of a view of the persistence of childhood innocence and desire at odds with its public message of how knowledge controls desire and leads to the end of childlike thinking. Similarly, albeit moving in an opposite direction, Alice seems unwilling to acknowledge the presence within it of a view of the complexity and capability of childhood at odds with its public view of the simple and enduring joys of childhood. Because both texts harbor within them the presence of attitudes antithetical to those they publicly proclaim, both leave room for some ambivalence about the relative value of childhood desire and innocence, adult knowledge and suppression of desire.

As defined here, childhood desire is devoid of the main quality that we identify with desire in adults. What Rosamond and Alice want—aesthetic pleasure and the power of knowledge—is not in any obvious way connected with sexuality, so the secrets closeted in these texts are not the sexuality-related ones Sedgwick focuses on. Or are they? Rosamond's wish for the jar represents a fulfillment of sensuous pleasure, and according to William Empson, "To make the dream-story from which *Wonderland* was elaborated seem Freudian one has only to tell it."[25] It is, in other words, an open secret, like the ones Sedgwick focuses on. Empson goes on to suggest that Alice "runs the whole gamut; she is a father in getting down the hole, a foetus at the bottom, and can only be born by becoming a mother and producing her own amniotic fluid" (217).

It might well be that the closets of texts of children's literature generally contain a theoretically repressed sexuality—a sexuality queer enough that it might represent what Freud identifies as the polymorphous perversity of childhood, the idea "that all the perverse tendencies have their roots in childhood, that children are disposed towards them all and practise them all to a degree conforming with their immaturity."[26] Viewed in these terms, children's literature might be viewed as a way in which adult writers, pretending to be childlike, gain access to their own inherent queerness. If so, however, it's instructive that the "happy endings" of children's literature tend, at least theoretically, to deny that queerness—to empty the purple from the jar.

The Story of Dr. Dolittle focuses on questions of knowledge just as obsessively as do "The Purple Jar" and *Alice* but is absolutely forthright about what *Alice* keeps more or less hidden: the idea that the openness to possibility supposedly characteristic of childlike thinking is actually wiser and more productive of happiness than the limited certainties of adult knowledge. Dr. Dolittle is a "clever" man (1) exactly to the extent that he ignores conventional adult views of what is and is not possible. The parrot Polynesia makes an explicit statement to this effect: "People make me sick. They think they're so wonderful. . . . And the only thing in animal-language that *people* have learned to understand is that when a dog wags his tail he means 'I'm glad!' . . . Such airs they put on—talking about 'the dumb animals.' *Dumb!*—Huh!" (16).

Not surprisingly, the supposedly dumb animals outwit and defeat the supposedly clever human beings throughout *Dr. Dolittle*. This represents a relationship between knowledge and desire different from those implied by the texts I've considered thus far: the confirmation that what the animals and Dr. Dolittle believe to be true about the relative value of regular adult knowledge and their own wisdom is true. I suggested earlier that this novel was a sort of wish-fulfillment fantasy. As long as Dr. Dolittle thinks like an animal (or a child) and ignores what adult humans consider to be true when they claim to know better, he gets what he wants and needs, and his life gets better and better. In this way the plot of *Dr. Dolittle* moves in the opposite direction from the plot of "The Purple Jar," in which adult knowledge turns out to be superior to Rosamond's desire-beclouded vision and works, readers are happily informed, to disperse it. Not only does Dr. Dolittle get what he wants, but his childlike lack of interest in what adults usually desire—money, as the text frequently points out—ends up making him incredibly rich. Thus, childlike wisdom, unimpeded by the error and constriction of adult knowledge, allows the fulfillment of childlike desire: wanting something more than or something different from what seems possible or rational to conventional wisdom turns out to be an act of real wisdom. That such wisdom should result in wealth represents a concern with capital at the heart of this book that seems central to many texts of children's literature. Consider, for instance, the degree to which Henry Huggins and Rosamond concern themselves with the buying and selling of things.

The celebration of childlike forms of knowledge seems far more open and one-sided in *Dr. Dolittle* than either the more veiled and ambivalent celebration of those forms in *Alice* or the publicly declared attack on childlike thinking in "The

Purple Jar." But as I suggested earlier, the conviction that childlike innocence is true wisdom does not mean that representations of adult knowledge and commentaries on them are absent from this novel; they must be present in order to be attacked. Being present, they then raise interesting questions about the nature of Lofting's celebration of their opposite.

Quite simply, adult knowledge is knowledge, and in being represented as the opposite of adult knowledge, childlike or animal wisdom can only be understood as a lack, a deficiency—a state of bliss defined by what is absent from it. In asking readers to admire this absence, Lofting makes a request quite different from the one Carroll seems to be making in regard to Alice. She wants always to know more of what adults claim to understand, whereas the animals and Dr. Dolittle become admirable by knowing less about it. Their condition is exactly like Rosamond's—except they triumph through their ignorance rather than losing out because of it.

But Dr. Dolittle—and most of the animals he interacts with—are, unlike Rosamond, adults; and Lofting himself was an adult when he wrote this book. Lofting and his characters had access to adult knowledge before they chose to dismiss its significance in favor of childlike or animal-like wisdom. All of them know enough, it seems, to know they know too much. I have a number of ways of thinking about this.

There is, for example, the question of praising those qualities that mark someone as other than and opposite to oneself, as a stick to beat oneself and one's kind with. What are readers to make of Lofting, clearly an adult, expressing such disdain for the wisdom of adults like himself? An adult cannot actually become a child again. That Dr. Dolittle does so makes Lofting's novel the most extreme form of wish-fulfillment fantasy, in which what is wished for is not only unlikely but actually beyond the realm of logic or possibility. There is something perverse in wishing for what cannot possibly be—and something peculiarly self-hating, even life-denying about wishing to be what one so clearly is not. To think as one imagines a child thinks, to be simple, to know less—all this means is that one is less conscious of the brute horror of the bare truth, despicable and unbearable reality itself. Lofting's attacks on typical adult knowledge represent an exceedingly negative and very ugly view of the world he knows and has no choice but knowing as an adult.

There might be a good reason for this. *The Story of Dr. Dolittle* had its genesis in illustrated letters Lofting sent home to his children while he served in World War I. It therefore represents an escape from a particularly horrific reality; it is an imagined utopia directly antithetical to the way things actually were in the world around Lofting as he wrote. My own knowledge of that horrific context for the golden utopia does much to change my understanding of the utopia. If the reality from which it escapes is one so clearly and completely brutal, then there seems to be more justice in attempting to escape from it and in indulging imaginatively in its impossible opposite. I can make sense of this text, and even admire it, if I, like Lofting, Dr. Dolittle, and the animals, have in my possession enough knowledge of the specific negative ways in which adults can and do actually behave in the real world. I can then see the justice of the wish to know less, even while I know it is impossible to do so.

But that raises, yet once more, the question of how the implied audience of child readers might be expected to respond to this text. Are they being expected to already know the context and understand the utopia in the light of it, as Lofting and Dolittle and I do? If not, how might they read *Dr. Dolittle*?

Let me consider the second possibility first and imagine a child reader who actually does not have knowledge of what the adult world is like. Such a child is quite different from the adult narrative voice implied by the text, which, in knowing the value of knowing less, is actually supposed to know more than most other adults rather than less—as do also Dr. Dolittle and his adult animal friends. These wise adults must know more than children usually do: they have known more and chosen to know less, whereas children presumably merely know less, period. The constant praising of childhood wisdom by these theoretically childlike adults distinguishes them from children, who simply are innocent without understanding why it is a good thing to be so.

If I imagine for a moment a child reader exactly that innocent, then I can see that the narrator addresses the reader something like this: "Take my word for it, as someone who knows better than you do: knowing less than I do is a good thing." Readers who accepted this position would not only be learning to be proud of their ignorance but also would be reaffirming, as does "The Purple Jar," the right of adults to define values for children by virtue of their superior knowledge. Paradoxically, the text would be contradicting and undermining its own message in the very act of promulgating that message successfully. It would be imposing a vision of childhood innocence and incapability on children in order to suit the needs and desires of adults—something that I have suggested texts of children's literature always and centrally do. And in doing so, of course, it would also be replacing actual childhood innocence with an adult vision of childhood innocence —inviting child readers to value their lack of knowledge, to develop an understanding of the meaning of the lack rather than just to lack it. And in doing that, it would be inviting readers to share the paradoxical double perspective of adults like the narrator and Dr. Dolittle: to have enough adult knowledge to know why not knowing very much of it is a good thing, to be un-innocent enough to value innocence.

For readers who accepted all this, the text in celebration of innocence would go some way toward dissipating their innocence, replacing it with a retrospective nostalgia for the innocence they have just lost in the very process of learning to value it. They would have learned to think about their own childhood more or less as adults who have moved beyond it do. That would place them in exactly the same category as the other group of child readers I have postulated—those who already possess enough adult knowledge to know why the childhood lack of knowledge they have moved beyond is desirable. As far as I can see, any child reader who makes sense of this text as it invites readers to do must both possess and deny the value of conventional adult knowledge and thus experience or at least think about childhood as both what he or she is experiencing and as nostalgia for what is already over.

Nostalgia, desire for and imaginary reveling in a golden, simpler time now past: I suspect that its presence is another key identifying characteristic of children's fiction. It is revealing that so many children's novels are historical fiction and that time-slip fantasies, in which children actually move into or have contact with people from an earlier time, have developed as a significant subgenre of children's fiction. Adults driven to write for children and about childhood are likely to be driven by nostalgia, for all were once children and are therefore revisiting a part of their own experience now past every time they write. As Valerie Krips suggests, however, "few adults would want to return to childhood as it was actually lived, with all its unremembered difficulties, humiliations, and problems, but returning to a past in which the problems of adulthood are by and large unknown is a different and much more enticing prospect."[27] Adults who understand childhood as a time they once experienced themselves, then left behind by growing more complex, tend to equate it with other mythic golden pasts—gardens of paradise, pastoral idylls, and so on. They view it in the same idyllic terms, in the golden glow of retrospective nostalgia.

But what interests me most here is the degree to which a text like *Dr. Dolittle* invites child readers to share the nostalgia—not just to enjoy descriptions of times in history now past but also, curiously, to view their own current childhoods nostalgically, as something to value for its relative innocence and simplicity. In a sense the text invites child readers to develop a double consciousness—to be both delightfully childlike and separate from that childlikeness, viewing and understanding it from an adult perspective. As I suggested earlier, *The Snowy Day* does this also—and so, in some ways, do *Alice's Adventures in Wonderland* (at least Alice's sister does) and *Henry Huggins*. Even "The Purple Jar" works to foster an adult memory of simple childhood inability on its child protagonist. The nostalgia of all these texts is a form of adult desire for a childlike lack of knowledge that adult authors are in one way or another inviting readers to share.

The Snowy Day makes the invitation by evoking and then thwarting childlike desire and then, finally, fulfilling it in terms that reinforce the adult desire for childlike incapacity. Peter feels a series of interconnected desires as the text proceeds. The first is to be able to play with the big boys, a desire thwarted when he is hit by one of their snowballs and realizes he is "[not] old enough—not yet." The second is to have a snowball for the next day—perhaps, although this is not ever said, when he imagines he will be old enough? The third, implied by his bad dream of the snow outside having melted, is for the snow to continue—perhaps a variation on the continuing wish to be grown up enough tomorrow to be able to join the big boys' game? What is clear here is that Peter's childlike desire—like Alice's—is for mastery. He wants to be older, more knowledgeable, more capable of manipulating his environment in order to get what he wants from it.

Meanwhile, the text and the pictures combine to reinforce the idea that Peter will not get what he wishes because he does not yet possess the appropriate degree of knowledge to make it possible—and that this lack is a good thing. When he enjoys the snowy day, he can do so because his childlike lack of conventional adult sense allows him to develop unconventional and more interesting uses for sticks and snowbanks. And when he suffers, it is either because of his ignorance (his lack of knowledge of the laws of physics that causes him to dump snow from a tree onto himself by hitting it with a stick or to assume he can keep a snowball overnight in his pocket) or his inadequacy (his inability to compete with the big boys). A picture even shows that the "great big tall heaping mountain of snow" he climbs up is really a not-so-large hill, thus reinforcing the deficiencies of his knowledge—and, of course, the charm and wonder of those deficiencies, for again and again, this book suggests that being innocent is wonderful, that even the trouble it gets you into is charming and delightful. Peter's ability to imagine a mountain out of a hill gives him pleasure, and his expression after he manages to dump snow on his head implies that even that disaster is a source of fun.

Finally, though, Peter gets what he wants—or rather, a version of it that leaches away his desire for maturity and mastery and replaces it with the nostalgic adult desire for simple innocence. Instead of the big boys, he gets a friend from across the hall to play with—a friend, the accompanying picture shows, his own size. Presumably, the games they will play together will be innocent ones, not the aggressively competitive and therefore, I assume, more adult games of the big boys. And instead of being able to preserve the snow, by an act of his own volition (and after his wish to do that reveals his ignorance), new snow simply falls, beyond his control.

This last strange development reminds me of the events of many of the well-known fairy tales whose adoption as texts for children in the nineteenth century seems to have set many of the guidelines for the characteristics of texts actually written for children. In stories like "Snow White" or "Cinderella" or "The Golden Bird," young people get what they want by not doing anything themselves to achieve it—and meanwhile, those who, like the step-relatives in "Cinderella" or the queen in "Snow White" or the older brothers in "The Golden Bird," trust themselves to make their own fates all fail miserably. In these stories, as in *The Snowy Day*, attempts to govern one's own fate by using one's knowledge lead to disaster; and passive trust in creatures such as talking foxes or fairy godmothers whose advice defies rational common sense (if you want transportation, simply provide a pumpkin; choose the dilapidated inn over the comfortable-looking one; and so on), or mere trust in fate itself, leads to reward. One could read these tales simply as wish-fulfillment fantasies, stories about surprisingly triumphant un-derdogs that are antithetical to the way real life usually is. Good but weak and not terribly knowledgeable characters get what they want, while self-seeking powerful people get punished. But it is also interesting that these tales circulated orally as folktales among adults, especially peasants, before they were written down as fairy tales for children. They may have acted to confirm the wisdom of a safely unquestioning passivity for their underclass audience that helped preserve the social structures that kept the underclass in its place and under the control of its wealthier and more powerful masters. *The Snowy Day* operates similarly, not only in terms of encouraging attitudes that keep children under the control of more powerful adults but also by encouraging children to think of themselves in terms of how adults see them: as charmingly inadequate, as delightfully without knowl-edge or the ability to govern themselves.

The Snowy Day thus works to fulfill the nostalgic adult desire that children think of themselves as innocent and celebrate their innocence. So, too, does *Henry Huggins*—and in similar terms. The events the book describes almost all emerge from Henry's childlike desires and almost always report how the fulfill-ment of those desires gets him into trouble. In the first story Henry gets the dog he wants and then has to cope with the disastrous consequences of having it. In the second he gets the fish he wants and then has to cope with the disastrous consequences of having them. After these two surprisingly similar episodes, each succeeding story represents a variation on the same theme of desire and its disastrous consequences. In the third story Henry gets to handle his friend's new football—exactly like the one he wants himself—and then has to cope with the disastrous consequences of losing it and having to replace it. The fourth story represents a reversal of this pattern: Henry does not want to play a Little Boy in the school play, and this time he enjoys the disastrous consequences of the means by which he gets his wish. The dog Ribsy manages to invade the school auditorium, the result of which is Henry's being covered in real green paint and therefore his being cast to play the only role appropriate for him: a green elf. In the fifth story, similarly, Henry's inept attempt to make his dog look clean by covering it in talcum powder that turns out, much to his surprise, to be pink, results in his getting his wish of having Ribsy win a prize in the dog show. Finally, the last story tells how Ribsy fulfills Henry's desire by choosing him over a former owner who suddenly appears to claim him.

In each of these stories Henry's lack of knowledge compounds the disastrous troubles into which his desire has led him. He acts to get what he wants because he does not know how difficult or impossible it might be; and he chooses counterproductive means of fulfilling his desires simply because he does not know enough to realize how counterproductive they are.

All of this seems to suggest a didactic pattern similar to the one in "The Purple Jar": childhood desires stem from childhood ignorance, and the getting of knowledge will reveal the inadequacy of the desires and make children wiser and better by expelling the desires. Unlike "The Purple Jar," however, desire is neither expelled here nor left unfulfilled. No matter how awful the consequences of Henry's desires, all of these stories end happily exactly because the desire is fulfilled. Henry gets what he wanted in the first place: the fish, the football, an acceptable role in the play, a dog show prize, and above all and in both the first story and the last one, the dog itself. Two important questions then arise. First, why, if it is so clearly an act of childlike ignorance and inadequacy to want what common (i.e., adult) sense suggests you can't have, does Henry get away with it? And second, what are the means by which he gets it? How and why are his desires fulfilled?

The answer to the first question is simply that Henry's childlike ignorance and inadequacy are being celebrated here. As in *Dr. Dolittle* and *The Snowy Day*, they are good things, not bad ones. If Henry actually did learn better, as Rosamond did, he would cease to be interesting or charming or delightful. The general effect of all these stories is to confirm the charm and the power of childhood inadequacy. Since Henry wins because or in spite of his misguided ignorance, and because that misguided ignorance leads him into such delightfully comic and never truly dangerous troubles, the ignorance emerges seeming more positive than negative —a source of pleasure for readers and profit for Henry. As I suggested earlier, of course, experiencing the pleasure requires readers to separate themselves from Henry exactly because, in order both to get the joke and acknowledge the wonderful charm of Henry's innocence, they must know more and see more than he does. Like *Dr. Dolittle* and *The Snowy Day*—and like many other comic narratives that chronicle the adventures of delightfully ignorant know-nothings (Don Quixote, Charlie Chaplin's tramp, Homer Simpson) innocently but happily making their way through life unconscious of the actual implications of the reality they move so blindly through—*Henry Huggins* implies readers who know enough to know that knowing less is better.

And this suggests the answer to my second question. Henry gets what he wants exactly because of his ignorant actions. They almost always backfire, but the backfiring turns out magically to be another path to the desired result. Thus, for instance, his ignorance of the logistics of fish reproduction, which leads him to having a bedroom full of guppies, results in his having enough cash to buy the more expensive fish he really wants; and his foolish application of pink talcum powder leads to Ribsy's winning the prize Henry wanted—albeit a prize for "the most unusual dog" (134). It almost always turns out that it is wise of Henry to be ignorant.

It also often turns out that Ribsy's uncontrollable animal urges have positive results. Henry had to apply the powder that resulted in the prize because Ribsy, foolishly unaware of the significance of being clean for the dog show, rolled in the dirt. It is Ribsy's uncontrolled and exuberant barking that prevents Henry from hearing the car that goes by just as he is tossing his friend's football, thus forcing Henry to earn the money that will eventually end up in his getting the football of his own that he wanted in the first place. And it is Ribsy's unrestrained scratching and barking that leads to Henry's getting out of the unwanted role in the school play. In all these instances Ribsy operates as a sort of exaggerated exterior surrogate for what the stories are asking readers to perceive and admire in Henry. Ribsy seems to be a physical manifestation of Henry's childlike desire and the ways in which it manages to defy and triumph over adult systems of knowledge and good behavior.

In a sense, then, Henry is most childlike, most lovable, and most triumphant when he acts most like an animal. Once more, as in *Dr. Dolittle,* the animal and the childlike are conflated and directly opposed to what come to be seen as the inadequacies of adult knowledge. Or perhaps it is not the childlike generally but the boyish in particular; I will explore how texts of children's literature typically work to construct the gender of their implied readers—and the extent to which texts for boys and texts for girls do that similarly or differently—in chapter 3.

I find it especially interesting that Henry is content with the role he finally does get in the school play—that of the Green Elf. "That was a good part," Henry thinks. "The Green Elf turned somersaults and didn't have to say anything" (106). As a freewheeling spirit of anarchy and of the color traditionally representative of nature and of giving in to one's natural or animal-like instincts, the elf Henry will enact is another manifestation of what Ribsy already is and what Henry really wants to be. The action of the story results in his being allowed to play out in public what he secretly already is, an essentially (and apparently unchangeably) childlike (i.e., animal-like or natural) spirit.

This series of events once more reverses the terms of "The Purple Jar." Whereas the jar loses its interesting but unnatural color and thus represents the inappropriate folly of Rosamond's desire, Henry gains a fascinating but unnatural color that represents the wisdom and therefore the appropriate fulfillment of his desire. Both texts operate in the same terms even though they work to express directly antithetical views of childhood, which may be what most clearly identifies them as texts of children's literature.

Henry prefers the part of the Green Elf to the one he was being forced to play earlier—a Little Boy: "It was worse than anything Henry had imagined. He would never live down the part of a little boy!" (85). But Henry *is* a little boy. Why does he find this part so objectionable? The answer is obvious: the Little Boy in the play wears pajamas and kisses his mother good night. These are things that Henry himself most likely does. But doing them in the play means doing them in public, in front of other people—acknowledging them; and acknowledging them is admitting to forms of boyish behavior embarrassingly unacceptable to other children. Furthermore, playing the part means doing these publicly unacceptable things in terms defined by the adult who wrote the script—enacting an adult version of a desirable childlikeness.

The child of the play is no more like the real Henry than the Green Elf is. It is instructive, for instance, that the script requires the Little Boy to address his mother by saying, "Yes, Mother" (93). Henry tries unsuccessfully to change the line to the less polite and less conventionally acceptable "Yeah, Ma"; but when he has a conversation with his own actual mother, he calls her neither Mother nor Ma, but Mom. That difference reveals that the sentimentalized Little Boy of the play diverges from Henry's normal reality just as much as the anarchic Green Elf, the kind of crude spirit who might call a mother Ma, does. But the Little Boy represents a fulfillment of adult desire—a grown-up's nostalgic version of desirable childhood; and the Green Elf is clearly meant to represent Henry's own desire. As he looks at himself covered with green paint, "He couldn't take his eyes off the mirror. Secretly he thought he looked fascinating. Like a leprechaun in a fairy tale" (105–106). The story then describes how Henry gets out of enacting the utopian and sentimentalized childhood that adults desire and replaces it with the fulfillment of his own utopian desire—a desire that, as I suggested earlier, equates childhood with energy and anarchy and animal spirits.

The Little Boy that Henry wants so desperately not to have to enact appears in a carbon-copy typescript—one copied so many times it is hard for him to read and make sense of it. But despite its blurriness, this often-duplicated adult script has power—it can force him to be what he does not want to be. His main effort to get out of being it is to attempt to produce his own script—a typewritten note presumably from his mother that will excuse him from appearing in the play. But Henry cannot produce an acceptable typescript. His typing is childishly inadequate to the task, a fact that seems to confirm the authority of the adult typescript over him. But then, of course, Ribsy saves the day by transforming Henry's appearance in a way that not only makes it impossible for him to enact the idealized child of the adult typescript but that accomplishes this by turning the exterior Henry into an actualized version of his own interior idealized self-image. Henry wins by being more childlike, not by being more adult.

The happiness of this happy ending is that Henry gets to play at the ideal childhood he wants rather than the ideal childhood adults want. Paradoxically, however, it is an adult, Cleary, who tells this story and who therefore both invents and confirms the validity of Henry's desire. I have to conclude that Cleary is in the business of doing the very thing the story so clearly criticizes—offering words that define readers, imposing a vision of idealized childhood on a child. Her vision is different from that of the school play, but the role with which she has Ribsy literally cover Henry—and, presumably, the role she invites child readers to impose upon themselves—is just as clearly idealized and artificial, an act of utopian wish-fulfillment and an invitation to child readers to share her adult sense of what they most happily might be.

This idealized image is peculiarly static. Elves and dogs never cease to be elflike or doglike. Unlike human children, they already are what they will always be, and they do not grow up or learn more than they already know. If Henry and the children who read about him are to think of themselves as being ideally elflike or animal-like, then they must also conceive of themselves as ideally unchanging and incapable of learning. Interestingly, Henry himself already seems to possess those supposed virtues. One of the reasons readers can enjoy the humor of his various traumas rather than respond to the horror of them is simply that Henry himself seems unaware of the horror: he simply soldiers on, undeterred. He also tends to remain blissfully ignorant of the implications of the chaos that his innocence and Ribsy's unruliness continually create—and he certainly does not learn to be different or better as a result of it. For instance, he arrives home from his bus trauma completely unaware of what kind of box would make a dog acceptable on a bus and quite happy to blame his mother for his troubles: "I just brought my dog home on the bus like you said" (29).

In this way, again, he is like other comic innocents, like Chaplin or Don Quixote. But those other innocents are adults who have remained childlike—and who are, therefore, like Dr. Dolittle, clearly removed from their intended audience, different—not so much to be identified with as to be admired and desired in a wish-fulfilling sort of way. The dynamic changes somewhat when the eternally childlike being is still a child and is being held up as an acceptable idea of childlikeness to child readers. As in "The Purple Jar" and *The Snowy Day, Henry Huggins* enforces a vision of childhood as a time of presumably permanent inadequacy and invites child readers to see themselves as more or less incapable of learning or changing, happy as a result of it, and therefore needing and ideally inviting the security of adult power over them. As I suggested earlier, it is instructive that the solution to Henry Huggins's bus problem is his mother's call to the police. Adult protectiveness means that he was always going to get out of the mess safely, no matter what he did, and this predisposition both leaves readers free to enjoy the chaos of his attempts to solve the problem himself and encourages them to perceive themselves as innocent enough to require and accept adult power over themselves.

Plain City has a quite different view of the potential for and significance of change and growth in children: not only can Buhlaire change; she must. At one point she remembers her mother saying, "Children are mutants. You don't remember childhood, Buhlaire, 'cause young people are all-time mutating to the next stage of young'un. You can't remember from one day to the next because your brain is in a state of flux. Flux? It's change. You are a mutant child, baby, here today and all fluxed tomorrow—heh, heh" (31). This statement is neatly undermined by the next thing Buhlaire thinks: "Remember her telling me that." If Buhlaire can remember being told why she cannot remember, then clearly the statement about her not remembering is not completely accurate. Readers later discover that it is something of a rationalization. Believing the knowledge will do her daughter harm, Buhlaire's mother has deliberately kept information about her past from her, particularly the fact that her father is still alive. Ironically, therefore, the real reason Buhlaire cannot remember her early years is not that she keeps mutating into somebody different but that her mother and aunts and uncles have deliberately tried to stop her from mutating, deliberately tried to hold Buhlaire in what they see as a safe static state of innocence. These adults in Buhlaire's life play out one more version of the adult effort described or performed in one way or another by so many of these texts: the effort to keep children statically and safely childlike by working to preserve their ignorance of the knowledge the adults possess.

In texts as diverse as "The Purple Jar" or *Henry Huggins* the adult belief that adult-imposed ignorance can keep children safely static is confirmed by child characters who don't actually know anything or learn anything, don't actually change, and are happy because of it. These texts work to confirm an adult vision of childhood as ideally static. In *Plain City* the opposite happens. The idea that childhood is safely static is undermined because, with yet one more level of irony, the mother's description of Buhlaire as being in a state of flux, which she clearly hopes is not true, actually is true. Buhlaire is in the process of changing right from the beginning of the novel; she is continually uncertain about everything, including who she is and what her life means. She therefore thinks constantly about what she knows and does not know. "Everybody probably knowing everything. But me, I, not knowing" (35), she thinks, and later, "How come everybody knew something before she did?" (42). Above all, she lacks certain knowledge of herself; when a teacher tells her that something she has done "isn't like you," she thinks, "How do you know what I'm like, when I don't even know?" (32).

Buhlaire's consciousness of her lack of self-knowledge and the uncertainty in which it results place her in a position much like the one Alice occupies in *Alice's Adventures in Wonderland*. As I suggested earlier, however, *Alice's Adventures in Wonderland* usually depicts the state of uncertainty as utopian. Most of the time Alice likes not knowing, and knowing she does not know, because it means she can work to find out more. In *Plain City* Buhlaire's actual state of knowing she does not know is no more utopian than the state of unknowing innocence that the adults in Buhlaire's life believe they have maintained for her. She is unhappy exactly because she does not know, and knows it, and wants to know more. As she eventually says, "I just wanted to know things. I didn't care what it was. I still don't. I just wanted to know" (160). She wants especially to know the very thing her mother wants to keep from her: knowledge of her "back time" or family history, and above all, who her father is or was.

Buhlaire wants to know because she is convinced of a truth opposite to the one her mother believes. Far from keeping her safely happy, her lack of knowledge has made her unhappy. Once she has the knowledge she lacks about her back time and her father, she thinks, she will also then know who she is. She will be certain, and she will be happy.

Buhlaire eventually gets the knowledge she desires; and like most fulfillments of childhood desire reported in these texts of children's literature, getting what she wants does not have the effect she imagined it would. It does not make her certain or rectify the lack of knowledge that her mother imposed on her. It does just the opposite—it unsettles her even more. In doing so, it reveals a paradox in Buhlaire's view of herself and her childhood. She has seen the secure cocoon that her relatives have worked to keep her in as the source of her insecurity and, therefore, as dangerous to her. She wants to escape the safety so that she can, paradoxically, be safe from it. Thus, she sees her house as an oppressive prison: "In her mind she locked sadness in that house, where it couldn't get her. . . . Everything was free and different outside" (95); and she thinks of the homeless shelter as another safe prison: "People went there, and it kept them penned up, she didn't know about safe" (99). She even finds herself doubting the wisdom of her uncle Sam, who unceremoniously gets rid of a stranger who approaches Buhlaire in a wooded area near her home, and whom she herself first sees as "a nightmare . . . bad news coming out of nowhere. Creeping up on her" (43). Sam tells her that "there are times when you can take no chances. You have to do the safe thing" (47). But Buhlaire, imagining the possibility that the man might have been her father, doubts that, and she doubts that safety is necessary: "Uncle Sam was mean. Maybe the man would've hurt me. Maybe not" (47).

It is not surprising that Buhlaire finds the new knowledge she gains so unsettling. She learns a series of interconnected things, all having to do with what it means to feel safe. First, her effort to escape the safety of home lands her in the middle of a whiteout outside of town, and she must realize how much she really wants and needs the safety: "I must be crazy to be out here" (102), she thinks, and, in language reminiscent of her earlier thoughts about the strange man who approached her, "It felt as if the white was tracking her down, that danger was just outside it. Something awful could get her" (104). Escaping the safety of home means feeling threatened, not strong. Second, and in the context of this threat, she finds the father she always wanted in the heart of the whiteout. As a homeless vagrant, his lifestyle represents exactly the freedom from stasis and suffocating security she thought she wanted, but in a desperately nonutopian form, and "the truth made her ache" (110).

Third, she learns that the theoretically impregnable safety in which the adults she lives with have cocooned her was never really impregnable. The "back time" she wants—represented by the photographs and trophies of her past that she lacks—has been stolen by her father, who has broken into the house to steal them: "He took my things. He took off with my back time" (127). The father she wanted knowledge of—and about whom she blamed her mother and aunts and uncles for keeping her ignorant—has himself conspired to deprive her of that knowledge. What she saw as opposite to the stultifying emptiness of home has contributed to the emptiness. Fourth, just as home was not a complete protected fortress, the world away from home was never a place of unprotected freedom. Her father has been following Buhlaire on her theoretically solitary rambles, just as her friend Grady has. She was always safe, even when she felt most free of the constrictions of safety.

In the light of the other texts I have been discussing here, I might expect Buhlaire to respond to her new knowledge in one of two ways. Fearing the dangers of the real world, she might accept the value of the ignorance the adults in her life worked to preserve and attempt to retreat back into the safety of the parental cocoon. Alternatively, accepting the danger as the price for the freedom she truly wants, she might confirm her distaste for the safety and ignorance of the cocoon and decide to leave it forever. Interestingly, Buhlaire does both and therefore neither of these.

She does, for a time, think of leaving home—all homes—by adopting her father's homeless lifestyle: "I don't have to go to anybody's shelter. . . . I can walk around all night if I have to and nobody can stop me. I can go live with my dad" (137). She even tries to persuade herself that "I am like my dad, can't stand the indoors for long. . . . Just an outside child!" (169). Meanwhile, however, this self-named "child" also thinks of her father as "a hurt child" (118) and sees herself in the role of his parental protector, which rather muddies the purity of the freedom this new life will bring her.

Finally, she realizes that she is not an "outside child"—that she would be "too scared" for a life on the road (177). But then the purity of this retreat into safety is muddied by Buhlaire's renegotiation of her position in the house. Not only is she no longer ignorant of the truth, but she has persuaded her mother that it was wrong to keep the truth from her. "I think I learned from you today, Buhlaire" (163), her mother says—making herself childlike in relation to Buhlaire's superior wisdom so that now Buhlaire is placed in the position of parenting both her parents. Even after deciding not to accompany her father on the road, she thinks about always watching over him, as he—and Grady and her mother and aunts and uncles—has watched over her: "If I can see him and be sure he's all right . . . I can live with it" (178).

As Buhlaire talks about leaving home, her mother says to her, "Whatever you are thinking to do, think about it knowing who and what he is" (167)—an invitation to act on knowledge rather than ignorance that transforms their relationship and the meaning of their life together. Finally, Buhlaire does just what her mother has advised—and because it is her own choice to remain at home, a space she has now renegotiated to include her own self-governance within it, it is no retreat, but a step forward into maturity. "Everything had changed, too," she finally thinks. "But not for the bad. *It's exciting, life is*" (191).

In these ways *Plain City* undermines and finally denies the validity of the oppositional relationships between a range of values and ideas it begins by seeming to support: home and away, safety and danger, innocence and knowledge. Home is a place of both safety and freedom, as is, to some degree, the world away from home. Children should feel as much responsibility for fostering the well-being of the adults in their lives as vice versa. Adults are in some ways as ignorant as children ("The hardest thing is understanding that our parents aren't perfectly good," Grady's father tells Buhlaire, "that they make mistakes. They're human" [147]). And children are in some ways as knowledgeable or more knowledgeable than adults ("Kids understand more than we think," Grady's father adds, confirming Buhlaire's earlier assertion to her school principal: "People think kids don't know. I could tell you things I bet you don't know" [24]).

All of this represents a move beyond the framework established earlier in *Plain City* and firmly in place throughout the other five texts I have been considering. Those texts are all built around similar sets of binary oppositions, and whether they end up honoring the wisdom of childhood innocence or the truth of adult knowledge, all tend either to choose one pole of the opposition as the correct one or else offer ambivalent attitudes toward the poles that confirm the validity of their polarity. The childlike remains opposed to the adult, innocence opposed to the knowledge of maturity, desire opposed to common sense. But *Plain City* collapses the opposition by finding the theoretically polar qualities intermingled in the two theoretically different categories.

Plain City ultimately denies the idea that children are really all that much different from adults—which seems to be the basic idea that underlies and engenders all the other polarities. The book begins with both Buhlaire and her adult relatives agreeing that she is different from and opposite to them because of her age; all they disagree about is which of the two poles knows better. (And that seems also to be the state of things asserted or implied in the other five texts.) Buhlaire's mother declares that childhood is a state of constant change, and readers learn that for Buhlaire at least, she was right. But Buhlaire herself finally concludes that being human is to be in a state of flux, and her realization is underscored by the unconventional cadence of her recognition, "*The whole world. Changes*" (182). She seems to equate the world with change itself, and later, when she declares to herself, "*You can't stop, me*" (193), she seems to imply that who she is equates with never stopping, being also eternally in flux. What was first asserted as a characteristic of childhood is finally acknowledged as merely the state of being human for both children and adults. Childhood as a state with distinguishing qualities simply disappears.

If childhood, as adults usually imagine it and invite children to imagine it, does not exist outside adult imaginations, and if readers accepted *Plain City*'s invitation to stop imagining it in that way, they would be denying the assumption on which children's literature is based. There is no need for a different literature if children are not different. This puts *Plain City* in the peculiar position of denying the reasons for its own existence.

Or does it? For as I suggested earlier, *Plain City* is what is usually identified not as children's fiction but as fiction "for young adults"—people in the process of changing from children to adults. It may not be accidental that its key difference from the other texts is its movement beyond the polarity between children and adults that the other texts all establish. As children presumably move past the characteristic of childhood in their teen years, this text for young adults begins with and then moves past what appears to be a characteristic of children's fiction.

I see two significant ramifications of this. First, it suggests that polar oppositions based on conceptions of the ways in which children and adults differ are characteristic of and possibly even essential to texts written for children. Second, it suggests a path for thinking about how young-adult fiction might both be similar to other texts written for children and vary from them. Perhaps young adults' texts are those that begin with the standard polarities of children's fiction but have the potential, at least, to deconstruct them.

Plain City deconstructs the polarities by clearly asserting an idea many readers manage to find in *Alice's Adventures in Wonderland*: the perception that the text's descriptions of Alice's childlike uncertainty in the face of a continually changing and always uncertain world might simply represent life as all human beings experience it. The idea that mature adult knowledge and experience really offers no more certainty or security than childhood innocence does—that both children and adults have less power to understand and control their world than adults like

Rosamond's mother like to imagine—appears to be what opens these texts to an audience not defined as purely childlike, to the no-longer-completely-childlike young-adult audience of *Plain City* or the purely adult audience that has found a place for *Alice's Adventures in Wonderland* in the canon of important literature for adults to read and think about. This reinforces how intermingled are conceptions of the need for a literature for children and the need for adults to reassure children about themselves and their position in relation to adults—to offer children comfort and/or to make adults comfortable about their power over children.

Home and Away: Essential Doubleness

In *Plain City* Buhlaire tends to explore her uncertain feelings about herself and her adult relatives most specifically in terms of how she feels about her home. It becomes her central image of oppression, and being away from it becomes her central image of escape from oppression: "Everything was free and different outside" (95). In *Alice's Adventures in Wonderland,* similarly, Alice, caught up in the anarchic freedom of Wonderland, thinks, "It was much pleasanter at home" (33). For her, too, home and away are significant images of safety and/or constraint as opposed to danger and/or freedom. Questions about the meanings of home and away are central to all six of these texts—as they seem to be central to cultural ideas about childhood in the time in which a specific children's literature has existed, ideas that tend to separate children from other human beings by imagining a space in which it is safe to be childlike and thus also a less safe space beyond it. All six texts take their main characters on trips away from home and back again. All six assert or imply that home and away represent opposing sets of values, and these values are the same or similar in all six texts.

Rosamond discovers the glory of the purple jar on a shopping expedition, in an unfamiliar place away from home. Later, the folly of her choice keeps her at home, deprived of the pleasure of other expeditions and unfamiliar experiences. It is especially interesting here that the practical choice she so foolishly rejects is, exactly, shoes: the most obvious equipment required for leaving home. Her desire for new and exciting experiences ironically deprives her of the ability to have such experiences.

In *Henry Huggins* Henry's wishes for something exciting to happen are fulfilled either by journeys away from home, and thus into the new and unexpected territory of unfamiliar experience, or else by his bringing something new, unfamiliar, and inevitably disruptive (like Ribsy or guppies) into his home. Home represents a framework of dependable normalcy Henry can always depart from and return to. It is always safely there, allowing him his desire for what he has not yet experienced by placing it in a context that renders the expression of that desire more or less harmless.

The section about Alice's sister at the end of *Alice's Adventures in Wonderland* does something similar. The sister imagines that the anarchy of Alice's wonderland has actually invaded the familiar landscape around her, just as Henry's multiplying guppies intrude on the usual calm of his home: "The whole place around her became alive with the strange creatures of her little sister's dream" (110). Everything Alice's sister imagines at this point is painful or violent—shrieks, chokes, sobs, demands for execution. Carroll then says, "She sat on, with closed eyes, and half believed herself in Wonderland, though she knew she had but to open them again, and all would change to dull reality" (111). This scene represents an ambivalent dismissal of everything Wonderland has come to represent. The sister reassures herself that it is not real at the same time as she calls reality "dull." It seems that, like the mothers of Henry Huggins and Rosamond, she actually favors the dull over the dangerous—she certainly seems to be reassuring herself about the lack of reality of what her sister has been experiencing. If Wonderland represents what one wonders about when one refuses to accept the limitations of conventional ideas about what is possible—a space of real freedom from the already known—then the sister is in the process of depriving wondering itself of its liberating dangers. She makes it merely illusory, not actually representative of any real possibilities or any actual danger. Alice enjoys the challenge of the unexpected that she finds away from home; Alice's sister transforms Alice's own opposition of home and away by, in effect, insisting that "away" does not actually exist—that there is really nothing new under the sun and that home is not only best but really all there is.

The Snowy Day is less dismissive of the value and possibility of unfamiliar experiences, but, like Henry Huggins, it carefully circumscribes them. The wonder (and possible danger) of the experiences afforded by the unfamiliar presence of snow outside occurs only within the comforting (but constricting?) presence of a warm and familiar home to leave from and return to, so inside and outside, home and away, represent clearly opposing values. Being outside is exciting but dangerous; home warms one but also melts and dissipates the exciting snow of outside.

Snow also figures prominently as an image of what home protects or imprisons one from in *Plain City*, but with different implications. The all-white jumpsuit Buhlaire favors implies her wish to identify with what she sees as the freeing qualities of the snow from the start. She worries a lot about how people see her, and the suit makes her, "at first glance, . . . invisible from the neck down" (2); and she sees her solitary walks outside town as ways of escaping the constricting frames imposed on her by other people: "Everything was free and different outside" (95). Later, her actual experience of being in a whiteout begins to show her the danger in her desires. Not so incidentally, one reason Buhlaire feels like an outsider is that her inheritance of her father's mixed parentage has made her skin lighter than everyone else's around her—more white-looking; and that adds race-related implications to her desire to be lost in whiteness.

The Story of Dr. Dolittle represents a somewhat different balancing of the same two opposites. At the start the doctor's home is a space controlled by the conventional adult values of his sister, who objects strenuously when he introduces the chaotic unconventionality of animals into the parlor—brings what conventionally belongs outside in. The sister then decamps altogether, leaving the space a utopian representation of a safe refuge for freeing unconventionality. In effect, this development reverses the dynamics of the opposing values: the doctor's home now represents what places away from home usually represent, and the sister's move away from it is a voyage into conventionally home-associated values. But for those the book identifies as being worthwhile—the animals and the doctor himself—home is still a place of safety and the sister's world away from it in conventional society a place of danger. Later in the book, the doctor's journeys into the wilds of Africa keep him in a place of safety, except when he becomes involved with places that seem more like conventional human homes—palaces and such. There he and friends of his confront the dangers of constraint and conventional values and must escape from them into the safety of the jungle or the ocean or anyplace not like home.

None of this is particularly surprising. A number of scholars have pointed to a favorite pattern in children's stories as beginning with their protagonists at home, taking them on a journey, and returning them home again at the end. In my own previous work in this area I have moved toward the conclusion that the pattern is worth paying attention to exactly because of the ways in which it works to attach opposing values to home and to being away from home, forcing child protagonists to confront the difference and make choices between the opposed values in terms of how they understand what they mean and, consequently, which of the two places they would rather be in.[28] Now, in the context of what I have written so far about these six texts, I begin to see other implications of this frequent focus on home and away.

One is simply the degree to which the narrative pattern reinforces the doubleness of these texts—makes the presence of opposed binaries within them seem a particularly significant characteristic. So far, I have suggested that the texts offer two versions of the stories they tell, the actual simple text itself and the more detailed shadow it implies; that they conventionally imply two different focalizations, one childlike and one more mature; and that they often represent the interplay of binary opposites such as constraint and freedom, safety and uncertainty, knowledge and innocence, desire and possibility, and so on. I can now add to all that the idea that the poles of these binaries tend to be associated either with home or with being away from home.

This makes the world of these texts inherently binary and incontrovertibly oppositional. Whatever else they do, these stories invite child readers to think of everything in terms of this or that—home or away, safety or danger, freedom or constraint, ignorance or knowledge—with, it usually seems (the exception in this group of six texts is *Plain City*), very little room for the occupation of moderating positions between the two poles. This is not a particularly subtle view of how things work, nor is it one that leaves much room for tolerance. Since the two poles are viewed as opposites, acceptance of one almost inevitably means rejection of the other. These texts tend to conclude with decisions made or implied, decisions that reinforce one pole or the other—home or away, black or white, never (except, again, in *Plain City*) home and away, black and white, part one and part the other. They tend to work toward establishing hierarchies. Once they divide what people experience into a question of two opposing values, they work toward a solution that privileges one over the other. In the struggle of opposites there are clear winners and losers.

A world perceived by means of binary opposites, however, is so inherently and thoroughly marked by struggle that the struggles can never really cease. The very act of declaring victory of one side over the other affirms the existence of that which is being defeated—acknowledges and defines it and thus renders it existent in order to render it nonexistent. Thus, as I suggested earlier, these texts tend to construct the theoretical victories of one pole over the other by allowing space for readers to reverse the dynamic and imagine a victory for the other pole. Eternally bipolar, they are therefore, and despite whatever else they might attempt, eternally *ambivalent*.

They are especially so in terms of the main opposition that seems to underpin all the others: the one between the childlike and the adult. Again and again, my discussions of other polarities have led me to questions about what adults know and want as opposed to what children know and want. The happy endings of the texts represent as true wisdom the understanding and acceptance of either an adult perspective or a childlike one, as well as both childlike and adult desire rightly fulfilled and/or rightly repudiated as a result of it. I begin to see that the primary reason why adults write literature for children—the idea that children are different from adults, and different in ways that require adults to write texts especially for them—marks those texts so deeply that it influences and controls everything they ever are, and it accounts for all the characteristics I have been exploring here. Whatever else they do, I am beginning to suspect, texts written by adults for children reaffirm and communicate the foundational idea that engendered them—the idea that children are different from and even opposite to adults. What distinguishes them from other texts is the extent to which they assume, inscribe, and reinforce assumptions about childhood that make their implied child readers different from their adult authors.

It is especially significant that a major expression of that which is different should come in terms of ideas of home and away. As I suggested earlier, these texts tend to be centrally concerned with justifying adult ideas of childhood to children—and in a sense, therefore, justifying their own existence. They work to persuade their readers that they are the kind of texts those readers need to read, exactly because those readers are the people the texts imply: children, opposite to adults in a number of significant ways and therefore in need of the adults to imagine safe spaces for them to be childlike and vulnerable within. As these texts tend to understand it, home is equivalent to what the texts are themselves: a controlled and limited space provided for a child by a more knowing and more capable adult in order to protect the child from the less limited but more dangerous world outside—the world away from home, the world as represented in literature for adults. As a result, the texts tend to focus frequently on justifying the need for home and the desirability of staying there. Their central thrust is, in a very real sense, a justification of their own existence—a celebration of safely limited places for children.

Being so inherently oppositional, however, these texts often proceed by means of describing opposition to the conclusion they might wish to reach and then moving toward the expulsion of the discontent. So they tend to begin by imagining children as being discontented with the restrictions of home, to equate childlike desire with lust for what lies beyond the safe walls adults provide, the constricting childhood adults imagine. Children, quite simply, are too immature to appreciate childhood as adults know it must be—which is why children need adults to protect them from themselves. In constructing children as opposite to adults, these texts tend to provide them with opposite desires, imagine them inevitably in conflict with adult values, and specifically adults' ideas about what children should be. Once more, children are imagined as double and divided—as what they should be according to adults and as what adults assume they already are and want them not to be. To be a child, according to these texts, is inevitably a matter of wanting to defy adult wisdom, wanting to emerge from adult protection, and wanting to move past adult ideas about what a child is and should be.

Specifically, therefore, these texts are about wanting to leave home. The way in which the texts center their disputes around ideas of home and away makes the actual spaces metaphoric by tying them to values and to certain recurring values in particular. Once having accepted the mythology underlying this group of texts, a reader can no longer think of a home as just a house or as just a backdrop for living, or of a space away as merely somewhere else. Each means something, something clearly defined. The physical world has been absorbed into the realm of meaning, the vehicle of the metaphor permeated with and inseparable from the tenor the texts attach to it. Both home and away from home as they function in children's literature are what Henri Lefebvre identifies as a "produced" space—a product, representation, and producer of social values: "The space thus produced also serves as a tool of thought and of action. . . . In addition to being a means of production it is also a means of control, and hence of domination, of power."[29] As Lefebvre argues, this space has profound ideological implications: "What is an ideology without a space to which it refers, a space which it describes, whose vocabulary and links it makes use of, and whose code it embodies? . . . What we call ideology only achieves consistency by intervening in social space and in its production, and by thus taking on body therein. Ideology *per se* might well be said to consist primarily in a discourse upon social space" (44). The home and away of children's literature clearly represent and intervene in such a discourse.

I might assert one further characteristic quality of texts written for children. They tend to make settings into produced social spaces, places representative of meanings, of ways of defining what the characters mean to themselves and to others. Their spaces are often, to that extent, allegorical, specifically in terms of places representing childlike and adult modes of perception. And perhaps that is why the plots of so many of them revolve around voyages from one place to another, especially to and from home. These voyages inevitably imply psychic journeys, moves from one state of mind to another, from one set of values to another—specifically from adult views of what childhood is and should be to child-centered ones and back again.

I repeat: and back again. Thus far in this section I have concentrated on the ways in which ideas of home and away in these texts replicate and reinforce oppositional patterns. But the patterns are so thoroughly opposed and so thoroughly dependent on each others' continuing existence in order to keep on being meaningful that the resolutions of the struggle between them can almost always be read as illusory or deceptive. "Home" needs "away" to define its meaning, and "away" means nothing in particular if there is no "home" to read it against. The ways in which these texts organize landscapes of home and away, and the way in which those organizations of space mirror other binary pairs such as child and adult, innocence and knowledge, and so on, imply a world held in stasis, its meanings always suspended between the two opposing poles and unable ever actually to move beyond them without ceasing to be children's literature.

But as narrative, these texts do have another movement beside the recurring one between the two poles: the sequential action of a plot. And that action also is built on ideas of home and away. In addition to always returning to and always confirming the eternal opposition of home and away, what adults create as a space for childhood and the places children want, the texts tend to move sequentially from home to away and then home again. In doing so, they muddy the apparently clear waters I have been describing. Viewed in terms of sequence rather than in terms of the shape of the ideational world of meaning they flesh out, there are not just two main components to the structure of the texts, but three: home and away, yes, but also, "home again." And the home one returns to after being away is not and cannot be the same home one left.

In a number of the traditional fairy tales that figure so prominently in the history of fiction for children, characters do quite literally end up in different homes after their journeys away. Consider, for instance, "Cinderella" and "Snow White." The characters in such tales gain their new residence as a result of a marriage—a marriage that not only ends any perception listeners and readers might have had of them as being children but that also gives them the power they earlier lacked in a home that stifled and oppressed them. These seem to be stories of people making the transition between childhood and maturity, and it is not accidental that their main characters now tend to occupy the positions in their new home that the adults who oppressed them occupied in their old home—*they* have the power, and *they* will be the parents to any children who happen to come along. In this way the tales confirm the idea that home is a good space to occupy for those with the power to control the space but not so good for those controlled within it— for adults but not for children. These tales thus present a rather one-sided view of childhood as imprisoning, maturity as empowering. The progress of movement forward triumphs over and dissipates the rigid strictures in place in the original home. This purely negative view of the spaces adults provide for children to inhabit suggests that there are likely to be far more young-adult novels than ones intended for younger children that end with their protagonists in a new home.

In all six texts I am focusing on, the characters end up in the same home from which they started out. But since they return with the experience of having been away, "home" still means something different, sometimes to them and almost always to their implied readers. The texts adopt and/or invite readers to adopt adult views of their need for the safe space and the constrictions adults have provided for them (most obviously in "The Purple Jar"). Or else they reveal the inadequacies of adult views in ways that allow their return to the childlike space of home to represent a victory for them and their childlike inability to adopt adult wisdom. This happens in *The Snowy Day, Henry Huggins,* and *Dr. Dolittle,* narratives that paradoxically treasure and reward childlike thinking by imagining as a home for it an enclosed utopian space protected from the dangerous world outside that it can continue to operate within—a space of childhood literally controlled in all three texts by adults, Henry's and Peter's parents in two cases and the doctor himself in the other. Or else, finally, the texts represent some ambivalent combination of the first two possibilities, a combination that changes what their homes mean to the child protagonists and to those who read about them *(The Snowy Day, Alice, Plain City).* In all three cases the home at the end is not the home of the beginning.

Home is different because of what has happened to the child while he or she has been away. At the end Rosamond and Buhlaire not only live in the protective safety of their homes, but they have had experiences that have forced them to become aware of and acknowledge the need for protection. While Henry Huggins and Peter of *The Snowy Day* never make such an acknowledgment, their readers are invited to develop a mature understanding of the meaning of their childlike innocence and the resultant need for a safe home to maintain it. Meanwhile, the homes of all these characters and also those of Alice and Dr. Dolittle have changed meaning at the end simply by coming to be understood as opposed to what is outside them, as opposite to the thrills or dangers of city buses or whiteouts or Wonderland, and therefore, to represent specific meanings they did not before have.

In all cases home changes. But paradoxically, viewed as one pole of a pair of binary opposites, home represents above all a place where change is unlikely or even impossible, a safely static enclosure designed to keep uncertainty and flux outside. The basic dynamic of the relationship of home and away is the opposition of the constriction and comfort of staying in the same place and the unfixed movement of journeying. It is no accident that home should be the metaphor for childhood as adults imagine it. As a constructed space, its purpose is above all to defy time, to prevent change from happening or at least from affecting those held within it, to keep children from the effects of change and time, to keep them safely as they now are for as long as possible.

This is clearly a doomed project, even theoretically. As Lefebvre suggests in talking about social spaces as a means of control, produced space "escapes in part from those who would make use of it. The social and political (state) forces which engendered this space now seek, but fail, to master it completely."[30] This happens in terms of the determinedly safe home spaces of children's literature especially because children do, must, grow up. The home at the end of these texts, although reaffirmed as better than the world outside, is a different home from the one the child protagonists imagine at the beginning. This difference represents a necessary acknowledgment of the inevitability of growth, particularly when child protagonists and child readers alike are invited to change their view of home. As a result, the home/away/home plot, which seems to represent a triumphant confirmation of the virtues of childhood as an enclosing and unchanging space, acknowledges and admits change in the very process of attempting to keep it out.

It may be for this reason that these texts are as ambivalent and double-voiced as I have found them to be throughout my exploration of them. They want to say two different things at the same time: that children can and must stay as they are at home in the enclosed space of childhood that adults provide for them but also that children do and must change even in order to appreciate the value of the enclosed space. There is a fatal contradiction at their heart.

I suspect it is the fatal contradiction at the heart of most adult views of childhood, which insist both that children are different from and even opposite to adults and that they are in the process of becoming more adult all the time. The same contradiction is commonly found in conventional assumptions about others thought of by powerful people, especially in the context of the European colonialist thinking that was the context in which children's literature as it currently exists developed, as belonging in less powerful categories: women traditionally by men, or racial and ethnic minorities by those in the majority. It intermingles two contradictory kinds of thinking. One kind of thinking is characterized by binary opposites. The less powerful are not only different from the more powerful but opposite to them in every way. Since the powerful clearly deserve their power, the less powerful must be perceived as weak exactly where the powerful are strong. And since the powerful define their strength in relation to the less powerful group's weakness, the less powerful must remain eternally and unavoidably weak so that the strong may continue to be perceived by themselves and others as strong enough to deserve power. But then, of course, a major responsibility of power is to work to teach that which is other, opposite, and inferior to learn better, to cease to be other, to become more like you. So there is also a second strain of thinking, this one evolutionary, which sees the deservedly less powerful groups as more primitive than the powerful ones but capable of evolving, in need of instruction and improvement. Ironically, however, this evolutionary strain of thinking works to doubly reinforce the oppression of the weak by the strong, for any inability of the oppressed group to evolve or change is viewed as further evidence of eternal intractability and inadequacy and thus further justification for the control of the weak by the strong and continued unsuccessful efforts to educate them.

When applied to disempowered groups, colonizing thinking of this sort often describes those disempowered by using metaphors of childhood. Conventional ideas about childhood appear to be the central model for this sort of colonial thinking about othered groups; it is not surprising that such thinking tends to be represented in parental metaphors like *paternalistic*. It is possible that the reverse is true, however, and that childhood as it has come to exist in a period concurrent with the colonial enterprise has been modeled on colonial thinking—or perhaps the two, as equivalent expressions of the capitalist societies that produce them, merely mirror each other. One way or the other, it is not surprising that texts written for children should view childhood as both eternally static and a place of change, children as both wonderfully incapable of learning and inevitably and always in the process of learning from adults who already know, home as both a place of safe fixity and a place where one learns to be different.

As I suggested before, the insistence that both contradictory positions be true—an insistence inherent in childhood as adults have come to construct it— seems to trouble and eventually undermine all attempts by these texts to come down on one side or the other. With the possible exception of *Plain City*, they are inherently and eternally double.

Variation

There is one further aspect of home/away/home patterns that interests me. The repetition of the first term in the third structural position implies something paradoxical about the latter occurrence: home is now both the same place it once was and at the same time a different place. As a different version of the same thing, it represents what I identify as a form of variation.

The *Oxford English Dictionary* defines *variation* in music as "a modification with regard to the tune, time, and harmony of a theme by which on repetition it appears in a new but still recognizable form; esp. in pl., embellishments in an air for giving variety on repetition after playing it in its simple form."[31] Like the structures of music, the structures of texts take shape over time, by means of sequential developments; they, too, can demonstrate variation. The home/away/ home pattern is one such structure; the reinterpretation of home at the end represents a modification that does not completely change its identity—while different, it is still home. These six texts often move forward by means of variations similar to this main underlying one. Their plots tend to consist of a series of discrete episodes, each of which represents a different version of the same or similar actions and a development of the same basic themes.

For instance, each double-page spread of *The Snowy Day* depicts a variation on the theme of playing with snow, finding out what it is and what one can and cannot do with it. The last sequence, in which Peter awakes to snow for a second time and goes out to play in it for a second time, but now with a friend his own size, is a variation on the events of the first few pages now intertwined with a new version of the central episode in which Peter wanted to play with the big boys. The text arrives at its happy ending by means of a replication of old elements in new relationships—by finding a satisfactory variation of what was earlier opposed that manages to unite the opposites.

"The Purple Jar" has a similarly episodic structure. There are a series of episodes in which Rosamond sees something in a shop, finds it attractive, and speaks to her mother of her desire for it, after which her mother explains why she will not purchase it, usually by making some reference to its potential usefulness. Although still versions of this basic situation, later episodes represent more extreme variations of it. The scene in which Rosamond gets what she wants rather than just expressing her desire for it still proceeds by means of a conversation in which she speaks of her desires and her mother responds by referring to usefulness. The final episode reverses various elements. A parent—this time Rosamond's father instead of her mother—speaks first yet still expresses reasons why Rosamond cannot have what she wants, and only then does Rosamond yet once more speak to her mother about what she wants. What she says suggests a way of resolving the war of previously irresolvable opposites, what Rosamond wants and what her parents know, for Rosamond's final declaration represents both at once. Nevertheless, the preservation of the basic dynamic here, the dialogue between parent and child about desire and usefulness in which the parent is right, undercuts the possibility implied by the sequence of changing events that something has actually changed in some significant way. The differences, however, undermine the stability of the basic dynamic.

Despite their episodic structure, "The Purple Jar" and *The Snowy Day* each contain just one complete action. *Henry Huggins, Alice's Adventures in Wonderland,* and *The Story of Dr. Dolittle* are more obviously episodic in that they consist of a number of such complete actions, each easily separable from the rest and all related to each other mainly because the same central characters appear in all of them. But these separate episodes or stories also have variational relationships to each other.

As well as being variations of each other, the episodes of *Henry Huggins* are variations on the pattern established in "The Purple Jar." In each episode Henry wants something and ends up defying adult values as a result of it. He then gets into and manages to get out of an anarchic mess. In four of the stories he can do so only with the fortuitous help of adults: the police officer and his parents in the first story, the neighbor who pays for worms in the second, the man who returns the football in the third story, the judge of the dog show in the fifth story. In all these stories adult intervention allows Henry to have what he wants but only on terms satisfying to adults. The fourth story, about the school play, represents an inversion of this pattern. Rather than Henry wanting something that defies adult values, an adult, the teacher, wants something that defies Henry's values; and it is not an adult who solves the problem but that which represents the opposite of adult order, Ribsy—and he does it by creating chaos rather than by dissipating it. In a different sort of variation, the final story involves no adults at all. It is the conflicting desires of two different children that causes the problem, and it is the community of children and the dog himself that solve it, without any adult interference. This rejuggling of previous components in a way that makes adult intervention unnecessary implies some progress beyond the stable world of static childhood that the earlier stories all end up reinforcing and thus seems like a good point at which to call the book ended.

Meanwhile, each of the stories in *Henry Huggins* also proceeds by means of a sequence of variations. In the first one, for instance, Henry makes a number of attempts to get on the bus, each one followed by an episode in which knowledge of Ribsy's presence leads to an ever-increasing amount of chaos and trouble and Henry's desire to get home being thwarted. Finally, Henry's wish is fulfilled by means of a journey on another means of transportation in which Ribsy's presence is acknowledged and allowed. Similarly in the second story, the episodes in which guppies produce more guppies and create ever larger problems are followed by an episode in which the abundance of guppies in the right place and for the right adult offer a solution to the very problem they created—and the next story represents another variation, replacing multiplying guppies with multiplying numbers of worms.

In *Dr. Dolittle* each episode involves some threat or danger to the doctor's life or lifestyle, almost always because of human pride or rigidity or folly—a threat that might prevent the doctor from going about his good work of healing sick animals. In each case animals find a way of solving the problem that shows up human inadequacies and allows the doctor to continue his good work; as the narrative itself reports, "People who made trouble for Polynesia or her friends were nearly always sorry for it afterwards" (89). These variations tend to be more or less repetitive so that the novel seems in the business of telling the same wish-fulfilling story about how humans are deeply flawed beings and how animals are smarter than humans again and again. And again and again the animals solve problems created by a human insistence on hierarchical distinctions between kinds of creatures by acting as a communal group of equals, helping each other without reference to a presumed scale of class or power.

The only real variations of this repeated pattern occur in terms of exploring the situations of creatures who do not quite fit into the rigidly imposed categories of bad human and good animal. When Dr. Dolittle requires animal help in dealing with sick monkeys, it is not a human that blocks his way but the Leader of the Lions, an animal but also "a very proud creature" who denies his own equality with monkeys in the fraternity of animals. In doing so, he sounds very much like a human aristocrat: " 'Do you dare to ask me, Sir?' he said, glaring at the Doctor. 'Do you dare to ask me—*ME, the King of the Beasts,* to wait on a lot of dirty monkeys? Why, I wouldn't even eat them between meals!' " (65). This humanized lion even expresses attitudes toward the serving classes typical of human aristocrats: "Help's pretty hard to get these days. . . . Animals don't seem to want to work any more" (69). Only after this animal has been persuaded to stop acting as stupidly as humans typically do can the story proceed in its typical form, with the lions playing their equal part along with the other animals helping the doctor to do his job of healing.

A more peculiar variation on the basic pattern involves an African prince whose help is needed in freeing Dr. Dolittle and his friends from imprisonment. As his name implies, Prince Bumpo is meant to be a comic character. But the source of the comedy is his supposedly ridiculous vision of himself in the typical role of a fairy-tale prince, able to awaken a sleeping princess with a kiss and make her happy forever after. It seems that Bumpo has already attempted to awaken a princess in the requisite way: " 'Tis true indeed she awoke. But when she saw my face she cried out, 'Oh, he's black!' And she ran away and wouldn't marry me" (96). Bumpo wishes that the doctor would make him into a white prince—a wish that, in the rhetoric of the text, seems to represent the equivalent of an animal wishing to be more like a human. For clearly, readers are meant to understand that a black human is somehow less human and more animal-like than a white one. If that were not true, then why would Bumpo's odd wish to be accepted for the prince he is be a source of humor? The perception that this is a joke requires an understanding that the only kind of prince an African can be is an inevitably unsuccessful imitation of the European model—and inevitably unsuccessful for the obvious reason of skin color.

If I were to use the logic that operates in relation to the Leader of the Lions, I would have to conclude that Bumpo is viewed as ridiculous here for not appreciating how much better off he is not to be as human as the white prince he wishes he were. And in a way that is the case: Dr. Dolittle has been imprisoned by Bumpo's father because he no longer trusts white men, after the one he once gave access to his lands indulged in behavior identified as typically human throughout the book: caring for nothing but money. But the opposite seems to be true also: Bumpo is ridiculous because he imagines he actually might be something so obviously superior to himself, something he can never be. Dab-Dab says, "He looked better the way he was, I thought. But he'd never be anything but ugly, no matter what color he was made" (100–101). The illustration of Bumpo presumably confirms the ugliness for readers, depicting him as the typically racist stereotype of an African, with outrageously thick, wide lips and an equally outrageous wide nose. Lofting clearly expected viewers in his time—an implied white, European audience—to laugh at this image and to feel superior to it. In any case, Bumpo represents both the inherent folly of being human and, as a not-quite-totally-human African, the folly of anyone not human aspiring to act like a human. In the episode about him, the doctor applies his medical skills, not to making sick animals better but to making the not-quite-human Bumpo worse by making him artificially white and more human.

This variation of the basic pattern repeated so often elsewhere in the book depends on Bumpo's being perceived as somehow both human and animal in a universe of discourse otherwise characterized by rigid oppositions between the two. It is instructive that the story of Bumpo's wish to desert his proper place in the scale of things is followed immediately by the statement that, although the doctor is on his way home, "Chee-Chee, Polynesia and the crocodile stayed behind, because Africa was their proper home, the land where they were born" (101). For all the utopian equality of animal behavior as described here, this text is still deeply conservative, using the repetitive sequencing of variations to promote and maintain its rigid categories in a variety of different circumstances.

For much of *Alice's Adventures in Wonderland*, each new situation involves Alice wanting to be bigger or smaller and getting her wish. Furthermore, almost every episode in the novel involves a conversation between Alice and one or more citizens of Wonderland; the novel in which she appears certainly fulfills Alice's desideratum of a book with conversations. In almost all of these conversations one speaker takes for granted something that the other person finds surprising so that they all represent variations on questions of dogmatism, the subjectivity of perception, and what one can never know for sure. The climactic moment, in which Alice dogmatically asserts her certain knowledge that her perception is the only true one and the other characters nothing but a pack of cards, brings all dialogues to an end by replacing the ambivalence of multivocal conversation with a single voice. It is like God saying the world into existence, except here Alice says her wonderland into not-existence. This is the one variation that renders further variation impossible (or so it seems; the sister's reinterpretation of the meaning of Alice's dream and of the relationships between Wonderland and normal reality imply yet a further variation and therefore a further opening of yet more possibilities).

Alice also contains subsets of variations, all having something to do with questions of uncertainty. For instance, Alice often finds herself misspeaking poems she has memorized; and much of the text hovers around questions of death, beginning with Alice's own concern that she might kill an animal if she drops a jar of marmalade during her original fall into Wonderland and then wondering what it would be like to be a candle and go out altogether, followed shortly after by her realization that she might drown in her own tears. She then disturbs a group of birds and mice by bragging about how her cat, Dinah, eats their kind, and then a pigeon by speaking of how she herself eats eggs. Later, the March Hare demands a change of subject when Alice raises the question of what happens after the members of the tea party have eaten their way around the table. Similarly, the Gryphon changes the subject when Alice asks what happens after the lessening lessons have gone from ten hours to none; and shortly after, the Mock Turtle interrupts Alice's poem about the panther and owl just, it seems, as Alice is about to announce that the panther has killed the owl. The queen's constant cries of "Off with her head" fit nicely in the midst of all this.

The plot of the last text, *Plain City*, represents a combination of the single unified action found in the short narratives and the episodic structure of the other longer texts. There is one overriding action, the story of Buhlaire learning the truth about her father and coming to terms with the knowledge. But this main action proceeds through a series of separate episodes—Buhlaire's day at school, her encounter with a stranger by the river, her visit to a nightclub to hear her mother sing, her adventure in the whiteout, her visit to the homeless shelter—and each of these bears enough similarities to the others so that they, too, seem like a set of variations.

In each of these episodes Buhlaire enters an environment where she feels alien and alone, usually in the midst of white or light—the school, the secluded spot by the riverbank, the nightclub where she is the only child, the whiteout in the countryside, her father's dwelling under the underpass, the homeless shelter, and, interspersed with all these, her own home. In each case something, usually a male, interrupts her solitude in a way that threatens her. After she responds to the threat by drawing attention to herself, another, frequently fatherly, male rescues her but in a way that leads her to question whether or not she really needed to be rescued.

At school, Grady teases her and therefore interrupts the invisibility she hopes her white suit gives her. After she lashes out at him, thus making her general uncertainty clear to the staff, the principal attempts to rescue her by giving her the knowledge she wants—that her father is alive. While she is grateful to the principal, the new knowledge has the reverse of the desired effect, making her feel more confused than ever. The following episode, in which Buhlaire is accosted by a strange homeless man, replicates these circumstances in different terms. The strange man who approaches her as she stands amidst the white snow in what seems like an attack, but what she later considers might have been a harmless call on her affection, replaces Grady. The rescuer this time is her uncle Sam, who as male head of her household is her surrogate father, an actual version of what the text reports she imagined as a younger child—that her previous rescuer, the principal, was actually her father. In an interesting reversal her response is to wonder if Sam did the right thing in keeping her safe by sending off the strange man rather than first finding out more about him. He might well have been her real father, she imagines. These variations around the same basic pattern keep foregrounding the question of fatherhood and of which sort of male involvement in Buhlaire's life might be either good for her or bad for her.

The same pattern is replicated yet again as Buhlaire stands singing beside her mother, but feeling alone, in the blinding brightness of stage lights, and a hand enters the light and reaches toward her. This time it is her mother who feels distress, not Buhlaire herself; she hisses, and another rescuing male, this time the club bouncer, pulls the hand away, leaving Buhlaire yet once more to wonder if the safety her relatives impose on her is the best thing for her. In the next episode, the blinding stage light is replaced by the blinding whiteout, which itself becomes the threat, something white tracking Buhlaire down now rather than making her feel safe, as the white suit once did. After Buhlaire calls out for help, her father's hand yet once more enters the light and grabs on to her but this time to rescue her. Her response now is yet more ambivalent; while she is happy to find him, she pushes him away, distressed by his odor—and then plans to join him in his homeless life.

At this point the variations become different from what has occurred so far. In the next episode Buhlaire's feeling that she is alone and belongs nowhere is interrupted by Grady's invitation to come with him to the homeless shelter—a positive variation on the teasing that interrupted her solitude earlier and of the rescue just performed by her own father. Once Buhlaire is at the shelter, another father, Grady's this time, replays a different version of the earlier scene with the principal, telling her more about her own father and offering further advice about what it means to have parents and grow older. In the next episode Buhlaire's discovery of her relatives dancing outside in a circle replicates her constant feeling of being an outsider and confirms her decision to stay outside, with her father; she now imagines him in the role of the fatherly rescuer. But after she actually goes outside to meet him, she realizes the danger in her action and, in the most significant variation on earlier themes, rescues herself from her father's life— puts herself in the position of her own wise parent. Finally, in the last sequence, it is Buhlaire's father and many others who need rescuing from the danger of outdoor forces, this time a flood, and Buhlaire now in the role of rescuer, assists her Uncle Sam in finding victims and ferrying them back to safety.

Like the other five texts, *Plain City* moves forward by means of a series of similar episodes that explore the same basic components by means of both repeating and varying their relationships to each other. In all six cases the variations become increasingly different as the narrative moves toward its conclusion so that any advance depends on a rejuggling and repositioning of components present from the start. That this is a particularly significant characteristic of a text intended for young readers is signaled by its presence in *Plain City*, which, as I suggested earlier, seems otherwise to diverge from the characteristics common in the other five texts.

It is possible that, once having discovered this quality of sequential variation in the texts under discussion, I might equally find it present in texts not intended for young readers. It might simply be a basic factor of the linear development of any attempt at unified narrative sequencing. But simply because I have not found myself so aware of it in my reading of texts intended for more sophisticated adult readers, I suspect this is not the case.

There can be no doubt that literary texts of all sorts contain variational elements such as rhyme and rhythm and patterns of recurring diction and imagery.

And while not all narratives intended for adult audiences move forward by means of variations on a sequence of discrete and similar episodes, some certainly do.[32] But when they do, they don't seem to be so blatantly focused on doing it in terms of such purely binary concerns. It appears to be the inability to choose between opposites and the resultant ongoing movement between them without ever really moving beyond them that distinguishes texts intended for young readers.

Unlike the vast majority of literary texts for adults, the texts I have been discussing here have one other quality in common. All but one of them have sequels. Rosamond appears in a number of other stories after her first appearance in "The Purple Jar," and Peter is the subject of a number of picture-book stories published after *The Snowy Day*. Alice's adventures in Wonderland are followed by the ones she has in *Through the Looking Glass*. Dr. Dolittle's adventures are the subject of eleven subsequent books, and *Henry Huggins* appears in numerous other books both about his own adventures and about those of his friend Beezus's sister Ramona. Only Buhlaire, the protagonist of a young-adult novel, seems to have changed enough so that a similar story about her is unlikely. Unless Hamilton chose to forget what Buhlaire had achieved by the end of *Plain City*, a story about what happens to her later would involve issues so different that it would be difficult to read as a variation. But despite any claims they might make as didactic texts for their protagonists having changed—learned to be better—the other five texts all apparently leave space for a similar story to be told again—for a child or childlike being to err in similar ways again, and to learn the same or a similar lesson from it again. Even after they end they are binary enough, and therefore potentially variational enough, to allow for further variations of themselves.

Summary

In the process of exploring these six texts, I have outlined a number of qualities that they share with each other and that also seem to me to be the qualities that lead to my identification of them as texts of children's literature. What follows is a summary of these qualities.

• The texts imply an audience of child readers—or, at least, of readers younger than their writers—and address them in terms that make their being younger a matter of significance, something that leads these readers to require special forms of address and special kinds of content.

• Their style is simple, at least in relation to the discourse of writing for more mature audiences.

- There is a focus on actions—on straightforward reports of what people do and what it leads to—and not much detailed description of people, places, or emotions.
- These simple, straightforward texts tend to "resonate"—to imply more subtle complexities than they actually say.
- They do so by implying a more complex shadow text—one readers can access by reading the actual simple text in the context of the repertoire of previously existing knowledge about life and literature it seems to demand and invite readers to engage with.
- The pictures that often accompany the texts also act as more complex shadows to them, providing the visual and emotional information about which the texts themselves remain silent.
- There is an inherent doubleness in picture books: they offer two different ways of viewing the same events. Simple texts and their more complex shadows possess a similar doubleness, so that the picture-book story and its two discrete channels of information, one simpler, one more dense, is a basic model of narrative intended for children.
- The tone of the texts tends to be matter-of-fact, often, therefore, not remarking on the strangeness of some of the strange events being described and thus inviting readers to be conscious of another doubleness: a distance between the response the events seem to demand and the actual response provided.
- The protagonists of these narratives are either children or childlike animals or adults.
- Most often, the texts invite readers to identify with their protagonists—to see themselves and their own lives in terms of what happens to the protagonists and what the protagonists come to understand about it.
- The texts are focalized through their child or childlike protagonists and thus offer a childlike view of the events described.
- While the focalization is childlike, the texts are not first-person narratives. They report the protagonists' perceptions by means of third-person narrators who often report or imply perceptions at odds with those of the protagonist.
- Since I presume that the narrator is an adult (like the adults who actually did write these texts intended for children), the texts tend to offer two different points of view, one childlike and one adult (a doubleness to go along with the other dualities already mentioned). In being different and often opposite, the two points of view imply a conflict between childlike and adult perceptions and values.
- Innocence, identified as a key characteristic of childhood, becomes a central subject of these texts—not just what they describe but what they work to suggest

attitudes about. They invite readers, not just adults but children also, to think not just about what it means to be a child but, specifically, about what it means to possess a child's relative lack of knowledge.

• The texts tend to work to encourage child readers to replace whatever sense they have of themselves and the meaning of their own behavior with adult conceptions of those matters.

• The texts assume that children can and do change and that childhood is by definition a time of change, a time in which young human beings undergo the process of becoming the adults they will eventually be. Because childhood is defined by change, the texts attempt to encourage children to change in the proper way.

• The texts assume the right of adults to wield power and influence over children; thus, they might represent a kind of thinking about less powerful beings that can be identified as "colonial."

• They represent colonialist thinking by making safety a central concern: a key question is whether children are capable of keeping themselves from danger. The usual answer is that they are not and that adults must therefore create safe havens for them, places where they can be safely childlike. (Such places are usually identified as "home.")

• The wish to have influence over children in order to transform them into adults is inherently contradictory. The texts often insist that children continue to need adult protection even though, or even because, they have been wise enough to acknowledge and accept adult interpretations of their behavior, the acceptance of which in effect makes them less childlike and therefore less in need of the protection they now are wise enough to acknowledge their need of.

• The texts suggest that childhood is a time of change, but despite changes, children continue to be childlike and in need of adult protection. Childhood is therefore paradoxically static as well as dynamic, always the same yet a continuing process of becoming different that does not actually result in difference until childhood is finally over.

• Since being childlike is identified with lack of knowledge and being adult with the possession of knowledge, the texts represent explorations of the relative merits of knowing and not knowing. While they arrive at differing conclusions— some view innocence as wisdom, some experience—the texts all present innocence and knowledge in clearly oppositional terms, and most of them end by privileging one over the other.

• The opposition of innocence and knowledge seems to survive attempts at closure: the texts leave space for readings that reverse the dynamic and imply meanings opposite to the ones they attempt to assert.

• Because the texts encourage children both to think of their behavior as childlike and to come to an adult understanding of childlike behavior, they tend to work to construct a divided subjectivity. They often seem to be encouraging children both to not know and to know enough to value or to dismiss the value of their not knowing.

• Because the texts encourage an adult understanding of childlike behavior in children, they often work to disperse innocence in the process of celebrating it. They thus encourage child readers, no longer purely childlike, to enact the childhood they have moved beyond.

• The enactment of childhood by young-adult readers is a form of nostalgia. The texts tend to emerge from and express an adult nostalgia for childhood as an idyll or Eden, a simpler and better time now over.

• They seem to conjure this sense of nostalgia in order to block out the knowledge of (or acknowledgment of the knowledge of?) the actual complexity and uncertainty of childhood for both children and adults.

• In terms of not acknowledging what children and adults actually do know about childhood, these texts work to silence child readers on the subject of any uncertainty or pain they might feel in being children or on the wisdom of allowing adults to have power over them. They have the effect of teaching children what not to say to adults about the realities of their lives as children.

• The nostalgic and idyllic qualities of these texts relate their conception of childhood to other forms of Edenic beginnings and mythic pasts. They invite children to view themselves in the terms by which the Euro-American culture from which they emerge has traditionally viewed its own historical past—in the process of experiencing a paradise they will eventually inevitably lose and regret the loss of. In this way they encourage children to be critical of adult thinking and thus undermine their own efforts to encourage it.

• In privileging past values over future developments, the texts tend to an inherent conservatism, a wish to keep things from changing and a dislike of it when it happens. Viewed from this angle, change is always for the worse, an idea that directly contradicts the idea that childhood is a time of change and that growth toward adult knowledge is a good thing. Once more, the texts are ambivalent, divided and self-contradictory about their central concerns.

• The texts deal centrally with questions of desire, as well as with questions of knowledge: what children or other childlike beings want and whether or not it is wise to want it; also, what adults want children to be (or to seem). As a result, they often depict the good or bad consequences of children's wishes being fulfilled; and they often report "happy endings" that represent adults' wishes for children being fulfilled.

• The texts tend to confirm the idea that it is adult knowledge that reveals the inadequacies of childhood desires. Children are innocent enough not to know the danger in what they desire and need to learn it.

• The texts also often harbor the possibility that the opposite might be true—that it is adult desires for children, attempts either to make them less innocent or to keep them from harm, that are dangerous and innocent childhood desires that are wise. In both celebrating and denigrating childhood desire and adult knowledge, the texts reveal the centrality of their ambivalence.

• The ambivalence emerges from the interplay of clearly established binary oppositions: home and away, safety and danger, desire and knowledge, adult and child. Even when one opposite triumphs, it tends to do so by negating its other entirely, thus still insisting on the inherent opposition. Because there seem to be clear winners and losers, the texts remain inherently and unceasingly bipolar. But the bipolarity means that losers never seem to go away. The texts confirm what they want to oppose in the very act of opposing it—that which needs to be imagined and introduced so that it can be denied.

• The bipolarity becomes particularly obvious in terms of the ways in which the texts focus on questions of home and make home meaningful.

• Home is a metaphor for childhood as adults invent and sustain it—a protective space in which children can enjoy being safely childlike on adult terms. Texts written for children seem to represent another version of the same space.

• The idea of home as a safe place is so centrally significant that it exists even in contexts where home is unsafe (as, perhaps, in *Plain City*). In such cases the thrust is almost always to focus on the lack of the safety that ought to exist but doesn't.

• In making home central, the texts imagine physical space as meaningful and symbolic—invest their settings with meanings, make them representations of what the characters mean to themselves and to each other. The physical worlds they describe tend toward allegory and have ideological import.

• In order to make the point that home is safe, the texts imagine children as not perceiving its benefits; childhood desire is equated with the desire for freedom from home and safety, childhood with rebellion against adult values.

• The plots usually follow a basic pattern of movement from home to away and then back home again.

• Home is identified with constriction, stasis, and safety; leaving it is identified with freedom, process, and danger. The return home at the end seems to
mean an acceptance of its constrictions in order to gain its benefits. But since
child protagonists must change in order to perceive that—cease being static—they
return home tainted by the journey. This is yet another version of the texts' central
ambivalence, their inability to decide whether childhood is and must be static or is
and must be a place of change, whether children are incapable of learning or
always learning, etc.

• These narratives are constructed as a series of variations, succeeding scenes
that replicate old elements in new, increasingly different relationships.

• The tendency to return and vary results in sequels; all but one of these texts
have sequels.

• The texts share many qualities with traditional European fairy tales.

• The texts are didactic and therefore have the shape of traditional fables,
stories in which what happens to characters is meant to represent a path for
future behavior in readers.

• Fairy tales are wish-fulfillment fantasies in which characters get what they
want and are happy with it. Fables tend to be stories about how characters are
wrong to want what they want and learn their error by getting the object of their
desire. Fiction for children, rooted historically both in the tradition of fables and
in the tradition of fairy tales, seems to represent an ambivalent combination of
the two opposite tendencies.

This is a long list of shared characteristics—a much longer one than I imagined when I embarked on this project. If my readings of these books have any
validity, the apparently different six texts have a great deal in common. And if they
are in fact, as I have claimed, representative texts, then I might well be safe in
making the assumption with which I began: the idea that fictional texts written by
adults for children and young people are enough like each other to be immediately recognizable as having been intended for their specific audiences—as
children's or young adults' literature.

If this is true, then children's literature might be something more than just an
indiscriminate body of quite different sorts of texts grouped together by adults for
convenience merely because of their intended audiences. It might, in fact, be a
specific genre of fiction whose defining characteristics seem to transcend specifics of time and place, cut across other generic categories such as fantasy or
realism, and even remain consistent despite variations in the ages of intended
audiences.

CHAPTER TWO

Exploring Assumptions

⁓

Reading as an Adult

In her introduction to *The Practice of Love* Theresa de Lauretis describes her own practice of reading: "I shall endeavor to remind the reader, as discreetly as it can be done without offense to critical and stylistic conventions, that my theoretical speculations and my reading of the texts follow the yellow brick road of my own fantasies, the less-than-royal road of my personal or experiential history."[1] De Lauretis is right to assert that being honest about the extent to which one's thinking emerges from personal experience is a defiance of convention, brave to defy it, and, I suspect, wise to be discreet about her defiance. In similar fashion I offer a warning: in what follows I am much less wise and much less discreet. The foundation of my argument in my own personal responses to texts seems to demand these breaches of convention.

The first assumption I made in pursuing the readings of chapter 1 was simply that my responses might matter. Do they? Why should or should not what I say matter? I am male, short of stature and slight of build, more or less masculine, and more or less heterosexual—my sense of the extent to which my own gender and sexuality and those of others exist in an always-fluid context of possibility and performance prevents me from being more definite. My family background is central European and Jewish but not religious. I am a North American—a Canadian born to Canadians born in Canada. My life began in the 1940s, which means that I moved toward adulthood at a time in the history of North American culture when a majority (or at least a majority of those with any power) assumed that heterosexual males of European background, especially North American (albeit not particularly Canadian or Jewish) ones, were the people most likely to occupy positions of authority, the ones most likely to speak of how they experienced the world and to expect others to listen to them and agree to view the world that way.

The culture that surrounds me has changed since I was young and, in one way at least, for the better. Any right to speak that someone like me might have presumed himself to have simply by virtue of his sex or his ethnic or cultural background has been effectively challenged, especially in the academy, by a range of previously disempowered or not-yet-existent discourses: deconstruction, feminism, African American and aboriginal studies, postcolonial theory, queer theory, and so on. I know that my right to speak about my responses to texts and my expectations that I will be listened to cannot and do not emerge from the accidents of birth that traditionally gave someone like me substantial power. I understand how specific and how personal my responses are and how little I can count on my authority as the basis for persuading others to agree with the conclusions I base on them.

I understand, for instance, that I came to my reading of the six texts described in chapter 1 as a member of what Stanley Fish calls an interpretive community—"a community made up of those who share interpretive strategies."[2] In my years of reading and studying literature, I have learned specific ways of making sense of texts—ways that I put into play when I read but ways not necessarily shared by others. Furthermore, I fully agree with Fredric Jameson's assertion that the historicizing always necessary in intellectual work (including work with literary texts) needs to consist not just of "the historical origins of the things themselves" but also "that more intangible historicity of the concepts and categories by which we attempt to understand those things."[3] In the light of that intangibility, I know that some of the strategies I use are ones that I am not consciously aware of using—that I am embedded in my particular interpretive community deeply enough that I perform operations of meaning-making without even knowing I am doing so.

There are, however, a range of strategies I *am* aware of and can name here. It seems important to do so, for they underpin the argument I want to make: that the characteristics I found in the six texts I've considered might be shared by enough other texts to be identified as the identifying markers of children's literature—what makes it a distinct literary genre.

I know, for instance, that the topics I chose to consider in my explorations of the texts relate to aspects of literary texts that my training in literature and discussions with other readers throughout my life have identified for me as significant elements—matters such as style, point of view and focalization, the relationships of events to each other (the plot) and of repetitive images to each other (the structure). Strictly speaking, these elements are ways of thinking about texts rather than actual separable components of them. But I believe they are ways of thinking shared by many readers, and because writers of fiction with a conscious or unconscious awareness of their craft know that, they write with the assumption that readers—even child readers—consciously or unconsciously know them and use them to make sense of what they read. I think I can safely assume that these elements can help me to arrive at ideas about the texts I have discussed that might potentially be convincing to others.

At the same time, they might make my project suspect. They require a consciousness of how fictional texts work that might interfere with a more visceral engagement with the worlds they create. Since my personal pleasure in reading fiction emerges less from the magic of a world made convincingly real by words than in an awareness of how the words work to make that magic seem to happen, I feel comfortable with this sort of response. But adults often assume that child readers are more likely to be intuitive readers than linguistically aware ones like me. For that matter, even linguistically aware child readers are unlikely to be as experienced and sophisticated in their linguistic awareness as a literary scholar ought to be—and I hope I am. These circumstances might limit the extent of what I can hope to accomplish here. How can I say anything useful about children's literature if I read it in ways child readers don't? As Jack Zipes asserts, "For us [he means teachers, librarians, and critics of children's literature], children's literature is a vast historical complex. For the young and their families, children's literature does not exist, but the single commodities exist for a moment of pleasurable or compulsive reading."[4] What I know of that vast historical complex, built up over many more years of diverse reading than an actual child could ever manage in the relatively brief time of childhood, prevents me from understanding texts as inexperienced readers might.

In response to this sort of concern, Peter Hunt mandates a "childist criticism"[5]—an attempt by adults to read as children would. In doing so, Hunt assumes it is possible not to know what one knows—that one can somehow imagine oneself to be less experienced and less sophisticated than one is. I don't believe I can or that, excepting amnesia, any adult can. As a result, I cannot accept another assumption Hunt makes—that it is possible for adults to know how children read. I simply don't know—can't know—how children might read, enjoy, and understand texts.

I might *ask* some children of course. But it seems unlikely that human beings in general experience only that which they are able to describe, and children with a limited experience of language might well know more and feel more than they can put into words. Even if I trusted what children told me, I would only know how *those* children respond. Childist criticism assumes that it is possible to generalize about children's abilities, tastes, and interests. But there are a range of critiques of the developmental assumptions of theorists like Piaget and Kohlberg—produced both by more recently active developmental psychologists like Charles Brainerd and William Kessen and by cultural theorists like Carol Gilligan, Erica Burman, John R. Morss, and Rex and Wendy Stainton Rogers—that seriously undermine the possibility that children generally, either throughout childhood or at any specific stage or age within childhood, might share specific and identifiable modes of thinking.[6] If adults can ever in any small or general way define childlike thinking, I am convinced it is only because the adults have imposed their own theoretical assumptions about children *on* children—constructed them as the limited creatures the adults have imagined them to be simply by interacting with them as if the imaginings were true. Speaking of the idea "that childhood is a biological 'reality'—it is an identifiable life-stage, manifested by both physical and psychological markers"—Rex and Wendy Stainton Rogers assert that "we can never know about such matters except within humanly constructed systems."[7] John Stephens agrees: "all developmental paths are ideologically constructed, involving conformity to societal norms."[8] Adults understand childhood only through their effort of making children into expressions of childhood as they assume it to be.

If there is no generalizable childlike response, then I can't pretend to read like a child. I could, I suppose, try to read like the child I once was or, as some adult readers of children's literature claim they do, like the child that remains within me. But the child I remember or imagine still being within me, viewed through inevitable lapses of memory and the filter of later knowledge and experience, is not the child I was. It is, inevitably, an adult's nostalgically reimagined version of a childhood, a version influenced by the same cultural conventions that, as I suggested in chapter 1, shape much writing for children and adult ideas about childhood in general. It is not, therefore, likely to provide accurate insights into real childhood experiences. The child that adults believe they were or still are might be of interest to other nostalgic adults and, as common adult constructions of childhood, might explain much about the implied readers of children's literature. But a "childist" criticism that explored how these imagined children respond without an acknowledgment of their fictional status is not likely to be productive of real knowledge about how actual children actually read.

Reading these texts as an adult places my attention exactly where I think it should be—on the constructed nature of the children involved in what we call children's literature. This forces me not to lose sight of the most startling fact about children's literature: that its creation is centrally and almost exclusively an activity of adults like myself. My topic in this study is texts written by other adults and usually purchased by other adults—and while I might wish for some brave and thoughtful child readers, I assume my audience will be other adults. As an adult writing for other adults about texts theoretically intended for children but created by still other adults, I have no choice but to replicate the literature in the process of discussing it—to read children's literature through my adult lens just as children's literature reads childhood through *its* adult lens.

My interpretive community, then, is not childlike and does not consist centrally of children. It is a community of scholars. As a member of that community I need, and have used, a range of knowledge not often possessed by children. In saying this I realize that I am leaving myself open to the accusation that I have now committed the sin for which I was castigating others just a few paragraphs ago: I have assumed the existence of a childhood at least generalizable enough for me to claim there is something children often do or don't do. Karín Lesnik-Oberstein would argue that my making such claims represents the extent to which I am a member of a specific community of scholars—those focused on children's literature criticism—and share the failings of that community. According to her, the one "aim or goal" of children's literature criticism—"the choosing of good books for children—does not change from critic to critic, no matter how much they claim that they will be doing things differently, or applying new approaches or methodologies"; and this goal is achieved, she says, by "each critic endlessly re-finding finally, through whatever route, a child who can be known, and to whom their good can then be done."[9] My statement about children not often possessing a certain range of knowledge might represent my rediscovery of that knowable child. Indeed, Lesnik-Oberstein says that "Nodelman's formulations . . . deploy simultaneously two ideas about childhood as identity. . . . On the one hand there are their overt arguments about the child as a construction, but on the other hand they also refer to a 'real child' " (ibid., 13).

Lesnik-Oberstein bases her conclusion on an article on deconstruction and fairy tales in which, after asserting that "there surely never was a childhood, in the sense of something surer and safer and happier than the world we perceive as adults," I go on to say that thinking there is means that "more significantly, we belittle childhood and allow ourselves to ignore our actual knowledge of real children."[10] Speaking of the same sentence, Neil Cocks agrees with Lesnik-Oberstein: "Nodelman argues for the notion of 'construction' before finally acknowledging the 'real child' and his unquestioned knowledge of it."[11] And Sue Walsh expresses the same concern: "Nodelman's essay co-opts the work of deconstruction to a liberal philosophy of education that resurrects the ignorant (innocent of language) child and the adult as the one who knows, and moreover knows what is good for the child, in this case 'deconstruction.' "[12]

What I find most interesting about all three of these comments is how they replace the "real children" of my original with a "real child"—replace a group of existing beings with a construct of representative childhood. As I have been arguing here, that supposedly "real child" does not exist. But surely, real children do. For Walsh, perhaps, they don't, at least not in any way describable in words. Elsewhere she objects to "a notion of language as reflecting the world rather than constitutive of it."[13] And it distresses her that for me and other children's literature critics, "there has to be some way out of discourse, some way of touching the 'real'; and this, curiously, is the rationalization for the teaching and practice of reading."[14]

I dwell on these matters here because I want to plead guilty. I do believe there is a world outside language—a world with which language interacts, even if language cannot ever accurately or completely represent it. I do believe there are real children in that real world and that the ways in which we describe them in language do have a real effect on them. If I replace Cocks's misrepresentation of my words with what I actually said, I arrive at this statement: Nodelman argues for the notion of "construction" before finally acknowledging real children and his unquestioned knowledge of them. Not only do I agree with the first of these ascriptions—there *are* children—but I also have to admit to the second. I do believe that parents, teachers, and other adults, including me, can know things about the children in their care and do use that knowledge to affect those children both negatively and positively. As Katharine Jones says about these critiques of me and of others, "Lesnik-Oberstein seems to miss the point that many of these critics are not, in fact, appealing to the 'real child' but might, instead, be seeking to talk about both the construction of 'children' *and* the difficult area of children's lives and experiences."[15] Once more: guilty.

Jones goes on to support Mary Galbraith's assertion that expunging all claims of "adult understanding of childhood experience" from children's literature criticism "would be to refuse the possibility of any meaningful interaction between adults and children."[16] Since I don't refuse that possibility, I also have to acknowledge the hope that my work here might actually affect how at least some adults assist at least some children in their interactions with children's literature. While I can't describe how a "real child" understands children's literature—or even how real children do—I can certainly use my knowledge of reading and textual practices to attempt a description of how the literature works to affect its implied readers—the child readers constructed by its texts. And I believe I have a moral responsibility to proceed with the conviction that such a project is pointless without a long-range goal of actually affecting how real people read and think about what they read—including, eventually, children. Finally, what Walsh finds curious—the assumption that literary work of the sort this book represents might hope to actually have an effect on real people—I find merely obvious but entirely essential.

Anyone familiar with literary theory and literary study will have read the last few pages with an awareness of how what I have been saying refers not just to deconstruction, as Walsh suggests, but to a broad range of recently powerful literary and theoretical discourse. In addition to my repertoire of knowledge of children's literature, I knew, even before I began to think about it, how the responses I was having to the six texts I was reading might relate to the wider context of ways of reading and thinking about texts in general and texts of children's literature in particular, described or assumed in the work of the literary theorists and specialists in children's literature with whom I was already familiar. Not able to not know what I know, I had no choice as I read but to make sense of my new experience in terms of the scholarship I knew already—particularly those parts of it that had excited my most intense agreement or disagreement. My work therefore evokes what Pierre Bourdieu calls "those *privileged interlocutors* implicit in the writings of every producer, those revered antecedents whose thought structures he has internalized to the point where he no longer thinks except in them and through them, to the point where they become intimate adversaries determining his thinking and imposing on him both the shape and the substance of conflict."[17]

This means that I was already entering a dialogue before I even began to imagine an audience and write for it, already understanding how what I was thinking might be like or unlike what I knew other readers did think or would be likely to think. Bourdieu says that "the most personal judgements it is possible to make of a work, even of one's own work, are always collective judgments in the sense of position-takings referring to other position-takings through the intermediary of the objective relations between the positions of their authors within the field."[18] My own judgments and understandings of these six texts are and always were similarly collective—communal. In chapter 3 I discuss how I understand myself to be located within this community, particularly in terms of ways in which other scholars have thought about what children's literature is and the positions I take in relation to those ways.

Because I do occupy my own position, that which is closest to me and most like myself inevitably seems most central and most relevant, and I have to resist marginalizing that which is further away. So, for instance, I have to continually force myself to realize that American or British specialists in children's literature are likely to be much less aware than I am as a Canadian and as editor of a journal concerned with Canadian children's literature and childhood studies of the Canadian texts that bulk so large in my own reading of children's literature. I also need to remember that the British specialists are probably less aware than I am of a spectrum of American texts, and the American specialists less aware than I am of the British ones.

The Canadian location I occupy might turn out to be an advantage. In the world of letters (and in the light of the peculiar nature of the Canadian economy in relation to world markets), we Canadians are uniquely blessed with easy access to the literatures of three countries, our own and that of the two major producers in the world of English-language literary culture. That the other two are so completely and oppressively major—especially the exceedingly powerful one that shares the North American continent with us—is also of significance. As I suggest in some detail in chapter 4, Canadians necessarily stand both inside of and outside of what citizens of Britain and of the United States take for granted about themselves. The extent to which Canadians share British and, especially, American values allows us to respond to both countries' texts with at least some of the familiarity of insiders reading about people like ourselves. But our outsider's view highlights any unspoken assumptions that readers on the inside share with writers on the inside and therefore never notice. My position as a Canadian on the margins allows me both some of the confidence of closeness and some of the objectivity of distance.

But I am not just a Canadian who writes most centrally for an audience of Americans. I am also a Jew beyond the edge of the non-Jewish mainstream, a nonpracticing child of nonpracticing Jews beyond the edge of the mainstream Jewish community. These aspects of my personal history have left me with a tendency to feel most comfortable on the margins, almost but not quite outside and looking in, and this exacerbates the effects of my position as a Canadian on the edge of the American behemoth and causes me to value my ability to remain separate enough from communities that claim me to be able to uncover what I then view as their true significance. My reading practices focus on thoughtful response and critical thinking. Perhaps I am merely unable to respond either as insiders naturally do, with relatively thoughtless involvement, or as complete outsiders do, with absolute objectivity. I then privilege my inability as a goal for others to aspire to.

I do, however, have to insist that I see it as a worthy goal—at least when it comes to a project like the one I am involved in here, trying to make sense of some literary texts. As I have suggested in my article "Pleasure and Genre," I deeply enjoy reading texts of fiction written for an audience of child readers (which is, as I noted above, another group that, as an adult, I stand outside of). But my passion for these texts is not predicated on or committed to blindness about them. I want to love them in the context of an awareness of their qualities and effects. I start with the assumption that they can withstand the scrutiny.

As I hope my earlier discussion of the reality of childhood and the moral responsibility of scholarship it gives rise to suggests, I believe that children, too, can share those modes of reading and understanding and might also be better off for it. Many children, not educated otherwise, might be intuitive readers of the sort I described above. But I have no reason to believe they *must* be intuitive readers—that they are incapable of being anything else, that they cannot become resisting readers and think at odds with the intentions of texts.

Whether their producers are aware of it or not, texts always operate in various deliberate and nondeliberate ways to give readers ideas about themselves and their needs and desires. The values texts most frequently support are ones that benefit those with the power to produce and distribute the texts—for producers would be foolish and therefore unlikely to promote values at odds with their own economic welfare; and texts surely do their ideological work best on those who are unaware of the possibility that that might happen and who are therefore less thoughtful about what they read. My work here is thus grounded in the effort to make other readers and me more aware. I believe that awareness is both benefi-cial and pleasurable—and that despite the quite different sort of pleasure they offer, intuitive readings are well worth sacrificing for awareness—even or espe-cially for children. "Rather than try to shield children from the world they live in," says Roderick McGillis, "we ought to be trying to give them the tools to read this world carefully and critically."[19] Once more risking the accusation of assuming real children exist, I have to say I agree. We adults ought, as Aidan Chambers asserts in discussing sharing literature with children, "to act on the assumption that children are potentially all that we are ourselves."[20]

Making Choices: Exploring Representativeness

The position I occupy forces other distortions on my thinking in addition to the one of my nationality. Surprisingly few texts of children's literature are trans-lated into other languages, and, as Emer O'Sullivan suggests, "Theoretical works on children's literature very seldom cross linguistic borders."[21] As an English-speaking resident of an English-speaking (at least in my part of it) country, my thoughts about texts written for children emerge primarily from my speculations about texts written in English based in my knowledge of a critical corpus written mostly in English. Any generalizations I find myself making might not seem so generally true for those working in the context of positions taken in the children's literature scholarship written in other languages or with knowledge of a body of texts produced in other languages or in other countries (or even in other parts of my own country). Or, for that matter, in other times: for not only does the bulk of my knowledge of children's literature relate to texts produced in the last century or so, but I read the texts I encounter from earlier periods of history in terms of my contemporary assumptions—inevitably, then, in ways different than readers of those earlier times would have made sense of them. In chapter 4 I consider the extent to which variations in children's literature written in other places and other times trouble my conclusions, but I go on now to discuss how the limitations of my context might have influenced my choice and perception of the six texts I have chosen to discuss.

My first decision was the one to limit myself to just five or six texts. I did so on the basis that keeping the list this short would force me to pay close attention to the texts, to read each of them carefully, and to think hard about the specifics of what I was reading before I presumed to leap to any conclusions about how the texts did or did not seem similar to each other or represent the field as a whole. This reveals a prejudice for a particular way of approaching questions about literature that says much about the kind of training I received as a student of literature. I was an undergraduate and graduate student in the early and middle 1960s—a time just before structuralism and deconstruction became significant forces in the North American academy. I do not recall ever even hearing words like *structuralism* or *Lévi-Strauss* or *Derrida* when I was a graduate student, let alone having any ideas to attach to them. My literary education consisted mainly of learning how to create interpretations focused on the close reading of texts, usually without much reference to any historical or cultural or literary or even theoretical context they might occupy. The object was to discover ironic paradoxes and structural intricacies; the more complex, the better. In other words, I was taught the theoretical approach to literature usually identified by the label "New Criticism." Since it was the only thing taught, however, I did not learn to think of it as a specific theoretical perspective. It was merely, as far as I knew, the one way literary study was always properly done. It is, therefore (and despite my later learning about other possibilities), the way I always begin. And I always find it revealing of how and what texts are capable of communicating.

As I have learned about and added other ways of reading to this New Critical approach, however, I have come to understand and to be fascinated by the extent to which matters of ideology and cultural content are embedded in the specific details of texts, what Jameson calls "the ideology of form."[22] I can see that my focus on binary opposites and on different texts replicating the same culturally central binaries has its roots in structuralism and later developments in poststructuralism and that the idea that the texts consist of a series of variations that describe differing relationships between the same binaries that provide the texts with both their meanings and their structure is based on Claude Lévi-Strauss's description of how myths operate as "bricolage."[23] And my constant suspicion about the motives adults might have in writing for children emerges from my knowledge of a range of ideological considerations of how texts represent shared cultural values and work to shape and/or repress individual difference by manipulating their readers for the benefit of those with the resources to publish and distribute books.

I assume, then, that however much it has a unique character, any literary text is inevitably representative of forces at play in the time or place of its writing and can therefore represent at least to some extent how literary texts of that time or place tend to operate. Even so, can six specific texts represent in any meaningful way the many hundreds of thousands of other texts written for audiences of child readers? Can they represent children's literature in general? What was I thinking while I made my choices? What principles allowed me to believe that my six texts might convincingly represent a wider body of other texts?

To make my case, I knew I needed to develop a list of texts as highly divergent from each other as possible. There would be no point in selecting, say, six picture books by Beatrix Potter. I also wanted there to be clear evidence that the text could legitimately be identified as children's literature. That such evidence exists might make my entire project seem rather beside the point. Why argue for the existence of children's literature as a distinct body of texts if people already agree that certain texts belong to such a body? But as I will show in the next chapter, it is possible to define children's literature in ways that accept its existence but deny that its texts necessarily share any qualities with each other. Children's literature might, for instance, be merely all the diverse books that children happen to read or all the diverse books produced by the children's divisions of publishing houses. As I saw it, my task was to establish that what people commonly identify as children's texts do share characteristics.

I decided that the texts I chose would have the following qualities:

• I wanted to approach unfamiliar texts with a determination to be open-minded about my readings of and responses to them. So I decided to choose texts I knew little about, beyond a first quick reading, prior to the experiment.

In addition to my childhood reading experiences, I have been reading, thinking about, and writing about texts for children for much of my adult life. This experiment was hardly going to be anything but the first time I had ever thought about children's literature—or even about the shared characteristics of texts identified by that label. I did, therefore, have to acknowledge that the exploration was not likely to be groundbreaking—that any discoveries I made about any of the texts I chose for my experiment would not be particularly new ones for me. (As it happened, I did make a number of new discoveries in the process of my thinking about the six texts I chose that surprised me, a fact that reaffirms my sense of the value of close readings of texts. It was the detailed consideration of a few specific texts that led me to new insights about texts written for children in general.) Since I was going to read these or any texts written for children in the light of my own previous speculations about children's literature, it would be surprising if I did not focus on qualities of these texts that had drawn my attention in other texts I had explored previously. I realized from the beginning that this was an aspect of my thinking that I would have to confront and address: how much would I be simply inventing, finding what I had consciously or unconsciously set out to look for? In a sense, I have to acknowledge, I did do that—my previous reading of other texts and of interpretations of them inevitably formed a context for my new readings this time. But I could at least avoid a mere replication of my own prejudices and previous discoveries by avoiding texts I had discussed extensively in other contexts.

• I knew I needed to choose texts whose status as children's literature would not be likely to be disputed by specialists in the field. They would therefore have to be texts by winners of awards for children's books or texts by writers often mentioned in histories of children's literature.

Here, in effect, I accepted the marginalization of texts usually marginalized. My conclusions would apply to what is conventionally accepted as good or ordinary— and might well not apply to, on the one hand, popular formula literature by less respected writers and, on the other, to experimental work by imaginative innovators. I would have the obligation of acknowledging that limitation—and the opportunity to consider such texts in the light of my conclusions about less marginalized materials. I do that in chapter 4.

• Although I wanted to focus on texts by writers whose status as writers for children was unquestionable, I did not want to include only the sort of highly distinct texts that most frequently attract the attention of literary scholars.

I am thinking of texts like Potter's *Tale of Peter Rabbit*, Frances Hodgson Burnett's *Secret Garden*, Kenneth Grahame's *The Wind in the Willows*, L. M. Montgomery's *Anne of Green Gables*, E. B. White's *Charlotte's Web*, Maurice Sendak's *Where the*

Wild Things Are—texts that are subject continually to new interpretations and ongoing scholarly discussion by specialists in the field. As I will show in chapter 4, the amount of attention that texts like these continually receive suggests to me that they are different from other texts—either actually different or made to seem different by their status as interpretable texts. They are too special to be representative of the mass of children's books they stand out from, and I realized any conclusions I might reach would be distorted by their specialness.

- I realized, however, that I would distort the whole picture by leaving out such books entirely, so I decided to include one—as it eventually turned out, *Alice's Adventures in Wonderland.*

In this light I am intrigued by the amount of time I spent trying to come to grips with ways in which *Alice* seemed different from the other five texts and, in particular, how it seemed to have a sort of metafictional relationship to the rest. This suggests something about the place of these sorts of especially canonical texts in the field of children's literature that I attempt to come to grips with in chapter 4.

- As I continued in my deliberations, I found myself deciding to restrict my list to fictional narratives.

I did so, I think, because I suspected that at least some of the qualities that led me to identify a text as being intended for children were facets of narrative—types or techniques of storytelling or plot patterns that might not be so readily apparent in nonnarrative poetry or in some nonfictional texts.

Nevertheless, nonfictional texts for child audiences tend to use simple language and offer utopian views of their subjects—and they often shape real events or situations into the narrative patterns typical of children's fiction. And a well-known and, to my mind, quite typical poem for children, Robert Louis Stevenson's "My Shadow," does tend to share a number of the qualities I discovered in the fictional texts of chapter 1. It offers someone's thoughts about his shadow in quite simple, straightforward language and from what clearly implies a childlike point of view—a viewpoint of innocence, as the speaker reveals no scientific understanding of why the shadow acts as it does and resorts instead to a literal way of thinking that many adults might most readily identify as childlike:

> He hasn't got a notion of how children ought to play,
> And can only make a fool of me in every sort of way.
> He stays so close beside me, he's a coward you can see;
> I'd think shame to stick to nursie as that shadow sticks to me![24]

Lines like these seem to invite a more informed response—a knowledge of how light travels and is blocked and how shadows change in relation to the relative positions of lights and blocking objects—so that the poet's strategy allows a reader to perceive the speaker's lack of knowledge and, I assume, find it amusing or charming or both. For adult readers this poem offers the kind of nostalgia for innocence that I found in many of the texts of chapter 1. For child readers the situation is more complex: they will either share the childlike ingenuousness of the narrator and miss much of the point of the poem or else possess the knowledge that allows something like the response that might more obviously be expected of adults—the response the poem seems more clearly intended to evoke. But having that response requires a child reader not only to understand more than the speaker but also to understand that the speaker is being childlike, and in a particularly desirable way. It requires that the child reader both know more and in knowing more perceive the value of knowing or pretending to know less. In other words, for the reader it most obviously implies, the poem about shadows evokes and depends on its own shadow text, one that works like the shadow texts of the narratives of chapter 1 both to establish hidden adult content and to reinforce the importance of hiding such content from adults. Thousands of poems for children from Stevenson's time until the present share many of these qualities: the childlike point of view, the nostalgia for innocence, the implication of hidden adult content. Many thousands of others offer narratives that echo the structures and concerns of fiction for children.

But while I sense the same commonality with other texts of children's literature when I read poetry or nonfiction identified as being written specifically for children, I decided to defer the question of how the specific demands of poetry or nonfiction affect the characteristics I am focusing on in this book. If I found shared qualities in exclusively fictional texts, I or other scholars could, once more, use them as a context to determine the extent to which children's literature in other genres fits the pattern or, perhaps, tends to diverge from it in characteristic ways.

My choice of fiction as the genre I would choose my texts from probably represents another dangerous assumption: that fiction is the essential, typical form of children's literature and that poetry, drama, and nonfiction are marginal subforms with specific distinguishing characteristics of their own. Yet I suspect most readers would have trouble accepting a set of generalizations about children's literature based solely on texts of poetry—and much less trouble accepting that generalizations based exclusively on fictional texts might well apply to children's literature in general. If my supposition is true, it might mean that widely popular assumptions about reading cause me and other readers to marginalize poetry and nonfiction.

Alternatively, it could simply be the case that children's literature tends to be a narrative form, in poetry and nonfiction as well as in fiction, so that the most typical or representative texts would have to be ones that contained a narrative. Meanwhile, other texts that, with or without a sustained narrative line, made a special claim to documentary truth or contained highly rhythmic sound patterns —qualities a large range of texts do not share—would have to be seen as less representative or typical, and therefore would be less wise choices to include in my group of six. The presence of a narrative line as a centrally expectable quality in texts for children in a variety of genres is a possibility I need to consider further.

• Even though they would all be fiction, I wanted the texts I chose to be as unlike each other as possible—to represent work done in different countries and different centuries, in different genres, for intended younger audiences of different ages.

I decided I had to include a picture book and a young-adult novel, some fantasies and some realistic books, some nineteenth-century books and some twentieth-century ones, and so on. I also decided that the texts I chose would include writers from different countries and of different sexes and ethnic backgrounds. My sense that these might be important variables told me much about my assumptions. They acknowledged a series of reasons why texts might be different in the very process of arguing for their inherent similarity.

In wanting to cover both fantasy and realism, both picture books and young-adult novels, I was revealing the major bias of my entire project: that there are significant likenesses among these admittedly different forms. Most commentary on children's books operates with the opposite assumption. Most people believe, for instance, that the books to which four-year-olds should have access are quite different from books intended for eight-year-olds. A trust in the principles of developmental psychology leads both writers and critics to imagine not one children's literature but a series of increasingly complex children's literatures, each one tied to a specific developmental stage or chronological age. It is in defense of such a position, and in opposition to my own convictions, that Caroline Hunt speaks: "Theorists in the wider field of children's literature often discuss young adult titles without distinguishing them as a separate group and without, therefore, indicating how theoretical issues in young adult literature might differ from those in literature for younger children."[25] And Roberta Trites suggests what those issues might be. Speaking of "the chief characteristic that distinguishes adolescent literature from children's literature," she argues that whereas "children's literature often affirms the child's sense of Self and her or his personal power," literature for adolescents involves "a recognition that social institutions are bigger and more powerful than individuals."[26]

Meanwhile, many scholars who specialize in fantasy literature tend to approach texts written for adults and those written for children indiscriminately, in the faith that children's fantasy is more like adult fantasy than like realistic fiction for children. And just plain common sense would suggest that a story communicated by means of pictures and very few words would have to be different from one told only in a great many more words.

I started with the idea that these assumptions are only part of the truth. I was convinced that, despite their differing degrees of complexity, all texts written by adults for an audience conceived of as children or as what the book trade identifies as "young adult" were not only similar to each other but also similarly different from other forms of literature. I did discover significant differences between *Plain City* and the other five texts—ones that might well be illuminated by Trites's argument. This suggests that the question of the differences between young-adult fiction and children's fiction, on the one hand, and adult fiction, on the other, requires further consideration. Young-adult literature seems to involve an intersection of the qualities of children's literature with ideas about adolescent readers and various types of adult fiction that turns it into a similar but distinct variation of literature for younger children.

I was equally convinced that children's fantasy, while sharing many qualities of adult fantasy fiction, differs from it exactly by virtue of the qualities it shares with other nonfantasy texts written for child readers. As for the differences between textual narrative and picture-book storytelling: that I found these significant is evidenced by *Words about Pictures*, my book on that subject. Nevertheless, my explorations of the six texts confirmed my sense of something important shared by bringing me to the perception of what I came to call the "shadow text" of text-based narratives and the ways in which it parallels the presence of illustrations in picture books. I could make discoveries of this sort only by trusting my basic intuition enough to include texts from all these usually distinguished categories. And I did my best to choose extreme cases, including both the extremely short and simple *The Snowy Day* and the much longer and more complex *Plain City*, the wildly fantastical *Alice's Adventures in Wonderland* and the doggedly realistic *Henry Huggins*.

For the same reason, I was careful to include two nineteenth-century texts and two books from the first half or so of the twentieth century in the group of six I chose to consider. Just as I can't claim that *The Snowy Day* represents all picture books or *Plain City* all young-adult novels, I can hardly make the case that the noncontemporary texts are representative of all the writing done for children in earlier times. They obviously are not, and I know they are not even despite my relatively limited knowledge of the vast range of writing for children of earlier times known to specialists.

To begin with, there is the question of why I chose no texts produced before the beginning of the nineteenth century. I made my decision in part because of a sense, based on my reading of earlier texts, that what I can most readily identify as children's literature similar to that still being written began to appear only in the last half of the eighteenth century. "The Purple Jar" comes early enough in the history of the genre so that including it along with later texts could at least begin to represent the historical scope of the genre. I am aware of how circular my thinking is here: I have avoided the possible problem of earlier texts differing from my sense of what children's literature is by asserting that those texts are not included in what I call children's literature. In chapter 4 I offer arguments for defining children's literature in this way.

But why did I choose the nineteenth-century texts I did? I did so in part because they represent two quite different points in that century—points that many scholars see as distinct periods in the evolution of children's literature. But I specifically chose "The Purple Jar" and *Alice's Adventures in Wonderland* because, despite my relative lack of expertise in early children's literature, I *do* know them. I am able to know them because they are so readily available for me to know, in currently purchasable reprints. In this sense, at least, they are texts of this time as much as they are texts of past times.

The fact of their availability raises questions about what makes these texts relevant, and thus perennially marketable, while so many other texts produced in their time are not. Most obviously, they continue to be available simply because they have been available before. They are among the relatively small number of texts that people who want to know something about literature—in the case of "The Purple Jar," specifically children's literature—are expected to know, so there continues to be a market for reprints of them. They are canonical texts, ones considered to be of some special significance; and the fact that they are special—distinct—may be exactly what makes them unrepresentative, unlike most other texts of their time, and what spoils any claim I might make for the conclusions I base in part on their having any general historical relevance.

It also might be the case that these texts are easily available simply because they are still readable—that they accord with readers' current assumptions about what makes for an interesting or characteristic or relevant text. The very fact of their canonicity might provide a good reason for that being so. Later writers might well have shaped their work in the knowledge of or in homage to these particular predecessors that had been singled out as admirable or otherwise noteworthy. Readers familiar with those later texts would then have a context for making sense of these particular earlier ones—a context that would make less admired and therefore less imitated texts of earlier times seem much less readable or "typical" and much less likely to share characteristics with texts of later times. My specific choices of two well-known texts from the past may well have distorted my argument before I even began to see what the argument was. History is a pursuit of the present, however, and those who pursue it do so for reasons of present significance that shapes what it describes and discovers. We are all always in the process of reimagining the past to suit our present needs. The trick is to be aware of that fact and its dangers and to consider the nature and validity of the needs— as, I hope, I am doing here.

In the case of my choice of these two texts, my awareness of the dangers leads me to make the qualifications I have just been making. I understand that the history I can account for in terms of an analysis of texts like "The Purple Jar" and *Alice's Adventures in Wonderland* does not stretch very far beyond those aspects of the past that remain most relevant for practitioners of children's literature and children's literature scholarship in the present. I am willing to accept that limitation, but I acknowledge the need for a consideration of other early texts that might confirm or deny the validity of my generalizations.

My perception of the dangers of this sort of choosing leads me to an awareness of another potential ramification of my project that I will need to consider: the very real possibility that I sensed commonalities between these nineteenth-century texts and more contemporary ones simply because my reading of and thinking about the more contemporary ones equipped me to look for and therefore, presumably, find qualities in them that may not actually be there at all or, if there, may not have been obvious or important to readers in earlier times.

In a sense, this sort of distorted reading was inevitable. I could not possibly have avoided imposing my own twenty-first century thought patterns on nineteenth-century texts. But I also remain convinced that what I uncovered is of value, that despite wide variations in the ideas about childhood that have led adults to produce texts written specifically for children over the last few centuries, logic suggests that at least two basic convictions about why such texts might need to exist have to have remained the same. The first is the idea that children are different from adults in ways that make them like each other: that children as a group display characteristics that are different from those of adults as a group. The second is the idea that the difference between children and adults is one that obligates adults to produce a special literature for children. All children's literature shares a common faith that there are such things as distinctive and different child readers, or a distinctive and different childlike way of thinking and reading, and that adults are not only capable of addressing that reader different from themselves but obligated to do so.

These perhaps obvious generalizations are, to my mind, highly significant. In ancient Greece or medieval Europe people clearly had ideas about childhood, specifically about how children differ from adults. But as the absence of texts easily identified as children's literature tells us, those ideas did not in any way obligate the people of those times to produce texts specifically marked as being intended for children. But from the seventeenth century up through the present in Europe and then in North America and elsewhere, a vast variety of different ideas of childhood have had one thing in common: each of them *did* lead adults to produce literature for children. That literature, whether it was Puritan religious tracts in seventeenth-century England or pop-up picture books intended to give sensuous pleasure to contemporary children in the United States, has at least that much in common. The most basic assumption of my experiment was that this particular commonality might well lead texts to share common forms of language usage or characteristic structures of organization or common subjects and thematic comment.

It was in the light of this assumption that I allowed myself to include the two nineteenth-century texts in my group and to take the chance of imposing my own twenty-first-century attitudes on them. If nothing else, my early twenty-first-century values share with those of Edgeworth and Carroll the double conviction that adults differ from children and that the difference requires adults to provide texts specifically for audiences of children. And since my focus remains fixed on that pair of central ideas and their ramifications, it remains possible that what I have to say might well have at least some validity for others beside myself.

• In addition to including texts from various times in my group of six, I made a conscious effort to include texts from a spectrum of other possible sources of difference.

My doing so relates to another set of assumptions, these about the possibility that matters such as a writer's gender or ethnicity or nationality, themselves shaped by ideological forces operating in the relevant communities, might well play a part in shaping the writer's work. I wanted therefore to choose texts by men and women and by writers of differing ethnic backgrounds and nationalities. In a limited number of texts I could do this only minimally. I ended up with three texts by women and three by men, three by writers from the British Isles (although one of them, Maria Edgeworth, was born in England but raised in Ireland) and three by American ones. The ethnic mix of my choices was less egalitarian: I managed to include just two texts about African American children, only one of them by an African American writer. But the second text about an African American child, by a Jewish author, increased the ethnic mix. In the light of the closeted history of homosexuality, I did not have access to trustworthy information about sexual orientation of writers to include it as a factor in my choices.

I allowed myself four books by writers who were, to the best of my knowledge, of British or European background by persuading myself that this disproportionate representation was representative of the field of children's literature as a whole. Even in recent decades, when publishers and educators have insisted on the importance of multicultural texts for children, surprisingly few are published in relation to the number of books published as a whole. For instance, a statistical survey by the Cooperative Children's Book Center of the University of Wisconsin reveals that of the up to five thousand or more American children's books published each year since 1994, fewer than two hundred each year were about Africans or African Americans and fewer than one hundred by Africans or African Americans.[27] In the business of isolating the most characteristic features of texts written for children, unfortunately, choosing texts from a wider variety of ethnic backgrounds would itself be a distortion.

Another major lapse of my list reveals a key fact about children's literature in general. As far as I am able to determine, all six of the texts are by writers of middle-class backgrounds; and with the possible exception of *The Snowy Day*, in which Peter's apartment home may represent existence on the edge of poverty that is nevertheless depicted as happily comfortable, all have middle-class protagonists who tend to take the comforts of their surroundings quite for granted. Since its beginning, in the eighteenth century, children's publishing has been primarily a middle-class venture, pursued by middle-class writers and intended most centrally and most often for audiences of middle-class children. For this reason more than any other, generalizations about children are dangerous—they construct as normal a middle-class vision of childhood for the vast population of children without the economic circumstances to be able to share it. Any conclusions I finally reach about children's literature will have to take that fact into account and make the middle-class bias that is so central to the literature equally central to any theories I develop about it.

There are at least two other important ways in which the texts I ended up choosing are highly unrepresentative of a variety of possible groups of people. They are all in the English language. And while half are from Great Britain and half from the United States, no other English-speaking nations are represented— not even my own country of Canada. Thus, only two of the many countries that produce texts for children are included.

I chose to limit my choices to books written in English primarily because English is the language with which I am most comfortable, and, by and large, English-language texts of children's literature are the texts I know. My choices are thus a blatant example of how my conclusions are limited by the boundaries of my knowledge.

I could, I suppose, make a case for the central significance of English-language texts in the history of children's literature throughout the world. The non-English-language children's literature of former British colonies such as India or Singapore will inevitably have been influenced by English-language examples provided by the colonial masters, and today the influence of American forms of children's storytelling as distributed not only in books but also by films and TV programs is international. The histories of children's literature I have read all tend to identify its seventeenth- and eighteenth-century originators as English-speaking inhabitants of England or the United States. It is also instructive that, according to Mary-Ann Farquhar, texts containing something like the characteristics of children's literature as I have outlined them did not appear in China until the beginning of the twentieth century, "and the proposed new literature for children was based on western models"[28]—on translations of European stories by writers like the French Jules Verne and the Danish Hans Christian Andersen. I tend to assume, then, that children's literature as it has developed in recent centuries is a product of England and the United States later exported elsewhere— that English-language children's literature is something like a normative base that led to and acted as a model for other children's literatures.

But is it? In the first edition of the *International Companion Encyclopedia of Children's Literature,* a context that implies an international scope for her work, Margaret Kinnell offers a survey titled "Early Texts Used by Children," which focuses almost exclusively on English-language books. She does, however, include English translations of texts like Comenius's *Orbis Sensualium Pictus* and Perrault's fairy tales—and thus more or less accidentally reveals that an otherwise unacknowledged children's literature did exist outside the English tradition she otherwise represents as universal. In his preface to the second edition of the *Encyclopedia,* Peter Hunt acknowledges that in the earlier version "the historical developments described and the examples given are overwhelmingly of English first-language-speaking countries and their empires," even though the *Encyclopedia* contained a "gathering of articles on separate countries and areas of the world in a separate section," a division that both acknowledges the existence of other literatures and histories and, as Hunt himself admits, "suggests that the 'rest' of the world is 'other'—that colonialism is not dead."[29] Similarly, Hunt reveals (and in this case, makes no apology for) something in the preface to his *Children's Literature: An Illustrated History* not specified by its title: "This book is about English-language children's literature."[30] Interestingly, the subtitle of the recent *Norton Anthology of Children's Literature,* edited by Jack Zipes, Hunt, and others, also makes explicit that it represents "The Tradition in English." I suspect that all the histories I have read by English-speaking British and American historians are as distorted by their linguistic and national biases as my own choices of representative texts so clearly are and that French or German or Chinese histories of children's literature would tell quite a different story, in which English-language texts would not play such a completely dominating part or seem so centrally normative.

Hunt, however, defends the focus on English children's literature even in the revised version of his *Encyclopedia:* "This is an English-language work, primarily written by scholars working in English, for a predominantly English-speaking audience. . . . Therefore, it is only natural (however theoretically regrettable) that the emphasis should fall upon English topics, writers, and historical concerns."[31] I find it regrettable in more than theory—but I have to admit to sharing Hunt's focus and its limitations. The best case I can make for my choices of texts to discuss in terms of their shared language is that they represent the egocentricity of an English speaker in an increasingly English-speaking world, a world that has allowed me, for instance, to address international conferences in the comfort of my own language while speakers of other languages at the same conferences, including speakers of the language of the country we were speaking in, were required to use mine. It is further evidence that colonialism is not dead.

The second edition of Hunt's *Encyclopedia* offers no English-centered overview of history and places its articles on the history of children's literature in the United Kingdom amidst those about children's literature internationally. The almost fifty articles on international literatures often confirm, but just as often challenge, my assumption that English texts play an especially significant role in both the history of children's literature and, in the light of the spread of English-language mass-media culture around the world, in the reading and viewing experiences of children internationally. If nothing else, my thoughtless assumption that English-language texts might be normative exposes the thoughtless colonialism of my assumptions and leaves room for scholars like those represented in the illuminating discussions of international children's literatures in the *Encyclopedia* to reveal the extent of my blindness. Their doing so might show more about the particular ways in which children's literature written in Finnish or Chinese does vary from the English-language texts I privilege and therefore help to make the English texts seem much less generally representative, and much less central. They might also reveal the extent to which childhood itself is not a generalizable phenomenon— how children in different places experience different childhoods.

My six texts represent only two nations, which gives rise to another way they might not be universally representative. According to the Swedish children's literature specialist Maria Nikolajeva, "The notion that there is a 'common' children's literature in all countries in the world is a misunderstanding. . . . With very few exceptions, children's literature in different countries has little in common."[32] I question this. It would be strange if texts that share an implied audience of readers younger than their writers did not share at least some qualities, despite national differences. As I said earlier, exploring that particular assumption is the main impetus behind this project. Nevertheless, it is hard not to believe that there are some, and perhaps many, significant differences in the children's literatures of different national groups. Why, then, did I compound the problem of my focus only on English-language texts by restricting myself just to British and American ones?

Part of my reason for doing so was the simple question of what I might expect readers of this book to know. Canadian or Australian readers would know and likely be willing to accept that texts of the sort I wished to investigate by Americans and British writers might well be somehow representative of children's literature in general. But American and British readers would be less likely to know Canadian or Australian texts and therefore would be more likely to suspect my identification of them as representative. In the world of English-language children's literature, I realized, the shared texts tend to be from Britain and the United States. Australians, as well as American or British readers, are less likely to know Canadian texts than British or American ones.

No matter what country they live in adults interested in children's literature tend to talk about the children's literature of countries like Canada and Australia as variations from a norm, even when they resist identifying specific distinguishing characteristics that might be accounted for by a text's country of origin. For instance, the Canadian students in my children's literature courses discuss texts like Sendak's *Where the Wild Things Are* or Potter's *Tale of Peter Rabbit* without reference to their national provenance. They are not American or British children's books, just children's books, period. But the students' discussions of books like Tim Wynne-Jones's *Zoom at Sea* or Brian Doyle's *Mary Ann Alice* almost always refer to the books as Canadian. Scholars tend to replicate these actions in their published work.

I have replicated them myself. In "Teaching Canadian Children's Literature: Learning to Know More," Mavis Reimer and I describe how we asked students in Canadian children's literature courses "to consider, in small groups, the ways in which these novels matched and did not match the ideas [about general characteristics of children's literature] presented in *Pleasures [of Children's Literature]*."[33] This classroom activity has resulted in further research that works to understand Canadian children's literature in terms of its divergence from international generic characteristics, including Reimer and Rusnak's "The Representation of Home in Canadian Children's Literature / La représentation du *chez-soi* dans la littérature de jeunesse canadienne."

Seeing Canadian books like *Zoom at Sea* in terms of their divergences from a generic pattern makes sense simply because the books have been written in that context. Canadian writers for children inevitably know books from elsewhere. Whatever its distinct qualities are, for instance, *Zoom at Sea* clearly emerges from a repertoire of children's picture-book story forms that includes books like *Peter Rabbit* or *Where the Wild Things Are*. Even so, putting *Zoom at Sea* on my list of representative texts would allow readers to doubt the list's representativeness, so I chose not to. My list replicates the tendency I described earlier in terms of speakers of the English language and historians of children's literature. It tends to be imperial in its basic assumptions, making texts produced in centers of power central and normative and marginalizing texts produced by less powerful people in less powerful places.

Paradoxically, however, it does reveal my position as a Canadian, in ways I have become aware of only as I discussed my choices of texts with my Australian colleague John Stephens. He pointed out to me that what I took for granted—that everyone with a knowledge of children's literature in the English-speaking world would have some familiarity with books like *Henry Huggins* and *The Snowy Day*—is not the case. These American books are not widely known in Australia. Stephens went on to point out an aspect of my choices that I had not been aware of: the three earlier ones are British, the three later ones American. My choices thus represented my unconscious assumption of a specifically Canadian view as a universally representative one. Canadians had access to many British children's books until Canadian economic and culture ties to Britain became less important than those to the United States. Then, as my list suggests, access to British books diminished, and the proportion of American ones increased. That has only begun to happen in Australia more recently, many decades after it did in Canada. I was more tied to my location than I knew, and my choices were more personal than I knew.

My choices of texts to discuss are inevitably tied to my own situation, inevitably marked by the ideological currents of my time and place. But in spite of or even because of that, they reveal not only the possible limitations but also the potential validity of what I can learn about children's literature in general from exploring just these six supposedly representative texts. The process of choosing that I have been describing here reveals not just my own biases but also, as I hope I have shown, how similar biases inform choices of what to produce and what to discuss that inform and shape the field of children's literature production and criticism generally. In those fields some texts are more powerful than others simply because they are perceived to be more representative than others—more "typical" of what children's literature is generally assumed to be. And that is actually my subject here—the ideas about what makes for a "typical" text for children, ideas that inform and encourage the production of yet more typical texts.

I am assuming, then, that a norm exists—that texts can be representative of children's literature in general exactly to the extent to which they conform to a set of characteristics recognizable and currently powerful in the field of children's literature. I am agreeing with Torben Weinreich: "I prefer to see children's literature as a *genre,* and by 'genre' I mean here a notion of a group of texts characterised by recurrent features."[34] This raises further important questions. Do genres exist? If not, what are the consequences of imagining that they do? If so, what are they, and why might it matter?

Assumptions about Genre

There are a number of reasons why literary texts share common traits. Writers might have similar interests with other writers they haven't even read that lead to similarities in their work. Or—and this possibility might turn out to be particularly relevant in terms of a discussion of children's literature—different writers might share ideas about an audience their text is directed toward and how and why that audience ought to be addressed. Most significant, however, those who produce the texts do so in the context of their experience of other texts. It is hard to imagine someone who had never read a novel independently conceiving of the idea of writing one, and it is inevitable that those who do decide to write one should do so in terms of consciously or unconsciously working to replicate those aspects of the novels they know that most interest them or give them most pleasure. A whole history of children's fantasies about talking animals played a part in determining the content, shape, and texture of E. B. White's *Charlotte's Web,* and that same history stands behind many similar fantasies written for children.

If texts can and do share characteristics, then groups of texts sharing similar characteristics might be thought of as a particular type or kind of literature—a genre. That numerous commentators have expressed ideas of this sort across the centuries may itself be one reason why texts that share certain attributes continue to emerge, for as David Fishelov says, genres "actually shape how writers produce, and readers respond to, literary works."[35] Once the idea that there are nameable kinds or types of books with similar properties circulates in critical discourse and educational practice, someone who has studied, say, drama may then work to produce a text that replicates what he or she perceives as the requisite features of a tragedy or a farce. In this way the idea that a genre exists and has some specific features can predate the existence of texts that contain those features.

As Jane Feuer says, however, "a genre is ultimately an abstract conception rather than something that exists empirically in the world."[36] There is no such thing as a "genre" in exactly the same sense as there is no such thing as "literature" or "sports" or "geological formations"—except in the minds of those who look at some specific unique entity, a poem or a game involving pucks or a rock, and think of it as being one example of a group of similar objects. In the same way and even more immediately, there is no such thing as a "poem" or a "puck" or a "rock," except in the minds of those who look at specific unique objects, understand them to be specific and unique, significantly separable from the perceptual field surrounding them, and then identify them as examples of the categories established by the existence of those words. "Literature" and "poem" are abstract conceptions in the minds of people, a way to make sense of the myriad of specific objects and experiences perceived by assigning them to categories based on their similarities to each other. As Jacques Derrida suggests, the operations of genres are just one example of how linguistic categories—language itself—always operates to establish guiding principles—rules or "law": "The question of the literary genre is not a formal one: it covers the motif of the law in general."[37]

Thinking in terms of such abstract conceptions seems to be a basic and unavoidable habit of human minds in making sense of the world they perceive. Cognitive psychology teaches that understanding proceeds in terms of the creation of "schemata"—generalized models based on the shared qualities of a range of objects or ideas believed to belong to the same class or group. One of the founders of cognitive psychology, Frederic Bartlett, defined a schema as "an active organisation of past reactions, or of past experiences, which must always be supposed to be operating in any well-adapted organic response. That is, whenever there is any order or regularity of behaviour, a particular response is possible only because it is related to other similar responses which have been serially organised, yet which operate, not simply as individual members coming one after another, but as a unitary mass."[38]

The unitary masses or generalized categories people derive from their previous experience of objects they have come to identify as being similar to each other allow them to identify a new object that comes into their perceptions as one example of a previously developed category—not just an indiscriminate something but a ball or a dog or a poem. In a mind without schemata, a round object or a group of words set out in rhythmic patterns could not be thought of as a ball or a poem. It could be only (and paradoxically) both forever irretrievably itself and forever inseparable from the entire field of perceptual information around it. It would be so completely individual yet so completely one with its surroundings as to be unthinkable and unthought about. The paradox is powerful: the placing of objects into preestablished groupings or types or categories is the very thing that allows understanding of how the objects are separate and distinct, the foreground to what then becomes their background. Without a perception of similarities to preestablished categories, distinctness itself is literally unthinkable.

I assume that all readers have a series of literary schemata—unitary masses based on their previous reading that cause them to identify the new texts they encounter as belonging to certain categories, such as, say, children's literature. In that context I must both accept that each and every literary text is singular and unique and dismiss the relevance of that uniqueness. It is not texts themselves that I want to describe here but how texts exist within the minds of writers and readers—how their creators and consumers understand what they are and what they do. And in the minds of readers and writers, texts inevitably exist in the context of their connections to other objects, specifically in the context of literary schemata: abstract conceptions of what literature is and what specific types of literature are—genres.

From this point of view an individual text is to genre as something like what the linguist Ferdinand de Saussure called *parole* is to *langue*—a specific individual utterance that exists within and can communicate effectively only in the context of a set of preestablished rules and relationships. For Alistair Fowler, "a literary work resembles the individual *parole* of ordinary speech. As with *parole*, its contingent and unique communication depends upon and embodies a previously shared system."[39] That system, suggests Fowler, is genre. A writer who writes a mystery novel or an epic poem does so with ideas about what mystery novels or epic poems can be, ideas that have been derived from previous readings of texts the writer has identified as belonging to the genre in question. A reader who approached a mystery novel or an epic poem with no previous knowledge of what mysteries or epics are might make some sort of sense out of the texts but not necessarily anything like the intended meanings. Communication always depends on a knowledge of codes, conventions, and grammatical relationships—what information theorists call "redundancies"; the pioneering information theorist C. E. Shannon claims that "the redundancy of ordinary English . . . is roughly 50%. This means that when we write English half of what we write is determined by the structure of the language and half is chosen freely"[40]—and so, then, is half of what we understand of what we read. In literature generic characteristics are the redundancies that allow readers to recognize a text as being of a certain sort, an epic poem or, I postulate, a children's novel, and then read and interpret it as such.

Understood most simply, literary genres are one particular form of schema recognizing one particular set of redundancies—the general models of types or kinds of literature readers develop from their encounters with specific individual texts. Genres operate like schemata in two ways. First, readers develop their ideas about genres from previous experience of texts they see as fitting into them. Second, they use those ideas to understand the new texts they encounter. Readers approach new children's novels in terms of expectations derived from the children's novels they have already read.

Cognitive schemata are individual constructs based on individual experience. Because the conceptions of genre that each person has in his or her individual mind are so dependent on past experience, they might well vary from each other. What I consider to be a tragedy or a children's novel is not necessarily what you would be willing to include as such. Perhaps each reader has his or her own private set of genres. If there is a "langue," it may be a relatively personal one—a system not necessarily as completely "shared" as Fowler suggests.

Significantly, however, experience teaches me that we are unlikely to allow each other our varying inclusions and exclusions without comment, discussion, and attempts to persuade. Ideas of inclusion and exclusion seem to be at the heart of what genre is and how it works. Derrida speaks of "a law of 'do' or 'do not' which, as everyone knows, occupies the concept or constitutes the value of *genre*. . . . Thus, as soon as genre announces itself, one must respect a norm, one must not cross a line of demarcation, one must not risk impurity, anomaly or monstrosity."[41] This concern with inclusions and, especially, exclusions is particularly powerful in relation to children's literature, a literature whose very nature seems tied up with the idea of exclusion, of existing in the first place exactly in order to leave things out. Proclamations by adults that certain texts they don't personally approve of are not actually children's literature at all—and therefore are not suitable candidates for their library or home or classroom—have been central to the discourse surrounding children's literature since it began.

Those who use restrictive ideas about genre to exclude certain texts are not content simply to accept that genre categories are personal or to be satisfied with their own categorizations; they want others to share their sense of what the genre is and is not. And this suggests what is lacking in my discussion so far: in focusing on genres as types of schema that allow each reader individually to make sense of literature, I have neglected to consider the ways in which genre categorizations are not merely personal. Like cognitive schemata or like a *langue,* they have a social dimension. The schema that allows me to identify a pencil as a pencil is not merely my own; if not exactly the same as the schema for pencil of many other people, it is very similar—if it were not, I couldn't usefully communicate with others about pencils, as I often do. I share a schema of pencils with others because my sense of what pencils are has been influenced not just by my encounters with actual pencils but also by my discourse with other people about pencils. I wouldn't call a pencil a pencil at all if I didn't share a language with other people that includes the word *pencil.*

As with pencils, so with genres: they have a communal, shared existence, as well as a set of private, individual ones. M. M. Bakhtin, who suggests that there is no utterance in or out of literature that does not refer to what he calls *speech genres*— "that is, certain relatively stable thematic, compositional, and stylistic types of utterances"—goes on to assert that any speaker always "presupposes not only the existence of the language system he is using, but also the existence of preceding utterances—his own and others'—with which his given utterance enters into one kind of relation or another (builds on them, polemicizes with them, or simply presumes that they are already known to the listener). Any utterance is a link to a very complexly organized chain of other utterances."[42] As a result, genres are an inherent component of the ways in which people communicate with each other. They are social and communal. Literary genres, being examples of the "secondary" speech genres Bakhtin understands as more complex combinations of the simply "primary" genres of conversation, inevitably possess these social aspects.

Producers and consumers of literature can develop expertise only by reading widely among the texts already in existence, so they tend to have schemata similar to the literary types that interest them. These shared schemata represent communal ideas about genres and their characteristics—not individual schemata but social ones. In any particular place or at any given moment in history, each member of the community of readers and writers that has an interest in a particular genre tends to have a fairly specific sense of what is or is not correctly considered appropriate or acceptable within that genre by the community at large—and polices that sense by what he or she is willing or not willing to read or write or recommend to other readers.[43] In terms of children's fiction, even a child who happened to read and enjoy James Joyce's *Ulysses* would likely know enough about genres to understand that the novel could not be identified as children's literature.

What I have just said implies the simultaneous existence of two different perceptions of genre that may or may not be equivalent: the communal view and the individual views of each of the community's members. And in this discussion so far, I have referred to two different systems of accounting for human thought and language to describe genres—the grammatical system that identifies them as parts of a *langue,* or as what information theorists call redundancies, and the system of cognitive psychology that identifies them as schemata. While similar, these two ways of describing the processes of thinking and writing are not completely congruent. A *langue* is a communally shared body of language, a set of conventions or redundancies shared by speakers or writers and hearers or listeners of the *langue.* Strictly speaking, a schema is a private matter, a construct developed by an individual as he or she goes about the act of making sense of his or her experience. While individuals refer to communal information in constructing schemata, the schemata remain individual. A schema is not a *langue,* and a *langue* is not a schema.

Yet I suspect that ideas about genre exist most interestingly in terms of the myriad shifting intersections of the private individual views and the more broadly shared definitions or understandings of the discourse community. It is this complex set of negotiations, this continuing dialogue among readers and writers and critics about what genres might be and what texts or textual qualities might or might not be seen to fit within them, this constant effort to transform personal schemata into aspects of a communal *langue,* that makes the exploration of generic considerations interesting and important. Marko Juvan offers a useful summary of the complex ways in which ideas of genre circulate within the community of writers and readers that suggests just how central to production and reception of texts they are:

Discriminating and identifying genres occur in literary life mainly through the daily practices that the individual, collective, and institutional agents conduct when dealing with particular texts. These practices are multiform: they can be seen in the readers' expectations and ideas of genres, in the author's or critic's genre naming of texts or in the intertextual evocation of family resemblances or significant discrepancy between the literary work and the corresponding patterns in other texts. The establishment, indication, reproduction, and recognition of generic features are therefore largely habitual tasks of authors and readers, as well as editors, journalists, opinion-makers, and others involved in presenting texts to the public and commenting on them critically.[44]

The ways in which producers and consumers of literature use ideas of genre are political activities with a communal function. As Tzvetan Todorov suggests, "In a society, the recurrence of certain discursive properties is institutionalized, and individual texts are produced and perceived in relation to the norm constituted by this codification. A genre . . . is nothing but this codification of discursive properties."[45] As social institutions genres need to be investigated in terms of their political effects on the community of readers and writers.

The most immediately noticeable feature of such an investigation is simply that it is possible. Unlike individual schemata—which might well remain private and unspoken—shared, communal understandings of genre are matters of public record. They are so most obviously in terms of explicit definitions or descriptions as laid out in critical and theoretical writing. But communal understandings of genre are also implied in the unspoken assumptions that govern reviews and other critical discourse about texts, and in the features of texts themselves, once someone postulates, as I did in chapter 1, that those features emerge from conceptions of genre. Seen from this point of view, my subject here is, exactly, what shared understandings practitioners and consumers have of children's literature —what conscious and unconscious agreements have been negotiated as this genre has developed since its beginnings a few centuries ago, and how those agreements may or may not be in the process of continual renegotiations.

Those agreements—and those renegotiations—have a huge influence on what can and cannot be published as children's literature. Concepts of genre as shared by large communities of writers and readers underlie all discussions of book selection and of what is or is not "appropriate" as children's reading; therefore, these concepts have a huge impact both on the economy of publishing and in the minds of writers for children and child readers. They need to be explored and understood, especially since many of the distinctive characteristics (and effects) of genres are features that readers and writers tend to take for granted as matters of course and are not explicitly aware of.

According to Carolyn Miller, each genre is a specific form of social action: "A genre is a rhetorical means for mediating private intentions and social exigence; it motivates by connecting the private with the public, the singular with the recurrent."[46] The act of engaging a genre—writing texts that purport to be examples of it or reading texts as if they are examples of it—is a matter of attempting to act on others or to be acted on by others in specific ways. As Aviva Freedman and Peter Medway suggest, "While recognizing that genres can be characterized by regularities in textual form and substance, current thinking looks at these regularities as surface traces of a different kind of underlying regularity. Genres have come to be seen as typical ways of engaging rhetorically with recurring situations. The similarities in textual form and substance are seen as deriving from the similarity in the social action undertaken."[47]

While Miller and Freedman and Medway are talking about genre in the context of teaching expository forms of writing like essays and science reports to children and other students, literary genres also exist as social actions—ways in which writers work to offer readers specific experiences of significance to a community and in which readers take part in or even are constructed as members of that community. Traditional ideas about, for instance, how tragedies are cathartic of emotions dangerous to the health of communities suggest how very much this particular genre is understood to be a form of social action. Thomas Beebee suggests that literary genres are differentiated by what he calls their "use-value"—the ways in which they invite readers to make use of them: "If the texts *mode-d'emploi* is not somehow marked, reading—in the sense of that word which transcends merely translating black marks on white paper into sounds—becomes impossible."[48] To the extent that genres are communally shared and communally mandated, their use-values tend to represent communal ideologies. Thus, children's literature functions as a way of offering young readers specific experiences for specific purposes of benefit to the community that the current child or the adult the child is becoming belongs to.

For that reason, the main generic markers of children's fiction might turn out to be the nature of the social actions it performs and encourages young readers to partake in—ways in which its shared surface characteristics operate to provide readers with a reading experience that encourages them to feel and think certain specific thoughts and work to make them think of themselves and others in certain specific ways that will affect their relationships with others. In Derrida's terms, genres establish what the law is and impose it on readers.

Nor is the law being promoted necessarily as something that either readers or writers are aware of. According to Richard M. Coe, "Much genre knowledge lives in the social unconscious of discourse community; for individual writers, genre knowledge is often at least partially subliminal. . . . One might say genre epitomizes the significance of approaching reading and writing as social processes in which individuals participate without being entirely conscious of how social the processes are."[49] For that reason, say Freedman and Medway, "because the social processes implicated in reading and writing are so often tacit, and because those involved in the processes are typically unaware at a conscious level of the social dimensions of what they are undertaking, it remains for researchers, teachers, and scholars to cast some light on what is actually going on when we participate in the use of written genres."[50] It is my intention here to do just that—to explore how the shared characteristics of texts of children's fiction constitute special forms of social action with significant effects both on individuals and on communities of writers, editors, publishers, booksellers, librarians, teachers, and both child and adult readers.

The idea that genres have ideological power suggests another important dimension of them. That power might represent a resistance to change. According to Juvan genre theories have "figured as a stronghold of essentialism ever since Aristotle."[51] They tended traditionally to operate in terms of viewing specific texts as trying to be representatives of an unchanging generic essence and, most often, judging them successful or not in terms of the degree to which they matched that essence. This sort of thinking still operates. In terms of children's literature, for instance, publishers and purchasers often proceed with the genre expectation that children's books are simple in style, and producers and consumers tend therefore to resist publishing or purchasing more complex ones. The ways in which ideas of genre act as law inevitably invite a clinging to essences that transcend history. Genres can be and often are stultifying, resistant to change.

But this is not to say that they don't change. As Derrida suggests, the law always fails to legislate. "What," he asks, "if there were, lodged within the heart of the law itself, a law of impurity or a principle of contamination?" He goes on to suggest that there is, that in order to declare its affiliation with a genre, a text must repeat a generic trait that inevitably in its obligatory presence implies others that are absent, different from it and exterior to itself: "The trait that marks membership inevitably divides, the boundary of the set comes to form, by invagination, an internal pocket larger than the whole."[52] In declaring its disaffiliation from that which is outside itself, the text evokes and demands the outside, brings the outside in and therefore allows what is on its inside out. In more general terms, the establishment of a border or boundary (or schema) implies and therefore inevitably allows that which it excludes—even depends for its existence and meaning on that which it excludes—for a schema for, say, children's fiction would be pointless without a context in which things existed that were neither fiction nor for children. As Thomas Beebee insists, "Since a 'single' genre is only recognizable as difference, as a foregrounding against the background of its neighboring genres, every work involves more than one genre, even if only implicitly."[53] Marking off genres implies everything outside the genres that might, and inevitably does, contaminate them, especially other genres. The outside might come in—as apparently it does when texts of children's literature like John Scieszka's *The Stinky Cheese Man* use postmodern techniques theoretically alien to the genre. More significant, the outside might come in in terms of the "hidden" adult knowledge I found in the texts I discussed in chapter 1. Alternatively, the inside might come out, as when wide adult audiences transgress genre boundaries by reading children's books like Rowling's Harry Potter series or when the makers of films for adults such as the Star Wars movies mirror the plot patterns and characteristic interests of children's fiction.

So genres have histories. They change, and readers' perceptions of them change, whatever their status in any given moment of history as fairly fixed *langues*. Readers' ideas of what a genre of literature might consist of change in relation to a spectrum of experiences of texts; a lover of mysteries finds ways either of accommodating new and different kinds of books as being mysteries or of assigning them to a separate category. Writers do the same thing; they find ways of accommodating new and different qualities into their new texts within a specific established genre. Fowler makes this clear in a phrase he adds to the sentence I quoted above, about how a genre embodies a previously shared system, "which, however, it modifies, initiating new departures that in turn become available as conventions or material for further literary *paroles*."[54] In this way, in allowing modification, the *langue* of a genre functions like a schema. What the people of Agamemnon's time called tragedy might well not have included something like the tragedies of Shakespeare—and although I want to argue that "The Purple Jar" shares characteristics with *The Snowy Day*, I have little doubt that Maria Edgeworth would have had trouble accepting *The Snowy Day* as a text of children's literature.

I, however, can see connections between *The Snowy Day* and "The Purple Jar" that Edgeworth, should she somehow have been able to read *The Snowy Day* without knowledge of a century and a half of intervening texts, could not see. And the connections I make allow me to become conscious of aspects of "The Purple

Jar" that I might well not have noticed without my knowledge of *The Snowy Day* to direct my attention toward them. There appears to be something central that remains, despite the obvious changes—something that resists change. And while I am aware of the possibility that I have misled myself by applying a schema derived from more recent texts onto the earlier ones, I sense that something more significant and less personal than that is happening here.

Fredric Jameson offers an intriguing explanation for what it might be. In describing how even the most apparently innovative literary texts sometimes express and support surprisingly conservative values, he suggests they can do so exactly because they maintain the marks of their genre—aspects of form that express conservative ideological content that shape and subvert content with which they are at odds. For Jameson, "it has become possible to grasp such formal processes [aspects of structure, language, etc.] as sedimented content in their own right, as carrying ideological messages of their own, distinct from the ostensible or manifest content of the works." As a result, "generic specification and description can, in a given historical text, be transformed into the detection of a host of distinct generic messages—some of them objectified survivals from older modes of cultural production, some anticipatory, but all together projecting a formal conjuncture through which the 'conjuncture' of coexisting modes of production at a given historical moment can be detected and allegorically articulated."[55] Jameson concludes, "The ideology of the form itself, thus sedimented, persists into the later, more complex structure as a generic message which coexists—either as a contradiction or, on the other hand, as a mediatory or harmonizing mechanism—with elements from later stages" (141). From this point of view, the shared characteristics that make up my schema for children's literature—most of them formal characteristics like shared plot patterns, structures based in binary opposition, and specific kinds of focalization—might well survive across history, sedimented in texts in ways that make it obvious that they are texts that belong to the genre of children's literature. And in so doing, they might be confirming or imposing theoretically outmoded models of childhood on contemporary children and adults.

Earlier I focused on the potential for change in Derrida's model of genres as always open to that which they define as being outside themselves. As Jameson suggests, this process might be viewed in less liberatory terms—as the conventional order outside entering in and imposing itself repressively on the inside. If that is the case, then it becomes important to understand how—to be aware both of the ideological content of the conventional generic markers of children's literature and of how that content enters and subverts the distinctness of individual and apparently innovative texts.

Genre and Field

Up to this point I have suggested that genres exist in the minds of readers and writers and that they operate there as schemata for specific ways of using language to affect others in specific ways that have social consequences—schemata that change in relation to the changing experiences both of individual writers and readers and also of the communities the writers and readers belong to, schemata that therefore have a history. Taken together, these qualities suggest some revealing connections between literary genres and what Bourdieu calls a "field."[56]

A "field" is an area of human interaction: economics, politics, culture, for instance, and also, within those larger fields, more specifically defined fields, such as, say, the field of banking or the field of municipal government—or the field of children's publishing. Seen from this point of view, children's publishing and its products—books for children—are sociological phenomena that can be accounted for in terms of operational characteristics and structural principles they share with other social activities.

For Bourdieu, each field takes its place in a shifting set of relationships with other existing fields and operates in terms of its own rules or conventions—some of them rules or conventions that also apply in other fields, some of them rules or conventions exclusive to a specific field itself. Bourdieu has written in detail about the specific conditions that operate within what he calls "the field of cultural production"—the production, distribution, and consumption of music, art, literature and so on.

While Bourdieu's theories are based on the specifics of cultural production in France, they account for characteristics of how capital operates that accord surprisingly well with the equivalent fields in other parts of Europe and North America, at least in terms of what I know of those fields from descriptions like those provided by Dan Hade and Michael Rosen and from my own experiences as a teacher, scholar, and reviewer, and especially as a writer of children's fiction.[57] They do so well enough, I believe, for me to make use of them here to discuss the production of children's literature.

In Bourdieu's terms the publishing, distribution, and consumption of children's literature would constitute a specific field within the larger field of cultural production, which is itself within the economic field and the overriding field of social interaction—what Bourdieu calls the field of power. Those who operate within a field do so in terms of what he calls a "habitus"—an implicit understanding of what forms of behavior are needed—appropriate or desirable or likely to be productive or have power—within that field. According to Bourdieu, a habitus is "necessity internalized and converted into a disposition that generates meaning-ful practices and meaning-giving perceptions; it is a general, transposable dis-position which carries out a systematic, universal application—beyond the limits of what has been directly learnt—of the necessity inherent in the learning condi-tions."[58] A habitus consists not merely of knowledge of explicitly stated rules and conventions but also an understanding, conscious and unconscious, of how best to operate in terms of those rules and conventions; in Randal Johnson's words, it is a "feel for the game":

> Bourdieu's theory of the cultural field might be characterized as a radical contextual-ization. It takes into consideration not only works themselves, seen relationally within the space of available possibilities and within the historical development of such possibilities, but also producers of works in terms of their strategies and trajec-tories, based on their individual and class habitus, as well as their objective position within the field. It also entails an analysis of the structure of the field itself, which includes the positions occupied by producers (e.g. writers, artists) as well as those occupied by all the instances of consecration and legitimation which make cultural products what they are (the public, publishers, critics, galleries, academies, and so forth). Finally, it involves an analysis of the position of the field within the broader field of power.[59]

What happens if "children's literature" is viewed as this sort of cultural field? Jack Zipes suggests, "The field of children's literature must include the interrela-tionships between children, teachers, librarians, parents, publishers, bookstore owners, vendors, business corporations, the mass media, and their various prac-tices of producing and consuming books intended for the young as commodi-ties."[60] In order to understand children's literature, I would also have to think about how the field relates to other fields—where children's literature sits in relation to various fields of adult literature and of movie and television production for audiences of children; how it fits within the overall fields of literary produc-tion, cultural production, economics and the field of power; in what ways its habitus mirrors or transforms the habitus of the fields it sits within or beside or shares some ground with. How is children's literature like or unlike, say, popular literature for adults? How is its publication and distribution connected with and divergent from the production and distribution of toys and of movies and video games for children or of popular literature for adults? I would also have to think about the structure of the field itself and the ways in which it disperses and organizes power—how specific writers, editors, publishers and so on function in relation to others in the field; how specific review journals or funding bodies or educational philosophies do and do not have power and influence over other people and organizations within the field. And I would have to attempt to develop some sense of the habitus of children's literature—what specific behaviors allow writers, editors, and others to gain success as they operate within the field, both in terms of what they write and what they admire in others' writing and in terms of how they behave in relation to each other.

All of this might seem to have more to do with larger questions of sociology and economics than with the literary matter of understanding specific texts or the characteristics of a genre of literature. But Bourdieu's "radical contextualization" reveals how the dispersal and organization of power in the field governs the nature of the texts produced and read. Bourdieu speaks of "the positional properties that any category of agents of cultural production or diffusion owes to its place within the structure of the field."[61] Every participant in the field occupies a specific position, the meaning of which is defined in terms of its relationship to other positions available within the field. To act as a writer or librarian, to write or purchase books, is a matter of occupying such a position, to take one's place in a complex set of relationships with others. Most significant, in terms of understanding literature, this means that individual texts must represent and contain the evidence of the positions their producers or purchasers occupy. Bourdieu calls the products of a field "position-takings" and speaks of the characteristics they "owe to the *positions* of their producers within the system of social relations of production and circulation and to the corresponding positions which they occupy within the system of *objectively possible cultural positions* within a given state of the field of production and circulation" (ibid.). Each text reveals in its characteristics the position taken by its writers and providers within the field it occupies, and it can be read by someone knowledgeable about the field in ways that reveal those positions and what they relate to—I was trying to do something like that as I described how I chose six texts to discuss. As a position taken, each text can be seen to represent one specific set of relationships with all the other texts in the field—both those currently available and those produced in the past and consigned to history. In its connections to and divergences from those other texts, in the specific position it takes in relation to them, each text contains information about the shape and structure of the group of texts produced by the field as a whole—of what might, perhaps, be called a genre.

Consider, for example, any specific children's book—let's say, for instance, an imaginary picture book about an Asian American child interacting with some fantasy monsters. Its writer and illustrator produce this text, and its editor chooses to publish it, in terms of how it manages to occupy certain positions already available to be filled—positions available because of preexisting understandings of possibilities within the field. Thus, a writer can choose to take the position of children's writer, write a text for children, and hope for an audience only because children's literature already exists as a possible form of writing—a position to be taken. The writer can produce a story told in few words and meant to be accompanied by a number of pictures because the picture book is an existing subcategory of the field—a more specific position to be taken. Editors often do literally know that they have a particular number of positions to be taken in a particular season—a certain number of picture books to publish, a certain number of those to be fiction or nonfiction, etc.—before they know which particular books will fill those slots and take those positions.

The writer of the picture book I described above probably arrived at a specific story line through an awareness of other yet more specific positions to be taken. The field of children's publishing exists to some extent within the larger field of education—much of the market for children's books in hardcover comprises schools and public libraries, which serve the interests of a clientele that attends the schools—and that means that it is influenced heavily by trends in education. A focus on multiculturalism in education in recent decades leads to a number of positions available in children's publishing to be taken by books that might be perceived to relate to multicultural concerns—positions that might well be taken by books about Asian American children.

Meanwhile, the existence of numerous successful books in which children meet with monsters of various kinds makes the depiction of monsters an acceptable position for a book to take. It was not always so. When Maurice Sendak's *Where the Wild Things Are* first appeared, in 1963, it created something of a controversy exactly because the depiction of monsters was perceived to be a new and unsettling idea. Sendak had, apparently, taken a position that was not actually there to be taken in the field of children's literature as it existed at that time.

Even so, he was able to take it. Presumably, the field, as then constituted, allowed at least the possibility that this position might exist (or perhaps, in Derrida's terms, the possibility that it be acceptably contaminated by the creation of this position). And in retrospect, it is relatively easy to see how it might. The appearance of this new book could reveal previously unavailable knowledge about the field in the past. For one thing, there is a long tradition in the history of the field of children's literature of children confronting monstrous horrific beings: consider Little Red Riding Hood confronting the wild wolf in Perrault's fairy tale, or Heinrich Hoffman's Conrad confronting the evil tailor who cuts off the thumbs of thumb-suckers in *Struwwelpeter*. In the early 1960s the field of children's literature was constructed around then currently powerful educational and psychological assumptions that made such depictions of monstrosity seem outmoded and counterproductive and therefore not conventionally acceptable positions to be taken. To take them—to revivify an aspect of the field that had come into disrepute at a moment when it might well be, and as it turned out, was possible to revivify it—represents Sendak's especially intense grasp of the habitus. He seems to have had the intuition to perceive that the way to gain power in this field was to defy its most firmly held shibboleths but to do so in ways that actually expressed some of the field's continuing central concerns. The dogma that violent monsters are definitely unacceptable in texts for children implies the field's continuing interest in violence and monstrosity just as firmly as does the freedom to depict violent monsters.

The field might even be seen to exist exactly in terms of adult concerns about how children need adult protection from violence and monstrosity. Texts written specifically for audiences of children came into existence at a point when adults decided that children were constituted in a way that required adult interference between them and the horrors of the adult world—as a protective act; and as my analysis in chapter 1 reveals, the texts I discussed there tend to replicate the need for adult protection that justifies the existence of theoretically unchildlike horrors within the stories they tell, as child protagonists come again and again to acknowledge their own weak innocence and their need for adult protection as a result of it.

In texts like "Little Red Riding Hood" and "Suck-a-Thumb," both violence and monstrosity and the wisdom that protects one from violence and monstrosity are exterior to the child protagonists, forces from outside them, antithetical to their own childishness. The violence and monstrosity are kept at the distance they occupy by adherence to adult rules and values enforced by adults. Little Red would not confront the wolf, nor Conrad have lost his thumbs, had they done what adults advised. The most unusual quality of *Wild Things* is that both the violence and monstrosity and the adult authority are Max's own. The story exteriorizes the violence and monstrosity that already reside within him; and the authority that controls and dissipates the violence and monstrosity is also his. Max fills all three roles available in the tradition within which the story positions itself: the threatened child, the force that threatens the child, the force that saves the child from the threat.

It is exactly this conflation of roles that seems to have allowed Sendak to reintroduce violent monstrosity into the field of picture books. By the early 1960s the influence of psychoanalytic views of the human mind and its unconscious on both writers and educators would have left a space open for the idea that the monsters children most need to be protected from are within rather than outside of them. And an educational climate heavily influenced by Piagetian and Montessorian ideas about how children teach themselves everything they come to know would have already been tolerant of the view that children might play roles traditionally assigned to adults in their own learning experiences. The position that a child might be both his own wild thing and his own adult savior from wildness is already there in the field waiting for someone with an acute enough sense of the habitus to take it.

Intriguingly, also, the apparently new position Sendak takes here reveals aspects of the older texts not necessarily apparent before. Viewed in the light of *Wild Things* (and with a little help from the psychoanalytical theories of Freud, also operating in the field in Sendak's time and now), the wolf might well be an exterior manifestation of Little Red's own divergence from the path on which her mother told her to stay—her own internal wildness. The thumb-cutting tailor could easily be seen as an exaggerated manifestation of Conrad's own unfortunate willingness to abuse his body parts. Both make choices allowing wildness to emerge from forces within themselves.

I have to admit I am less easily able to see ways in which Little Red and Suck-a-Thumb might be seen to have adult wisdom and be instrumental in their own salvation—although there do exist versions of the ever-adaptable "Little Red" in which something like that happens, in which the little girl herself tricks and scares off the wolf. And it might be worth noting that the wild forest that Little Red chooses against adult advice contains not just a dangerous wolf but a protective huntsman, so it is possible to conclude that in leaving the path, Red chooses the medium of both her problem and her salvation from it—and thus, in a way, occupies all three available roles also. As for Conrad, the choice of defying adult advice allows the entry not just of that which threatens him but that which ends the threat: his thumbs gone, he will no longer be able to suck his way into trouble. He, too, might be seen to have taken an adult role in engendering his own future protection from monstrous violence. The significant characters in both texts might be viewed as the id, ego, and superego of one child.

These interpretations strike me as being rather far-fetched, however. They would not have occurred to me had I not thought of these texts in the light of *Wild Things*. But far-fetched or not, they are not totally implausible. The taking of this new position reveals some less obvious aspects of the old ones; the field as a whole changes shape with each new position taken within it and thus retains integrity and consistency as a field.

In *Wild Things*, in any case, Sendak both defied and mirrored the conventions of the field, and he did so in ways that represent both continuity in the field—a confirmation of the principal underlying rules or shared understandings that give the field its shape and its boundaries—and startling but acceptable innovation within it. He knew how to take a position in relation both to older positions and to current ones that was intensely powerful. And in taking this position, *Wild Things* itself reveals some significant characteristics of the field within which it positions itself and of its relationship to other fields of which it is a part, including, especially, the field of education and the field of power.

Once *Where the Wild Things Are* was published and praised, it came to represent a position that could more conventionally, and more obviously, be taken by others. In a post–*Wild Things* world in which Grovers and Elmos, Pokémons and Sponge-Bobs, Mercer Mayer monsters and Anthony Browne gorillas seem merely conventional, my imaginary picture-book writer would have little trouble finding a publisher for his book about monsters or for a story in which a child saves himself from the threat of his childishness.

Unless, of course, he described the wrong kind of monsters—monsters made of human feces come to life, perhaps, or monsters who made children happy by fondling their privates or who encouraged children to brush their teeth every day and to refuse all candy and then turned out to be evil and wrong. A writer with a feel for the subtleties of the game would reject such ideas outright, for they are simply not currently possible.

Writers find success in proportion to their understanding of the field's habitus—their feel for what kinds of children's texts are possible or useful to produce or recommend or disperse. And as I hope my discussion of *Wild Things* reveals, this means that the habitus is inscribed in the texts themselves. Each new text that successfully enters the field will demonstrate a feel for the game of children's books, both by following rules and by putting them into play in new and different ways—taking new positions in relation to the established ones. As Bourdieu says, "Few works do not bear within them the imprint of the system of positions in relation to which their originality is defined; few works do not contain indications of the manner in which the author conceived the novelty of his undertaking or of what, in his own eyes, distinguished it from his contemporaries and precursors."[62]

To develop the most thorough understanding of the significance of any given text, readers must attempt to see what position it takes—how it exists relationally within a field of available possibilities or understandings of other texts and kinds of texts and within the historical development of such possibilities, how the various kinds of texts came into existence and grew and changed, and why they did so in relation both to other texts and to the economic and social conditions that influenced their character. As Randal Johnson says in his description of Bourdieu's argument, "The full explanation of artistic works is to be found neither in the text itself, nor in some sort of determinant social structure. Rather, it is found in the history and structure of the field itself, with its multiple components, and in the relationship between that field and the field of power."[63]

How might questions that deal specifically with genre relate to Bourdieu's description of fields? As I have now come to understand it, *genre* refers to the evidence of the nature of the field inscribed in the texts produced within the field. To focus on questions of genre is to look specifically at texts themselves in order to seek that evidence in them, to discover how they imply, in their language and subject and structure, relationships with other texts and with the field as a whole. Since the characteristics that mark a text as belonging to a specific genre might well result from the influence of economic or cultural forces at work in the field but exterior to texts themselves, such forces will need to be considered in attempts to account for the characteristics. But in a consideration of genre specifically, the focus will remain on the literary evidence—on exploring the distinctive characteristics of individual texts as evidence of a habitus and as positions taken in relation to other texts and to the field as a whole.

My wish to maintain such a focus defines the boundaries of my project here. An exploration of the field of children's literature as a field might well centrally concern itself with issues of power—with who gets it and how and why, with the sociology of the production and distribution of children's books, with what Randal Johnson calls "the complex network of social relations that makes the very existence of the texts possible."[64] But while the exploration of children's literature as a genre necessarily has implications in terms of an understanding of the field as a whole, it concerns itself centrally with the field as inscribed in texts and deals with the qualities texts share and the positions texts take in relation to other texts. My interest here is less centrally in unveiling the ideology of children's literature production or adult dealings with children than in exploring one specific aspect of such questions: what effects they have on the texts produced, as evidenced primarily by the qualities of the texts themselves viewed in terms of their relationships to each other—and thus, as a result of these position-takings, what effect the texts might have on their audience. While my attempts to account for distinctive generic markers or position-takings might lead me into considerations of economic context or cultural values, the discovery of such contexts is not my main goal. My main goal is knowledge of the texts themselves and, specifically, of their various relationships with each other.

The exploration of genre as a specific aspect of a field seems to me to be an eminently useful project for several reasons. Such an approach makes it clear that concepts of genre are more than just Platonic ideas preexisting and more perfect than actual texts—that descriptions of genre are not merely acts of essentializing. It firmly grounds genre in specific human contexts, as matters of shared social understandings, ways of acting socially and having or intending to have specific effects on specific other people or groups of people. Exploration of children's literature as a genre should provide information about what powerful forces in society, rightly or wrongly, believe literature should be and do and, therefore, about what child readers should be and do. It focuses on the distinctness of children's literature as the medium of a transaction between two divergent social groups, adults and children.

In doing so, this sort of approach should show how specific texts of children's literature are complex sites of social action—how, far from being purely distinctive products of uniquely individual human minds, they find their place in and contain within themselves the manifestations of numerous power relationships—not just between children and adults but also among writers, editors, reviewers, and purchasers, as well as between the field of children's literature and various other fields: adult literature, the toy industry, the field of education, the economy, and so on.

In focusing specifically on these matters as aspects of a habitus, however, this approach avoids the one-sided assumption that literature exists only as a manifestation of societal forces. It ascribes some agency to individual writers who possess varying degrees of a feel for the field and are able to express that feel by drawing on methods that emerge from their own personal history and experience. It might, of course, be argued that the writer's habitus is itself a product of social forces, the agency mainly illusory. But at the very least, it is important to distinguish between what people think they control and what merely more obviously controls them. And it is also important to understand why some positions taken in a literary field seem like unmediated and obvious responses to general social forces, while others at least seem cagier and more individual.

This approach provides a way of focusing on texts both in terms of their individual distinctness and in terms of how they are similar to and have connections with other texts. To read a text as a position taken is to understand it as a site where the personal (or at least the local) and the communal interact. The act of doing so understands the communal not as a rigid set of shared characteristics but as a complex, ever-shifting set of connections and relationships. It focuses less on the unity of the unitary mass than on what varies from that unity. While all texts identified with the genre do have connections and relationships to each other, each text remains distinct, a unique position being taken. Genre thus becomes something like a matter of familial relationships. While all members of a family have similarities with other members of the family, no two members necessarily share the same characteristics as each other. Some are closely connected, some more distantly; and sometimes, as in my discussion of *Wild Things* in relation to "Suck-a-Thumb," it takes some consideration of a series of members with closer relationships to determine what connects more distant and less obviously related members.

Like families, genres change over time. New elements enter and cause shifts in the relationships among those already present (although perhaps, as Jameson suggests, in ways that reinscribe the implications of the old elements). The approach to genre I envisage here acknowledges not just that genres have histories but that new developments in the present provoke new developments in the past—or at least in the present view of the past. Consider for example, the fact that Mary Shelley's *Frankenstein*, which predates the idea that there might be a genre of literature called "science fiction" by almost a century, is often nowadays labeled in discussions of the genre as science fiction—and seems to readers in the present to be an obvious and unquestionable example of this genre—a clear expression of its central defining traits. A similar logic operates in attempts by current children's literature scholars like Gillian Adams to find the characteristics of children's literature as it is now in texts written centuries before children's literature came to be identified as such. As I suggested earlier, it might also operate in my own attempt to read texts like "The Purple Jar" as similar to more recent texts. The field claims a past for itself in a way that changes what the past meant for those in past times. The genre does not so much evolve as it imagines at each new moment of its existence a rejuggled and somewhat different version of the past that accounts for its current interests. A new position taken causes a remapping of the past in terms of the new positioning.

Northrop Frye once spoke of two "obviously fallacious" conceptions of genre. "One is the pseudo-Platonic conception of genres as existing prior to and independently of their creation. . . . The other is that pseudo-biological conception of them as evolving species."[65] The first of these is obviously limited and obviously expanded by the concept of genres as the textual aspect of fields. I feel less comfortable about the obviousness of the second.

Frye found the second conception fallacious because he wanted to insist that texts were shaped by something more than just the forces of history and culture, by what he identified as basic archetypal myths, so that "we glimpse the possibility of seeing literature as a complication of a relatively restricted and simple group of formulas that can be studied in primitive culture" (ibid., 12). Frye replaced the pseudo-Platonic conception of ideal genres with what appears to be an equally ahistorical entity—something permanent and permanently beyond the ravages of historical change. I find it hard to reject the evidence of the permanence of the basic patterns. There is no question that such formulas exist and that texts of children's fiction do tend to share the use of them with stories told throughout history, from fairy tales to contemporary fiction. But as my earlier discussion of Jameson's ideas about the persistence of old ideologies suggests, I find it equally hard to attribute the permanence of these formulas to their existence outside of history. As far as they can be rationally known and apprehended, archetypes exist only in their specific manifestations. There is no logical reason not to believe that they do so simply because writers know and replicate the patterns of earlier texts they know—that what Frye calls archetypes are actually products of human history. Jameson offers a way of understanding that history.

One way or the other, however, the idea that archetypes exist is a useful one. It allows a focus on the relationships between the two aspects of texts that most interest me here—the ways in which they are similar to each other and the ways in which they are different despite their similarities. Frye's interest in archetypes as common features of quite different texts shares with Bourdieu's ideas about fields and position-takings the advantage of allowing perceptions of texts that share a genre as being similar but not the same—as, in fact, variations of each other. That might be another way of describing the view I am postulating here: genres consist of texts that operate as variations of each other.

While allowing and accounting for variety—for distinct qualities in texts and for vast divergences among texts included in a genre—this approach insists that a genre does exist, that there is a shared field, and that the texts that take their positions within that field do have significant relationships with each other. The main point of my argument here is that texts of children's literature written in different times and places do tend to share some key features.

Genre and Genres

That children's literature can be understood as a genre suggests two additional problems. Both pertain to the relationship between this genre and others.

First, if children's literature is a genre, then how can it contain other genres? How can a text belong to the genre of mystery or science fiction and to the genre of children's literature at the same time? While marketed for and read by young readers, texts like Donald Sobol's Encyclopedia Brown books or Carolyn Keene's

Nancy Drew books are readily identifiable as mysteries, Robert Heinlein's *Rocket Ship Galileo* or Madeleine L'Engle's *A Wrinkle in Time* as science fiction—and that might seem to undermine the validity of the idea that children's literature has generic characteristics. If one text clearly represents the characteristics typical of mystery and another those typical of science fiction, how can they both represent the characteristics of a third, notably different, genre at the same time?

Yet they do. The Encyclopedia Brown books, for instance, clearly operate as mysteries. Each story provides Encyclopedia with a crime to solve. But I suspect that most adults readers familiar with mysteries would perceive them as noticeably diverging from their expectations for standard adult mysteries and would probably even account for the divergence as the result of an intended audience of children.

That might mean merely that they are shorter, contain larger print, and are noticeably more simple and straightforward than, say, the novels of P. D. James. The adaptation theories popular with German and Scandinavian children's literature theorists would suggest that this is the case. As Maria Nikolajeva says, "by adaptation in children's literature we usually mean . . . a conscious endeavour on the part of writers to make their texts accessible for young readers through the use of shorter sentences, easier and shorter words, uncomplicated syntax, abundant dialogue, straight plots, a limited number of characters, and few abstract notions."[66] But I suspect it is more than that—that a closer look at the Encyclopedia Brown books will reveal that, because they are versions of mystery as channeled through and shaped by the adult ideas about childhood that shape children's literature, they share many of the characteristics I identified in chapter 1.

The series takes place in a town with "four banks, three movie theaters, and a Little League. . . . the usual number of gasoline stations, churches, schools, stores, and comfortable houses on shady streets."[67] Although a later book in the series branches out into the exotic by adding "two delicatessens" and a "synagogue" to this folksy list,[68] the residents of Idaville all seem to be white and of European descent. This is a town out of an Andy Hardy movie or a Henry Huggins novel, reminiscent of the relatively pastoral and pleasant small towns of so many other novels for children—a nostalgic vision of what presents itself as utopian, home as many adults like to remember it and like to imagine children imagine it. It is clichéd but not surprising that Encyclopedia Brown, the son of the town's police chief, lives in "a red brick house with a white picket fence in front."[69]

In this innocent and idyllic place young Encyclopedia Brown does what crime fiction detectives usually do. He solves crimes. Even though Idaville "had the average number of crimes for a community of its size . . . for nearly a whole year no criminal had escaped arrest and no boy or girl got away with breaking a single law in Idaville."[70] Apparently, however, the average number of crimes is surprisingly high—ten per book in book after book, for the series is, after all, detective fiction. In an adult mystery that amount of evil-doing would imply some cynicism about just how idyllic the town is, for a paranoid suspicion that all people everywhere are inherently prone to evil and therefore possible suspects is central to the mystery genre. But in Idaville, crime is always understood to be an unusual aberration from the law-abiding norm, even though it happens all the time. Furthermore, the villains tend to be people already marked as villainous. Many of the crimes against children are committed by the conveniently named Bugs Meany, and Encyclopedia is right when he tells his father that a man who sells ice cream and has been accused of kidnapping a child must be innocent:

> "No, Dad. Izzy couldn't do anything so terrible."
>
> "What do you know about Izzy?" asked Chief Brown gently. "Do you know what kind of man he really is? Do you even know where he lives?"
>
> "I know he loves children," insisted Encyclopedia. "Otherwise he wouldn't do what he does for a living."[71]

In Idaville, unlike the locales of many adult mysteries, it's easy to tell good from bad.

This is also a world without sex and almost without violence. Murder or incest or prostitution or dope addiction never occur. The police are never on the take. The crimes are almost always crimes of property—people trying to take things that don't belong to them or cheating to win competitions they don't deserve to win. Such competitions—counting jelly beans in a jar, being the champion at breath-holding underwater, winning the Idaville Mumblety-Peg championship or the photography prize or the tennis or golf or rifle competition—are a recurring fixture; three of the ten stories in *Encyclopedia Brown and the Case of the Jumping Frogs,* the latest book in the series, deal with a lawn-mower race, a frog-jumping contest, and an air guitar contest. In Idaville, as in the locales of much children's fiction, mainstream assumptions about ownership and desert are simply taken for granted by everybody, even the criminals, who always seem to understand that their crimes are in fact criminal acts. There are no radicals or anarchists or any questions about how idyllic the world already generally is.

While the stories alternate between crimes that Encyclopedia helps his father solve and ones children hire him to solve, there is no sense of any difference between the adults' crimes and the children's crimes. Whether one steals jewels or roller skates, crime is crime. Unlike the morally uncertain quagmire implied by much adult mystery writing, this is a world with a fixed shape, firm values that never shift or get questioned. Good is good, and good always triumphs.

The series offers the sort of wish-fulfillment fantasy conventional in children's literature: innocence, as adults wish children experienced it, sees the way things really are. This is exactly and most centrally the pleasure the series offers. Encyclopedia Brown always sees the truth. A child sees more and knows more than supposedly wise adults do.

But he can do so because he possesses what is clearly an unchildlike knowledge: "Leroy Brown's head was like an encyclopedia. It was filled with facts he had learned from books. He was like a complete library walking around in sneakers."[72] As a child hiding a body of adult knowledge, he is a walking metaphor of what I have called the hidden adult: "Who would believe that the guiding hand behind Idaville's crime cleanup wore a junior-size baseball mitt?"[73] The adult masked in the childlike, he uses his powers in support of adult norms, acting always for the values represented by the police and by his police chief father. There is no celebration of anarchy here nor of anything abnormal. Innocence is conservative. Innocence is normative.

Encyclopedia Brown himself is normal and revels in his normalcy: "Encyclopedia never let out the secret [about helping his father] either. He didn't want to seem different from other fifth-graders."[74] Even though he shares the unusual body of knowledge and uniquely acute observational powers of the gloriously eccentric Sherlock Holmes, the novels insist always on his not being truly different. Unlike Holmes or Hercule Poirot or Nero Wolfe or many other strange detectives in adult mysteries, he is no outsider, not marked as someone strangely unlike the rest of us, blessed or cursed with abnormal powers. The sneakers outside matter as much as the knowledge inside. He is really just a child, like the implied readers of the stories he appears in.

A major function of the books is to invite child readers to become more like Encyclopedia—to observe the details provided in each story and attempt to solve the case before turning to the end of the book to find Encyclopedia's solution. He is a role model in a way that the peculiar Holmes and Poirot are not, offering a didactic lesson about the value of knowledge and observation that papers over the way they inevitably remove one from the more usual kinds of interactions with others—something many adult mysteries make a central concern. And in making Encyclopedia a role model, the series works to engage child readers in the hidden adult subjectivity represented by his hidden encyclopedic knowledge—for like Encyclopedia, readers are clearly expected to buy into his version of what is normal and right and, despite acute powers of observation, never to question the adequacy of Idaville values. The conservative innocence of children's literature thus strangely bends some central conventions of the mystery genre.

Science fiction for children often represents a similar reshaping of conventions. In my article "Out There in Children's Science Fiction" I describe how a number of texts of science fiction produced by the children's divisions of publishing houses offer versions of a common story pattern—the emergence of young people from an enclosed space, which they and their ancestors have inhabited for a long time, into the larger world beyond. The children's versions of this resilient story typically undermine the optimistic view of a technologically sophisticated future, a future that is more common in adult versions of the story, and replace it with an antitechnological pastoral nostalgia. I conclude that "the shortage of good SF for young readers may be accounted for by generic differences between SF and fiction intended for young readers—one of those differences being the characteristic ambivalence of fiction for young readers about acceptance of things as they are, and the liberating potentiality of SF that tends above all to question things as they are."[75]

In the process of contaminating the values of another genre, the characteristics of children's literature make themselves and their ideological implications apparent. This suggests how powerful they are, how widely the ideas about childhood that shape children's literature are shared and taken for granted. As theorists of popular literature like John Cawelti and Tania Modleski have shown, genres like mystery and science fiction also tend to share ideological implications, but in the versions that are written for children, those values tend to be trumped by the values common in writing for children generally.

That shared ideology suggests the second problem raised by thinking of children's literature as a genre. Derrida's claim that genres operate in terms of what they mark off as being left out means that they necessarily evoke what is deliberately not present. For that reason Beebee suggests that readers can identify genres only by distinguishing them from other genres and that, therefore, "the use-value of any single genre depends on our recognition of other genres that oppose it. . . . To say a work's genre is to say what it is not."[76] But children's literature exists because those who have the means and inclination to produce it believe that children need a specific kind of book. At least in theory, child readers are not likely to be, or at least not supposed to be, aware of the other genres that are unlike or opposed to it and therefore automatically unsuitable for then. Logically, this means that, for the child readers for whom it is intended, children's literature cannot be identified or understood as a genre—that whatever the use of texts in this genre is for child readers, it is not the "use-value" that readers able to distinguish it as a genre—that is, those who are able to compare it with and be aware of its difference from other sorts of texts—perceive.

If that is true—and, logically, it has to be—it means that thinking about children's literature as a genre must be exclusively an act of adult readers, whom I define here simply as those equipped to distinguish texts for children from those belonging to genres that are unlike it or, as Beebee suggests, opposed to it—texts that are, put simply, adult literature. The use-value of children's literature is most exactly stated in terms of that opposition: its marked lack of those qualities that would make it "adult" and therefore, presumably, unsuitable for child readers. Its very existence as a genre implies an act of censorship. It also implies a dependence on the "adult" content it presumes to mark off and leave out, as well as a dual audience, consisting of those who cannot perceive it as a genre and those with the knowledge of other kinds of literature who can. As the next chapter demonstrates, these three qualities turn out to be central to how adult theorists have understood the genre.

CHAPTER THREE

Children's Literature as a Genre

Defining Children's Literature

At the end of chapter 1, I listed a number of characteristics shared by the six texts I discussed there, and I postulated that those characteristics might be some of the defining generic elements of children's fiction. In the last chapter I made a case for viewing literary genres as the evidence of a field of literary production embedded within the texts produced within that field, and I postulated that children's fiction might be such a genre. While these interpretations of texts and views of genre emerged from my personal history and values, that history and the development of those values inevitably involved interactions with others—not just with family and friends and children I have met but also, centrally, with many adults in the fields of children's literature and of children's literature criticism. Over the years I have often engaged in discourse about children's literature with those who write, edit, publish, review, select, sell, buy, teach, study, research, critique, and otherwise involve themselves with children's books, sometimes in person and sometimes in terms of my responses to their published writing about it.

All of these people have inevitably had general understandings of what children's literature is, how it operates, what matters about it. They could not have had opinions about specific books without consciously or unconsciously having such a general understanding, for even the frequently expressed sort of view that children should read a certain book because it will teach them the right way to think about dental care or people of color or shoplifting implies a general view that children's literature is ideally didactic. In Bourdieu's terms, all of these people have taken positions about the generic characteristics of children's literature, some less consciously than others; and my own views have developed as a position taken in relationship to all those others—a position in the field of children's literature, especially in the field of children's literature criticism. My own position relates to and intersects with all the others in ways that can reveal much about the nature and potential of my own views and much about the fields of children's literature and children's literature criticism generally.

If I am right in thinking that the genre represents the evidence of the field inscribed in the texts it produces, then understanding more about positions taken by those who work with it ought to lead to a better understanding of the genre. Most centrally for my concerns in this book, understanding more about positions taken in the field of children's literature criticism should lead to a better understanding of the texts the field deals with. Critics and reviewers not only have the job of trying to make sense of children's books, but also, and just as centrally, their opinions and choices tend to shape what texts have power and how those texts might be read; thus, what texts critics and reviewers consume and how they consume them profoundly affect the nature of what producers choose to produce.

For these reasons it seems important for me to attempt to reveal the relationships between my own ideas as expressed here and those of others as positions taken in relationship to each other. It is so, first of all, because the relationships do exist.

People have been discussing children's literature ever since it emerged some centuries ago, and positions like the one about the value and usefulness of texts encouraging good dental hygiene or discouraging shoplifting have a long history. Consider, for instance, the advice recently offered on the PABBIS (Parents Against Bad Books in Schools) Web site. Parents are encouraged to "monitor what your child reads like a paranoid hawk" on the basis that "this will also significantly reduce the chance of your child being exposed to objectionable material."[1] Such counsel echoes Sarah Trimmer's conviction, expressed more than two centuries ago, that "children should not be permitted to make their own choice, or to read any books that may accidentally be thrown in their way, or offered for their perusal; but should be taught to consider it as a *duty*, to consult their parents in this momentous concern."[2]

But despite its long history, children's literature criticism also has a habit of forgetting its own past or even, sometimes, utterly lacks awareness of that past's existence. In the years in which I edited the *Children's Literature Association Quarterly*, I often found myself reading submissions about *Charlotte's Web* or *Peter Rabbit* by professors of American literature or Renaissance drama writing about books they shared with their children. Often these scholars were blithely unconscious of the fact that other serious scholars had come before them—a phenomenon that I find repeating itself in my recent work as editor of *CCL/LCJ: Canadian Children's Literature / Littérature canadienne pour la jeunesse* in terms of submissions about, for instance, L. M. Montgomery's Anne books.

Even scholars within the field often tend to ignore the possibility that they have had precursors. In a review of Zohar Shavit's *Poetics of Children's Literature* published in 1986, I expressed my concern that "in the last decade, many scholars have indeed been examining exactly the questions that Shavit says have been ignored. . . . Shavit seems to be unconscious of most of this work."[3] A decade later, in a review of Karín Lesnik-Oberstein's *Children's Literature: Criticism and the Fictional Child*, I expressed almost exactly the same concern. Commenting on Lesnik-Oberstein's assertion that "it is possible to reject children's fiction criticism as it stands,"[4] I say, "She means all of it, bar none. . . . In order for readers to accept this conclusion, they would have to be convinced that the fairly short list of critics that Lesnik-Oberstein actually manages to quote or to mention do indeed represent children's-literature criticism as a whole. They don't."[5] In a later publication another decade later, Lesnik-Oberstein herself confirms the ongoing ancestry-amnesia of children's literature criticism: "This claim . . . that the encounter between discussions about children's fiction and (adult) literary criticism and theory is new, or only just starting out, may, curiously, be seen to recur as a theme. . . . Children's literature critics in various ways claim repeatedly that this meeting of children's literature, literary criticism, and theory (however they define them), is yet to begin, or has only recently started."[6]

These absences may mean merely that the field of children's literature studies is still too young to have firmly established means of circulating information about new research—that ignorance of other work is all too possible. In my work as an editor of academic articles, I often have to steer writers toward previous work on their topics they simply hadn't known about. But I suspect there is something about children's literature itself that causes those who choose to involve themselves with it to replicate its qualities. It is revealing, for instance, that even those who want to write *for* children often express the lack of awareness I have observed in critics. The pop star Madonna echoes many newcomers to writing for children when she blithely announces that she has taken up her new pursuit after reading a few books to her son: "I couldn't believe how vapid and vacant and empty all the stories were. . . . There's like no books about anything."[7] As I have been claiming, children's literature tends to see things from the viewpoint of innocence—as children theoretically see them. Adults who find themselves attracted to it as a field of interest might well tend to be people who enjoy imaginatively experiencing in it the freedom of an innocence they themselves no longer possess—an innocence manifested not only by the assumption that they are ever and always pioneers breaking new ground but also by the replication in their work of the qualities of and assumptions about childhood they themselves produce in the texts they write or find in the texts they explore. New writers tend to produce books that are not about anything much—books innocent of or carefully hiding all vestiges of sophisticated and supposedly unchildlike knowledge. And critical work on texts for children often reproduces the attitudes it examines in the very process of analyzing and exposing them and theoretically, therefore, moving beyond them. Children's literature criticism thus tends to maintain an innocence of its own by hiding—or completely forgetting—any awareness of its past adulthood.

That it does this suggests the enduring strength of the most common cultural assumptions that operate in thinking about children and the objects of childhood. Like all manifestations of powerful ideologies, these assumptions are tenaciously resilient, resistant to change or eradication. I have to suspect that whatever they try to repress or erase must be important. My effort to understand the intersections between my own ideas and those of others is an attempt to understand what is important and how and why it matters. I want to acknowledge the existence of the field I am taking a position in—to fight the tendency toward scholarly amnesia and insist that the discussion about children's literature and (adult) literary criticism is not new or only just starting. I want to explore the rich diversity of the field, the myriad ways people account for children's literature and the connections between those ways. I want to consider the implications of all these accounts—what values they support or undermine. And I want to try to perceive the genealogy of my own ideas, to understand how they emerge from the field and represent responses to and borrowings and divergences from it, and how I might account for and justify those divergences. I want not just to take a position but, having taken it, to try to stand back and understand the implications of having done so.

I try to do that in the pages that follow by focusing specifically on a series of ways in which various people have defined children's literature or otherwise made statements that imply definitions of what children's literature is and on how those definitions do and do not relate to my own conclusions about the characteristics that, for me, define a text as being children's literature. I have included definitions from a variety of different places: in theoretical work by critics of children's literature, in textbooks for college-level children's literature courses, and in discussions of their work by children's authors.

Focusing specifically on definitions allows me to cover a wide range of possibilities fairly efficiently—especially because defining children's literature has been a major activity of children's literature criticism throughout its history. As Torben Weinreich says, it is "an area of research and an endless debate that is as old as research into children's literature itself. It is both the simplest and the most complex question we can ask: What is children's literature? The answers to this question are many and various. There are not quite as many answers as there are researchers, but it is a close call."[8]

According to Weinreich there is a good reason for this: "We cannot avoid the definitional path. If we are to produce statistics on how many books are published a year in one country or what percentage of the total production children's books constitute, we have to have a working definition of what a children's book is. If we are to set up special libraries of children's books we have to consider which books should be allocated to the respective library, and so on" (ibid.). Definition allows exclusion. There is a sense in which Sarah Trimmer's insistence on parental selection, referred to earlier, implies a definition: children's literature is, or ought to be, only and exclusively that literature that parents consider suitable for their children. Here, as in almost all definitions, children's literature is that smaller group of texts singled out from the larger mass of all literature for possessing (or, perhaps more often, not possessing) certain specific qualities. But the qualities change from definition to definition—which is why, it seems, definition is such a significant aspect of the criticism. "Clearly," says Katharine Jones, "fundamental definitional problems with the term continually create difficulties for anyone who wants to discuss the genre." Jones concludes: "I agree with [Jacqueline] Rose that the *term* 'children's literature' is impossible because the possibilities of a children's literature are irrevocably undermined by the confusion created by the term."[9]

Obviously, I don't agree. I believe that the term *children's literature* creates confusion because children's literature as a genre *is* confusing—richly and complicatedly so. The confusions make the genre seem impossible only with the assumption that the differing definitions must be mutually exclusive and that one must be right in ways that makes the others wrong, which makes them all mutually defeating. But what if all the differing definitions suggest some part of the more complex truth? What if the contradictions of the definitions are suggestive of contradictions—or, possibly, paradoxes—inherent in the genre itself? What if children's literature as a genre represents the complex field of shifting position-takings of the field that engenders it?

It is these latter possibilities that I focus on here. I believe that an attempt to understand differing definitions in terms of their complex relationships with each other will reveal not just how they interconnect but also how their connections imply an underlying and ongoing set of concerns—concerns significantly related to ideas about children and about the place of literature in the lives of children—that give shape and consistency to the genre of children's literature as a whole and reveal ways in which apparently quite different texts similarly belong to that genre.

In the pages that follow, therefore, I consider a spectrum of definitions of children's literature or descriptions of its distinguishing characteristics by looking at many quotations from other critics and theorists and responding to them. The chapter maps the complex network of endlessly intricate relationships among positions taken in the fields of children's literature and children's literature criticism, as well as the position I take in relation to them all. I have come to realize that working in this way—defining my position as it relates to others—makes me seem rather ungenerous, far more likely to dissent from than to agree with my colleagues. I insist, however, that I couldn't have developed my own understanding without access to all these others, without figuring out the relatively small but, I believe, significant ways in which I diverge from the massive amount I did learn and accept from them—the ways in which the position I take departs from yet depends on and is sustained by the other positions it relates to. For those reasons, although I may find fault with aspects of the specific words I quote and discuss here, they represent powerful ideas in children's literature criticism and in the field of children's literature production as a whole. Together they provide a concise and revealing overview of how adults over the past century or so in Europe, North America, and elsewhere have generally tended to think about children and literature.

Because I believe all the positions I have represented here currently have power in the field, and because I want to show the theoretical connections between them, my overview is more synchronic than diachronic. I have not presented my quotations in the chronological order of their original appearances but in what I hope is a logical order that clarifies both the separate threads and their relationships to each other. Nevertheless, the ideas that underpin the notion of writing specifically for an audience of children and that lead to what I have come to understand as characteristic features of children's literature are connected to each other in complex ways, and I often find myself having to promise that I will pick up various threads that have emerged from my speculations later or referring back to threads I have developed earlier. The path I have chosen to follow through this chapter is, then, more or less arbitrary—just one of many possible paths through this network of interrelated assumptions about children, about literature, and about children's literature; but it is one that I hope, even in its repetitiveness and endless looking forward and circling back, reveals the nature of the network as a whole.

No Genre

While there can be no question that children's literature exists—that there is a body of literary texts labeled as intended for an audience of children—a surprising number of adults question the existence of children's literature as a genre with definable characteristics. As Robert Bator says, "Critics often shun definition entirely. . . . It is unfashionable to hold *any* definition of children's literature."[10] Critics offer a variety of revealing reasons for their refusal to define.

According to Roger Sale, "Everyone knows what children's literature is until asked to define it. . . . We are better off saying we all have a pretty good idea of what children's literature includes and letting the matter rest there."[11] What "we all have a pretty good idea of" is pretty well what the ideological theorist Louis Althusser means when he speaks of obviousnesses: "It is indeed a peculiarity of ideology that it imposes (without appearing to do so, since these are 'obvious-nesses') obviousnesses as obviousnesses, which we cannot *fail to recognize* and before which we have the inevitable and natural reaction of crying out (aloud or in the 'still, small voice of conscience'): 'That's obvious! That's right! That's true!' "[12] What is obvious is what people are invited *not* to think about—presumably be-cause thinking about it would reveal aspects of it they might not like.

In Sale's case the invitation not to think emerges from the nature of his project—a book about children's literature that denies it has any significant con-nection to children or their reading. "I write as an adult," he says, "and for other adults . . . often regardless of any experience any of us had as children. . . . Here are these books, I want to say, good books, and we read them essentially as we read any book."[13] John Rowe Townsend agrees: "Since any line-drawing must be arbi-trary, one is tempted to abandon the attempt and say that there is no such thing as children's literature, there is just literature. And in an important sense, that is true. Children are not a separate form of life from people; no more than children's books are a separate form of literature from just books."[14] Townsend, Sale, and the many others who share such views disregard the fact that there would be no such thing as children's literature—even just as an arbitrary line drawn, a label, or a publishing category imposed on a body of diverse texts—if adults did not believe that children are different enough from adults to need a special group of books and imagine a category to contain them. As Bator says, "To avoid definition may be to flee 'rigid' constraints. But what constrains, delimits. Any literature directed at a special audience is a necessarily limited literature. Literature for children will remain largely a critically uncharted and confusing territory if its limitations are not defined."[15]

Why, then, do so many critics refuse to delimit? Many do so as a defense against the widespread assumption that children's literature is too childish for adults to consider seriously. Zohar Shavit's theories about the characteristics of children's literature center on this phenomenon and on what she calls the "poor self-image" of children's literature.[16] For Sale and others it *can* be taken seriously exactly because it *isn't* unlike other literature. Adults can read it just as they read other, more adult-oriented, books.

A number of writers of fiction make this view apparent in their refusal to accept the idea that they do write something distinguishable as children's literature. Pamela Travers, author of the Mary Poppins books, says, "Nor have they [her books] anything to do with that other label 'Literature for children,' which suggests that this is something different from literature in general, something that pens off both child and author from the main stream of writing."[17] Scott O'Dell says, "Books of mine which are classified officially as books for children were not written *for* children."[18] L. M. Boston makes a similar claim: "Is there a conscious difference in the way I write for grown-ups and children? No, there is no difference of approach, style, vocabulary or standard."[19]

Comments like these distressingly confirm what they purport to counter. Rather than consider the implications of widespread assumptions about what too many people disrespectfully call "kiddy lit" in terms of the lack of respect it implies for both children and children's literature, these adults declare that the literature is not actually limited to a child audience—not actually childlike and for that reason a respectable subject for adult discourse.

To take this position, however, they have to add a proviso that implies a somewhat different definition—that it is only the *good* children's literature they find respectable. Thus, Sale specifies "good books" as the ones he feels comfortable about reading as an adult—and presumably, therefore, excludes from consideration as children's literature all the books written for children that he doesn't consider good. The author Jane Gardam, who claims that the question of whether or not her books are for children "has never occurred to me," says, "I have never liked children's books very much. I don't read very many."[20] Gardam is saying, in effect, that her books are good children's literature because they are not like most children's books. The issue here is what *literature* is—it is not all the works of fiction or poetry written but rather only the ones of all those texts that perceptive, sophisticated readers admire or view as possessing quality. And that cannot possibly include most books written for children. As C. S. Lewis says, "I am almost inclined to set it up as a canon that a children's story which is enjoyed only by children is a bad children's story."[21]

In terms of understanding children's literature, the main negative effect of this position is exactly what it allows adult readers of children's books to ignore. Reading a text intended for children with a determined refusal to be aware of the child reader it implies and the efforts made to address and thus work to construct actual child readers seems like willed and dangerous blindness. Nor is it much of a stretch to suggest that a text might be both good and at the same time a characteristic text of children's literature—even good *because* it is a characteristic text of children's literature. To assume otherwise is to harbor elitist assumptions about the taste and interests of children—at least insofar as those tastes and interests are accurately evoked in the texts adults conventionally write for children.

Michael Steig offers an intriguing variation on the possibility that a book can both be good and possess the characteristics of children's literature: "I would go so far as to say that in a sense all imaginative literature has the qualities of the best children's literature and reading it the quality of childhood experience: language as play, invention, and discovery, and life represented as a series of internal and external conflicts. . . . Having begun by questioning the possibility of children's literature, I find myself coming close to claiming that all literature is 'children's' in a fundamental sense."[22] This is cleverly paradoxical. Because children's literature has unique qualities that relate to childhood, it is not actually unique at all, except insofar as it shares with other good literature a childlike implied reader. Steig seems to be turning Lewis's canon upside down: the only good adult books are the ones that children also enjoy. But as the quotation marks he places around *children's* make clear, that is not what he is saying. The versions of language as play that appear in the prose of Steig's examples, James Joyce and Thomas Carlyle, are quite different in content and complexity from the ones that appear in texts written for children—different enough to make their "childlike" adult readers quite different from the implied child readers of children's literature. Adults who take on the "childlikeness" invited by the kind of adult texts Steig names are assumed to have a more usual, less playful adult way of thinking that they are being invited to move beyond. Texts for children presume, on the surface at least, to be addressing children as they usually already are and often invite them to move beyond their childlikeness into theoretically more adult forms of thinking.

Underlying their apparent similarity, then, texts for children and "childlike" texts for adults tend to have quite different agendas, and Steig's formulation suggests important distinctions that it appears to be claiming to erase.[23] Although I worry about the restrictiveness of Paul Heins's focus only on children's literature "at its best," I find myself more comfortable with his views: "children's literature—at its best—is worthy of consideration with the rest of literature . . . [but] the term *children's* remains a specifying term and, willy nilly, must be respected."[24]

Different but Not Distinct

A few common ways of respecting the term *children's literature* still avoid the question of definition and distinctness. According to John Stephens, "The literature written for children . . . has no special discourse of its own. While the literature is subject to some constraints on certain kinds of linguistic complexity (in syntax, lexis, and figurative language . . . these features aren't enough to constitute a distinctive discourse."[25] In other words, children's literature is like adult literature but simpler. Rebecca Lukens offers an explanation for this sort of position: "Children are not little adults. They are different from adults in experience, but not in species, or to put it differently, in degree but not in kind. We can say then of literature for young readers that it differs from literature for adults in degree but not in kind."[26] Torben Weinreich—who identifies " 'adaptation,' the writer's and perhaps the publishers' matching of the text to the assumed reader," as a key idea in recent European theories of what defines children's literature—describes the usual explanations theorists offer for it in a way that implies a similar insistence on differences of degree rather than kind: "Writers do not primarily adapt because children have *other* experiences and *other* knowledge, but because they lack experience and knowledge."[27]

Arguing against the idea that children's texts represent different degrees of the qualities of adult literature, Weinreich himself says, "I prefer to see children's literature as a *genre* and by 'genre' I mean here a notion of a group of texts characterised by recurrent features."[28] Not surprisingly, I believe there are good reasons why he might do so. If adults actually believed that children differed from themselves only in degree, then there would be no need for disciplines like child psychology that focus obsessively on the otherness of children and of childlike thinking, no conceptions of differing stages of cognitive development or characterizations of who children at various ages are and what they like or need—probably not even any literature for children. All of these institutions of culture presume differences significant enough to transcend mere degree.

Even when adults do produce literature for children that represents differences of degree, literature, for example, that caters to their supposed shorter attention spans or lesser ability to make sense of complexity, the differences in degree very quickly turn into differences in kind. Consider, for instance, the assumptions of lack Weinreich mentions and the resulting constraints on linguistic complexity to which Stephens refers. Texts for adults don't usually presume to tell less of the truth than their writers know, as texts for children characteristically do. In telling less than their authors know, these texts represent a holding back, a reticence about saying too much in too much detail that might well leave its traces within the text and that might well turn out to be a defining characteristic of children's literature. The holding back makes for a style of storytelling with a quite specific set of characteristic moves, a style distinct enough and used consistently in enough texts written for children to be more than just a difference of degree. These texts are not just less complex than adult ones. As my explorations in chapter 1 revealed, they are less complex in some very characteristic ways.

In telling less than their authors know, these texts evoke—for knowledgeable adult readers, at least, and perhaps, as I suggested in chapter 1, for the child readers implied by the texts—the more complex truths they leave unspoken. Their tendency to imply a more complex shadow text that transcends the presumably childlike view they purport to represent becomes a significant distinguishing characteristic of texts for children—a difference of kind, for even when adult literature hides great depths, it tends to speak much more and more complexly of all it knows, to leave, therefore, proportionately less in the shadow and therefore to be much less likely to hinge on the significance of the difference between the simplicity of what is said and the complexity of what isn't—on questions of childlike and adult knowledge. In addition, adult literature says less in ways that transparently invite readers to be aware that there is more and to figure out what it is: what is hidden in the metaphors of many poems and literary texts of fiction is hidden with the object of public interpretation and exposure, not the unacknowledged awareness that texts of children's literature more typically invite from readers. Once more, differences of degree lead to differences of kind.

Another way of acknowledging that children's literature is distinct from adult literature that avoids an investigation of distinguishing characteristics is the pragmatic procedure of trusting the judgment of those involved in its marketing and distribution. As Emer O'Sullivan suggests, "According to this theory, the definition of children's literature is determined not on the level of the text itself, that is to say in the form of specific textual features, but on the level of the actions and actors involved: texts are identified by various social authorities as being suitable for children and young people. These include educational institutions both ecclesiastical and secular, figures active in the literary market (publishers, distributors, etc.) and those who produce the books (editors, authors, etc.)."[29]

Despite (or perhaps because of) their claims that children's books are basically books like all other books, both Michael Steig and John Rowe Townsend make a plea for this sort of pragmatism. "In commercial publishing," says Steig, "children's literature and its various subcategories can be seen as artificially generated designations intended to target certain members of the reading public—parents, perhaps, more than children. The designation 'children's literature,' in other words, is a constructed category whose content [is] determined by those who make professional use of it, rather than the children who supposedly read it."[30] Townsend says, "The only practical definition of a children's book today—absurd as it sounds—is 'a book which appears on the children's list of a publisher.' "[31]

Even a cursory glance at publishers' catalogues reveals how many different kinds of texts some publisher or other believes might be suitable for children: fantasy, nonfictional texts, floating bath books, books of poems, and so on. As a result, John Warren Stewig says that "the diversity of children's literature is probably its most striking characteristic. The term *children's literature* would more accurately indicate the myriad facets this field includes."[32] Similarly, after saying that " 'children' includes any and all persons who fall between the ages from birth to eighteen," Roderick McGillis claims that children's literature "includes all books published and marketed for people falling between the ages I set out above."[33] And in an article published in 1974, Peter Hunt offers a variation of this idea, focused on writers rather than publishers: "If a book, in the intention of the author, was for children, then it is within our frame of reference."[34]

In suggesting that children's literature is too expansive for consistency, comments like these last few tend to assume that the vast spectrum of possibilities makes definition impossible and thus have the effect of closing off further thinking about what children's literature as a whole tends to be and to do. But as my analysis of six quite different texts in chapter 1 demonstrated, there is no reason to assume that a wide variety of books cannot possess commonalities despite their apparent differences. What Stewig calls "myriad facets" are all within a recognizable spectrum that allows people to recognize them as facets of literature for children. What Steig calls a "constructed category" is still a category—a way of making sense of things shared by a number of people that therefore implies some kinds of consistency among the items included in the category.

The pseudonymous "Pelorus" shrewdly suggests one reason why: "Whether we like it or not, children's writers are, unconsciously or otherwise, subject to the atmosphere generated by reviewers, critics, coterie friends. Writers tend to produce what the readers they value most look for."[35] To put this in the terms suggested by Bourdieu that I discussed in the last chapter: writers write with a knowledge of the field they occupy that tends to make the texts they produce replicate features of other texts within the field. The artificiality of the category is less significant than its very real effect on the texts included in it, which inevitably, as productions within a defined field, tend to have numerous intertextual relationships and a great deal in common with each other.

For this reason, I think, Clifton Fadiman, who makes a case for children's literature as a genre with its own history, its own canonical masterpieces, and so on, is correct to assert that children's literature is "identifiable as an entity."[36] That the entity is identifiable logically implies a range of specific characteristics in the texts the entity includes that allow the identification and therefore open the door to definition.

Peter Hunt reveals the difficulty of embracing an open-ended inclusiveness that eschews definition by quickly retreating from it. In work published later (and discussed later in this chapter), Hunt significantly changed his views about these matters. But even in his early article, after asserting all-out pragmatism, he goes on to propose a variation on the idea I discussed earlier—that children's literature is just good literature: "It is not simply reading matter—educational, moral or otherwise. It is not, for example, Enid Blyton. . . . I would as much consider including her in a study of children's literature as I would consider including, say, Mickey Spillane on a literature degree course."[37] Children's literature consists only of those texts that the adult Hunt is willing to identify as being literature. Here Hunt goes one step further than Lewis; not only are the good children's books the ones adults like, but all the books that *only* children like aren't children's literature at all.

The early Hunt is not alone in this sort of act of restriction. Carl Tomlinson and Carol Lynch-Brown say, "*Children's literature* is good-quality trade books for children from birth to adolescence, covering topics of relevance and interest to children of those ages."[38] Judith Hillman offers an explanation for this sort of focus on quality: "The term *literature* suggests that some judgment, or critical evaluation has been applied to a book. There are many children's books, but how many do we consider to be literature? . . . To distinguish between books and literature is the duty of the adult and child who read and want to recognize the best."[39] These writers share a focus on what Steig calls "the best children's literature"[40] and Heins calls children's literature "at its best," and they assert that good children's books have more in common with good adult books than they do with not-so-good children's books.

Good children's books might well have something in common with good adult books, if only because "quality" or "the best" are so tied up in subjective opinion. The adults who make these claims tend to admire the same features in all the texts they read—to value subtlety or inventiveness or the play of language in children's books as they do in adult books. For instance, Hillman speaks of "engaging the intellect," "beautiful language," and "deep and subtle human motives" as qualities of the texts she is willing to identify as literature.[41] But that is no reason to assume that the "good" children's books don't also share qualities and have important relationships with the not-so-good ones. I believe that as products of a shared field, they must and that their doing so is at least as worthy of note as what they share with the presumably quality books for adults. Truly generic characteristics are likely to appear in some way in all texts of a genre, regardless of how anyone might judge the quality of any of the texts. The apprentice sonnets of a mediocre poet are no less members of the sonnet genre than the sonnets of Shakespeare; indeed, it would be hard to understand the status of Shakespeare's sonnets as quality work without the existence of more mediocre examples of the genre that they can be perceived as surpassing. Presumably, therefore, Enid Blyton's novels, or more recent series like K. A. Applegate's Animorphs books or R. L. Stine's Goosebumps books, are no less texts of children's literature than the winner of a Newbery Medal and must have significant intertextual relationships with the medal-winning texts.

This does not mean they might not be different experiences, different sorts of books. In chapter 4 I argue that the differences between run-of-the-mill texts of children's literature and those singled out constantly for critical attention and admiration might reveal something of significance about the workings of the field and the nature of the genre. But that significance can be understood only by first understanding that these different texts are all children's literature—that they have the characteristics I am attempting to identify here and that they represent different position-takings in relation to each other and to the genre and the field as a whole.

For this reason I happily accept the pragmatic definition that children's literature is the literature published as such. In defining the scope of the field, such a definition provides an excellent place to begin. While it doesn't necessarily reveal *why* any of these texts might have been chosen for publication—what their publishers imagined children's literature to be—it does define where to look for the evidence about that. Any acceptable view of the characteristic tendencies of children's literature as a genre will have to account in some way for all of that vast range of apparently divergent texts. I suspect that part of the accounting will be a matter of explaining apparent divergences or exceptions—but doing so in a way that makes sense of some key recurring characteristics and the relationships possible between any and all individual texts and the genre and field as a whole.

Literature and Children

There is one further—and particularly revealing—reason that some critics offer for avoiding a definition of children's literature: it can't be done. The literature is distinct, all right, but in ways that place it beyond analysis. According to Joan Glazer and Gurney Williams, "Children cannot be easily defined. Nor can their literature."[42] Similarly, Lillian Smith, who speaks of "the eager, reaching, elusive spirit of childhood which has its own far horizons, and a friendly and familiar acquaintance with miracle," claims that the "magic" of children's literature "eludes definition."[43] For these writers the indefinability of children's literature represents its accurate mirroring of childhood. Childhood cannot be defined because definition is an act of logic and reason, and childhood is presumably the antithesis of logic and reason—a time of innocence, the glory of which is exactly its irrationality, the lack of knowledge and understanding that presumably offers insight into a greater wisdom. These objections to attempts at defining children and children's literature have close connections with Wordsworth's objection to acts of rational analysis—"we murder to dissect"[44]—and to his postulation in "Ode: Intimations on Immortality" and elsewhere of childhood as a joyfully non-analytic time.[45] They represent a long-standing and still-powerful tradition that views childhood as idyllic exactly in terms of its lack of adult knowledge.

Despite their refusal to define, most people who occupy this position actually have a quite firm conception of children's literature, in its representation of ideal childhood innocence, as a specific literary type: a form of pastoral or utopian idyll. I will say more about this sort of view of children's literature later, as I discuss positions that openly espouse it. What interests me at this point is the basic assumption behind Smith and Glazer's refusal to define—an assumption quite different from those of the definition-abstainers I have considered thus far. It is the important idea that children's literature is what it is because children are what they are.

Marjorie R. Hancock represents a position taken by many people in the field when she says, "Children's literature can be defined as literature that appeals to the interests, needs, and reading preferences of children and captivates children as its major audience."[46] Hancock assumes that children's literature works—that the adults who produce it do accurately understand what children need and are interested in; thus, children are captivated by what they produce. As I suggested earlier in this book, these are questionable assumptions. What adults believe they understand about the nature and needs of children in general is not necessarily accurate. It tends usually to consist of a series of unconsidered and untested assumptions about the nature of childhood that, even if they might to some degree represent tendencies in the general populace of young people, are not all that likely to be accurate descriptions of individual children—which accounts for why some children are not captivated by what adults expect them to find captivating.

But whatever children actually are, there can be no question that it is adult *ideas* about childhood that shape the literature and provide it with its characteristic features. Speaking of genres in general, including all those found beyond the confines of the literary, Bakhtin says, "Each speech genre in each area of speech communication has its own typical conception of the addressee, and this defines it as a genre."[47] If children's literature is a genre—in this case, a specifically literary speech genre—then it might be best defined by the nature of its addressee: what it suggests about the audience it speaks to. And if texts for children written in different times and places for different purposes and for children of different ages are in any way similar, it can only be so because the ideas that the adults in those different times and places have about children are similar and because the addressees of the texts those adults write for children are therefore similar.

They are, as I have suggested, similar in two key ways. First, in order to produce children's literature at all, adults have to believe that children need such a literature—that there is something specifically unadultlike in children that requires a special form of literary engagement, texts different from the ones adults produce for each other. Second, adults who produce children's literature must also believe that children are not able to produce such texts themselves, that it is something adults must do for them.

That last key quality raises the question of whether children themselves can or do write children's literature—a significant issue in considering the genre if the literature seems more usefully identifiable as literature written by adults. "In terms of children's literature," David Rudd says, "it might still be argued that, unlike women and other minority groups, children still have no voice, their literature being created for them, rather than creating their own. But this is nonsense. Children produce literature in vast quantities."[48] But can this literature by children be correctly identified as "children's literature"?

According to the kind of views I am discussing here, it can't. I have suggested that children's literature represents the evidence of the field of children's literature publication embedded in texts—and most writing by children has not been produced in the context of that field. As Roderick McGillis rightly suggests, "When it comes to children's literature, the chance of our economic system making room for children's voices in any coherent and expansive manner seems slim. In other words, we don't expect to see a run of children's books written and illustrated by children appearing soon in your local bookstores."[49] The appearance of books by children in bookstores is unlikely, I think, not primarily because customers might assume such books would lack interest or artistry but because there is no guarantee the books would safely represent the usual experienced adult views of what it is acceptable for children to read. The values of the field might not be acceptably embedded in them. In being authentically childlike, they might transgress the boundaries of children's literature. Consider, for instance, the vast differences between texts produced for children by adults and the fan fiction by youngsters on the Internet. As Kimberley Reynolds, says, "It is perhaps not surprising that a generation that has grown up with online pornography, web cams that allow them to send intimate pictures of themselves into cyberspace and many of whom send and receive sexually explicit text messages is producing writers who seem uninhibited about producing sexually graphic material and posting it (albeit anonymously) for the world to read."[50] As I am discussing it here, children's literature centrally represents adult views of childhood, not those of children themselves. A text genuinely expressive of childhood or childlike thinking as experienced by a child would lack a fundamental defining quality of children's literature.

It is possible, of course, that children might have learned, from personal experience and from reading children's and other literature by adults, adult views of childhood that they then mimic (or even challenge) in their writing. My own reading of many children's stories and poems suggests they often do, and Rudd speaks of how the literature children produce "comes from reworking the discourses around them, through which children negotiate their social and embodied positioning."[51] Commenting on her studies of writing by children (especially those who later became published writers as adults), Juliet McMaster agrees: "When a child writes, I suspect, she's not usually writing for other children. . . . The child is not trying to produce 'children's literature' (whatever that is). She has her eye on the Canon."[52] The child is imitating and perhaps interacting with the literature by adults that she has already read—which for many children usually includes texts of children's literature. The implied audience is not necessarily or even centrally other children, except insofar as the literature being imitated implies such an audience. McMaster rightly, I believe, concludes that "literature *by* children is a different matter from literature *for* children" (280).

If literature written by children isn't necessarily children's literature, how about the literature *read* by children? Over the centuries children have frequently chosen to read texts not originally published as children's literature: various fairy tales, novels like *Robinson Crusoe* or the ones McMaster reports the writers of juvenilia she discusses reading, poems like Blake's *Songs of Innocence,* or collections of *Peanuts* cartoons. Those who argue that children's literature cannot be defined have a habit of naming such texts as evidence for the genre's lack of clear-cut boundaries and, hence, its indefinability. How can anyone know what children's literature is, these arguments go, if a child I know likes to read James Joyce, say, or Ernest Hemingway? Or, how can anyone know what children's literature is, if a lot of children's libraries include books like Defoe's *Robinson Crusoe* or *Peanuts* cartoons that were originally intended for adults? These arguments deconstruct themselves in revealing ways.

What is most telling about the fact that some children read Hemingway is that it wouldn't seem so telling if Hemingway's writing weren't so different from what is usually understood to be children's literature. The focus of my interest here is precisely that: what people usually understand as children's literature. That some children don't read children's literature and some children read nonchildren's literature is germane to my concerns only insofar as it makes clear that it is not necessarily or immediately children's reading that I hope to make sense of. It is, once more, what adults have imagined as appropriate for children. As Steig accurately suggests, the category is defined by adult use, not by what children read.

The inclusion of texts like the Grimm fairy tales or *Robinson Crusoe* in children's literature reinforces that truth. In the oral tradition the folktales that the Grimm brothers collected were not restricted to audiences of children, and their first published collection of them was a scholarly volume intended for adults. As John Ellis and Jack Zipes reveal, however, once the Grimm brothers understood that children might be a potential audience, they selected and edited tales they thought might be appropriate, and the editions of Grimm tales now found in children's libraries almost always consist of revised versions even more bowdlerized than the Grimms' own.[53] The editions of books like *Gulliver's Travels* and *Robinson Crusoe* to be found in children's libraries are revised also, and in similar ways—to accord with adult perceptions of what might be suitable for or interesting to children. They have been changed, that is, to match adult perceptions of the characteristics of children's literature. I conclude that books not originally intended for children that are generally accepted as suitable literature for children without amendment or expurgation are acceptable simply because they *already* accord with adult genre expectations. For instance, *Peanuts* cartoons offer the child's (or childlike animal's) focalization and the idyllic view of the world as supposedly perceived by innocence characteristic of texts produced specifically for children. If they didn't, many adults would be horrified by children reading them, as they are horrified by children reading, say, pornography or *Doonesbury* cartoons. Adult perceptions are the key to what children's literature is.

According to Peter Hollindale, "Children's literature does not denote a text but a reading event. Whenever a successful voluntary transaction takes place between any text and any one child, that text is for that occasion 'children's literature.' "[54]

From the viewpoint of adults hoping to encourage children's reading and writing, Hollindale's is a practical position to take—but in terms of my purposes here it represents a counterproductive use of the term *children's literature*—one more likely to confuse the issue than clarify it. Assuming that what any child reads constitutes children's literature prevents the development of a deeper knowledge of the texts specifically marketed as children's literature and of the institutional forms and structures mandated to produce and deliver such texts to children. "Without wishing to diminish the importance of the works that speak about how the child is constructed—or 'implied'—in its literature," says Rudd, "it would be a mistake to see them as the whole story: they miss, precisely, half of it, in neglecting the constructive powers of the child."[55] Before focusing on these constructive powers—what children make of the literature adults provide for them—adults need a better understanding of the ways in which the texts invite responses in the reader they imply. My concern with what the texts offer readers rather than with how readers take up the offer makes my work less immediately practical in terms of understanding how children interact with children's literature (although I admit, based on my own experiences with young people, that I expect they most often do react as institutions invite and as mediators like parents and teachers teach them to). But not exploring what Rudd identifies as "half" allows a revealing degree of attention to the specific nature and implications of the adult investment in the production of texts for children that will then, I hope, provide a basis for a sounder understanding of that missing half.

In any case, the ideas about children's literature that I discuss in the rest of this chapter all work with the same basic assumptions—that children's literature is written by adults and that it is what it is because of how it addresses its audience, because of what adults believe children are—adult constructions of childhood. Interestingly, however, different ideas about children lead to a range of different ideas about what children's literature is and how it might be defined.

For instance, some definitions focus on the pragmatic idea that children's literature is merely the literature children like. Children are the intended audience, after all, and the purpose of literature is to give readers pleasure, isn't it? So the books adults appropriately label as children's literature must surely be the ones children will actually enjoy reading. Ideas like this are another variation of the refusal to define. If children's literature consists of what children enjoy, then it must be too diffuse to have specific qualities—unless, of course, all children's tastes and interests are highly similar.

But those who take this position do tend to believe that most children's tastes and interests are more alike than not. As Karín Lesnik-Oberstein suggests in a misleadingly sweeping generalization that does possess some degree of truth, "Children's literature criticism is about saying, 'I know what children like to read / are able to read / should read, *because I know what children are like.*'"[56] Claiming to know what children like is claiming that children are alike and, for that reason, knowable as a group entity possessing a limited range of generalized characteristics—and with therefore a limited range of shared likes and dislikes. As a result, the apparent accepting pragmatism of those who make such claims usually disguises a consistent and often quite rigid set of characteristics that define what children's literature is or ideally should be.

Not surprisingly, this is almost always an exclusionary ploy—as it was for Mrs. Trimmer and as it is in just about all the definitions I discuss from now on. It is clear that almost always critics define exactly in order to exclude—to find ways of not admitting into the field certain books that others might consider to be children's literature. The central purpose of the vast bulk of adult discussion of children's books is almost always the matter of knowing *what* to exclude. The range of excludable texts and properties within texts is wide and various: books adults think children won't like, books adults think children will like but shouldn't, nonchildist books or nonquality books, books with language too complex for children's limited cognitive abilities, texts too long for children's limited attention spans, material too violent for children's tender sensibilities or too sexy for children's innocent purity—or, alternatively, material violent enough and sexy enough to dangerously arouse children's uncontrollable passions. In each case some perceived limitation of children leads to some necessary exclusion from children's literature.

That is important. A special literature for children seems to have come into existence in Europe somewhere around the end of the sixteenth century at the point at which adults perceived a need for expurgated editions of classics for children.[57] Children's literature remains a literature that excludes. It is, as Bator suggests, "a necessarily limited literature,"[58] and any persuasive understanding of its generic qualities will have to deal with the implications of that. Not only do I wish to understand how exclusionary ideas affect conceptions of childhood and children's literature in the time in which it has existed, but I also want to find a way of defining the genre of children's literature that excludes as little as possible of what has been published for children.

What gets excluded in terms of thinking about what children like is that which critics believe children will not enjoy reading or will refuse to read at all. Consider, for instance, this definition of the term *children's literature* by the influential historian of children's literature Harvey Darton: "Printed works produced ostensibly to give children spontaneous pleasure, and not primarily to teach them, not solely to make them good, nor to keep them *profitably* quiet."[59] From this point of view, a vast body of educational texts produced specifically for audiences of children, many of them novels or poems, are not children's literature at all. This is a position shared by many historians of children's literature who propose a gradual evolution of the only true form of children's literature—the current and presumably nondidactic kind—out of a mass of other, more blatantly didactic, writing that does not deserve to be identified as children's literature. From this point of view, for instance, "The Purple Jar" is not children's literature. This position echoes that taken by Hunt and others: such obviously didactic texts are not children's literature simply because they are not literature. Literature includes only quality texts, and, presumably, quality texts are not obviously didactic.

Many critics who believe that children's literature consists of the texts that children enjoy tend to move in the opposite direction, however, *excluding* the books that Hunt would label as literature. Educators and librarians who work with children often focus their attention on books that are popular with children or that they believe will be popular with children—and question that Newbery Medal winners or the novels of innovative writers for children like Alan Garner or Lynne Rae Perkins are actually children's literature, since so few of the children the educators and librarians know (or imagine) care to read them.

On this model one might argue that the poems of Wallace Stevens—or just about any poems, for that matter—or the novels of Russell Banks or Julian Barnes are not literature for adults, since so relatively few adults read them. The true adult literature must be by Danielle Steel and Stephen King—what is sometimes called popular literature exactly because vast numbers of people read it. I suspect few literary scholars would accept that idea. It leaves too many questions unanswered—as does the idea that children's literature is just what children like. Should adults trust that children's taste is inviolably fixed, that what they currently like is all they are capable of liking or, for that matter, what they ought to like? According to whom, and why? Why do so many children seem to share similar tastes, particularly at any given moment in time? Are human children somehow biologically wired to share these tastes, or are there cultural factors that work to shape and influence their tastes and interests? If there are, who controls these cultural factors? Whose power does popular taste emerge from and depend on? That a text is popular is important information. But before anyone can understand what children's literature is, they need to know why children like what they like and consider the implications of their liking it.

Or their not liking it. To say that explicitly didactic books or the medal winners that adults admire are not children's literature is a form of wish-fulfillment fantasy by adults who would like to believe that these things ought to be true, that wise adults can and do know what children enjoy and that children's literature ideally consists of nothing but that. The fact is that many texts produced for children in the past and in the present *are* primarily didactic. The fact is that the Newbery Medal winners *have* won the medals. The field of children's literature as currently constituted does include all these texts, in spite or even because of their unpopularity with many children. To dismiss them from discussion is to misrepresent the field. An understanding of the genre as the textual evidence of the field will necessarily include all these texts.

I suggested earlier that the distinctions between good children's books and not-so-good ones were of less significance as defining characteristics than the distinctions between adult texts and ones intended for children. I am tempted here to make the same point from the opposite direction and say that the differences between popular texts and unpopular ones are also of less significance as defining characteristics than the distinctions between children's texts and ones intended for adults. But I find myself not quite able to do so. As I said in the first chapter, children's literature shares with popular literature the fact that it is named for its audience. As I also suggested there, however, the names of these kinds of literature relate most significantly not to the actual characteristics of their intended audiences but to the ideas that their producers have about those audiences: what constitutes and satisfies popular taste in one case, what children might like to read or be able to read—what children are—in the other. From this point of view texts can be considered popular literature without actually being popular or widely read. Widely read or not, they can maintain the distinct characteristics of what has become a recognizable genre because so many producers share an idea of what their potential adult audience might like. Viewed in this way, "popular literature" is exactly equivalent to what I mean by "children's literature" —not so much what children actually read or enjoy or benefit from as what adults imagine for them to read and enjoy and benefit from.

I also suspect the ideas about audience that sustain children's literature and popular literature tend to be similar, and my reading of theoretical studies of popular literature by writers like John Cawelti and Tania Modleski and of children's literature and children's literature criticism suggest that the two literatures tend to share characteristics. Both are "simple" literatures, focused on action rather than on subtleties of character or linguistic complexity. Both offer protagonists with whom readers are intended to identify, and both tend to depict events from the protagonist's point of view. Both tend to operate in terms of plots that do not diverge greatly from the same basic story patterns. I will discuss how texts of children's literature reveal these qualities later in this chapter. Meanwhile, I need to point out that these qualities appear almost as often in the didactic children's books and the medal winners as it does in the popular ones. They appear, for instance, in all of the six texts I discussed in chapter 1, some of which are didactic, some popular, and some medal winners.[60] I might propose the possibility that, popular or not, most children's literature has more in common with popular literature for adults than with quality literature for adults. In defining and understanding it, then, popularity might be a significant issue—but because of the generic characteristics of what tends to be popular or imagined for popular audiences, not because of the popular tastes of most children or even the tastes of any specific children.

In his book *Criticism, Theory, and Children's Literature,* Peter Hunt offers a controversial variation on the kind of thinking that excludes texts from children's literature on the basis of what children read and like. Here he offers a different sort of exclusionary view from the one he presented in the article I discussed earlier and argues that the books not currently read by children are not actually children's literature any longer, even if they once were. In the chapter titled "Defining Children's Literature" Hunt bases his argument on what I have been arguing here—the undeniable fact that children's books emerge from adult concepts of childhood: "Concepts of childhood change so rapidly that there is a sense in which books no longer applicable to childhood must fall into a limbo in which they are the preserve of the bibliographer, since they are of no interest to the current librarian or child. . . . On the whole, then, that a particular text was written expressly for children who are recognizably children, with a childhood recognizable today, must be part of the definition."[61] This appears, once more, to be pragmatic—and Hunt clearly intends it to be so. His focus is less on what children's literature is as a distinct form of literature than on how children might read it. He imagines a "childist" form of children's literature criticism, in which adults would work to move past their adult habits of thought and "cross the gap, to see what is really happening on the child's terms," and read, "as far as possible, from a child's point of view."[62]

What Hunt recommends here is, I suspect, not actually possible at all, except as a self-fulfilling prophecy. People can only know how children as a group will read by imagining that groups of children do share reading practices—and if they do share such practices, surely it can only be because adults have taught them to do so or are in the process of teaching them to do so simply by operating on the assumption that they do so already. The flaw of "childist" criticism is its dependence on assumptions about children that distort and limit the vast spectrum of actual or potential childhood capabilities and experiences. A more useful criticism might focus on the assumptions themselves and consider their history, their validity, and their implications in terms of adult involvement in children's reading experiences.

In this particular case the theoretically pragmatic assumptions are surprisingly utopian. Hunt's discussions of children's reading are filled with comments about their wonderful ability to indulge in imaginative play and escape repressive manipulation. For instance, "It is likely that child-readers . . . will read against societal norms" (11); or, "The adult mind . . . is far less likely than the mind of a child to accept images and atmosphere and undirected allusions" (197). This is an idyllic vision of what Hunt believes childhood ideally ought to be, imagined as what children already are. It is pleasant to imagine children in general so blessed, and as I suggested in my first chapter, many texts for children imagine just that and work to encourage children either to believe it of themselves or to perform it for adults. Hunt's childist reading is thus a transposition of a view of childhood common in children's literature from the texts onto readers. Operating as an adult version of the implied child reader of many texts of children's literature, Hunt reads children in terms of how the texts work to have children read themselves.

Hunt's privileging of this particular reading of children as the one that defines the boundaries of children's literature emerges from his assumption that other, older readings are not accurate descriptions of childhood today. He avoids the question of how his own reading might be equally inaccurate. There are certainly differences in how Maria Edgeworth or Lewis Carroll imagined childhood and how Peter Hunt imagines it now. But Edgeworth, Carroll, and Hunt all do have specific readings of childhood—and in all three cases it is a reading that allows them to imagine a special literature for children to be provided by adults. As I keep insisting, it is the continuity of this one major characteristic that underlies my work here. Seen in the light of this one powerful similarity, the differences that separate Edgeworth's view of childhood from Hunt's are not all that huge. They both tend to see children and adults as different and opposite on the base of their differing levels of knowledge—Hunt, for instance, says that children's "approach to life and text stems from a different set of cultural standards from those of adult readers, one that may be in opposition."[63] And although they place opposite labels on the same qualities, so that what Edgeworth sees as a dangerous removal from clear-sightedness Hunt admires as a saving playfulness, both have just about the same idea about how children think.

For the Good of Children

Edgeworth's and Hunt's views of children's literature share another central principle: children's literature exists as a way for adults to influence children for the children's good. "The Purple Jar" exists in the faith that reading the right text can make children better people; "childist" criticism exists in the faith that understanding childlike thinking will allow adults to understand which texts are really the ones children will benefit from reading.

What adults most frequently believe children need from their literature is education. Understood as innocent and inexperienced, children know less about the world they live in than they might, less about how to think about themselves and others than they might, less about how to behave than they might. Adults thus have a duty to teach children what they don't yet know, so, from this point of view, children's literature is primarily a didactic literature.

Most texts for children view their audience as in need of education, and as Maria Nikolajeva suggests, that perception accounts for many of their characteristic qualities: she argues, for instance, that "in children's fiction, the function of characters is closely connected with overall didactic purposes: characters are supposed to provide models and statute examples."[64] Certainly, most commentaries about children's literature tend to concentrate on how it might or might not help to make its target audience better, more educated people. When adults not professionally involved with children's books talk about children's literature, they almost always focus on what they see as its obvious "morals" or "messages" and tend to base their judgments of texts on whether they agree with those obvious teachings. There are also more sophisticated ways of talking about the educational impact of less obviously didactic aspects of children's literature. For instance, Fred Inglis sees children's novels as particular instances of the imaginative structures of consciousness and social interaction that, as an adherent of F. R. Leavis, he believes worthwhile fictional narratives generally offer readers to help them shape their understandings of themselves in the world and in the specific society they belong to: "Novels are the disciplined and public versions of the fictions we must have if we are to think at all. Children's novels are proposed by adults as the imaginative forms of life which they may work with and turn into their future lives."[65] As I will describe later, however, a whole range of less optimistic theorists focus on what children's literature teaches beyond its obvious messages by describing the repressively manipulative mechanisms by which texts shape individuals' subjectivities into conforming with societal constraints.

It has been fashionable for the last hundred or more years for commentators to express dislike of "didactic" children's books. But the often proclaimed distaste for the didactic is usually actually just dismay about the *obviously* didactic, on the assumption that, ideally, children's literature ought to teach without seeming to do so. For instance, Charles Temple and his collaborators repeat some oft-repeated conventional wisdom: "Many children's books turn out to be about something, and it is often possible to derive a lesson from them. But if a book seems too obviously contrived to teach a lesson, children (and critics) will not tolerate it."[66] From this point of view, the best children's literature is sneaky about its didactic agenda. It manipulates its readers into being educated by not being obviously educational, by giving children what they need by appearing to give them what they like.

But there is something else that adults commonly believe children need from their literature: protection, both from knowledge and from experience. From this point of view children's literature exists in order to offer children this protection, to exclude things they ought not to know about. As I have suggested, what children's literature excludes varies from time to time and from adult to adult. What has remained almost universally constant from the sixteenth century on is the idea that there is something or other that children should not learn, should not or cannot know—some knowledge they need to be protected from and that children's literature exists exactly in order to exclude. It can be defined as that literature that gives children what they need by *not* being didactic about the wrong things—by *not* teaching them what they cannot or should not know.

But as I have already established, as well as preventing children from knowing more, adults also believe they have an obligation to help them know more—to teach them what they can and should know. As a result, children's literature tends to be both exclusionary *and* didactic. As Torben Weinreich suggests, it tends to contain not just "something the child should learn or be influenced by" but also "something the child should be protected against or something society should prevent the child from finding out about.[67] Paradoxically, children's literature characteristically attempts both to make children better than they are and to keep them the same as they are already.

But in both cases the issue is still centrally about what adults desire for children—want them to know and not know, want them to be. What adults believe is good for children is essentially what is good for adults, and what I have identified as the literature children need might be better defined as the literature adults want and need children to need.

And, of course, children's literature must be exactly that—if it weren't, adults would not be in the business of producing it. Some decades ago, John Rowe

Townsend suggested a division among adults interested in children's literature between "child people" and "book people."[68] The "child people"—educators, psychologists, librarians, many parents—claim to have knowledge of what children in general are like and base their discussions of children's literature on that supposed knowledge. The "book people"—literary scholars and many children's writers—claim to believe that children are too individual to be known as a group and focus on evaluating books on their own terms, recommending what they identify as quality literature. But as Karín Lesnik-Oberstein points out, the book people also imagine a generalized child, one who needs and who ought to respond positively to the books they admire. Thus, "both 'book people' and 'child people' are 'child people,' ultimately unable to escape relying on the existence of the 'real' child."[69]

On the basis of this shrewd perception, Lesnik-Oberstein eventually concludes that all adult attempts to do criticism of children's literature are doomed to be pointless: "If children's literature criticism depends on, and is defined by, its claim to the existence of the 'real child' . . . then it is indeed dead. . . . As children's literature criticism operates at present, I can only conclude it makes non-statements, for its own purposes. In making judgments and criticisms on behalf of a 'real child' who does not exist, its writings are useless to the fulfillment of its own professed aims" (ibid., 163). I don't accept this conclusion, simply because it is illogical (and overly optimistic) to assume that critics' imaginings of a fictional "real" child do not accomplish their aims. If the critic is persuasive, numerous adults, and no doubt many children also, will come to believe that the child imagined by the critic is what children actually are. The fiction will become a reality, the books recommended will be the right ones to recommend, and, possibly, the implied child readers of those books will guide children about how to understand themselves. This is not necessarily a good thing, but it certainly represents the fulfillment of the goals the criticism claims for itself: to ensure that the children and the childhood reading that it imagines will operate in the ways it imagines.

I have to assume that ideas about childhood that are shared by many adults and the children they influence are so widespread exactly because they are useful to adults and to their society as a whole. It is important to explore why so many adults want to imagine children as joyfully creative or incapable of complex thought exactly because those imaginings have so much power to control reality.

Indeed, it is hard to conceive how such imaginings might be avoided. Lesnik-Oberstein herself acknowledges that the psychotherapists whose work with children she admires also have constructs of childhood: "Psychotherapy works with specific theoretical models of general human emotional structure and development, which, however, have to be translated into an application in therapy to the differing cases of distinct 'individuals'" (ibid., 171). How this differs from what many children's literature critics do in imagining a generalized child reader and then struggling to understand real individual readers in terms of it is hard to fathom—although Lesnik-Oberstein does make the outrageous claim that "children's literature criticism is inextricably tied to a *prescriptive* role (even when it does not want to be), whereas psychotherapy is extensively concerned with functioning non-prescriptively" (ibid., 176). There are certainly as many bad prescriptive therapists with normative assumptions about desirable mental health as there are bad prescriptive critics with normative assumptions about children. Virginia Blum far more persuasively sees "psychoanalysis itself as yet another mythmaker, another story of the child that talks about the adult instead, another discourse that employs the child as a vehicle to effect the theory's own adult ends." And I share Blum's conclusion: "Despite all efforts to sidestep definitions of the child, such avoidance is itself a theoretical gridlock, in many ways as tyrannical as those [definitions] I repudiate."[70]

Even the conviction that "childhood" is a nonexistent generalization leads to general conceptions of what children are that will inevitably influence how one talks about children's literature, especially in terms of children's reading. But the generalization that children are most significantly a body of differing individuals with different needs, tastes, and so forth and with the potential to respond to a wide range of literary experiences seems to me a positive and useful one. I consider it the best construct to have if one must—and one surely must—have a construct. It allows no claims about how children as a group may actually read books or what books they should be reading as a result of that—merely claims about how books imply they should be read. I imagine children capable of perceiving and separating themselves from those implied readers—though not, I hasten to add, all children. To deny the idea that all children are incapable of certain behaviors by virtue merely of their being children in no way implies that each and every one of them is capable. It merely requires one to operate without the possibility that each one might be.

Although Lesnik-Oberstein's claim that the focus on an imagined child mars and must inevitably mar any and all attempts to do criticism of children's literature is overstated and unfounded, it does point toward a more revealing way of understanding the idea that children's literature is what adults want children to want. It might well be so, not in terms of what specific texts critics choose to recommend but in terms of the nature of the literature itself. One of its defining characteristics may well be its imagining of a fictional child as its reader—a fictional child it proposes as a model for the actual children who read it.

Anyone familiar with theoretical studies of children's literature will recognize Lesnik-Oberstein's thesis about the fictionality of the constructed child of criticism as a variation on Jacqueline Rose's idea of the "impossibility" of children's fiction—impossible because the readers implied in books written by adults for children will always be constructed out of adult wishes and desires. Lesnik-Oberstein says that Rose "closes down the field of children's fiction and therefore, by implication, children's literature criticism, by questioning the status of the 'existence' of the child."[71] But this closing down is hardly inevitable. The opposite possibility seems more likely. As Rose's own provocative discussion reveals, children's literature criticism becomes valuable exactly at the point at which the constructedness of the child readers implied by children's literature becomes a focus of attention.

And the constructedness of its child characters is a crucial consideration here as well, for a corollary of the idea that children's literature constructs child readers is that it constructs child characters for readers to identify with, in order to satisfy adult wants and needs in regard to children. According to Rose, "If children's fiction builds an image of the child inside the book, it does so in order to secure the child who is outside the book, the one who does not come so easily within its grasp."[72] The child is "secured"—made to understand him- or herself in terms of the fictional construct of the text—by identifying with the child characters the text describes and thereby becoming the reader it implies.

Notice the paradox hidden here—an echo of the paradoxical relationship I discussed earlier between teaching children and protecting them from knowledge. Children's literature might be didactic exactly insofar as it attempts to teach children an image of childhood with which to understand themselves that defines them as incapable of knowing or learning certain kinds of "adult" knowledge. Its key lesson might be to teach children how *not* to know.

According to Rose, adults attempt to teach this lesson and thus "secure" child readers because, left unsecured, children threaten adult constructions of adulthood. Central among these is how adults understand themselves as sexual beings, an understanding that requires children not to be sexual at all, and certainly not to be sexual in ways that might threaten conceptions of (or convictions about) adult normalcy: "Freud is known to have undermined the concept of childhood innocence, but his real challenge is easily lost if we see in the child merely a miniature version of what our sexuality eventually comes to be. The child is sexual, but its sexuality (bisexual, polymorphous, perverse) threatens our own at its very roots.

Setting up the child as innocent is not, therefore, repressing its sexuality—it is above all holding off any possible challenge to our own."[73] If adults can persuade children that they are as innocent as the children in the texts adults provide for them, then the adults can keep themselves from acknowledging aspects of their own sexuality that they have themselves repressed and prefer to keep repressed. Very explicitly, adults produce and distribute literature to children exactly in order to teach children to know less and exactly in order to suit their own adult wants and needs.

For Rose, what matters about the fictional children imagined as characters and implied readers of children's literature is not the characteristics they possess but the ones they lack. This idea is insightful and important. I spoke earlier of how definitions of children's literature based on assumptions about children tend to operate primarily to exclude. Clearly, this is so because common assumptions about children are in themselves exclusionary—built on ideas about how children are what they are in terms of how they lack qualities or characteristics or depths or experiences possessed by adults. That exclusionary vision of childhood accounts for many of the shared characteristics of the texts I explored in chapter 1. These include, among others, their simplicity of language, their implied shadow texts, their reinforcement of innocence, their postulation of binary oppositions that seem to relate to a basic opposition between child and adult. Later in this chapter I consider how various of these characteristics are the focus of a range of definitions of and theories about children's literature.

At this point, though, I want to explore the implication of the mechanism Rose proposes: the way in which texts by adults work to "secure" their intended child readers. From this point of view, what most defines children's literature is its existence as a force to shape and control children—to make them into the children —and eventually, presumably, the adults—that adults want them to be.

Why do adults want children to be less or seem less than they might be capable of being? I can imagine a lot of adults rejecting Freudian interpretations of the motivation behind the need for control. In North American culture today, as throughout the past few centuries, the slightest suggestion that children might be sexual beings in any way whatsoever tends to infuriate the vast proportion of adults.[74] It is a possibility so threatening to a typical adult's sense of well-being that there seems little choice but to wonder about what unconscious or perhaps merely unspoken (and unspeakable) fears or desires it represses.[75] Rose might well be right simply because so many people want her to be wrong.

But there's no need to accept Rose's interpretation of what motivates the need for control in order to believe that control is a central issue in, and a central characteristic of, children's literature. Most discussions of children's literature in terms of the role it plays as a conveyer and shaper of ideology tend to share that belief also. Thus, according to John Stephens, "Writing for children is usually purposeful, its intention being to foster in the child reader a positive apperception of some socio-cultural values which, it is assumed, are shared by author and audience."[76] And Roderick McGillis suggests, "What every society wants is a quiet and satisfied collection of people. Perhaps for this reason, many books for young children displace aggression and offer substitutes for desire."[77]

Rose herself sees connections between these attempts by knowing adults to shape less knowing children and the entire enterprise of European colonialism: "children's fiction has a set of long-established links with the colonialism which identified the new world with the infantile state of man."[78] If colonialist thinking tends to conceive of people as colonizable in part by perceiving them as childlike, it seems logical to suggest that adult thinking about childhood is inherently colonialist already. The metaphor of childlikeness applies most immediately to children themselves—and children's literature might be best characterized as that literature that works to colonize children by persuading them that they are as innocent and in need of adult control as adults would like them to believe.

This is not to say that children do not often have less knowledge of the world than older people do or that they are not often in need of adult protection. As Alan Richardson quite logically asserts, "Any argument that, noting the historical in-fantilization of women, slaves, the working classes, racial minorities, and colo-nized peoples within modern social discourses, attempts uncritically to portray children themselves as a colonized group (Nodelman), which child-centered dis-courses 'infantilize' (Suransky 8), loses sight of the undeniable fact that children, unlike the various adult groups oppressed in their name, *are* in legitimate need of protection and guidance."[79]

But this is not completely accurate. There is an important distinction between many children's obvious need of protection and guidance and the constructions of childhood that adults have invented to justify those needs—particularly in texts intended for child readers. Children are certainly not as universally uninformed or incapable as texts of children's literature conventionally assume, nor are they always uninformed and incapable exactly in the ways those texts tend so consis-tently to describe them. It is instructive that children's literature works so typically to persuade them that they are uninformed enough to need protection—that they are the innocent children adults imagine—to colonize them with childhood.

The idea that children's literature is colonialist is more than just a pretentious way of saying that it is literature in which adults attempt to manipulate children.

A hopefully not-too-uncritical consideration of Edward Said's influential analysis of colonialist thinking, *Orientalism,* reveals a number of intriguing aspects of colonialist thought that might well reveal or account for some of the equally intriguing aspects of children's literature that emerged from my explorations in chapter 1. In what follows I explore how very suggestive metaphors of colonization—and particularly the ones Said considers—are in attempting to understand what children's literature might be.

Before I proceed, however, I need to make it clear that the metaphor is just that—that colonialist thinking in the age of empire and beyond has been complex and multifaceted and that it has varied significantly in different places and in different times during the colonial period. And as Mavis Reimer suggests, "When we turn to texts specifically produced for children of the colonizers by adult colonizers, the simple analogy between the child and the racialized other begins to break down,"[80] for the implied reader is being "colonized" as a child in the process of becoming a colonizer. But while the parallels between Orientalist thinking and adult conceptions of childhood are inexact, they are extraordinarily suggestive.

The most obvious of these suggestive parallels relate to the nature of children's literature as a field. Said says, "The Orientalist is outside the Orient, both as an existential and a moral fact."[81] So, too, are adult practitioners of children's literature—writers, editors, librarians, scholars—outside of childhood. This has a number of consequences for the field and for the texts that inscribe the field.

First, adult practitioners of children's literature must speak for and about and to children, who are presumed, as Orientals are by Orientalists, to be unable to speak for and about and even (in the form of literary texts, at least) to themselves. As a field, children's literature is an adult activity. Its most important discourses and dialogues are those between adults, not necessarily those with children. Even the texts produced by all this activity, which purport to speak to children, do so indirectly. Their first and most influential readers are adult editors and then adult reviewers. Consequently, the texts must necessarily and inevitably appeal to the tastes and needs of those adults—which accounts for their focus on transforming children into what the adults who control children's reading want and need children to be. The texts might well be understood to have these adults as their implied audience, instead of or in addition to the children they purport to be addressed to.

Second, as Said says, Orientalist thinking "is weighted heavily with all the orthodox attitudes, perspectives, and moods of Orientalism" (104). Colonialist thinking deals with colonized peoples as conventionally understood by their colonizers. Since Orientals are assumed to be unable to speak for themselves, knowledge about them can only be that which is engendered by and shared by Orientalists. For the same reason, the children that children's literature purports to address must be the children of shared adult wisdom. For this reason children's literature characteristically and inevitably depends on conventional adult constructions of childhood. "What the Orientalist does," says Said, "is to *confirm* the Orient in his readers' eyes; he neither tries nor wants to unsettle already firm convictions" (65). Neither do most children's writers and most adult experts in aspects of childhood. Each new text tends therefore to re-express and reconfirm the basic assumptions already operative in the field.

Third, Said says, "the Orientalist remained outside the Orient, which, however much it was made to appear intelligible, remained beyond the Occident. This cultural, temporal, and geographical distance was expressed in metaphors of depth, secrecy, and sexual promise: phrases like 'the veils of an Eastern bride' or 'the inscrutable Orient' passed into the common language" (222). Just as the constructions of the Orient that emerge from an outsider's perspective focus on the mysterious unknowability of the alien other, so, too, do the constructions of childhood found in adult thought about children and often, consequently, in children's literature. Consider the comments about the mysteriousness of childhood and children's literature I referred to earlier.

That conviction of mystery also helps to account for the self-replicating nature of the field of children's literature, as well as of related fields like child psychology, education, and so on. The more people say about what they understand, the more they understand that they can't understand. The more adults claim to know about childhood, the more they find themselves insisting on its mysterious otherness— its silence about itself—and the more they feel the need to observe yet more, interpret yet further, say yet more. And by filling the space with their own words, they encourage yet more childhood silence for them to worry about and speak about. The adult observation of the child as an other that does not observe itself is always doomed to fail to understand and thus doomed to continue replicating itself.

It also, therefore, must replicate itself in children's books. At first that seems impossible: children's literature is nothing if not clear about what adults think children are. But what matters is the content of that knowledge—a construction of childhood centered paradoxically on the *lack* of knowledge.

Earlier, I referred to Lillian Smith's view of "the eager, reaching, elusive spirit of childhood."[82] Children elude adult understanding exactly because of their own lack of understanding. Their innocence of the ways in which adults think makes the ways in which children think unknowable—tantalizingly unknowable—to adults. Paradoxically, the claim of superior adult knowledge creates the circumstances in which what is known is, centrally, unknowability—that which is beyond or before knowledge itself as adults understand it. James Kincaid suggests that this view places "at the center of the child a kind of purity, an absence and an incapacity, an inability to do."[83] Texts of children's literature characteristically work to describe this absence—to capture an accurate view of how childhood innocence thinks—or, perhaps better, does not think.

I have just been discussing how children's literature tends to be didactic, and as I demonstrated in chapter 1, many texts of children's literature have the obvious purpose of moving children beyond innocence—making them know and thus, presumably as sharers in adult knowledge, making them knowable. But I have also just explored how exclusion balances didacticism; and as I also demonstrated in chapter 1, the declared invitation to know is undermined by a less clearly spoken invitation either to keep on not knowing or, more often, to pretend not to know. Said's descriptions of Orientalism help to account for this characteristic ambivalence.

"For a number of evident reasons," he says, "the Orient was always in the position both of outsider and of incorporated weak partner for the West."[84] This suggests two contradictory modes by which Europeans address Orientals. On the one hand, the Orientals imagined by Orientalism are the opposite of Europeans in ways so basic and unchanging that "the Oriental mind" transcends differences of specific places and times and always in ways that define European superiority. If there were no more colonies to colonize, imperialists could no longer perceive themselves as being imperial; so in a very basic sense *Oriental* means "eternally and inalterably opposite to human." Those identified as Orientals must be addressed in terms of the self-confirming enterprise of educating them into being what Europeans have always imagined them to be—typical representatives of "the Oriental mind." On the other hand, however, part of the European's superior humanity is a more evolved sense of obligation to others less superior. This leads to the evolutionary enterprise of educating Orientals into being more like Europeans. The strong must colonize the weak to help them become stronger, so, in a very basic sense, *Oriental* means "a less evolved being with the potential to become human."

A nonhuman in the process of becoming more human. There is no way to resolve this contradiction: Orientals cannot be both the unchanging opposite of Europeans and in the process of changing into Europeans. The same contradiction is so central to adult discourse about children and children's literature that it might well be their defining characteristic. On the one hand, the declared themes and messages of most texts for children are almost always about becoming less egocentric, more rational, and so on—less childlike. They teach children how to be adults. On the other hand, however, they also teach children how to be childlike by providing them with images of childhood and secretly or not so secretly recommending that child readers maintain or adopt them. They work ambivalently both to make children more like adults and to keep them opposite to adults—both to move children past innocence and encourage them to keep on being innocent. As Peter Hollindale suggests, it is "a noticeable feature of some major 'classic' children's books that they test and undermine some of the values which they superficially appear to be celebrating."[85] I suspect that this is true of more texts than just the classic ones in which it is most obvious.

The conscious or unconscious wish to keep children innocent clearly suggests how central adult needs are. Children need to be innocent less than adults need to believe that children are innocent—that childhood is a matter of not being human in the ways that adults are human. A century or so ago, the British colonial official Lord Cromer summed up his knowledge of the East by saying, "I content myself with noting the fact that somehow or other the Oriental generally acts, speaks, and thinks in a manner exactly opposite to the European."[86] Or, in other words, I define who I am myself as a European by seeing the Oriental as everything I am not. A main purpose of a discourse of the other is always this sort of self-definition. People characterize the other as other in order to define themselves. "The Oriental is irrational, depraved (fallen), childlike, 'different,' " says Said; "thus the European is rational, virtuous, mature, 'normal.' "[87] Similarly, adults can see themselves as rational, virtuous, mature, and normal exactly because they have irrational, depraved (fallen), childlike, different children to compare themselves to.

This is a version of Rose's view that adults imagine children in certain ways in order to confirm and establish their own rationality as adults. But Rose tends to focus on a different version of the meaning of childhood—not its depravity so much as its innocent freedom from depravity. In yet a further variation on this theme, a fairly sizable stream of commentary on children's literature focuses on the depraved, fallen nature of adulthood, the desperately unimaginative and limited adult overtrust in reason in comparison to blissfully irrational, not-yet-fallen, not-yet-limited children.

Paul Hazard begins his book about children's literature, first published in 1944, with this formulation: "Children and grownups belong to different worlds. . . . How far removed is the world of childhood! Its inhabitants seem of another species. . . . Reason does not curb them, for they have not yet learned its restraints.

Happy beings, they live in the clouds, playing light-heartedly without a care."[88] This sounds like praise for the different world of childhood; indeed, Hazard goes on to assert that childhood "remains healthy because it has not yet reached the age for analyzing the soul's emotions" (167). Analysis is not healthy, it seems—and Hazard makes this comment in the midst of a presumably rational adult analysis; thus, he identifies himself as a sick being envying the health of those in a category so opposite to himself that he could not possibly enter it. For, of course, no matter how much adults admire the health of childhood, an adult cannot become a child, cannot without debilitating loss of memory know less than he or she has already learned. Is it possible that the habit I have identified as colonialist—imagining children as opposite to adults—might actually have the noncolonialist result of imagining children as superior to adults and of imagining children's literature to be inviting children to think of themselves as beings superior to their elders? Just who is colonizing whom?

The answer to that question emerges from a consideration of who benefits from the conviction that children in their innocence are wiser than adults. It is unlikely to be children, for, exactly like the idea that children are inferior to adults in their lack of knowledge, the idea that children might be superior because of their lack of knowledge still confines them to a lack of knowledge. What is being celebrated is, exactly, inadequacy, inhumanity, incapacity—the state of being less than completely human; and as Mavis Reimer suggests in discussing the adult discourse surrounding the cancellation in 1994 by a Canadian TV network of the *Mighty Morphin Power Rangers* show for its excessive violence, "The meaning of the *Power Rangers* debate would seem to be either that adults define children as powerless in order to see themselves as powerful or that adults define children as powerful in order to access what is seen as their power."[89] The act of celebration most clearly benefits the person who does the celebrating; in fact, Hazard directly asserts a benefit for adults: "It is sweet, sometimes," he says, "to see the world again with a child's eyes."[90] Children must be childlike primarily so that adults can imagine themselves, sometimes, to be children.

But only sometimes. Hazard goes on to say, "It is true that they lure us away from the feast of ideas, taking no pleasure there themselves. They place small value on the abstractions that are so useful to our grown-up pastimes" (166). But it is clear that what he presents here supposedly as a qualification is exactly the reason why he wants to think like a child: "let us admit that they have no skill in handling ideas. What they have is enough for them" (166). It would be enough for him too, it seems, if only he weren't cursed with his awful adult superiority—the terrible knowledge of how very bad knowledge is that prevents him from being more than a fleeting guest in the wonderful world of childhood. Thus, Hazard has it both ways: he is superior to children, and he knows how bad it is to be superior enough to hate it—which, presumably, makes him even more superior than other adults. This particular version of colonialist thinking is still surprisingly common in children's literature criticism, in which sophisticated adults often celebrate the wise innocence of childhood as a way of attacking other less wise adults.

There is a good reason for this insistence on the wise innocence of childhood. As Rose argues, and as Kincaid says, "If the child is not distinguished from the adult, we imagine that we are seriously threatened, threatened in such a way as to put at risk our very being, what it means to be an adult in the first place."[91] Childhood exists, then, to allow adults to be adults—so children's literature exists in order to impose childhood on children.

My assumption here is that adults, identified as such, can only exist—and adulthood can only come to be—in a system that insists on beings known as children who are significantly different from those labeled, in contrast, "adult." Without a concept of a definable childhood, adults could not think of themselves as such, for they would have no one specifically and significantly different from themselves to see themselves as different from in terms of their adulthood; there-fore, they would have no hope of coming to some understanding of themselves as not being children or childlike—of being, that is, adults. If adults need children to be childlike in order to understand and confirm their own adulthood, then chil-dren's literature exists most significantly as part of a system that confirms the childlikeness of children in order to confirm the adulthood—and the power and authority—of adults.

Said's discussion of how Orientalists approached their subject reveals how it might do so—the mechanism by which children's literature claims its audience: "Proper knowledge of the Orient proceeded from a thorough study of the classical texts, and only after that to an application of those texts to the modern Orient. Faced with the obvious decrepitude and political impotence of the modern Orien-tal, the European Orientalist found it his duty to rescue some portion of a lost, past classical Oriental grandeur in order to 'facilitate ameliorations' in the present Orient."[92] The parallel "classical texts" of childhood fall into two categories. First, there are written descriptions of children, in children's books but also in psychol-ogy textbooks and such. Second, there are adults' personal versions of their own childhoods: what they identify as childhood memories. As Beverly Lyon Clark suggests, "We are so adult centered that the only child we adults can see is ourselves; we do not recognize what it means to attend to children's perspec-tives."[93] Believing that these self-regarding texts of nostalgic memory describe an ideal childhood—childhood as it ought to be—and perceiving a gulf between this ideal childhood and the real behavior of children they know, adults work in literature and life to make children more like the ideal—to restore to them a "childhood" that they appear to have lost sight of.

In *Inside Picture Books* Ellen Handler Spitz offers a revealing example of this sort of logic, as she justifies her focus on books published some decades ago. She acknowledges that "many of the images and stories we will encounter in this book reflect a world at least superficially different from that which swirls around us today,"[94] and she offers an example as she discusses books about grandparents and comments on the absence of grandparents from many contemporary children's lives. But, she says, "these books may even serve as a substitute for what once was or might have been—a kind of compensatory experience, in other words —a providing of imaginary grandparenting when in fact those important kin are missing from children's everyday lives" (101). The benefit of picture books for children with childhoods unlike, I assume, her own is to offer them imaginary versions of that presumably required childhood. Picture books don't describe universal childhood experiences so much as create them for children deprived of them in reality.

But did Ellen Handler Spitz or any other adult really experience childhood as they claim to remember it? Or have they come to believe they did because they themselves, in both their childhood and their adult lives, have also read books by and had interactions with adults who worked to impose preexisting visions of childhood upon them?

One central and particularly instructive vision of childhood is the one that appears in psychoanalysis. According to Virginia L. Blum, "Psychoanalysis is the story of the adult's relationship with an internalized, repudiated, but nevertheless ceaselessly desired child—not the actual child the adult has been, but rather the 'dead' child mourned by a present-tense self which is constituted on the past this child at once represents and withholds."[95] Psychoanalysis invents, without knowing it is doing so, a version of childhood that it then invites adults to impose on their own past as a universal history of all mature human beings. This child, being "dead," cannot speak—cannot be communicated with—yet communication with it is the theoretical source of psychoanalytical health. "As long as psychoanalysis submits to its unconscious fantasy of the child as both the origin and guarantor of desire," Blum concludes, "it will continue to validate its fictions as stories of real life. And, as long as psychoanalysis hoards its darkest secrets in the mute child-subject, it is fated to repeat its distortions in the form of a lived agenda for living human subjects, both adults and children" (23). Psychoanalysis is then merely one more particularly telling example of how colonialist thinking imposes a fictional childhood on children for adult purposes—a story for adults that tells the same story with the same purpose as does children's literature for children. Kenneth Kidd asserts that it might be "productive to treat psychoanalysis and children's literature as discourses that revolve around similar concerns and themes, and which may be mutually constitutive."[96]

In any case, all of the views I have been describing have in common the implication that there is something wrong with the processes being described. Merely identifying them with something as universally condemned as the act of colonization now is reveals how distasteful people find them, and how repressive. But Kidd asks, "If adults write children's books, as is routinely pointed out by more suspicious critics of the field, couldn't adult intentions be more generous (less manipulative) than we often assume?"[97] As I suggested earlier, there can be little doubt that young children need adult concern and supervision; and while, perhaps ungenerously, I tend to find much popular discourse about childhood and in children's literature unnecessarily repressive, I have to acknowledge that there are more positive ways of viewing these matters and to take those ways into account.

In her discussion in *Looking Glasses and Neverlands* of how Lacan's version of psychoanalysis might offer insights into the effects of children's literature on child readers, Karen Coats suggests that what others call "colonizing" is inevitable, inescapable—part and parcel of the human condition. Yes, literary texts— indeed, all the stories adults tell to children and each other—shape their audiences in the repressive forms of the subjectivities acceptable within the social world they occupy. But there is no other form of subjectivity available: "The only way we come to make sense of the world is through the stories we are told. They pattern the world we have fallen into, effectively replacing its terrors and inconsistencies with structured images that assure us of its manageability. And in the process of structuring the world, stories structure us as beings in that world."[98]

Texts of children's literature thus teach exactly what all stories always teach: "colonization" or, a Lacanian would say, their audience's coming into existence as subjects, as everyone always does. This may be repressive—it defines who people are in ways that leave them with a sense of lack, of something more about themselves that they want to know or be but can't express. But it is equally repressive for all human beings, not some specific quality of texts for children to be especially condemned and gotten rid of.

Is there anything distinctive about those texts in the development of subjectivity? Coats suggests there is, in two ways. First, texts for children "will probably be read at a time in the life of a person when she is less structured, or, if you like, when her boundaries are more porous, her mental architecture less crowded or filled in with images that define and stabilize her sense of reality and the self" (4). Second, the texts have been written in terms of their adult author's conscious or unconscious acceptance of the means by which subjectivity develops in childhood, and thus describe events able to operate as allegories of development for child readers to identify with. Suggesting that E. B. White's *Charlotte's Web* is "an allegorical story of the advent of subjectivity," Coats adds that such stories "not only show how the theory works, but also actually facilitate the process whereby the modernist subject comes into being by taking the reader, by way of identification, on a journey through what counts as the normal development of subjectivity" (37). I might generalize to suggest another definition of children's literature: that literature that teaches child readers subjectivity by offering them opportunities for identification with characters undergoing normative processes of coming into selfhood.

This is essentially a more nuanced way of repeating one of my earlier formulations: children's literature is that literature that constructs child characters in order to satisfy adult wants and needs in regard to children. But Coats goes on to provide some very specific descriptions both of what normative patterns of psychic development texts for children most often express and of how these texts operate to engage readers in their processes. She suggests, for instance, that the texts tend "to 'capture' the child into the world of signification and to channel that child's vision through identification into certain signifiers that mark modernist culture—the loss of the mother, with salvation coming through fantasy on the one hand, and capitulation to the Law on the other" (55).

The Law Coats speaks of here is the Law of the Father, the Lacanian version of the regime subjectivity as people know it exists within—a regime clearly connected with traditional male power and male-dominated social structures even though Lacan insists it can be held by both males and females. As Coats describes them, texts for children tend to move their protagonists from female maternal spaces into male paternal ones. In following the patterns they tend to follow, these texts imply and sustain traditional assumptions about gender and power. This is, to my mind, both normative and repressive. My utopian optimism urges me to see it as avoidable and therefore worthy of consideration as colonialist, with a view to opening up liberatory possibilities.

Literature for Boys and Literature for Girls

The reinforcement of traditional gender assumptions is one particular and particularly important aspect of the colonizing work of children's literature—so much so that a defining characteristic of children's literature is that it intends to teach what it means for girls to be girls and boys to be boys. A fairly large proportion of children's literature consists of books specifically for boys or girls that act to address—or produce—the presumably different tastes and interests of male and female children. Whether novels for adolescents or picture books for younger children, texts about—and therefore, people often assume, for—boys still tend to replicate the strenuous adventures in the larger world out there of older texts like Stevenson's *Treasure Island*. Books about—and therefore, people often assume, for—girls tend to replicate the domestic settings and relationship intrigues of older texts like *Anne of Green Gables*.

Suggesting that the gender divisions that still mark texts for children emerged in the later decades of the nineteenth century in response to specific cultural concerns of that time, Kimberley Reynolds argues that "the importance of the separation of children's literature on the basis of gender has had profound and lasting implications, although the reasons which initially lay behind it are no longer relevant at the end of the twentieth century."[99] While ensuring that children understand culturally significant differences between males and females remains a significant goal in the socialization of children—and therefore in children's publishing—current understandings of those differences seem quite different from late Victorian ones. The continuing existence of separate categories of books for boys and girls might be an example of Jameson's ideology of form—the preservation of outmoded ideologies in the characteristic structures of a genre. Despite the contemporary feminist concerns that find expression in many contemporary books for and about girls—Lynne Rae Perkins's recent Newbery Medal–winning *Criss Cross* is an example—the fact that they *are* clearly intended to be books primarily for girls and that they *do* tend to focus on traditionally feminine concerns (romance rather than adventure, conversation about relationships rather than physical activity, and so on) might well dilute their anticonservative effect—and reveal the generic consistency of children's literature across time. As Reynolds says, "There remained a mainstream of juvenile fiction which appealed equally to both sexes and there continued to be women writers who exploited the subversive potential of the genre . . . but for the most part the patterns of juvenile publishing were to remain unchanged until the closing decades of the twentieth century" (34). Some years after Reynolds wrote that, and in another century, I believe they still do.

Speaking of the late Victorian period, Reynolds says, "Future defenders of the empire needed to be masters of fact, highly rational, independent, and completely in charge of their emotions. Clearly fiction, with its interest in relationships and the inner life, was of less use in creating the right kind of boy than was non-fiction" (31). And if I set aside for a moment specifically boy-oriented adventure stories, the mainstream of children's fiction—the writing meant to appeal equally to both sexes—has tended, at least since then, to have fewer boys than girls in its audience. The very existence of children's literature is dependent on questions of caregiving for young people, and as Beverly Clark says, "Certainly most of those who write, edit, buy, and critique children's literature, at least in this century, are women."[100] It is possible, as I once suggested, that children's literature, whether written by women or men, is a form of what theorists identify as women's writing.[101] Mavis Reimer says, "To claim girls' books as part of children's literature, we must allow them to interrogate the theories of children's literature we are developing."[102] One way of proceeding with that interrogation might be to consider whether any text recognizably characteristic of children's literature—perhaps even *Treasure Island*—is actually a "girl's book."

Many of the characteristics I described in chapter 1 and discuss throughout this chapter emerge from a privileging of the domestic, female-administered space of home over an often masculinized world away from home: consider how a mother controls the home space of *The Snowy Day*, while the most tempting adventures outside involve aggressive boys, and how in *Alice's Adventures in Wonderland* Alice's sister functions as a safely uncomprehending destination after the wild anarchy opened up to Alice by a traveling male rabbit. According to Lissa Paul, "Feminist texts are about private space, home and nurturing, while male-order books are about public space, ownership, and winning."[103] Certainly, the privileging of female space over male journeying happens most obviously in Montgomery's *Anne of Green Gables*, Alcott's *Little Women*, and many other books about and intended especially for girls, where it especially implies an allegiance to traditionally feminine concerns and values. But it tends to be a quality of children's literature generally. Even in *Treasure Island* Jim Hawkins renounces his own earlier lust for adventure and comes to prefer the virtues of home—as the requisite "happy ending" of literature for young people demands.

In an analysis of how ideas about *écriture féminine* put forth by the French feminists Hélène Cixous and Luce Irigaray might apply to children's literature, Christine Wilkie-Stibbs says, "Within a certain body of children's fiction, *the feminine* functions as a consciously corporeal use of language that manifests itself in the physical, psychical, material, and textual landscapes."[104] Although Wilkie-Stibbs's study focuses on books that "happen to be both written and read by women" (xii), she insists that "the critical perspectives . . . adopted here . . . are not reducible to biological or sexual definition: to men's and boys' versus women's and girls' versions of writing and/or reading and/or characterization" (2). And while the specific texts she discusses are relatively complex, having "narrative patterning . . . intrinsically linked to the great mother myths" and favoring "circularity, fluidity, mutability, intertextuality, and specularity through doubling and metafictional modes" (xiv), Wilkie-Stibbs implies that readers might expect to find aspects of *écriture féminine* in children's literature generally, "because in the system of literature, children's literature, like the theorizations of women's literature in patriarchal discourse, is positioned as Other, as all that is repressed and disavowed and struggles to find a meta-language" (43). If this is even minimally true, then children's literature by and about both males and females might well be a form of women's writing—as a form adopted even by males unsympathetic to women's issues who nevertheless engage characteristics of the genre that have their origins in the primal scene of children's literature, now understood not just as an adult writing for children but specifically as a female adult writing for children. The complaint of parents and teachers, heard across the decades, that boys don't read might have something to do with an inherent disavowal of conventional masculinity in characteristic texts for children.

But while conventional texts of children's literature, like the six I discussed in chapter 1, possess the circularity of home/away/home plots, they less obviously exhibit the fluidity, mutability, intertextuality, and metafictional qualities Wilkie-Stibbs identifies as qualities that make the books she discusses identifiable as *écriture féminine.* If they represent an othered response to patriarchal discourse, it is rarely a very rebellious one. And as I suggested in chapter 1, Henry Huggins's dislike of the Little Boy he is supposed to perform in the school play represents an objection to performing a sentimentalized—and effeminized—version of childhood mandated by his elders, an objection that turns out to be justified. The Green Elf that he prefers to play is more akin to at least one traditional view of masculinity as active, energetic, anticivilizing, just as the wild things in Sendak's picture book tend to represent an exuberantly masculine alternative to the conservative feminine repression of Max's mother and as the ship without women in *Treasure Island* represents an exuberantly masculine alternative to the repressive place where both men and women live back home. And books for girls have traditionally featured admirably tomboyish heroines, even if the books often find ways of feminizing them by the end. These and many other texts for children tend to view the feminine as a force of repressive conservatism, something to be subverted rather than celebrated. Perhaps the gender bias characteristic of children's literature is illusory or only half the truth.

Often, however, the tomboys do get feminized in ways that don't represent much resistance to the repressions of patriarchal convention; and Reynolds makes a good case for the idea that late Victorian girls' fiction "reconciled changes in life-style and opportunities for girls with a conservative definition of femininity . . . [and] encouraged girl readers to react against change, collude in their own containment, and uphold a moral ambience based on feminine idealism."[105] The deflection of Henry Huggins's urge to wildness into an acceptably defanged stage representation might have similar implications. Perhaps the subversion of gender conservatism is only half the truth. I suspect conservatism wins out here, as it does in many other aspects of children's literature, and I suspect it is the conservatism of children's literature that marks it as feminine, not its resistance to patriarchy.

At any rate, there is no question that children's literature is characteristically marked by gender concerns. As I have already pointed out, however, it is also marked by its construction of childhood as asexual. In children's literature gender is at least theoretically divorced from sexuality, and boys must be boyish and girls girlish for reasons that have nothing to do with the underlying reasons that there are gender categories at all. The focus on gender implies a hidden awareness of children as at least potentially sexual beings and suggests the possibility that sexuality is at least part of the sublimated, hidden adult content of children's literature.

Middle-Class Subjectivity

Coats's suggestion that people can only make sense of the world through the stories they are told raises the issue of the universality of those stories. As many commentators have suggested, psychoanalytical concepts like the Oedipal complex might not be as universal as theorists like Freud and Lacan supposed but may draw on specific facets or underpinnings of the European and middle-class milieu in which they and the patients on whom they based their theories moved. For Coats, a different milieu embedded in different stories might produce different kinds of subjects, and "trends in postmodern children's literature . . . may have a significant impact on the kinds of subjects our children become"[106]—yet another reason for optimism about moving past the repressive qualities characteristic of children's literature. In the next chapter I will consider just how different these "postmodern" texts are, but the significant issue at this point is the extent to which children's literature as it currently exists does tend to encourage or assume or invite or construct the same form of subjectivity in its readers.

Speaking about children's literature of Australia, John Stephens outlines how certain "principles, for which Australian society in general ideally strives, together construct an ideology of childhood, which is to some extent common to Western societies because these principles are also basic tenets of Western liberal humanism."[107] It is not difficult to see some of Stephens's principles operating in texts as diverse as "The Purple Jar" and *The Snowy Day*:

1. Autonomous selfhood is necessary to quality of life, and it is desirable, if not essential, for individuals to strive for it.
2. Such a selfhood is intersubjective, not solipsistic; altruistic, not self-serving.
3. Democratically organized political and social structures are preferable to overt or implicit sociopolitical hierarchies, hegemonies or forms of tyranny.
4. The emotional health of human beings, especially children, is best served by life within some, perhaps broadly conceived, version of the nuclear family.[108]

I might conclude that children's literature, at least children's literature as it currently exists, emerges from and is an expression of the values Stephens identifies as "Western liberal humanism"—the values most common in the contemporary middle-class homes of Europe and European settler societies. I might define it as the literature produced for and in order to construct the subjectivity of the children of the middle class.

The historical and ongoing relationships between the existence of that class and an economic system that puts a lot of value in the getting and keeping of property reveals another significant aspect of the subjectivity children's literature tends to construct and support. Suggesting that "visions of the snug place abound in Children's Literature," Jerry Griswold says, "The security of the guarded place is also associated with private property. . . . With every use [by a child protecting a snug space] of the words 'No!' and 'Mine!' likewise comes a healthy assertion of privacy and private property; a declaration of the self fortified and snug behind defense mechanisms. Playing alone, engaging in solitary games in private enclosures, the child rehearses individuality."[109] It is not surprising that so many of the events in texts as diverse as "The Purple Jar" and *Henry Huggins* revolve around issues of getting and spending money.

Griswold's description of the assertion of private property as "healthy" and Stephens's emphasis on autonomous selfhood and democratic structures seem at odds with the oppressiveness of the colonial practices I have been describing. Paradoxically, adults might be understood to be repressing children into an understanding of their autonomy—colonizing them into ideas about freedom and privacy. As I have already suggested, the process by which young humans enter into the social world might be unavoidable, less an objectionable act of repression than a necessary condition of subjectivity; and perhaps repression into a view of oneself as free and autonomous is not all that repressive.

Peter Hollindale's concept of "childness" suggests it isn't. Offering his own word for "the quality of being a child—dynamic, imaginative, experimental, interactive and unstable," he claims that "childness is the distinguishing quality of a text of children's literature, setting it apart from other literature as a genre."[110] But he goes on to add that "it is also the property that the child brings to the reading of a text" (47). Not only do texts of children's literature offer readers adult constructions of childhood, but "children also construct childhood as they go along, and they do it from fictions of various kinds, not merely from social experience" (14). As negotiations between the constructions of childhood that texts offer and the ones that child readers already have or are developing, readings of children's literature allow room for choice and even autonomy.

Whether derived from what Hollindale calls "social experience" or from books written by adults, however, the choices are almost always among adult constructions; even the theoretically subversive versions of being childlike that children often share with each other tend to have been engendered by and allowed by adults. As Hollindale himself acknowledges, his positive view of the room for negotiation available in what he identifies as the "event" (29) of children's literature—the interaction of text and child readers—depends on "a variegated imaginary world of childhood, a multiplicity of childhood possibilities, which will enrich and diversify their sense of what it can mean to be a child" (15). My readings of six apparently various texts suggest to me that children's literature is not all that variegated, nor is it often all that indulgent of variety in the versions of childhood subjectivity it offers.

Children's literature *is* interested in the gender distinctions I have just been considering. Its ideals of autonomy and equality are contaminated by the need for girls to be girlish and boys to be boyish. Those ideals are also contaminated by its clinging to the ideas of class, race, the possession of property, and many other of the registers of difference that have limited and continue to limit the power of individuals to be individuals in the time children's literature has existed. If children's literature works to construct mainstream democratic subjectivities, it does so in the terms of current hegemonic values that limit freedom as well as allow it.

Doubleness

Perhaps what people call "childhood" is always an imaginative construct of the adult mind, always being moved not only outward to blind adults to their actual perceptions of contemporary children but also backward, into the past, to blind them to their memories of their actual past experiences. Perhaps there never was a childhood as innocent, as creative, as spontaneous, as egocentric, as Oedipal as adults like to imagine. Perhaps children are always more like adults in their individual humanity or potential for repression than adults are ever able to see.

If they are, then children's literature as a whole is a dangerous imposition on children, an immoral manipulation of them to serve adult ends—an unwholesome enterprise altogether. I am now some distance away from the optimistic conviction that adults produce texts for children merely to offer children pleasure, no strings attached. Colonialist theory suggests there are nothing but strings attached, yet colonialist theory is hard to ignore.

Not surprisingly, some frequently expressed ideas about the generic nature of children's literature try to have it both ways—to see children's literature as simultaneously fulfilling both adult and child desire, simultaneously offering children what they like and adults what they believe children need. "These days," says Humphrey Carpenter, "we are accustomed to books which fulfil both needs at once. For more than a century it has been possible to pick up stories which both satisfy the child's desire for excitement and contain some moral truth or lesson. In fact, we would think fairly poorly of a modern children's novel which did not satisfy both criteria."[111] I suspect he is right—most of "us" would think just that. It is an assumption common in the field.

What is most interesting about this idea is the absolute degree of its doubleness. It perceives adult needs as different from and opposite to children's needs. It perceives pleasure as inherently and inalterably opposed to learning. And it sees children as themselves double and divided.

The opposition of adult and child is, most significantly, a question of knowledge. Adults know enough not to be governed by their desires. Children do not. For that reason adults need to offer children pleasure in order to teach them—they will not desire to learn because learning is inherently not pleasurable.

The disjunction of learning and pleasure reveals the intrinsic ambivalence of the adult project of what Rose calls securing the child. Despite the claim that one can both please and teach a child at the same time, it is clear that what adults almost always want children to learn is some form of controlling their pleasure, thwarting their desire, being mature enough and moral enough not to seek excitement and self-gratification. So pleasing and teaching are almost always primarily a matter of teaching: adults offer children specific forms of literary pleasure in order to destroy their desire to be pleased in more or less exactly those ways.

This formulation, however, imagines that a child cannot learn not to desire excitement, adventure, instant gratification, and so on unless the child does desire those things in the first place so that the pleasing can be an effective means to the teaching. If the teaching actually occurred, the desire would no longer exist, and the child could no longer be taught by this means. Texts could no longer please a child by offering excitement, adventure, instant gratification. Yet texts purporting to do that are, as Carpenter rightly suggests, the most predominant form of children's literature, and adults tend to hope that child readers will read book after book that claims to operate in this way. Presumably, then, child readers are untaught enough by each one to enjoy the process of the next book's attempt to please and thus teach them. All this suggests how little adults trust that the learning ever does actually occur. It might even suggest a hidden or unconscious wish on the part of adults involved with children's literature for the teaching always to fail—for children to be triumphantly ineducable, so thoroughly creatures of desire that they never will learn the knowledge or possess the wisdom that opposes desire. From this point of view, pleasing and teaching is almost always primarily a matter of pleasing: adults offer children specific forms of literary pleasure in order to fail at the purported purpose of destroying their desire to be pleased in more or less exactly those ways.

In the last two paragraphs I seem to have reached two opposite conclusions. I think both are true. Even the most aggressively pleasurable of texts for children—popular series books like Carolyn Keene's Nancy Drew or K. A. Applegate's Animorphs, for instance, or texts like *Henry Huggins*—make educational claims or establish theoretically moral frameworks that allow the pleasure. Characters act violently and/or adventurously, and readers experience violence and/or adventure, in the context of a declared defense of goodness, justice, and reason against violence, injustice, and chaos so that the texts invite children to disapprove of what the texts themselves offer. Meanwhile, the most assertively didactic of texts for children—Sunday school fables, for instance, or tales like "The Purple Jar"—tend almost always to be based on assumptions about children's inevitable desire for pleasure that undermines their faith in their own ability to manipulate those readers into being different. Such texts unconsciously invite child readers to remain uncontaminated by the very things they seem to be most intent on teaching.

If texts that seem most intent on pleasing pretend to teach and texts that seem most intent on teaching purport to please, then it is logical to conclude that the less extreme texts that occupy the middle part of the spectrum of possible degrees of pleasing or teaching always do both. The double goal of pleasing and teaching means that texts of children's literature tend characteristically and ambivalently to work to both teach and please their implied readers.

Consequently, their vision of childhood is divided. On the one hand, the child of this vision wants nothing but to enjoy, is capable only of enjoying—and does not ever, it seems, enjoy learning about morality or being moral. On the other hand, this child is capable of learning about morality and, presumably, of being moral; otherwise, there would be no point in trying to teach it against its desires. This child is the childlike being of the colonial project: at the same time a creature with the potential to become an adult and a creature alien from and opposite to adult humanity. And children's literature is a literature that characteristically possesses a double vision of childhood.

More specifically, it tends simultaneously to celebrate and denigrate both childhood desire and adult knowledge. As a didactic literature—giving children the knowledge adults think they need—it wants to urge children to stop being childish and learn to be better and different. As a literature of childhood wish-fulfillment fantasy—giving children the protection from knowledge adults think they need and the indulgence in childishness adults think or hope they like—it wants children to stay exactly as they so wonderfully already are. Therefore, and as I have found myself suggesting a number of times in this chapter, children's literature is inherently and centrally ambivalent—and its ambivalence results from these pulls in opposite directions.

Commentators tend, typically, to emphasize one pull over the other. Some, focusing on the ways in which children's literature allows or invites children to be childlike, emphasize ways in which it questions or allows space for the questioning of adult authority and adult values. Remember, for instance, Peter Hunt's conviction that "child readers . . . will read against societal norms."[112] Kimberley Reynolds suggests that the literature itself often encourages them to do just that, that it "is both a breeding ground and an incubator for innovation. There are certainly many ordinary children's books—at least as many as there are banal books for adults—but there are also aspects about writing for children that result in a kind of wild zone where new ways of writing are explored, given

shape, and so made part of the intellectual and aesthetic currency of that generation of child readers."[113] Among these aspects are ideas about childhood creativity
and rebelliousness that encourage writers to be creative and rebellious: "there is
abundant textual evidence suggesting that addressing a child audience removes
some of the censors and filters that come into play when writing for adults"
(ibid., 16).

Speaking of her own childhood reading, Alison Lurie remembers "the sacred
texts of childhood, whose authors had not forgotten what it was like to be a child,"
and says, "The great subversive works of children's literature suggest that there
are other views of human life beside those of the shopping mall and the corporation. They mock current assumptions and express the imaginative, unconventional, noncommercial view of the world in its simplest and purest form. They
appeal to the imaginative, questioning, rebellious child within all of us, renew our
instinctive energy, and act as a force for change."[114] For Lurie, as for Reynolds,
children's literature at its best, and when it is most characteristic, represents a
subversive attack on conventional adult wisdom.

If it does this, of course, it can only be because its adult writers wish to be free
from and attack the conventions of other adults. It is a rebellion by some adults
against other adults under the banner of something here identified as childhood.
It is interesting that Lurie should focus on childhood as a quality inherent "in all
of us"—including, obviously, adults—but needing to be appealed to and, presumably, awakened in everyone—including, it seems, children—by the right sort of
texts. For her, being childlike is curiously separable from the mere fact of being a
child. Lurie confirms some of my conclusions in chapter 1 by suggesting that
children's literature has the purpose of teaching children—and in this case, also,
adults—how to be the right kind of childlike being.

What Lurie calls subversive—and to some extent what Reynolds calls radical—
is a variation on Paul Hazard's worship of the alien otherness of children, their
refusal to operate by adult understandings of reason and logic. It is not surprising
that Lurie should see children's literature as portraying "an ideal world of perfect-
ible beings . . . a paradisal universe"[115]—a place defined exactly by its difference
from reality and real possibilities. It subverts, it seems, not so much by seeing
through conventional adult claims to truth and showing things as they truly are
but rather by imagining an unreal utopian alternative that Lurie believes opens
minds to new, not-actually-existing possibilities. It would be just as logical to
assume that this utopia might be less subversive of convention than supportive of
it, in that it represents an escape from conventional understandings that leaves

those understandings intact and in control of how powerful adults perceive the world and administer the lives of children and other less powerful adults.

Lurie often identifies the subversive elements in the children's books that she discusses as existing alongside other elements supportive of conventional adult values. She speaks, for instance, of the "concealed moral" of Beatrix Potter's *Tale of Peter Rabbit*: "That disobedience and exploration are more fun than good behavior, and not really all that dangerous, whatever Mother may say."[116] The subversive tends to exist alongside and in the context of the nonsubversive, and, I believe, the nonsubversive is just as likely to subvert the subversive as vice versa. Even in Lurie's own readings of them, these texts are more ambivalent than Lurie would like to claim. Reynolds is much more up-front about that ambivalence, focusing on the "radical" qualities of children's books but speaking also of Salman Rushdie's *Haroun and the Sea of Stories* as representative of "the dichotomous nature of children's literature itself. On the one hand, it is dependent on and respectful of the education system and the didactic tradition; on the other, it is subversive and liberating, mocking and critiquing the values and practices of those same systems."[117]

Other commentators tend to emphasize the respectful side of this ambivalence and focus on ways in which children's literature not only works to impose adult values on children but also manages to subvert what appears to be subversive about it. Beverly Lyon Clark asserts that "there's a strong temptation, when one is consciously addressing children, not to be subversive but to be preservationist."[118] As a result, children's literature most characteristically reinforces conventional adult values in ways that tend to subvert any potentially subversive elements within it.

"To ensure the conditions of production (and hence the condition of financial solvency)," says Roderick McGillis, "the publisher must ensure nothing in the books he or she publishes alienates prospective book buyers. One way to do this is to perpetuate the values and cultural conceptions of the ruling group within the pages of the books turned out by the publisher's production line."[119] Speaking of so-called postmodern books, works such as the Ahlbergs' *The Jolly Postman* (1986) and Jon Scieszka's *The Stinky Cheese Man and Other Fairly Stupid Tales* (1992), McGillis asks, "Are these books in any political sense radical, or do they too put to rest the transgressive instincts of their readers?" (112). Like, I suspect, McGillis himself, Jill May would say the latter: "Children's authors are also aware that just as they are not children, neither are the professionals who will publish and evaluate the worth of their stories. . . . Their messages must be constructed around the child's perceptions, but they must be couched in a familiar structure that will appeal to adults. And so, children's literature texts hold traditional patterns and seem to address acceptable societal concerns about childhood and growing up, even when they are subversive."[120]

It is important not to lose sight of what McGillis and May are suggesting here, important to be suspicious of claims that children's literature might have some sort of revolutionary force opposed to conventional adult wisdom. Consider, for instance, Herbert Kohl, the author of *Should We Burn Babar?* who asks, "Are there any books written for young people that question the economic and social basis for our society?"[121] His own answer is, very few, and he speaks of "a need that exists in children's literature, a hole that exists in the body of the work" (68). But as Kohl goes on to outline the features of the literature he finds "so necessary and so lacking" (78), he recommends the inclusion of "a stranger, usually an adult, who offers protection, kindness, and a new vision of how to solve problems and grow up. This adult is not like other adults, but a character whose life allows her or him to have special insight into the inner workings of the human mind or the social world" (83). In Kohl's "radical literature," as in the conventional literature he opposes, child readers are invited to accept an adult vision of who they are. As does Lurie, Kohl imagines subversions of conventional adult values by means of a nonsubversive acquiescence to another adult's views.

Logically speaking, however, it is just as possible to believe that the subversive elements subvert the attempts to subvert them as it is to believe that those attempts are successful. This is especially likely in light of the reasons I have laid out throughout this chapter for identifying a central and perhaps inescapable ambivalence in the thinking about childhood that led to and still sustains the production of children's literature. This thinking celebrates childhood innocence and also wishes to disperse it; wants to please children as they are and also make them feel guilty about their pleasure; wants to admire childhood wisdom and replace it with something different and better; wants to protect children from harm and also offer them exciting adventures; and so on and so on. The literature could not exist without these ambivalences, and it is likely to be itself ambivalent and to express ambivalence about the relative merits of the subversive and the nonsubversive. As Reynolds suggests, it is "dichotomous."

I have returned, once more, to the idea of doubleness and to that word: *ambivalence*. According to Zohar Shavit, texts of children's literature are ambivalent when they "belong simultaneously to more than one system [a version of what Bourdieu calls a field of literary production] and consequently are read differently (though concurrently), by at least two groups of readers."[122] Shavit views texts originally written for adults that have become children's classics as the model for most other children's literature. She therefore accounts for its ambivalence in terms of its aspiration to be understood one way by its presumed audience of children and a different way by its other audience of adults who purchase the books and award the prizes. I am struck by the implication in Shavit's reading of children's literature that each of its audiences sees only one of the two differing meanings. Paradoxically, it is an ambivalent literature whose ambivalence is not apparent to any of its implied readers. The arguments I have been pursuing here suggest the opposite conclusion: that the dichotomous ambivalence of children's literature is so thoroughgoing that an awareness of it is invited from all its implied readers.

To produce and / or recommend texts that will make sense to less sophisticated children, the adults who admire the ways in which texts of children's literature share the qualities of serious texts of adult literature can and, indeed, must still presume to have the ability to imagine how these children will understand the texts. More significant, the children capable of understanding the less sophisticated half of the ambivalent meaning of these texts are not necessarily unaware of the more sophisticated half. As my arguments in chapter 1 suggest—and as Rose's ideas about securing children and Lurie's views on subversion do also— these texts characteristically invite children to enact adult-engendered versions of childhood that require various kinds of moves beyond their own inherent childishness. The readers these texts imply are very much aware of the shadow texts of complex adult knowledge that underpin the apparent simplicity of the actual texts and, therefore, are aware of the ways in which the texts are ambivalent about childhood and invite ambivalence about it in child readers.

For adult readers, an ambivalence about childhood is external to oneself, more or less merely theoretical. But for children, to be ambivalent about childhood is, exactly, to be ambivalent about oneself—to have a divided sense of what one is or ought to be. Children's literature not only expresses ambivalence about childhood but also, and perhaps most centrally, invites its readers to share it. It is characteristically a literature that addresses a divided child reader.

One the one hand, the implied readers characteristic of children's literature expect to be gratified by the text's ability to please the people they already are—to, perhaps thoughtlessly, enjoy being who they are and wish to stay that way. On the other hand, these implied readers are also expected to be willing to be unsettled by new knowledge and open to learning to be different and presumably better from it. The inevitable result of experiencing these contradictory impulses is to be pulled between them. Characteristically, the texts seem to resolve the tension by, eventually, dismissing the value either of the pleasure or of the need to learn one's way past it; they achieve their happy endings by denying one-half of the divided subjects they imply and work to construct. But also characteristically, the apparent resolution is only apparent. As long as the ambivalence in adult ideas about childhood remains, the division in the implied child reader remains. Children's literature characteristically works to construct a child like its central characters—characters like Edgeworth's Rosamond and Cleary's Henry Huggins, who simultaneously and continuously experience the opposing pulls of thoughtless (and possibly subversive) self-satisfaction and an interest in and acquiescence to communally shared adult understandings and the constraint of individual desire they inevitably require. Canonical texts—the ones many children know and enjoy and most adult experts admire—tend to be those that present this division in its most irresolvable terms. As didactic fables, they want to urge children to stop being childish and learn to be better and different. As subversive wish-fulfillment fantasies, they want children to stay exactly as they already are and offer depictions of what Maria Nikolajeva identifies as "resisting growing up—the eternal 'Peter Pan complex' of children's fiction, in which adulthood is presented as undesirable and threatening."[123] Such texts happily inform readers that Potter's Peter Rabbit or Max of Sendak's *Where the Wild Things Are* mature through the process of being triumphantly wild and childlike or that Montgomery's Anne can grow up without actually changing or growing up at all: as Anne herself says toward the end of *Anne of Green Gables*, "I'm not a bit changed—not really. I'm only just pruned down and branched out. The real *me*—back here—is just the same."[124]

Endings of this sort emerge from what Roni Natov calls "the central question of much of children's literature: How can we grow up without losing the spontaneity of our natural responses?"[125] Indeed, the triumphal exuberance of texts of this sort suggests the possibility that the ambivalence and the division I have been describing might be intended and desirable effects of the discourse about childhood from which children's literature emerges—might be the very thing that discourse is most centrally designed to produce.

Analyzing the subjectivity typically constructed by colonial discourse, Homi Bhabha describes it as a form of mimicry that in some important ways echoes the process I have been describing here—the ways in which children's literature and other products of adult discourse about childhood invite child readers to mimic not, in this case, the behavior of the adults themselves but rather the childhood that adults imagine for them. Bhabha says:

The discourse of mimicry is constructed around an *ambivalence;* in order to be effective, mimicry must continually produce its slippage, its excess, its difference. . . . Mimicry is thus the sign of a double articulation; a complex strategy of reform, regulation and discipline, which "appropriates" the Other as it visualizes power. Mimicry is also the sign of the inappropriate, however, a difference of recalcitrance which coheres the dominant strategic function of colonial power, intensifies surveillance, and poses an immanent threat to both "normalized" knowledges and disciplinary powers. . . . The success of colonial appropriation depends on a proliferation of inappropriate objects that ensure its strategic failure, so that mimicry is at once resemblance and menace.[126]

If I rehearse this argument in terms of adult colonizations of children, I arrive at the following. Adults offer children images of childhood that they expect children to mimic in order to be the right kind of children. The necessity of this process itself inscribes its inevitable failure: children are not yet and not actually what adults wish them to pretend to be, which is exactly why adults wish them to pretend to be it, for their own good. The mask of mimicry therefore peculiarly requires and confirms the necessity and necessary continuance of that which it hides. That which the mimicry hides survives the act of hiding and thus reinforces the need for the hiding to take place. In other words, children can be understood to need to pretend to be better than they actually are and occupy a childhood they don't actually experience only by continuing to be what they actually are in spite of or because of the pretense. They are necessarily double and divided—both that which they mimic, childhood as envisaged and imposed on them by adults, and that which underlies and survives and transgresses that adult version of childhood. The adult impulse to control children, to keep them "safe"— the impulse I believe to be at the heart of children's literature—requires that children be both controllable and uncontrollable, both what adults want them to be and incapable of being what adults want them to be. Children's literature can continue to attempt to secure children only as long as it believes them to be both securable and not securable.

Or, in other words, divided. The divided child is the only possible child constructed by children's literature. And this explains, I think, how children's literature characteristically manages both to confirm adult culture and subvert what it confirms, both to be subversive and to subvert its own subversions—and why, therefore, its success always implies its failure. As Bhabha says of the mimicry of the colonized, "The *menace* of mimicry is its *double* vision which in disclosing the ambivalence of colonial discourse also disrupts its authority."[127] That children need a children's literature to police them firmly establishes both the policing itself and the unlikelihood of their ever being permanently policed.

Specific Markers

I have clearly rejected the possibility that a range of common adult assumptions about children and childhood might be generically or universally true or that such assumptions might accurately be used to establish what children should read or what texts should fall within the boundaries of children's literature. But because these assumptions about children are so widespread among the adult writers, editors, and librarians who occupy the field of children's literature, I have also postulated that they might well lead to and account for the characteristic qualities of the texts produced in the field. This suggests an important definition of children's literature that deserves more detailed investigation: the idea that it is a genre of literature whose defining characteristics can be accounted for by conventional assumptions about and constructions of childhood. The issue here is not what children do actually like or do need. It is how adult perceptions of what children like or need shape the literature that adults provide for children in ways that provide it with distinct markers that allow it to be identified as a genre.

If widely held assumptions about what children like or need operate in the field—if ideas about the intended audience shape the texts the field produces—then the genre's characteristic markers are likely to be present even in texts by writers who do not consciously share the assumptions. According to Mike Cadden, "It is both easy and sensible to combine the notions of genre and audience when one is writing in a genre named for an audience—text and context necessarily become conflated. Genre and audience are combined rather than confused with each other."[128] Cadden goes on to suggest that the genre might itself then function as an audience: "Perhaps it isn't odd to talk about genre as an audience. Genre is an audience in its own way, an audience to which people write. It is a living tradition with clear rules and expectations for discursive behavior. It is as much a context for conversation as that provided by an audience of children" (137). The paradox here is that a "conversation" with a genre shaped by its allegiance to commonly held assumptions about children is already a conversation with children—albeit the generalized children of convention.

As a result, and as Cadden concludes, "The conflation of audience and genre . . . is a phenomenon that itself marks literature for children as a unique genre shaped in part by its own demands" (146). In the pages that follow, I consider various specific qualities of children's literature that seem to emerge from assumptions about children and that operate as defining markers for the genre. Clifton Fadiman implies the existence of such features when he speaks of "the medium's high esthetic capacity to embody certain specific themes and symbolic structures, often more imaginatively than does the mainstream."[129] But what are these themes and symbolic structures?

According to Judith Hillman, texts of children's literature commonly display five specific characteristics:

- Typical childhood experiences written from a child's perspective
- Children or childlike characters
- Simple and direct plots that focus on action
- A feeling of optimism and innocence (e.g., happy endings are the norm)
- A tendency toward combining reality and fantasy.[130]

This is an insightful list. Unfortunately, Hillman makes no attempt to explain *why* these qualities might be so characteristic of this literature. Although Fred Inglis does snappishly assert that "too much genre-chopping is a tedious side-industry of literary theory. . . . Let us rather count as children's fiction whatever children read," he does go on to admit that "it is simply ignorant not to claim that children's novelists have developed a set of conventions for their work,"[131] and he does provide some idea of what they might be: shorter and simpler texts, child protagonists, a relative lack of concern about probability in plotting. But he explains these primarily as natural extensions of how adults generally talk to children. Myles McDowell offers a somewhat more detailed list of characteristics: "children's books are generally shorter; they tend to favour an active rather than a passive treatment, with dialogue and incident rather than description and introspection; child protagonists are the rule; conventions are much used; the story develops within a clear-cut moral schematism which much adult fiction ignores; children's books tend to be optimistic rather than depressive; language is child-oriented; plots are of a distinctive order, probability is often disregarded; and one could go on endlessly talking of magic, and fantasy, and simplicity, and adventure."[132] McDowell claims that these "essential" differences between children's books and ones for adults exist "simply because children think quantitatively differently from adults" (52). While it is true that the adult assumption about childlike thinking plays an important part in making children's literature what it is, that doesn't explain how all the specific characteristics McDowell lists result from these assumptions.

I assume it is such explanations Robert Bator is after when he says that "those who perceive juvenile literature as a single genre, as do Isabelle Jan and Perry

Nodelman, would do well to plot its distinctive features."[133] The rest of this chapter is a response to this invitation. It deals with definitions such as Hillman's that focus on one or more of these distinctive features, in an effort to account for their status as characteristic markers of children's literature as a genre.

About Children

Some commentators view children's literature as marked significantly by its subjects: it is about children and/or childhood. Tomlinson and Lynch-Brown say, "Children's books are about the experiences of childhood," and Temple and his collaborators list as one of the usual qualities of children's books "[a] child protagonist and an issue that concerns children."[134] While it is true that texts for children do most often purport to be about the experiences of childhood, they are actually so only in relation to the extent to which adult authors' readings of the nature of childhood experience accord with that of actual children themselves. They may do so successfully for two reasons. First, adult authors might accurately remember or observe childlike experiences shared by large numbers of children. Second, as I suggested earlier, the childhood imagined by children's books might be the means by which actual children learn how to be suitably childlike. The version of childhood presented by children's literature may be accurate as a self-fulfilling prophecy.

In any case, and as Tomlinson and Lynch-Brown go on to suggest, children's books deal with an "amazingly diverse" range of other subjects beside childhood. Many stories for children are about not children but animals. Fairy tales like "Cinderella" and "Snow White"—which, despite their history as orally circulated folktales with an audience including adults, must surely be included in any accepted sense of what children's literature has been and currently is—are about marriageable young adults. And children's nonfiction deals with any and all aspects of reality, not just childhood.

But it does so, of course, with what its authors perceive as the specific needs of child readers in mind—it addresses itself to what the authors understand to be a childlike understanding; thus it encourages a theoretically childlike view of its vast range of unchildlike topics. Similarly, fairy tales discuss the romantic entanglements of young adults from a viewpoint that many adults see as suitably childlike enough to be shared with children. The tales appear to be suitable literature for children because their central supposedly adult characters and their implied child readers are innocent enough to understand adult sexual attraction in apparently nonsexual ways untypical of adults but presumably typical of children. The many children's stories about animals also tend to describe the animals as childlike (as the childlike is conventionally understood) and assume their child readers will think of the animals as being somehow like themselves. Even though they do not focus on child characters, these three kinds of texts do deal with childhood experience.

The Eyes of Children

Or they deal, at least, with experience as understood "childishly." I might propose a variation on this kind of definition of children's literature—that children's literature characteristically describes things from a childlike point of view. As the children's writer Nina Bawden says, "The only real difference between writing for adults or for children is whose eyes I am looking through."[135] Aidan Chambers suggests that this concept might be technically true—that texts written for children tend literally to be focalized through the point of view of a child: "In books where the implied reader is a child, authors tend to reinforce the relationship [between adult author and child reader] by adopting in their second self—giving the book, if you prefer—a very sharply focused point of view. They tend to achieve that focus by putting at the centre of the story a child through whose being everything is seen and felt."[136]

The basic assumption here is that childlike perception is different from adult perception but that adults can retain it and draw on it—as, presumably, writers for children do and even must. Thus, C. S. Lewis says, "We must write for children out of those elements in our own imagination which we share with children."[137] Childlike perception—presumably a result of immaturity—is something that can, curiously, survive the maturing process. Adults can continue not to think as adults and to think in childlike ways at least part of the time. This is a clear signal that the childlikeness under consideration here is an intellectual construct of adults just as much as or even more than it is a characteristic behavior of inexperienced human beings destroyed by the process of maturation.

The continuance of childlike thinking in adults may be simply a matter of memory. The children's novelist Phillipa Pearce says, "Writing about and for children, one should have a view almost from the inside, to re-create—not what childhood looks like now—but what it felt like then."[138] The children's novelist William Mayne agrees: "I write for myself, but myself of long ago."[139] So does the children's novelist Ivan Southall: "I am wholly *with* the child, I become a child, in the pages of a book my heart beats with the pulse of a child, I become a child. . . . Putting away childish things, surely, has nothing to do with putting away the child. It is a total distortion of terms. The child should go on inside you."[140] The children's writer Meindert de Jong also agrees: "To get back to the essence [of childhood] you can only go down. You can only go in—deep in. Down through all the deep, mystic intuitive layers of the subconscious back into your own childhood. And if you go deep enough, get basic enough, become again the child you were, it seems reasonable that by way of the subconscious you have come into what must be the universal child. Then, and only then, do you write for the child."[141] Numerous other writers echo this opinion and suggest that they write for the child they once were, still hidden within them. According to Jerry Griswold, "Because they are still connected to their childhoods and sympathetic, then, the best writers for children can speak to the young. . . . Simply said, the great writers for children know—and their stories speak of and reveal—what it feels like to be a kid."[142]

All of these comments assume that what appeals to the child the authors once were will appeal to the children they hope for as an audience—that childlike perception is a universal experience. Not surprisingly, writers who express this view do not hesitate to define exactly what that childlike vision is. Eleanor Cameron, who says a writer "cannot look back; he has got to enter in," goes on to say that the essence of childhood is "the dimension of amazement" and quotes Rachel Carson: "A child's world is fresh and new and beautiful, full of wonder and excitement."[143] Fred Inglis uses a similar string of adjectives when he speaks about a group of children's novels he admires: "The joy they bring revives in us the childlike qualities of freshness and innocence and delight."[144]

Inglis's comment suggests another definition. Since children's literature is written by adults no longer children, no longer innocent, and since it seems to focus so much on what is beautiful about innocence, children's literature is a literature of nostalgia. According to Julia Dusinberre, "Mark Twain set in *The Adventures of Tom Sawyer* a fashion for writing about children not only for the amusement of the child reader, but in order too that the adult might recapture the child that he had been."[145] Children's literature in this tradition—or any text for children read by adults in this traditional way—represents what Valerie Krips identifies as an act of "returning to a past in which the problems of adulthood are by and large unknown."[146] Suggesting that Grahame's *The Wind in the Willows* "is redolent of a nostalgia which is strongest when grown-ups remember their childhood at its best," Inglis adds, "That nostalgia deeply and necessarily stains a great many books for children and is a source of strength as much as weakness. It is a cadence in which to judge the present against its own ideal antecedents."[147]

As I suggested earlier, Paul Hazard also nostalgically asserts that there is a separate "world of childhood." He goes on to suggest that the stories that will appeal to the lighthearted irrational creatures who inhabit that world are "those that offer to children an intuitive and direct way of knowledge, a simple beauty capable of being perceived immediately, arousing in their souls a vibration which will endure all their lives."[148] What is interesting here is that it is adults who are doing the offering of this "intuitive and direct way of knowledge." It must come *in*directly from adults, presumably because it is not so intuitive after all. If it were, then children would have it already and would not need to be offered it. So there is a double paradox here. Adults, theoretically nonintuitive by virtue of their adulthood, must provide intuitive knowledge for theoretically intuitive children. Children, theoretically intuitive by virtue of their childhood, must get intuitive knowledge from theoretically nonintuitive adults. Childhood and a childlike point of view are, once more, constructs of adult minds that adults work to impose on children, in part by means of children's literature.

In engaging with the adult constructions of childhood offered by texts of children's literature, the implied child readers of children's literature might be said to be learning to perform childhood, somewhat as Judith Butler suggests people generally learn to perform gender: "Gender is the repeated stylization of the body, a set of repeated acts within a highly rigid regulatory frame that congeal over time to produce the appearance of a substance, of a natural sort of being."[149] So, too, childhood is a set of acts represented repetitively not only in literature but in all other adult communications with children. This suggests another definition, with other implications: children's literature is literature that encourages child readers to perform specific versions of childhood.

Despite the suggestion of playfulness and the freedom to play otherwise suggested by the idea of performing, this sort of performativity is inherently repressive (or, to use more positive language, normativizing). If successful, the "repeated acts" do "congeal"—become what those performing them believe themselves to naturally be. Suggesting that "adult writers construct childhood when they write for and about children," Peter Hollindale adds that "children also construct childhood as they go along."[150] Ideas of performativity make it clear that the mechanisms of construction—identification, mimicry, repetition—do implicate children themselves in their adoption of adult versions of childhood. But as I suggested earlier, that involvement doesn't necessarily represent much freedom: the childhood adults generally and children's literature specifically most often invite children to perform is and has been fairly stable across the centuries.

There is, however, liberatory potential in the realization that, as Butler says, "the inner truth of gender is a fabrication and . . . a true gender is a fantasy instituted and inscribed on the surface of bodies."[151] So, too, is childhood, as most often understood and as most often depicted in texts of children's literature and inscribed on children's bodies, a fabrication and a fantasy.

Roni Natov offers insights into how the invitation to readers to perform childhood and adopt the fantasy works. On the one hand, she sees adults as separated from their own childhood, "severed, to one degree or another, from childhood memory, and therefore, from the imagination—from a natural sense of wonder and originality of thought." But, she adds, "Behind the fractured adult a child hides, estranged from his or her own history."[152] Adults write about childhood in an effort to regain contact with this hidden child—more or less the same child that writers for children speak of as being within them. As Inglis says, "The best children's books reawaken our innocence."[153]

Natov argues that the "literature of childhood" that does this sort of reawakening consists both of texts written for children and ones written for adults. But she shows surprisingly little interest in child readers or in how they might read the texts identified as being for them. "The majority of works considered here," she says, "belong as much to adults as to children." In honor of what she calls her "focus on the imagination of childhood, on how its formation and development is portrayed,"[154] her readings even of children's books focus on what readers can learn from them *about* childhood.

That makes some sense for adults—but what about children? Why do children need to have the experience Inglis suggests children's fiction offers readers of having their innocence restored? Why do they need adults to teach them about childhood? If childhood imagination is, as Natov claims, "natural," why must adults do the imagining of it for them?

Inglis focuses much of his work on what fiction teaches children: speaking of the importance of having "a way of understanding the world and living honorably in it," he asserts that "the best guides to it for children are the best novelists for children."[155] Although this might make sense in terms of children growing into more mature understandings of themselves, it doesn't account for why they need to be "restored" to adult understandings of their current innocence as children. How is being restored to innocence during childhood a movement into usefully mature understanding?

According to Inglis, "The re-enchantment of the universe is the point of a great deal of what is written for and read to children."[156] Similarly, Natov frequently reads texts for both children and adults in terms of how, as in her description of a tale by Hoffman, they offer opportunities for readers to "explore and reclaim the internal child-spirit who will guide us into the substantive imaginative realm."[157] But while she often suggests that adults don't allow children to act "naturally," she never really explains how it is that child readers might be divorced enough from their "internal child-spirit" to be aware of their separation from it or be in continual need of guidance toward finding it. For her, it seems, "childhood" is not necessarily or even very often what children experience but instead what they *ought* to experience, what all human beings ought to experience. According to Natov, *The Diary of Opal Whitely*, which may or may not have actually been written by a young child, "resonates with authenticity perhaps because it is told through the metaphoric language and with the intensity that ordinary children may feel but be unable to articulate" (40). Paradoxically, this text seems real to Natov because it misrepresents childhood reality in ways that satisfy her adult understanding of it. In offering what Natov sees as similarly adult articulations of childhood, the texts for children she discusses must inevitably be understood as teaching children how to be acceptably childlike. She sees them as therapeutic in exactly that way: "My concern here is to find in the imaginative expression of childhood a poetics for children. How is their experience captured so that it becomes a landscape where they can turn for solace as well as inspiration?" (220). One clear answer to her question is that these texts offer children what are identified as acceptably childlike points of view as models for how to understand themselves as children—they teach children how to be childlike.

There are, of course, texts of adult literature that describe things from a childlike point of view—not just nostalgic and sentimental evocations of the joys of childhood like the poems of Eugene Field, not just more poetic evocations of childhood like many of the adult texts Natov focuses on, but also less reassuring literary texts like James Joyce's *Portrait of the Artist as a Young Man*, Margaret Atwood's *Cat's Eye*, Roddy Doyle's *Paddy Clarke Ha Ha Ha*, and William Blake's *Songs of Innocence*. In these and other adult texts, however, the implied reader is clearly not a child who might be understood to be sharing that childlike view. As Tomlinson and Lynch-Brown say, and contrary to Natov, "Stories *about* childhood told in nostalgic or overly sentimental terms are inappropriate"[158]—not within the boundaries of what we usually mean by "children's literature."

Yet children's literature is about childhood and is, in fact, often sentimental and nostalgic. Witness Inglis's focus on reawakening and reenactment and the various comments I quoted earlier from writers like Cameron and Hazard. In what way might adult texts that offer a childlike point of view be different from characteristic texts written for children?

The difference, I think, emerges from the readers these adult texts about children imply. Their readers are almost always being invited to see through and beyond what the focalized children in them see—to understand the limitations and errors of childlike innocence, either in order to celebrate the joy of, or to bemoan the tragedy of, its blindness to life's complexities. There is another and different version of what the events described mean, implied exactly by the blindness and limitations of what the focalized characters believe to be the truth. In texts for children the implied reader usually appears not to be required to have—even seems to be assumed not to have—such awareness. It seems that readers are expected to identify with characters like Henry Huggins or Peter of *The Snowy Day*, to see and understand what Henry and Peter experience as Henry and Peter see and understand the world. For these implied readers, it seems, the blindness and limitation do not appear to be blind or limited.

According to Andrea Wyile, this limited point of view is a key feature of children's literature, which she sees as working primarily to engage readers by discouraging a perception of ways in which they might differ from child characters—particularly first-person narrators of their own stories: "Engaging narration privileges the focalizer, who sees and speaks in the narrative, and distancing narration privileges the voice of the narrating agent, who sees and comments on the actions of the focalizer from a (noticeable) distance at the time of narration. Most, if not all, narration for children and young adults is engaging and not distancing. Distancing narration is not prevalent in children's literature; it is most suited to adult narratives.[159] Wyile's descriptions of this state of affairs leave unspoken the obvious reason why immediate engagement might be suited to and characteristic of children's literature. In engaging readers in this immediate way, adult authors can more easily encourage child readers to accept the child characters they have constructed from their adult understanding of childhood as accurate versions of what it means to be young. Wyile rightly claims that first-person narratives in which events are narrated shortly after they have taken place are more engaging than ones (like the novels by Joyce, Atwood, and Doyle) in which an adult remembers childhood experiences from the distance of years. But they can be more engaging exactly to the extent that they conceal the actual fact of an adult writer's distance from a child's or teenager's experience.

But what is concealed is not necessarily absent. There remains the question of the shadow texts that I postulated in chapter 1 as aspects of *Henry Huggins* and *The Snowy Day* and that I believe characteristically hover around most texts of children's literature. These shadow texts imply a less innocent point of view that qualifies and changes the meaning of the childlike focalization. If shadow texts exist—and surely they almost always do—then texts of children's literature do not operate in a significantly different way from the way in which texts for adults with child focalizations do. In both cases the texts invite readers to perceive the limitations of the focalization in order to encourage an attitude toward childlikeness.

But there is an important difference in terms of what appears to be the significance of that attitude—what the purpose of adopting it might be for readers invited to adopt it. The adult readers of Joyce or Blake or Doyle are being invited to develop attitudes to the significance of a way of thinking and being clearly separate from themselves and unobtainable by them. Experienced adults cannot become innocent children, so finding cause to bemoan the blindness of childlike innocence invites adults to celebrate their lack of innocence, and finding cause to celebrate the joys of childlike innocence invites adults to bemoan their inescapable experience. One way or the other, childhood is the other that allows adults to understand their existence as adults. In texts for children, however, the shadow of a less innocent point of view that hovers around apparently innocent focalizations appears to have the opposite purpose. These texts assume that their implied readers can somehow both understand how a noninnocent adult outsider might view innocence and yet still be innocent in the terms they describe. In texts for children, then, finding cause to bemoan the blindness of childlike innocence invites child readers to bemoan their own blindness but not necessarily to become less blind. Finding cause to celebrate the joys of childlike innocence invites child readers to celebrate their own innocence and, as I suggested in chapter 1, to imagine themselves to be (or, perhaps more exactly, to pretend to imagine themselves to be) innocent in order to please adults. To use Wyile's terms, children's literature characteristically offers child readers distancing experiences that masquerade as immediate ones and invite them to reinvent their own actual immediate experiences in terms of distanced adult imaginings of childhood immediacy.

According to Anne Lundin, "Children's books are the site of adult re-creation of an earlier geography. The locales of many children's books are the enshrouded landscapes of childhood, remade, re-visioned."[160] The remembering automatically implies a transformation into something different. This sort of formulation makes apparent a thread running through much of what I have been saying here: that childhood as characteristically presented in texts of children's literature is a fictional construct for *both* children and adults. It is an invention of adults, the main quality of which is exactly the way in which it is conceived to be opposite to adulthood. It is an imposition on children, the main quality of which might well be the ways in which it is conceived to be different from, even opposite to, the actual perceptions and experiences of the children it is designed consciously or unconsciously to police. The childhood of children's literature might turn out to be a mind-set that never actually exists for either children or adults except in the presence of and in comparison to two other mind-sets—that presumed to be normal in adults and that presumed to exist in real children prior to their reading of the literature. In other words, the childhood of children's literature has its own shadow texts. Inherently conceived as one component of a pair of binary opposites, it cannot exist without those shadow texts.

Simplicity and Sublimation

The most widespread way in contemporary culture of enunciating what distinguishes children's literature from other texts is to say, simply, that children's literature is simple literature. Students in the children's literature classes I have taught frequently express the idea that texts for children are short because children have short attention spans, use simple language because children can't understand complex language, and have large, bright pictures because children are incapable of responding to small or dark ones. And there is certainly some truth to these perceptions, at least in terms of how common adult assumptions about what children lack do lead to characteristic qualities in texts of children's literature.

They certainly lie behind one particularly famous formulation of what children's literature is: children's literature is literature that leaves things out. This is the position that Bator implies when he speaks of "a necessarily limited literature" and that C. S. Lewis adopts when he famously says, "This form permits, or compels, one to leave out things I wanted to leave out. It compels one to throw all the force of the book into what was done and said. It checks what a kind but discerning critic called 'the expository demon' in me."[161] Nina Bawden agrees: "You can, and should, leave out things that are beyond their comprehension."[162] As I suggested earlier in discussing definitions of children's literature built on excluding certain kinds of texts or certain kinds of knowledge, texts for children form a literature built on exclusions and limitations, of saying less to children than adults know or are capable of hearing themselves. As Maria Nikolajeva suggests, "One of the strongest conventions of children's fiction is the absence of all the prominent aspects of human (i.e., adult) civilization, including law, money, and labor. . . . Children, real as well as fictional, are supposed to grow up unaware of and unrestricted by these tokens of adulthood."[163]

But saying less than one knows means knowing more. Something can be simple only in relation to something less simple, so "simple" almost inevitably means "simpler." Logic suggests that only those with knowledge of more complex texts can identify children's literature as simple. In theory, at least, adults certainly don't expect children to perceive them as simple. For children, theoretically, the texts represent as much of the truth about the world as adults assume children are capable of knowing. But as I have just suggested, the childhood of children's literature makes sense only in terms of its implied binary opposites, shadows that imply a different and more complex knowledge in child readers and in adults in general—so the simplicity of the texts themselves inevitably implies more complex shadows such as those I proposed in chapter 1. The simple implies and invites awareness of the less simple, even if only, as is often the case in children's literature, to confirm the virtues of simplicity for either children or adults or both.

The idea that texts of children's literature written by adults imply shadow texts relates to another powerful take on leaving things out as a central characteristic of children's literature: the idea that children's literature is a literature of sublimation. The idea is Freud's as understood by Peter Brooks, who proposes that "novels define themselves as children's literature through a kind of lack, an absence, or perhaps more accurately, a sublimation."[164] In psychoanalytical discourse "sublimation" is a capacity of the sexual instinct, which has, Freud says, "the power to replace its immediate aim by other aims which may be valued more highly and which are not sexual."[165] That which has been sublimated in a text remains, housed in what might be called the unconscious of the text—that aspect of it that it does not appear to know or wish to assert but that is apparent to readers who learn how to perceive its traces, to read through that in which it is sublimated. For such readers its presence is implied by the very fact of its apparent absence—for of course the absence can be perceived as an absence only by those who know what might have been present and isn't. I reiterate my view that this group includes the implied readers characteristic of texts written for children.

But what exactly is being sublimated in this way? A Freudian such as Brooks or Jacqueline Rose would argue that it is the true and truly disturbing fact of and nature of childhood sexuality—bisexual, polymorphous, perverse; as Freud himself says, "The Unconscious is the infantile mental life."[166] Many critics have read a wide variety of texts of children's literature in terms of the unconscious "infantile" content they sublimate, with a variety of degrees of persuasiveness. Among them, of course, is Brooks, who argues that the uncanny or *unheimlich* aspects of children's books—the strange monsters and extreme circumstances—are actually familiar fears disguised:

> Through the play of repression, the adult writing for children consciously or unconsciously, possibly because he is unwilling or unable to assume the burden of adult sexuality, metamorphoses the erotic quest into a quest for adventure which takes the

hero far from the *heimisch,* into a world where Woman and Mother are only implicit presences, to do battle with monsters, enigmas, and cataclysms, through his victory to find triumphant peace. Does the child reader unconsciously decode the story, respond to the adventure because he interiorizes the *unheimisch* and feels its relevance to the *heimisch?*[167]

This line of argument is interesting for a number of reasons.

First, such a theory foregrounds—and accounts for—some fundamental aspects of children's literature. "While I am generally not one who espouses Grand Unification theories," Roberta Trites says, "I do see the potential in our recognizing the primacy of the *unheimlich,* the uncanny, in determining the form and content of much children's literature." Trites identifies the uncanny with "that unknowable and unreasonable fear—of death, speculates Heidegger; of castration, speculates Freud—that lurks in the subconscious for everyone."[168]

Second, the idea that unconscious content shadows simple texts helps to account specifically for the conventional lacks of children's literature—especially sexuality. There is no question that explicit sexual content is characteristically absent or that the children characteristically constructed as the implied readers of children's literature tend to be beings without any apparent interest in or awareness of their own sexuality or that of others around them. But it is also true that texts of children's literature often strike adult readers (and in my experience some honest child readers) as implying unstated sexual concerns. Consider, for instance, readings like those provided by Coats or by critics like Lucy Rollin and Mark West.[169] For these readers the absence does seem to invite consideration of the texts in terms of exactly what is being left out. The shadow texts might seem to contain sexuality merely because the text itself as read by sex-aware human beings so obviously does not include it.

I might, at this point, evoke James Kincaid's view of common constructions of childhood as an equally appropriate description of texts of children's literature: "Unencumbered by any necessary traits, this emptiness called a child can be construed in about any way we like."[170] Texts of children's literature might be so empty, lack so much, be so full of absence that it is possible to imagine an entire range of shadow texts to be resident in their unconscious. What a Freudian interpreter like Brooks or Rollin finds there might be merely one of a range of possible ideas about what they hide but nevertheless contain.

But as Kincaid himself argues—and as Rose does also—the apparent emptiness of childhood as conventionally imagined, its constitution as a lack or absence, does seem to be closely bound up with an adult need to believe that what children most specifically lack is sexuality. For this reason many adults (in North America, at least) become distressed when a picture book like Maurice Sendak's *In the Night Kitchen* dares to break convention by depicting the genitalia of a naked boy.[171] It is also for this reason that, as Kincaid suggests, so many adults are enraged at any whiff of suggestion that some children might in some way—not necessarily wisely or for their own good—enjoy the attentions of pedophiles. There may or may not be an unconscious resident in human beings that contains repressed sexual material. But it is true that widely held ideas about childhood do elide any reference to the incontrovertible presence of bodily pleasures and interests in children, and these ideas demand that that presence be closeted away from public avowal. It is therefore equally true that texts of children's literature tend to make similar elisions. What Kimberley Reynolds says of Victorian texts is equally true today: "real children and real children's bodies were made to disappear in children's literature and were replaced by more spiritualized, ethereal, and idealized images."[172] But the absence of sexuality in such images makes obvious what it ignores just by ignoring it. As Roderick McGillis suggests in his discussion of how children's books relate to Northrop Frye's theory of modes, "Most books for children are romances with the sexual aspects displaced into respectable relationships between the hero and authority figures such as parents, wizards, wise old men, white rabbits, or kindly fairies."[173] The need for displacement onto what is "respectable" is a matter of not saying what one knows should not be said. Children's literature might well have the unacknowledged purpose of teaching children not to reveal their sexuality to adults.

Brooks's specific argument about the sublimation of the *heimisch* in the *unheimlisch* is intriguing primarily for its unstated assumptions. The "he" that Brooks identifies as the hero of texts of children's literature is, quite clearly, male and clearly fleeing specifically feminine ("Woman and Mother") attempts to ensnare him by means of his sexuality. So, too, apparently, is the "he" Brooks identifies as the author of children's books. Yet as my explorations in chapter 1 reveal, texts such as "The Purple Jar" and *Plain City,* which are by women and about female protagonists, also describe confrontations with the *unheimlich* away from home. If these encounters sublimate sexual content, it is unlikely to be the content Brooks envisages.

What might it be, then? While it doesn't take much imagination to read Buhlaire's desire for her literally un-homed and therefore literally *unheimlich* father as Oedipal attraction, it is hardly a sublimation. It is quite explicitly and exactly her father she seeks, and she does so because she doesn't actually know him, has never met him, and, consequently, cannot actually have any sexual feelings for him that she needs to repress. As for "The Purple Jar," well, if I were determined to read the jar itself as evidence of sublimated content, I could suppose it represents Rosamond's repressed desire to acknowledge publicly her clearly forbidden fascination with the *unheimlich* exoticism of her own container-like genitalia.

But what would I then make of the fact that the most significant aspect of the jar turns out to be that it is not *unheimlich* at all? Does this early nineteenth-century story have a sublimated subtext about teaching children healthy attitudes to their own sexuality, now understood as actually acceptably *heimlich*? Or would it be implying that the genitalia are simply not interesting, just as the jar is not purple, and that children should therefore not have (or at least reveal) any interest in them—an interpretation that would support the idea that the desire being sublimated is shameful and needs to be sublimated?

One way or the other, the interesting thing about both "The Purple Jar" and *Plain City* is that their protagonists are brought to reject the *unheimlich* that first attracts them—as do the characters in a number of the other texts I discussed in chapter 1 and many other texts of children's literature. According to Brooks, the heroes of texts of children's literature "find triumphant peace"—conquer and presumably then eliminate the repressed sexuality their stories sublimate. If this is in any way true, then the happy endings characteristic of children's literature postulate sexuality as that which is dangerous and a triumph to conquer—a rejection of the adult world that keeps them imprisoned in childhood. Children's literature is, then, all about keeping children safe from the horrors of adulthood.

But as my explorations in chapter 1 reveal, that is not necessarily the whole truth about texts of children's literature. Or consider the animal characters featured in Potter's *Tale of Peter Rabbit*, E. B. White's *Charlotte's Web*, and so many other children's stories, characters that so often represent what children instinctually are prior to adult attempts to civilize them into acceptably socialized human beings. Might such characters be sublimated versions of child sexuality? If they are, the many texts that admire or allow animality or express ambivalence about the extent to which being an animal or being animal-like is desirable are actually in the process of allowing space for children to imagine themselves as sexual beings, albeit in sublimated form. Sublimated sexuality is not necessarily purged in texts of children's literature.

But the extent to which sexuality is purged—or more usually, as I have argued, appears to be purged but actually isn't—leads me to what most interests me about Brooks's theory of sublimation. He appears to assume that being free of sexuality, defeating disguised versions of Woman and Mother, might be a positive condition, a happy ending for child protagonists because it represents freedom (apparently because Woman and Mother constitute that which ties one down). "Is it perhaps true," he asks, "that because of the presumed innocence of children, their lack of contact with corruption, and the assumed restrictions of any writer addressing himself to them, children's literature gains an equal and (seemingly) opposite liberation of the imagination?"[174] Imaginative liberation here equals freedom from the constraints of sexuality. One confronts one's fearsome and therefore sublimated sexuality not in order to cease to fear it but in order to rid oneself of it altogether. No wonder Brooks imagines writers for children as being afraid of sex.

He also imagines children as having the same fear, as he speaks of children unconsciously decoding the sublimated material and understanding its relevance to their own supposedly real concerns. Logically speaking, the unconscious content of a text of children's literature must emerge from its *author's* unconscious— and must therefore represent the adult's repressed infantility, not necessarily the infantility or childlikeness anyone might logically expect to be present in unrepressed form in the conscious minds of child readers. What Brooks is suggesting here is another version of the colonialist project. Children's literature is a means by which adults teach children how to be childlike and, specifically, how to repress their sexuality. According to him, adults immature enough to fear sexuality themselves tell children stories that replicate and affirm the rightness of that fear in audiences of children. The end result of the sublimation of sexual content in children's literature is not a move beyond sublimation into a more mature understanding and acceptance of sexuality but, rather, an affirmation of the value of sublimation. The affirmation insists that children are deeply concerned with sexual matters but equally insists that they keep their sexuality properly repressed —just as the texts they are supposed to read and learn from do.

One further thing that interests me about Brooks's comment is his suggestion that writers for children sublimate sexual material "consciously or unconsciously." Many writers do this quite consciously—remember Lewis's comment about deliberately leaving things out. The possibility that it might be a conscious choice casts doubt on its actually being an act of sublimation at all. I suspect sublimated sexual content is merely one part of a vast range of materials that texts of children's literature characteristically imply by their absence.

They might, for instance, imply not sexual content repressed by an individual psyche but, rather, archetypes of the collective unconscious as described in the work of Carl Jung. Speaking of stories he identifies as "quest narratives," Elliot Gose says, "The child will probably be pulled into a tale by the simple excitement of heroes facing a series of adventures. Behind the excitement lie . . . patterns and depths of which the child—and sometimes the author—is unaware."[175] For a Jungian like Gose, these deeper matters affect readers whether they are aware of it or not: "The reader is invited to share a world of imagination with the implicit offer that he or she may thereby come in contact with a potential that lies below the surface nature of each of us" (115). As does Brooks, Gose postulates that the shadow text of unconscious material affects readers beyond their conscious awareness—that they understand more than the simplified information presumably designed to suit their childish needs. At least this one particular aspect of the shadow text does communicate to child readers.

I have little faith in the existence of a collective unconscious outside or beyond the shared memory of members of human cultures across time. But I also have little doubt that shared memory does act as a sort of unconscious of texts of literature in general and therefore of texts of children's literature. For their writers and many of their adult readers, apparently simple texts of children's literature exist in the complex context of a range of previously existing texts. These include not just texts of children's literature but any and all texts that an individual writer might have encountered in the process of developing a cognitive schema for what stories are, what literature is.

And more than that. Northrop Frye asserts, "Poetry can only be made out of other poems, novels out of other novels. Literature shapes itself, and is not shaped externally: the *forms* of literature can no more exist outside literature than the forms of sonata and fugue and rondo can exist outside music."[176] To the extent that a writer is aware of and shapes a text in terms of these forms, the texts that influence the writer include not only the texts that the writer knows but also the texts known by the writers of the texts the writer knows and, thus, eventually, the vast body of literature as a whole, along with all the plot patterns and conventions and generic characteristics that any one story emerges from, relates to, and evokes merely in the act of being told. Literature as a whole—and specifically, the literary aspects of it—is the shadow text of any one text of children's literature and operates to make the text meaningful both in terms of how it evokes conventions and patterns and how it departs from them.

Once more, here, I have to raise the question of the degree to which the implied child readers of texts of children's literature are aware of this shadow. They must, surely, be somewhat aware of it, in order to understand that a plot is a plot, a character a character, and so on, well enough to enjoy the narrative they communicate—to make sense of the wide variety of ways in which any literary text engages specifically literary textual practices not necessarily found in the world children and adults inhabit outside literary texts. One can, of course, engage texts with a variety of levels of understanding of its intertextual relationships with literature as a whole; but making something like the expected sense of even the simplest of books for babies requires some degree of engagement with the formal conventions of literature. These forms and conventions, the shadow texts of the specific details that manifest them in texts of children's literature, are part of the repertoire of the child readers the texts construct. Once again, child readers are assumed to be capable of understanding the simplicities of a text in terms of the more complex knowledge that sustains it and makes it comprehensible.

There is at least one other component of the shadow texts that children's literature characteristically evokes. If children's literature possesses a literary unconscious—an unspoken body of knowledge about literary forms and conventions that underlies the surface features and allows those features to be meaningful—so, too, must the literature possess a political or cultural unconscious. The specific gestures and appearances of characters, the details of settings and objects described, derive their import from the ways in which they refer to unspoken assumptions about race, class, gender, and a range of other registers of difference that legislate how power is distributed within any specific cultural context. Like all products of human thought, texts of children's literature exist within, represent, and tend to work to reinforce the ideology of the culture that produces them.

The most powerful aspects of ideology are the ones people are least aware of. What people take for granted as true—so true they don't need to think consciously about it—is what most firmly defines their sense of themselves and the world they live in and what most consistently governs their behavior within that world. In this way ideology is the shadow text of people's dealings with each other—the unspoken knowledge that allows them to engage in the actions they know about and tend usually and incorrectly to believe they engender out of their own wishes. If unconscious and unspoken ideological knowledge is the shadow text of everyone's conscious interactions with their environment and other people, then it must also form part of the shadow text of literary texts, including texts of children's literature. Such texts can be read as intended only by those immersed enough in the ideology of their culture to properly read its traces in what the text actually says. Once more logic suggests that the implied readers of children's literature must possess some knowledge of the complex ideological shadow text—knowledge they might well not be consciously aware of—in order to make sense of the apparently simple texts themselves. The implied readers characteristic of these texts must know more than the limited and presumably childlike in order to make sense of that which is limited and presumably childlike. It is interesting, therefore, that real readers of these texts often don't know all the texts imply.

There is a sense in which the texts exist exactly to allow adult readers to share knowledge of the shadow with children.

The Hidden Adult

I keep arriving at the same conclusion. The simplicity of texts of children's literature is only half the truth about them. They also possess a shadow, an unconscious—a more complex and more complete understanding of the world and people that remains unspoken beyond the simple surface but provides that simple surface with its comprehensibility. The simple surface sublimates—hides but still manages to imply the presence of—something less simple.

That something might well be identified as nonchildlike or beyond the ken of childlike consciousness—which might well be *why* it remains in the shadow. It is, by definition, not childlike. Inextricably tied up in binary habits of thinking, the childlike can be constructed and understood only in relation to that which it is not—the nonchildlike or, more directly, the adult. David Rudd draws on Derrida's concept of différance to explain how this dichotomy affects children's literature: "Without a recognition of what it is different from, differences cannot be sustained. Hence difference is always tainted by 'the other,' and must always be dependent upon it. . . . Children's literature is different, certainly, yet intimately bound to its parent literature, hence the constant slippage."[177]

That slippage allows the hidden adult. What texts of children's literature might be understood to sublimate or keep present but leave unsaid is a variety of forms of knowledge—sexual, cultural, historical—theoretically only available to and only understandable by adults. Brooks's suggestion that adult authors might consciously or unconsciously repress material that children might respond to only unconsciously is instructive here. It implies that what might be sublimated for an imagined child reader—not available to the child's conscious perception—is quite possibly not sublimated at all for the adult but rather consciously known and consciously left out. As with readers, so with texts. The unconscious of a text of children's literature is the adult consciousness that makes its childlikeness meaningful and comprehendible, so children's literature can be understood as simple literature that communicates by means of reference to a complex repertoire of unspoken but implied adult knowledge.

This might be the key to the aesthetic pleasure offered by texts of children's literature. According to Francelia Butler, "Much of the best [children's] literature can be enjoyed by children and adults as well. But more time needs to be spent studying the reason for this—that literature which appeals to this dual audience rises to a higher sophistication in its absolute simplicity."[178] What Butler does not say here is that only sophisticated minds would be able to perceive the sophistication being manifested in the simplicity. Such minds would gain a quite different pleasure from simple narratives with sophisticated depths than from obviously complex narratives with obviously difficult surfaces. At least part of the pleasure would emerge from the lack of obviousness—from the fact that the sophistication is hidden from obvious view and must be discovered by minds equipped with the knowledge and ability to do so. Such texts offer readers the pleasure of mastery, of knowing more than the narrative itself is claiming to tell, of seeing through and beyond its apparent simplicity. Convention would suggest that child readers understand only the simple surface, adults the complex depths. But as my discussions of sublimated and unconscious material suggest, children must have access to at least some of the complexities in order to make sense of the apparent simplicities. Expecting that of implied readers is a defining characteristic of children's literature. They too have access to this characteristic pleasure.

In any case, the idea that children's literature might have—indeed, might characteristically and even inherently and unavoidably imply—an adult audience as well as a childlike one is a key feature of some important theories of children's literature. It would not be surprising if that were true, simply because the field of children's literature—its production and consumption—is so overwhelmingly occupied by adults. In practical and economic terms, the actual audience for texts of children's literature is not children but rather the adult editors, publishers, reviewers, librarians, and parents who produce, market, distribute, recommend, select, and purchase children's books. In terms of picture books intended for younger child readers, it is often an adult who actually does the reading of the text and therefore experiences the book along with a child; and many adult teachers share the experience of texts intended for children in their classrooms. It is obvious that the child audience these texts characteristically imply would have to accord with what all these adult consumers conventionally view as relevantly childlike. The advertising and marketing of these texts, the reviews of and professional discourses about them, and the peritextual material present in the books themselves—the jacket design and copy, the specifications of reading levels, and so on—are far more clearly directed at this adult audience than at child readers themselves. It seems logical to assume that the texts themselves do imply an adult audience along with the child one, that, as Beverley Lyon Clark claims, "children's literature is always written for both children and adults; to be published it needs to please at least some adults."[179]

As I suggested earlier, Zohar Shavit argues in *Poetics of Children's Literature* that speaking to adults and children at the same time may not be simply a matter of the interpretive habits of differing people: "The children's writer is perhaps the only one who is asked to address one particular audience and at the same time appeal to another. Society expects the children's writer to be appreciated by both adults (and especially by 'the people in culture') and children. Yet this demand is both complex and even contradictory by nature because of the different and even incompatible tastes of children and adults."[180] Shavit's work is based in the concept of "literary systems" as developed by semiotic thinkers like Roman Jakobson and Yuri Lotman, another way of thinking about what Bourdieu calls fields of cultural production based less in questions of economic power but still concerned with the socioliterary constraints that define how texts are produced and understood. Shavit focuses her attention on what she calls ambivalent texts—those that, like *Alice's Adventures in Wonderland,* operate within two different literary "systems," the system of children's literature and the "canonized system" of serious literature for adults. Such texts follow the conventional forms and structures expected of children's literature but also offer something beyond that, variations on or additions to those conventions. Despite these differences, such texts maintain the conventions firmly enough that they can be read not necessarily in a variety of ways but in two different but quite specific ones—with an ignorance of the variations and with a consciousness of them. For Shavit, that means the texts have "two implied readers: a pseudo addressee and a real one. The child, the official reader of the text, is not meant to realize it fully and is much more an excuse for the text rather than its genuine addressee" (71). Because of adult acclaim for and interest in them, such texts become the model for other texts of children's literature. This sort of doubleness is a central fact of children's literature as a genre.

Shavit concludes, "This forces the children's writer to compromise between two addressees who differ both in their literary tastes as well as in their norms of realization for the text. The writer must skillfully craft this compromise, employing a complicated range of 'compensation strategies' while remaining within the limits of the system's prevalent norms, in order to reach both addressees" (93); thus, ambivalence is the normal condition of texts of children's literature.

I have already established that I believe it is. Furthermore, as Shavit claims, the ambivalence does seem to be based in the evocation of two implied readers with two different levels of knowledge and two different capacities for complexity—the readers of text and the readers of shadow text. And the ambivalence might well emerge in particular cases from the specific causes Shavit suggests, including her main focus, the insecurity of writers for children desperate to establish their credentials as serious producers of literature and their consequent efforts to move past the constraints that define children's literature. But I think that the ambivalence and the double addressee emerge from something much more basic than what Shavit identifies as "the poor self-image of the children's system" (59). It is, surely, inherent in the binarism that underlies all adult thinking about children in the centuries in which a special children's literature has existed—the understanding of childhood purely in terms of its opposition to, lack of, and subordination to maturity, and the double task of pleasing children as they are and transforming them into something better. Writers don't have to feel inferior or to ape those who felt inferior in order to produce texts of children's literature that speak to adults as well as children. As adults writing for children imagined as less knowledgeable than themselves, they can hardly do otherwise.

Shavit's argument is also marred by her fairly unquestioning acceptance of the stark division between the two addressees and of the idea that one must be a child and the other an adult, based on what she calls "the different and even incompatible tastes of children and adults." Speaking specifically about one children's novel, Thomas Hughes's *Tom Brown's Schooldays*, Mavis Reimer points to a flaw in Shavit's argument generally: "The assumptions that there are only two reading positions available, that these are closely correlated with the ages of actual readers, and that 'the child' can be linked with the simple and conventional and 'the adult' with the complicated and innovative are insupportable."[181] Many adults—myself among them—have a taste for children's books that depends to a great extent on what distinguishes them from adult texts: the presence within them of a supposed childlike point of view. That childlike viewpoint is available to me as an adult. And as I have been arguing here, the supposedly adult material present as the shadow of texts of children's literature is potentially available to child readers as well as adult ones. In some important ways it is *necessarily* available to them, as a condition for their comprehension of the texts. It is possibly even *intentionally* available to them, as a requisite part of the process by which adults use non-childlike knowledge in their efforts to teach children how to be childlike. There can be no doubt that there is a theoretically childlike set of perceptions and also a more complex second set of perceptions characteristically present or implied in children's literature; and there can be no doubt that these two streams are theoretically associated, one with an implied child reader, the other with an implied adult reader. But there is no reason to ignore another possibility: that the single implied reader of these texts, whether a child or an adult, is expected to experience a double awareness of the events described, seeing them simultaneously or, perhaps, in turn, in both "childlike" and non-"childlike" ways. What distinguishes these texts is not necessarily that they can be read in one way or the other but that they seem to invite a reading by both child and adult readers with an awareness of both. As Alan Richardson suggests in speaking of things like the parodic elements in *Alice's Adventures in Wonderland,* "In order to understand children's satire, we must relocate that doubleness or ambivalence within the *child reader.*"[182]

Consider, for instance, Shavit's assertion that Charles Perrault addressed his fairy tales "officially to children as the main consumers, while at the same time using the notion of the child as a source of amusement to allow adults (mainly highbrows) to enjoy the text, too."[183] This works only on the assumption that Perrault did not expect the children in his audience to understand and enjoy the sophisticated ironies with which he describes the unsophisticated characters in the folktales he is retelling. There is little reason to believe that. The history of attitudes toward children in Perrault's time and the kind of experiences the upper-class children he wrote for were consequently allowed would suggest otherwise.[184] I suspect that the experience these stories intended to offer both children and adults is the double experience of seeing innocently and simultaneously seeing through innocence—of being both "child" audience and "adult" audience. What Reimer says of *Tom Brown's Schooldays* might be a more widespread phenomenon in texts of children's literature generally: they tend to imply a reader who is "asked to repress some of the knowledge he is given."[185] Alternatively, Richardson suggests that some Victorian writers of texts for children "construct an 'ambivalent' child reader in order to subvert the fiction of an innocent child self."[186] As subversive of innocence or as an act of shoring it up through a process of repression, the presence of knowledge that a text invites its readers to know but pretend not to know seems available to the readers of all ages that texts of children's literature most characteristically imply.

Narrator and Narratee

The double implied reader of children's literature emerges from adult authors' need to speak from their adult experience—indeed, their inability to avoid doing so, for any effort to speak in a manner understandable to their child audience will be filtered through adult ideas of what it means to be childlike. As a result, the narrator most characteristically implied in texts of children's literature is someone much like the actual author: an adult, and more specifically, an adult speaking to children. The adult narrators of many texts of children's literature share a distinctive set of character traits. Aidan Chambers explains how Roald Dahl revised a story originally intended for adults to make it into a story for children:

What he aims to achieve—and does—is a tone of voice which is clear, uncluttered, unobtrusive, not very demanding linguistically, and which sets up a sense of intimate, yet adult-controlled, relationship between his second self [the author as represented in the text] and his implied child reader. It is a voice often heard in children's books of the kind deliberately written for them: it is the voice of speech rather than of interior monologue or no-holds-barred private confession. It is, in fact, the tone of a friendly adult storyteller who knows how to entertain children while at the same time keeping them in their place."[187]

It is not hard to understand why the narrators of so many texts of children's literature might share these traits. They emerge from the basic dynamics of the writing situation, from the conviction that children are different from adults and that the difference relates to the ways in which children are weaker than, less experienced than, less knowledgeable than adults.

Because the audience is perceived as inherently different from the author, it is logical to address it in terms of dialogue, on the model of conversation with someone unlike oneself and not likely to share one's internal thought processes as they might be expressed in interior monologue. Adults expect children to identify with the central child characters of texts of children's literature but not in any direct way with their characteristically adult narrators.

Because the audience is perceived as lacking in relation to the author's own adult knowledge or experience, it is logical to believe in one's obligation to speak for it. As my earlier discussions of the colonialist tendencies of children's literature revealed, it presumably cannot do so itself. But it is equally logical to avoid speaking for it or to it in complicated language or confessing to it about adult matters that might well be beyond its comprehension.

As dog-training manuals and the guides for dealing with servants produced in earlier times reveal, one can best speak to those whom one perceives as less than oneself in terms that one can expect the lesser beings to respond to positively—not peremptorily but in terms of proclaimed friendship and apparent sympathy and with an effort to make them feel comfortable and pliant by pleasing them on their own terms. Happy dogs, servants, and children are more likely to accept supervision. On the other hand, however, one must supervise. One has an obligation to control those beings understood by definition to lack control—to police their unsophisticated tendencies, teach them about their own inadequacies, not allow them to escape the bounds of the reason and good sense they so clearly lack—keep them, as Chambers says, in their place. The voice of many adult narrators of texts for children is the voice of a benevolent colonial official dealing with those in need of being colonized in a friendly but firmly controlling way.

As Jacqueline Rose suggests, this voice is most characteristically present in texts of children's literature produced in earlier times: "There has . . . been one fairly consistent progression in children's writing. I would call it an increasing 'narrativisation' of children's fiction, and a gradual dropping of the conspicuous narrating voice—the voice which in the very earliest books revealed itself as so explicitly didactic and repressive."[188] A number of commentators see this progression as an advance and proclaim the lack of obviously didactic adult speech as a standard of quality. For instance, Barbara Wall praises Arthur Ransome because in his children's novels "the voice of the narrator is unobtrusive, undogmatic, uncondescending, but distinctly adult too, in its unwavering intention to make clear what is described."[189]

But as Rose goes on to say, the sort of tone Wall admires here doesn't necessarily mean that the texts have become less didactic or less repressive; instead, "the adult intention has more and more been absorbed into the story and, apparently, rendered invisible."[190] It is perhaps least visible in the increasingly larger proportion of children's fiction that presents first-person child narrators telling their own stories, so that the fact of an adult storyteller is hidden, masked within what claims to be not only a child's thoughts but also the child's words.

But perhaps this adult storyteller is not so hidden and invisible as all that. Children's novels characteristically provide information and even photographs on their covers that make their status as fiction clear and clearly inform readers that their authors are adults. It is a common activity in language arts classes in North America for children to do author studies, to find out information about authors and write to them, and so on. All of this implies how important many adults think it is that children understand that children's literature is provided for them by adults and that the authors of the books they read are not themselves children.

If authors and their status as adults are so highly visible in the culture surrounding their texts, it is worth asking if they are really so invisible in the texts themselves. It seems unlikely that the children imagined as readers even for texts with first-person child narrators are expected to actually believe that a child wrote the words. Instead, surely, the texts imply a competent reader's understanding of their fictional status. They invite readers to realize that the narrator is the product of an adult imagination, to accept the truthfulness of the adult's imagining, and, in the very act of acceptance, to acknowledge their own inability to imagine themselves and their own childishness so well. As John Stephens says, this process is meant to occur whether narrators are obviously present or not: "A narrator either by direct address exerts overt control over the reader . . . or by means of the apparent absence of a narrator implies that particular assumptions are a matter of common knowledge, shared between narrator and narratee."[191] This common knowledge is inevitably adult knowledge, what adults believe the world to be and want children to believe the world to be. If what children already knew from their childish point of view were adequate, then adults would not need to provide books for them in order to make the superiority of adult wisdom clear to them. That children acknowledge the basis in adult perceptions of the child characters and narrators they read about is an inherent and necessary part of the way in which children's literature functions.

This means two things about the readers that texts of children's fiction characteristically imply. First, those readers are assumed to be aware of the ways in which the adults who write them are in control as adults and in the process of enacting childhood—pretending to see and think as children in terms of the characteristic focalization of children's novels and stories I discussed earlier, and to be writing as children in terms of the child narrators of first-person texts. Second, they are assumed to understand the prime purpose of this adult enactment, its didactic function as a model for their own enactment of childhood as wiser and more perceptive adults would like them to understand it. Once more, the childhood characteristically described in children's books is primarily significant for its fictionality—its status as constructed both for adult writers and child readers—and for the attention it invites readers to bring to its fictionality. And for that reason, the fact of an adult narrator and an invited awareness of the presence of that adult voice even in texts in which it seems invisible are likely to be recurring features of texts written by adults for children.

But a key part of the process that texts of children's literature characteristically invite their readers to undergo is hiding their knowledge of the fictionality of the childhood in question—rendering it invisible. If children are to pretend to occupy the childhood that adults imagine for them, then they must mask their awareness of the extent to which it is a product of adult minds and does not jibe with their own actual perceptions—or accept it as true and forget any of those actual perceptions that don't jibe with it. That seems likely to work best when the texts themselves mask the extent to which their childhood is a product of an adult mind— when their narrators are rendered invisible. Thus, as Rose says, "The writing that is currently being promoted for children is that form of writing which asks its reader to enter into the story and to take its world as real, without questioning how that world has been constituted, or where, or who, it comes from."[192] Like Rose, Stephens sees this process as effective on its own terms: "Narrative [of this sort] secures the identification of the child with something to which it does not necessarily belong. And it does so without the child being given the chance to notice, let alone question, the smoothness and ease of that process."[193] In light of my conviction that implied child readers are aware of the shadow thrown by the only apparently simple texts of children's literature, I want to suggest that it works exactly to the extent to which the child *does* notice it. The implied readers of texts of children's literature tend to be not gullible but adept at pretending to be gullible, not ignorant enough to be easily manipulated but wise enough to know how to be manipulated into pretending to be ignorant.

In the last few pages I have been referring to a characteristic I discussed earlier—that the attempt to address children often involves enacting childhood, presenting events as authors believe or hope a child might see them. It is precisely this paradoxical situation—the narrator speaking simultaneously as both child and adult—that most clearly reinforces the fictionality of the childhood of children's literature.

Showing, Not Telling

One further ramification of a childlike focalization is that it limits what Lewis refers to as "the expository demon." If, as popular assumptions suggest, children see less and know less than adults, then a text with a childlike focalization—or any text with a child audience—will have less exposition, less detail of all sorts. Its author must, as Lewis said, "throw all the force of the book into what was done and said."[194] Thus, as Lewis and a number of other commentators suggest, children's literature characteristically focuses on showing rather than telling.

This wish to show, rather than tell, results in a number of characteristic features that combine to define the style of children's literature. I have already discussed the question of simplicity of language. I can add a characteristic focus on events rather than on description or character revelation. Temple and his collaborators suggest that "readers see more of what characters do than of what they say, and certainly than of what they think."[195] Peter Brooks talks about how "everything is subordinated to narrative fictionalizing, the way any didactic intent, any characterization, any metaphor or symbolism, is held in check by a desire to make the tale do all the work."[196] And Hugh Crago speaks of how "children's literature has in a sense taken over the tradition of fiction as a primarily *narrative* experience."[197]

What Crago is suggesting here is that children's literature is different from the mainstream of serious literature for adults because its focus on narrative represents a retention of a quality that adult fiction (except, of course, popular literature) once had and has moved away from. Felicity Hughes describes this movement as a deliberate act, a key turning point in the history of adult fiction. She describes how influential discussions of fiction produced by writers like Henry James in the latter decades of the last century defined worthwhile adult fiction exactly in terms of its difference from what might be suitable reading for the less sophisticated minds of women and children. "The children are to be sent away to play, with their mothers presumably, so that the serious novelist can be free to pursue his art and write about sex."[198]

According to Hughes, "the view that the serious novel is one that children cannot read was generally accepted among writers and critics. The impact that this exclusion has had not only on the development of children's literature but on attitudes towards it is still overwhelming. The segregation of adult's and children's literature is rationalised, even celebrated on all sides. It has assumed the status of a fact, a piece of knowledge about the world, that children read books in a different way and have to have special books written for them" (32). This is an intriguing reversal of usual assumptions: not that children's books came into existence in response to already-present perceptions of the needs of children but that the existence of the books leads adults to assume and establish the existence of the needs they presume to fulfill. In a sense, the literature precedes and produces the children it purports to address. I think that in an important way it does: many adults tend to acquire their views of childhood at least in part from the books for (and also, of course, the books about) children produced by other adults. And so, too, do children.

But what is significant here in terms of genre characteristics is the identification of children's literature—and its implied audience of children—with, once more, a wide range of lacks and absences. As I suggested earlier, it is by definition less complex than adult literature and allowed a smaller range of topics, excluding, above all, sexuality. Also, its focus on narrative represents something it shares with a less evolved state of adult literature and becomes evidence of its appropriateness as literature for a less evolved form of humanity. In terms of how the genre of children's literature fits into literature as a whole, it is not merely different—it is inherently and by definition less evolved. As it was for Henry James, its main function for many adults currently at work in the field of literary production is to reveal by their absences the distinguishing qualities of mature, evolved, sophisticated, serious, and important literature.

Hughes goes on to suggest, "The exclusion of children's literature from the class of serious literature has of course resulted in its being classed as a branch of popular literature" (34). As I have suggested, the classification is not inaccurate. The two literatures do tend to share characteristics, including a focus on narrative action based on a lack of details about characters and settings. For many readers this means that children's literature is *not* serious, *not* important—its lack of importance inherent in its existence as a literature defined by lack. But as Hugh Crago says, "It is partly *because* of the displacements and constraints we have been considering [i.e., that it is written by adults for children, shaped by perceptions of the audience, necessarily simple, and so on] that a peripheral area like children's literature has been able to develop its particular achievement."[199] This echoes Francelia Butler's comments about "the higher sophistication in its absolute simplicity." As my discussion of shadow texts reveals, the peculiar achievement of children's literature is surely to show more than it says or appears to be telling—to imply a lot by saying little. At its best, and despite the inherent presence of an adult voice within it apparently speaking down to its implied child audience, it is a literature that actually talks up to readers rather than down to them. In its evocation of and dependence on shadow texts, it assumes those readers will be able to see more than superficially appears to be there, including, as I concluded a few pages ago, the adult voice and vision it closets.

Happy Endings

According to Maria Nikolajeva, "Children's fiction is basically about play. It can be serious and dangerous play, involving killing dragons in faraway mythical worlds, but the young characters are inevitably brought back to the security of home and the protection of adults."[200] A number of theorists see happy endings not only as a key characteristic of the texts but the main import of their existence. And since a happy ending inevitably implies an optimistic view of reality, children's literature is characteristically hopeful and optimistic in tone. As the children's novelist Natalie Babbitt says, a happy ending "turns a story ultimately toward hope rather than resignation and contains within it a difference not only between the two literatures [for adults and for children] but also between youth and age. . . . When one learns to compromise, one learns to abandon the happy ending as a pipe dream, or—a children's story."[201]

Speaking of Northrop Frye's stages of myth displacement, which end with ironic narratives—one defined as centrally concerning characters inferior to others—Nikolajeva says, "By this definition, all characters in children's fiction would appear at the ironic stage, since they naturally lack experience and knowledge and are therefore inferior to adults."[202] But she quickly goes on to say that "even a brief glance at a number of classic and contemporary children's novels demonstrates that this is not the case" (26) because the texts view their central characters' apparent inferiority as superiority; and as a result, "the romantic hero . . . is one of the most common character types in children's fiction" (30). Similarly, Roderick McGillis suggests that of the four basic modes of literature that Frye postulates, romance is more suitable for children than comedy, tragedy, and satire because it is about idealized people in an idealized world. "Romance is appropriate for children . . . because its plots turn on adventures that tend to end happily, thus reassuring the reader that the world is, ultimately, human in shape and meaning."[203] It confirms that the world is what human beings optimistically hope it to be.

Sara Smedman focuses on that "human" meaning as a key feature: "Hope is a vital dimension of a children's book, for it recognizes, at least implicitly, that readers are at the beginning of life, in crucial areas still uncommitted, even to their own personalities, and that for such readers growth and change are still to come. In a fictional world which purports to appropriate the world as we know it, the resolution must leave scope for such growth and change."[204] In a similar vein Tomlinson and Lynch-Brown propose that "when stories show children as victims of natural and human disasters, the stories should emphasize the hope for a better future rather than the hopelessness and utter despair of the moment."[205] Humphrey Carpenter sums up the reason for this focus on hope in the very first sentence of his book about children's literature: "All children's books are about ideals. Adult fiction sets out to portray and explain the world as it really is; books for children present it as it should be."[206]

What is most interesting about this group of assertions is the degree to which they both acknowledge the dishonesty of the hopefulness they praise—the degree to which it is a "pipe dream" or not "the world as it really is"—and view it as beneficial for children. Put in less positive terms, what is being recommended here is that adult writers lie to child readers—for their own good. I spoke earlier in this chapter about how that works as a means of protecting adults from children's knowledge of the actual truth, for the adults' own good. At this point my focus is on the characteristic qualities in texts that this process leads to. It makes texts for children's literature into utopian fantasy, a description of what the writer knows or thinks is a better world than the actual less ideal one of which the writer is conscious.

I have to add a proviso here. The assumption being made is that the optimistic world characteristic of children's literature is a fantasy only for those readers possessed of (and controlled by) adult knowledge of reality. For child readers, it is usually assumed, the fantasy will or should appear to *be* the reality, not fantastic at all. It purports to be the real word of childhood, itself a fantasy from the viewpoint of adult knowledge of reality (except for those adults who follow Wordsworth in viewing it as the actual spiritual truth hidden behind mere facts). But in the light of the singularly nonutopian ways I know far too many children have lived and still live on this planet, I suspect that what adults view as fantasy might well appear equally fantastic to child readers—a childhood more utopian than the one they are actually experiencing. For that reason Maria Nikolajeva even suggests that the true audience of children's literature is not children but adults: "the notion of childhood that we meet in children's fiction reflects adults' views, which may or may not correspond to the real status of children and childhood in any given society. The central concept seems to be that childhood is something irretrievably lost for adults, and this lost Arcadia can only be restored in fiction. With this premise, children's fiction is not, as it is commonly defined, literature addressed to children, but a sort of storytelling therapy for frustrated adults."[207]

Indeed, children's literature offers a myth of childhood as utopian in itself. More specifically, it constructs childhood as the period in individual human lives parallel to an earlier period in the history of civilization when, it is often assumed, things were simpler and better: a form of Eden. As Jacqueline Rose points out, "Andrew Lang published his fairy tales in the nineteenth century as the uncontaminated record of our cultural infancy . . . to which, it was assumed, the child had a direct and privileged access."[208] This sort of assumption has been widespread in European culture throughout the time in which children's literature has existed. It still remains powerful. For instance, Peter Hunt argues that children share with preliterate peoples what Walter J. Ong identifies as oral culture, a culture quite different from that associated with literacy, with quite different views of what stories are: "We are dealing not with a lesser ability, but with a different kind of ability, one that seems likely to view narrative (consequently perceive its structures) in a way not accounted for in conventional [i.e., literature-based] theory."[209]

Assumptions such as this one have resulted in the fact that writing for children characteristically attempts to imitate the literary forms of what is understood to be cultural infancy. A lot of the literature published for children actually consists of retellings of materials from earlier literatures—ancient epics and sagas, Aesopian fables, and fairy tales based on oral folk stories. Much of the rest of children's literature has characteristics in common with that early literature: its repetitive nature, its focus on showing actions and not telling about what motivates them,

its depiction of idealized people and settings, its tendency to utopian wish-fulfillment, its tendency to include fantastic elements in relatively realistic settings—
but also, as Ong suggests, its ongoing "close reference to the human lifeworld,
assimilating the alien, objective world to the more immediate familiar interaction
of human beings."[210] In children's literature, as in traditional oral literature, what
is strange and new emerges amid and interacts with what is familiar—talking
animals or strange visitors at home or in the garden, magical jars on the street. In
the light of characteristics like these, Torben Weinreich concludes that "some
written literature for children, especially for smaller children, clearly retains an
orality in the narrative as a result of a narrative strategy and the use of literary
devices; I see this as a consequence of a particular perception, partly of the child,
partly of the literature and partly of the situation that arises when narrator, narrative and reader or listener meet."[211]

Presumably, those now identified as primitive peoples produced primitive
texts automatically, as a result and echo of their own supposedly primitive world-
views. No matter how much children's literature replicates the primitive, it cannot
replicate this consonance of text and author mind-set. As an act of imitation of
something different from one's own current circumstances, it is—it can only be—
produced by nonprimitives. For this reason a number of commentators see it as a
version of one specific form of utopian literature, one that describes a life more
primitive and more innocent than the ones actually lived by its authors: the
pastoral idyll, a traditional form of poem that celebrates the joys of the unsophisticated rural life, close to nature and in the company of friends. Many children's
books seem to function in this way. Anita Moss suggests that William Steig's
children's novel *Dominic* represents "the pastoral values of childhood"; and according to Geraldine Poss, Grahame's *Wind in the Willows* is like many texts for
children in making potentially disturbing events seem safe by placing them
"within an innocent pastoral milieu."[212] Even books that don't describe idyllic
natural environments allow children to find them in the midst of urban blight: in
tree houses or backyard hideaways or on days that fill the urban streets with snow.
Maria Nikolajeva suggests that "the vast majority of children's fiction, classic as
well as contemporary, shows the same unmistakable features of pastoral: the
importance of a particular setting; autonomy of the 'felicitous space' from the rest
of the world; a special significance of home; absence of death and sexuality; and,
as a result, a general sense of innocence."[213]

Clifton Fadiman offers an explanation for the pastoral nature of children's
literature that reveals its roots in assumptions about childhood. He speaks of "a

group of themes, freighted with symbolic content, that find powerful development in children's literature [because of] the child's affinity for the nonartificial,
or for places man has abandoned to nature. A vast apparatus is needed to condition the human being to the fabricated, technological surround to which he now
seems fated. But, until so conditioned, the child normally relates himself to a
nontechnological world, or its nearest approximation."[214] Fadiman is clearly writing of a time before cell phones and PlayStations. But the evolutionary assumption here that childhood replicates the childhood of civilization signals the degree
to which a focus on nonartificial and nontechnological nature is a form of nostalgia—and specifically nostalgia for what one has never actually experienced. The
key significance of the traditional pastoral idyll was its representation of just this
form of nostalgia. The writers of and audience for pastoral idylls among ancient
Greeks or Renaissance Europeans were sophisticated urban aristocrats who enjoyed the idylls exactly because they evoked a way of life purer and simpler than
their own—a way of life that surely never existed. Speaking of pastoral as the
representation of a "golden age," W. W. Greg suggests that it springs from "the
yearning of the tired soul to escape, if it were but in imagination and for a
moment, to a life of simplicity and innocence from the bitter luxury of the court
and the menial bread of princes."[215]

Many texts for children express exactly this kind of nostalgia for a better world
that never actually existed; they describe a childhood more sweet and innocent
than most if not all children ever experience, far from the bitter complexities of
adulthood and the menial bread of multinational corporations. According to Roni
Natov, "As in all literary pastoral, the green world in the literature of childhood is a
response to the worldliness of the world"[216]—and it seems inevitably to evoke the
worldliness it responds to and opposes, for as Sarah Gilead suggests, even the
most idyllic of texts for children imply a more painful adult knowledge, simply by
being so determined to leave it out: "However successfully evoked, the projected
child's experiences, mentality, or feelings reflect an adult's need for escape from
necessity, conflict, or compromise. Determined cheerfulness or confident morality [masks] a guilty poignancy. An ostensibly unambiguous realm, the idyll is
filtered by adult intellectuality, by an awareness of irony, sexuality, conflicts, and
social power arrangements."[217] What Gilead suggests here is the way in which the
similar dynamics that underpin the writing of pastoral idyll and the writing of
children's literature cause them to have similar shadow texts of more sophisticated knowledge that similarly then constitute innocence as a utopian escape for
adults from adult sophistication.

According to William Empson,

The essential trick of the old pastoral, which was felt to imply a beautiful relation between rich and poor, was to make simple people express strong feelings (felt as the most universal subject, something fundamentally true about everybody) in learned and fashionable language (so that you wrote about the best subject in the best way). From seeing the two sorts of people combined like this you thought better of both; the best parts of both were used. The effect was in some degree to combine in the reader or author the merits of the two sorts; he was made to mirror in himself more completely the effective elements of the society he lived in.[218]

This description of pastoral works surprisingly well as a description of common tendencies of texts for children. They, too, often present children as pure representatives of basic human feelings as yet uncomplicated by the veneer of over-sophistication. As Natov suggests, "In the literature of childhood, the child actually can serve as the green world itself. . . . The retreat from the worldly world is the child himself, the figure of escape, renewal, and possibility."[219] Like pastorals, texts for children also require adult writers with the wisdom to perceive the delights of simplicity and the sophisticated grasp of language that will allow them to represent the simplicity well and beautifully. They also tend to be produced by writers who see themselves as combinations of sophisticate and nonsophisticate—as adults with a child hidden within them. And above all, they work to produce readers who see themselves as combining the "best" qualities of the two sorts of people—as themselves, child or adult, and also as children in the ways in which children are most perceptively understood by adult minds. It is not surprising that Empson should conclude that what he calls "child-cult"—the adult worship of the joys of childhood so prevalent as a thread of children's literature—is "a version of pastoral."[220] Speaking of *Alice's Adventures in Wonderland* and *Through the Looking Glass,* Empson asserts that "the essential idea of the books is a shift onto the child, which Dodgson did not invent, of the obscure tradition of the pastoral."[221] One might generalize that statement as a way of accounting for a number of central features of children's literature.

There is, however, an important difference between pastoral and children's literature. The rustics of traditional idylls were not expected to read the idylls that theoretically described their lives or to accept their utopian vision as truth. The implied child readers of children's literature are expected to do just that—to be the sophisticated readers, as well as the unsophisticated subjects, of the texts. Children's literature offers what must seem like a utopian fantasy or idyll for adults, one that operates with the assumption that children will take that fantasy for truth.

Or, I reiterate, pretend to take it for truth. As with the sophisticated implied audiences of traditional pastoral, the child readers implied by children's literature might well be in the process of being invited to indulge in the masquerade of pretending to be less sophisticated than they actually are.

Achieving Utopia

My speculations about the relationships between pastoral and children's literature began with a focus on the happy endings of texts of children's literature and the idyllic mood of optimism they help to engender. But texts can have noticeably happy endings only if what precedes the ending is not quite so happy. It is difficult to imagine any even barely satisfying story that did not involve its central characters in some kind of unhappiness—a difficult situation to be solved or transcended—and texts of children's fiction are no exception. Simply because they are so plot-oriented, then, texts of children's fiction are less thoroughly utopian than poems in the pastoral tradition. If the worlds they describe are in any way idyllic, the idyll tends to be less than idyllic for much of the story. I therefore offer this variation of the idea that children's literature is a form of pastoral—that it is literature in which an idyllic utopia is eventually achieved. If the stories start in a place of comfort and repose, then discomforting elements enter it, and must be gotten rid of; or else the protagonists leave the idyllic place for a less comfortable one and then, finally, return to it again. In some stories there is nothing utopian to begin with, and the idyll comes into existence only at the end.

By and large, the idyllic place left or sought or achieved tends to be identified with the idea of home. Characters leave safe or constricting homes to have adventures (as tends to happen in the texts I discussed in chapter 1), or else their safe or constricting homes are invaded by something exciting and/or upsetting (as happens occasionally in *Henry Huggins* and *Plain City*). According to Christopher Clausen, "When home is a privileged place, exempt from the most serious problems of life and civilization—when home is where we ought, on the whole, to stay—we are probably dealing with a story for children. When home is the chief place from which we must escape, either to grow up or . . . to remain innocent, then we are involved in a story for adolescents or adults."[222] As a result, it is a place or state of being clearly understood as a safe home that child characters in texts written for children almost always come to at the end—either the one they willingly or unwillingly left at the beginning and have now learned to appreciate or a new one more idyllic than the disrupted one they left.

In *The Pleasures of Children's Literature* Mavis Reimer and I suggest that "characters in texts of children's fiction tend to learn the value of home by losing it and then finding it again. This home/away/home pattern is the most common story line in children's literature."[223] Various commentators offer explanations for the recurrence of this pattern. Anita Moss and Jon Stott suggest that stories from the folk tradition, important models for much later children's literature, have "two basic narrative patterns. . . . In both linear and circular journeys, the central character . . . is displaced from the home environment."[224] Margery Hourihan suggests that children's literature continually retells something like Joseph Campbell's archetypal story of "the hero with a thousand faces," a story that "has been with us since the emergence of Western culture."[225] In this story, says Hourihan, someone "leaves the civilized order of home to venture into the wilderness in pursuit of a goal" and, at the end, "returns home" again (9–10). Hourihan sees this story as a repressive manifestation of patriarchal culture: "The hero story has dominated children's and young adult literature, passing on the traditional values to each new generation. . . . If Western society is to become less violent, less destructive of nature, more genuinely equitable, we need to tell different stories, especially to children" (3–4).

Perhaps we do. But Hourihan's focus on what children's stories share with other fiction misses some significant aspects of how these patterns are deployed specifically in writing for children. Discussing stories in which children have to leave home, John Stephens offers an explanation that is both more positive and more specifically related to children's literature: "Displacement or relocation are common strategies in children's fiction by which main characters are forced to come to terms with their own subjectivity through a new context of intersubjective relations."[226] What is instructive, though, is that the end result in most stories of this sort is that what the newly aware children tend to become most aware of is the value of home, the place designed to protect them from their own previous lack of awareness. As Hourihan suggests, the supposedly happy ending of a return home does seem to represent some kind of potentially repressive adherence to adult views of childhood.

Stories of children who leave home, have adventures, and return happily home at the end are found so frequently in children's literature that the pattern can usefully operate as a cognitive model with which to make sense of the many texts that vary from it. It seems to act in just that way for the authors of a lot of stories about, say, child characters with abusive parents or child characters whose lives are disrupted by war or poverty. Such stories tend to proceed by inviting readers to see the homes these characters have in terms of how they differ from what a home ought ideally (or idyllically) to be. One way or another, children's literature characteristically tends to focus on exploring what home might mean or ought to be for child characters and readers.

In terms of its function in texts written for children, home means, most significantly, two things. First, it is a place of safety, a protective enclosure that is meant to be a shield from the dangers of the world outside. Second, it is a place provided for children by adults: it is where adults, specifically, keep children safe by not allowing them contact with nonchildlike dangers. It is utopian, theoretically an idyllic place even in its relationship to the world outside it, a relationship implied by the mere fact of its existence as something desirable. As such, it tends to operate within children's stories in much the same way that the stories themselves are meant to operate in the lives of children. They are safe places for children to play, to be irresponsible, to be childlike—safe because adults have eliminated discomfiting aspects of the world from them, made them comparatively idyllic. Each is the space in which a vulnerable and innocent childhood as adults conceive of it can safely exist.

Nevertheless, the simple fact that supposedly safe places can be and most often are left behind in children's stories—that protagonists go away from home to have an adventure—suggests they are not so completely safe and impregnable and good for those who inhabit them as they seem to claim. As Derrida suggests of the "Law" of genre, the law of home implies what it leaves outside merely by insisting it be left outside. The outside is already inside. It is there as the *unheimlich*—translated literally, the unhomely—it denies but sublimates. It is there most of all in the potential for those who inhabit it to feel like outsiders inside it (because, perhaps, they have more access to what is being sublimated within it than adults might hope?). The hero of a thousand faces leaves home because he is already an outsider in the place where he was born, and like Max in *Where the Wild Things Are* or like Alice, Dr. Doolittle, and Buhlaire in the texts I examined in chapter 1, the protagonists of children's literature already have unhomely desires while at home that precede and cause their leaving. In the repressions that provide it with its security, home itself almost always houses and causes the "unhoming" it exists to prevent.

That it does so reveals a significant assumption about the child readers children's literature implies. Children are by definition irresponsible and childish— they would need neither safe homes nor special safe texts if they weren't. In a way children themselves are understood as the *unheimlich* in the home. They don't appreciate the safety of the safe places that more responsible beings have created for them. They are likely to question the need for a home or for any adult control over them and require frequent reaffirmation of it. Paradoxically, then, texts written specifically for children in order to create safe literary experiences for them almost inevitably focus on the *unheimlich*—on ways in which children lack safe homes or question the values of homes or have the safety of their homes disrupted. The children in these texts achieve happiness by finally getting home— arriving at the happy ending of a safe childhood that adults hope they will then accept as the right and proper one, as, in fact, a happy one. At the end of children's stories home finally becomes the safe place it was always supposed to be, a place for innocent childhood, with whatever was *unheimlich*—or childish—about it at the start expelled at least temporarily by the journey away, the unhoming the unfortunate presence of the *unheimlich* led to. Childhood expels the childish as home expels the *unheimlich*.

Speaking of novels by Dickens in which orphaned or otherwise homeless child protagonists undergo danger before they finally, at the end of their stories, achieve happiness in what is purported to be a normal, happy, family home, Virginia Blum says that "the family the child gains at the end retrospectively founds a past; it is in the end that the pattern is forged for the beginning. Such a reversal obtains because the narrative is located in *adult* fantasy that artificially resuscitates a child's perspective."[227] What Blum finds in these novels by Dickens obtains also in many texts written for children. Texts of children's literature most typically reverse the supposedly normal chronology of childhood so that their child protagonists experience the adult world away before they gain the safe and more limited world of childhood.

As my arguments earlier in this chapter suggest, this happens because the childhood of children's literature is so clearly an adult fantasy, an attempted imposition of adult views of childhood on children—adult views that see childhood as a safe place but also see children themselves as inherently and dangerously *unheimlich*. What is especially revealing is that, in focusing on the *unheimlich* qualities of children and then on child characters' experiences away from home and in a very real sense *out* of childhood, the characteristic plots of children's literature replicate in a highly visible way the relationship between text and shadow text that underlies its nature as a genre. They show children more than what is childlike in the process of imposing a more limited childhood on them. They move beyond childhood in order to confirm the value of childhood and celebrate its achievements or its return.

And yet, of course, it remains an adult version of childhood that child protagonists and, presumably, child readers accept at the end—a childlikeness that supposedly erases the childish. In accepting that these are happy endings and thus agreeing to this interpretation of their own childlikeness, child protagonists and their implied readers come to share adult thinking. Paradoxically, their arrival at, or supposed return to, this particular form of childhood can be viewed as, and is often explicitly presented as, an act of maturation.

The happy endings of texts of children's literature most characteristically involve two interrelated and apparently contrary events. First, there is their protagonists' stated or implied realization that the childish desires for freedom, adventure, and so on that have driven the plot of their stories thus far were misguided and immature—a moment defined as an end to childishness and an entry into maturity. Second, and as a consequence of this, there is the reward of a safe home in which to be safely childlike—the happy acceptance of which is a sign of true maturity.

A maturity that results in an acceptance of one's childlike need to be protected from the dangerous adult world of freedom might well not be so one-sidedly mature as texts usually wish to claim for it. This is yet another way in which adult ambivalence about the relative desirability of childhood and maturity expresses itself. Questions like those Beverly Lyon Clark asks of the ending of Baum's *Wizard of Oz* might well be asked of many texts for children: "Is it good to be home in Kansas? Or is Dorothy's true home in Oz—where, indeed, she returns and stays in subsequent books in the Oz series? Is Dorothy's return to Kansas a token of maturity or a regression to childhood dependency?"[228] One way or the other, the mere fact that Dorothy and many other protagonists of children's literature return home happy to be there doesn't erase its potential for being *unheimlich* in the first place. Despite claims to the contrary, it is still the same place it was at the beginning, with the same structurally unavoidable inclusion of what it claims to leave out and therefore insists on invoking.

Whether or not any individual text is ambivalent, the experience that children's literature offers its readers tends to reinforce ambivalence simply because so many texts follow the pattern I just outlined. Most child readers read many more than just one text of children's literature. In their reading lives they often return from the mature understanding offered at the end of one story back to the childish desire characteristically in force at the beginning of the next one. In real life, for each human being, the voyage from childhood to adulthood, innocence to maturity, happens only once. But in children's book after children's book, characters get into trouble and learn wisdom from it, only to be superseded by the next innocent character moving beyond innocence in the next book. The central characters of many stories for children that appear in series replicate this pattern. In each of H. A. Rey's books about Curious George, George gets into trouble and learns, in theory, not to be so curious. In almost every chapter of L. M. Montgomery's *Anne of Green Gables,* Anne gets into trouble and learns not to be so enthusiastic and unrestrained.

There are a number of Jungian interpretations of children's novels like the one offered by Elliot Gose, which work to identify various characters as the protagonist's shadow or anima, and describe how the story replicates an individual's move toward psychic integration. Such interpretations usually make the assumption that the fictional representation of this psychic voyage somehow takes readers along the same path, through chaos toward mental health. If they do, though, why would a reader who has gone through the process once and become an integrated whole as a result of it ever again need or want to read another, similar book that replicated the same experience? The answer might be found in the inevitable presence of the *unheimlich* in the home, the adult ambivalence about childishness and childlikeness, expressing itself in the body of children's literature as an invitation for child readers to share the ambivalence. In the reading of children's fiction, the theoretically one-directional move from innocence to wisdom, ignorance to knowledge, youth to age and inevitably death is replaced by endless recurrence. Age succeeds youth only to be succeeded by youth once more. Beginning to read a children's book, each reader, adult or child, is invited once more to view the world supposedly as a child does, become at least in imagination childish yet again, innocent yet again, or free yet again. And as each reader moves toward the end of a children's book, each one, child or adult, can grow wise and learn more than children know (which might, as I have been suggesting, actually be less than the implied child readers of the texts actually do know). Anyone in the act of continuing to read such texts is invited to think of herself or himself as ever again young and innocent, ever again older and wiser, ever again more mature than the child he or she is supposed to pretend to be and ever again more childish than the adult wisdom he or she is supposed to agree to—ever ambivalent about the relative wisdom of childhood and adulthood. Children's literature is ambivalent as a genre even without taking into account the characteristic ambivalence of its individual texts.

Binaries

This ambivalence relates to several sets of apparently opposing dualities that are held at the same time. Some texts of children's literature do at least appear to be less ambivalent—seem to dismiss the value either of the childlike ("The Purple Jar," for instance, or many texts with explicitly didactic purposes) or the adult (various chapters of *Henry Huggins,* for instance, or many series adventures in which children triumph without the help of adults). But even then, these texts reach their conclusions by including and then dismissing one of a pair of opposites and celebrating the other. Underlying the ambivalence is a view of the world as consisting of various opposed and interacting forces, the relative value of which it is one's central business in life to decide.

Furthermore, while the forces that actually define human existence might more realistically be understood as an infinite range of possible positions with a myriad of differing kinds of relationships to each other, the ones that operate most centrally in the worlds characteristically described in children's literature come in pairs. Children's literature is binary in structure and in theme.

In an article written in the mid-1980s, I suggested that, "if children's fiction is different from other kinds of fiction (and it obviously is), then the main distinguishing factor may be . . . a fascination with the same basic sets of opposing ideas, and a propensity for bringing them into balance, so that both can be included in a vision of what life is."[229] I still consider this fascination a central characteristic of children's literature as a whole, even though further consideration has led me to ascribe the propensity to balance less to a unifying desire for wholeness than to an uneasy and complex ambivalence about the constituent pairs. In *The Pleasures of Children's Literature* Mavis Reimer and I list a number of the binaries frequently found in conventional texts for children, including childishness and maturity, nature and civilization, disobedience and obedience, ignorance and wisdom, good and evil.[230]

Other commentators also focus on the central significance of such pairs of opposites to children's literature. In *The Nimble Reader,* for instance, Roderick McGillis offers tables of the binary opposites implied by Sendak's *Where the Wild Things Are* and E. B. White's *Charlotte's Web.* According to McGillis,

The structure of binaries in *Where the Wild Things Are* might look something like this:

child	adult
wild	civilized
animal	human
food (raw)	food (cooked)
bedroom	forest (and sea)
pictures	printed words
dream	reality
powerlessness	power
night (moon)	day (sun)
son	mother

But McGillis insists that "this analysis of the structural pattern and its 'meaning' in *Where the Wild Things Are* is repeatable with any book"[231]—not just any children's book. It is a characteristic of all literature, not just this one kind. Margery Hourihan, who sees the archetypal hero story as central to children's literature, would agree with McGillis that its binaries are merely those found conventionally in most literature produced over the centuries: "The conceptual centre of a hero story consists of a set of binary oppositions: the qualities ascribed to the hero on the one hand and to his 'wild' opponents on the other."[232] She provides a list of a number of crucial, interrelated dualisms that effectively reinforce each other, forming a fracture that runs through our culture:

reason	emotion
civilization	wilderness
reason	nature
order	chaos
mind (soul)	body
male	female
human	non-human
master	slave (17)

The degree to which this list (borrowed from Val Plumwood's *Feminism and the Mastery of Nature*) might amplify McGillis's reading of the binaries in *Where the Wild Things Are* is provocative.

But as both Hourihan and McGillis suggest, the recurrence of these binaries might be merely because they are so prevalent in most products of human endeavor. Structuralist theory postulates that understanding in terms of the relationships of pairs is basic to human thought—and therefore presumably, and as McGillis agues, basic to all literary texts. It is, certainly, characteristic of the thought of the great canonical tradition of Western thought and literature, which tends to view the world in terms of binary categories such as old and young, rich and poor, appearance and reality, good and evil—and perhaps most centrally, masculine and feminine. The structural anthropologist Claude Lévi-Strauss claimed to find it in the various other civilizations about which he wrote also.

It is possible, however, that Lévi-Strauss might merely have seen what his own mind-set prepared him to see. The binaries might have been in his thought processes, not necessarily in the alien cultures he investigated. As Hourihan and a number of commentators have pointed out, binary thinking might be basic only to the thought of Europeans, and patriarchal male Europeans at that; this is the basic argument of Hourihan's book about the destructive nature of the hero story.

But children's literature as we know it came into existence in the context of European patriarchal thinking, and in terms of its traditional conventions, at least, it could hardly be expected to represent anything other than that thinking—which, as I pointed out earlier, is inherently binary. Adults who know that—and who allow themselves an awareness of its overwhelming presence in so many texts for children—are in a position to defend themselves against it and help children to do so as well. As Katharine Jones suggests, "The adult/child opposition, therefore, becomes a problematic rather than a given for understanding the world. We cannot move beyond dualistic thinking, but we can challenge and resist it: look at how the adult/child opposition arises rather than just accepting it as 'a taken-for-granted template for understanding the world.' "[233]

One path of resistance is awareness of how such templates operate. Speaking of pairs such as "the opposition between the child and the adult," Jacqueline Rose says, "these are structural oppositions in the strictest sense, in that each term only has meaning in relation to the one to which it is opposed. They do not reflect an essential truth about the child; . . . instead they produce a certain conception of childhood which simply carries the weight of one half of the contradictions which we experience in relation to ourselves."[234] If that conception of childhood is essentially and inherently just half of something, meaningful only in relation to the other half it insists on not being, it inevitably requires and always brings with it the very things it proposes to leave out. Literature written to enforce and produce such a conception of childhood inevitably expresses the other half it wishes to exclude—the *unheimlich* in the *heimlich* once again.

The binaries of children's literature that I have been discussing here—innocence and experience or, alternately, ignorance and adult wisdom or, alternately, childlike wisdom and corrupt sophistication; freedom and safety; knowledge and lack of knowledge; text and shadow text; didacticism and utopianism; home and away from home—all tend to represent versions of this sort of opposition. They all seem to derive from the primal scene of children's literature, the adult author in the act of engendering texts for child readers. The writing situation is itself inherently binary, inherently based on an insistence on the difference between two groups of people and therefore prone to be oppositional. McGillis's lists of binary pairs for both *Where the Wild Things Are* and *Charlotte's Web* include the child/adult opposition, and it would not be difficult to figure out where to put these terms in Hourihan's lists: the hero achieves mastery by leaving the emotional, wild, slavish world of childhood for the reasonable, civilized world of adults.

According to McGillis, "At least one commentator on early childhood education, Kieran Egan, argues strenuously that this pattern of binary opposites conforms neatly with young children's thinking. . . . For this reason, Egan advises teachers to cast their lessons in the form of stories, stories in which binary opposites are the structuring feature."[235] What interests me here is less the possibility that Egan might be right than the fact that he believes he is. He does so on the basis, clearly, that there is such a thing as childlike thinking, that it is different from adult thinking, that the primary difference has to do with lesser degrees of complexity, and that binaries are a less complicated habit of thought. Many adults share these ideas. As a result, texts for children might contain the binary patterns I and others find in them because adults who don't necessarily think in binaries themselves imagine that children do, and they therefore provide them with texts containing them. One way or the other (or both), the texts end up being binary in theme and in structure.

In terms of structure, I have already described how the homes of children's literature tend to represent meanings and values opposite to places away from those homes. The plots of these texts tend to center around characters moving from one of these places, home or not-home, to the other and opposite place, in order to explore their meanings—the protagonists' attraction to and hostility to each place. Here I can repeat a statement about children's literature I made in chapter 1—that children's literature is literature that tends to attach specific meanings and values to its settings and tends to include two main settings opposed in meaning to each other. Characteristically, the texts work to make a public declaration of support for one of the settings over the other—almost always the place identified at the end as safely homelike—and imply a less forthrightly spoken espousal of the opposite conclusion, so that they remain resolutely binary and ambivalent.

The binary obsession at the heart of children's literature manifests itself in a variety of other ways also. Consider, for instance, the characters found most frequently as protagonists: they almost always represent some strange combination of binary oppositions. They are wild animals who also have human personalities and the capability of human speech. Or they are manufactured toys or dolls but, again, with human personalities and the capability of human speech. Or they are orphans or temporarily orphaned and forced to fend for themselves—vulnerable children but with what we conventionally view as the life circumstances and often the self-reliance of adults. As beings inherently divided by the oppositions implied by their binary nature, characters of these sorts express the central ambivalence about childhood as understood in adult thought. As combinations of two halves, one of which is identified as childlike and one of which isn't, these characters both express and deny the wholeness of the adult conception of childhood as, in Rose's words, "one half of the contradictions which we [adults] experience in relation to ourselves." They thus allow for the constant and unending exploration of the ambivalence that most significantly characterizes the genre of literature in which they appear.

Repetition

That the exploration is constant and unending—a seemingly unchanging characteristic of texts in the genre—suggests another defining statement about children's literature: it is repetitive, in a range of ways. Some texts are internally repetitive: cumulative nursery rhymes like "This is the house that Jack built" or texts like Sendak's *Where the Wild Things Are,* with its repeated "terrible," or books for beginning readers with their limited and often-repeated vocabularies; fairy tales involving the adventures of three brothers or three voyages or three encounters with a prince and novels with repetitive events like Henry's misadventures in *Henry Huggins* or Anne's freeing encounters with repressed older people in *Anne of Green Gables.* By definition, picture books repeat the same story in two media, words and pictures. There are also many texts that more or less repeat each other: those with common story patterns like the hero tale or fairy tales about displaced princesses; series novels about the same characters in almost the same situations.

For Maria Nikolajeva, children's literature is a form of what Yuri Lotman identifies as "canonic" art: "According to Lotman, there are two principal types of art. The first is based on the canonic system and can be called 'ritual,' 'canonical,' or 'traditional' art. The other is based on violations of the canon, that is, the prevailing norms. This type is called 'modern' art."[236] As a canonic literature, children's literature is inherently conservative and therefore inherently repetitive. Texts are more like each other than not.

Hans-Heino Ewers offers a different set of terms, based as are Lotman's in the work of structural semioticians like Roman Jakobson, to account for the same distinctions. He also distinguishes between two types of narrative art, folklore and literature, but introduces a third: "written folklore."[237] Texts of literature, on the one hand, are distinct, individual, marked less by their practical usefulness than by their distinctiveness of style, and therefore less prone to adaptation and retelling by others. Folklore, on the other hand, operates by means of rewriting, retelling, adaptation, "selective excerpting and recombination" (87)—all because it is inherently practical, more significantly shaped by the needs of its audience than by the artistry of its producer. For Ewers, these qualities are shared by "the mode of textual use 'written folklore,' to which I believe a large part of children's and young adult literature belongs" (88). As I suggested some decades ago, "Most children's books are 'simple,' undetailed, and consequently, so similar to each other that their generic similarities and their evocations of archetypes are breathtakingly obvious."[238]

Nikolajeva ascribes the canonical nature of children's literature to "the dominating norms in subject matter, . . . behavior, . . . and language."[239] There is so much that cannot be said that what *is* said remains more or less the same. I see a number of related but more specific factors at work here.

The first of these has to do with the significant place repetition occupies in pedagogical practice. One of the clichés of educational thought is that we learn actions or thought processes by repeating them and being thus imprinted by them. The didacticism of children's literature accounts for much of its repetitiveness. I have already mentioned the ways in which books intended for early readers use repetitive vocabularies. Nikolajeva argues that the canonic repetitiousness of children's literature acts as a sort of cognitive schema, in that it "structures and organizes unstructured information in the recipient's brain."[240] Child readers come to understand what they already know—including their sense of themselves—in terms of the repetitive patterns of the literature they read. The repetition of ambivalent attitudes toward childhood, attitudes occurring repetitively because of adult inability to ever permanently solve the ambivalence, construct each child reader's view of himself or herself as another repetition of what is being so obsessively repeated.

But repetition emerges as much from the attempt to provide children with pleasure as it does from the wish to teach them. Whatever its pedagogical benefits, repetition is also a source of enjoyment. Witness the pleasure of repetitive rhythmic patterns in music and language; nor is it accidental that the most popular forms of literature for adults, such as romances or action thrillers, are the ones that are most repetitive, repeating conventional plots, character types, and forms of language. Repetition is inherently reassuring, pleasurably comforting—a matter of knowing what to expect and therefore not being unsettled by uncertainty. In a very real sense, repetition is parallel to what adults writing children's literature conceive of as the virtues of home. Home is a desirable place exactly because it allows repetitive responses to repetitive experiences. The happy endings of characteristic texts of children's literature almost inevitably suggest that, after a series of unexpected, unusual, and unsettling events, what has been achieved is the expectable, usual, safe daily round. Utopia, or childhood viewed as utopian, is most centrally defined as freedom from randomness—the freedom to repeat without interruption or end, without any need to change or learn or mature beyond the maturity of accepting sameness. In repeating words and sounds and story patterns, children's literature itself replicates this utopian nirvana of freedom from randomness. Perhaps paradoxically, it even characteristically repeats the move from the random world of adventures to the repetitive world of home in text after text, thus catching up the random in its web of repetitiveness.

In this way it operates as a series of repetitions of the child's game Freud describes in *Beyond the Pleasure Principle,* in which a young boy repetitively hides a toy while saying "fort" ("gone") and then pretends to find it again while saying "da" ("here"). Freud sees this game as the child's way of dealing with his mother's leaving him on his own and offers a series of possible interpretations for this behavior. First, the child merely reenacts the going away in order to experience the pleasure of the return; there must be a *fort* moment in order to have a *da* moment. Second, the child achieves mastery by transforming his mother's uncontrollable departures into something he himself controls. Third, the child expresses hostility toward the mother and gets revenge for her not behaving as he desires; in a sense the *da* moments occur so that the *fort* moments can be repeated. Freud himself suggests that literature often acts as a repetition of this *fort/da* pattern: "the artistic play and artistic imitation carried out by adults, which, unlike children's, are aimed at an audience, do not spare the spectators (for instance, in tragedy) the most painful experiences and yet can be felt by them as highly enjoyable."[241]

But what happens when the "artistic imitation" of adults is of children and directed at an audience of children? What are we to make of its repeated *fort/da* of nonrepetitive events/arrival at repetitively utopian home? The repeated pattern implies an adult compulsion to repeat some real or merely feared desertion by children—children absenting themselves from the comfort of adult security in ways that make adults feel insecure. All three of Freud's suggestions about how to interpret the pattern are provocative. First, the adult authors send child protagonists away from a safe childhood in order to allow themselves the pleasure of the happy return and, perhaps, persuade child readers that the return is happy. Second, the authors gain mastery over what distresses them—the knowledge of the *unheimlich* in the *heimlich,* the fear that children might be left unprotected, or, just as frightening, be capable of dealing with being unprotected, by enacting what they fear, making it happen. Third, the authors express hostility toward children for not being what the adults want children to be and get revenge for their not behaving as desired by removing them from the comforts of childhood as conceived of by adults. The three possibilities, combined as I suspect they tend to be in adult writing for children, represent one more version of the self-contradictory ambivalence of children's literature.

In all three cases adults purport to offer children pleasure by depriving child characters of comfort—and as Freud suggests, the results for the child readers that the texts imply can be "highly enjoyable." But for them, the pleasure might be in imagining as utopian wish-fulfillment what adults are more likely to acknowledge consciously as deprivation. Reading about children being sent away from home is as likely to please implied child readers as distress them—particularly when the texts themselves so often confirm that children are likely (wrongly, of course, as it usually turns out) to like the idea of freedom from adult protection. For actual children who read, reading about children being sent away from home repeatedly, again and again, reinforces two contradictory pleasures: the pleasure of imagining being away from home and the pleasure of coming home again.

In any case, what Freud calls "the compulsion to repeat" is a central characteristic of children's literature, one that makes it doubly (i.e., repetitively) ambivalent. It repeats both to teach child readers and to please them; and in each case, the repetitions ambivalently reinscribe repetitively opposite ideas of what children are and what adults want them to be.

Variation

One might argue from a more theoretically purist perspective, however, that children's literature is not repetitive at all—and for one simple reason: repetition is impossible. I suggested in chapter 1 that the return home after a visit away was not a return to the same place. No repeated occurrence of the same event can ever possibly be merely a repetition of it. Repeated the second time, it comes accompanied for those who experienced it earlier by the knowledge that it occurred once before, that it is in fact a repetition and therefore significantly unlike the first occurrence, which repeated nothing. For this reason every repeated occurrence of anything is less a repetition of it than a variation on it—different despite its apparent similarity.

Furthermore, the knowledge that a repeated act is repetitive might be a spur *not* to repeat—to try to change the act in some way merely so that one might escape whatever it was that compelled one to repeat it in the first place. Those forced to perform repetitive tasks—mowing the lawn or washing the dishes— often attempt to escape boredom by inventing small divergences from what is being repeated—changing the sequence in which one mows or rinsing everything

236 The Hidden Adult

all at once at the end rather than individually as one washes. Those who repeat because of the kind of ambivalence I outlined above—unable to decide between two alternative viewpoints and therefore condemned to try to decide between them again and yet again—might well attempt to move forward by varying the ways in which the terms relate to each other. In these circumstances one repeats without being exactly repetitive, performs the same task differently. And these seem to be the kind of circumstances that encourage adults to produce texts of children's literature.

I propose a variation on the idea that children's literature is repetitive—that it is variational. I described in chapter 1 how the events in the texts discussed there can be read as variations on each other, their repeating elements juggled into a series of new patterns as their plots unfold. I believe this is true of children's literature in general. In the paragraphs that follow I explore how variational form emerges from and relates to a wide variety of the statements about children's literature that I have been discussing in this chapter and the previous two.

Variational form is characteristic of the kinds of texts that Nikolajeva identifies as canonic and that Ewers calls folklore. For instance, fairy tales are variational: consider how the Grimms' "Snow White" consists of a series of scenes involving people looking at or through windows, mirrors, and other forms of glass. A traditional epic like *The Odyssey* is also variational, involving its hero in a series of adventures in which he is held captive by powerful beings and made to act like some form of animal. Also, many forms of popular fiction for adults tend to be variational in form. The plots of romance novels consist of a series of similar but different encounters in which a man and woman resist and then give in to the strong feelings they have for each other, and mystery stories tend to consist of a number of similar but different episodes in which a detective explores a space or interrogates suspects and focuses on seemingly insignificant details that turn out to be of great importance. Individual romances, mysteries, or fairy tales tend to be similar to, albeit not exactly the same as, other romances, mysteries, or fairy tales. Each one can be read as a variation of the same ritualistic pattern and of all the others of its type, and, this variational nature is a main source of the pleasure each offers readers. Discussing his childhood reading of comic books, one popular form of variational literature, Jon C. Stott says, "As I look back, I think that what I most enjoyed about the comic heroes was the ritual of finding the familiar characters, drawn by familiar artists, undertaking new but familiar adventures."[242] The pleasure Stott describes here—reading about familiar characters undertaking new but familiar adventures in a series of episodes that then act as variations of each other—might well describe exactly what the plots of *Henry Huggins* and *Alice's Adventures in Wonderland* offer their readers.

I might reach two related conclusions here. First, as a simple and canonic form of literature, fiction for children shares the characteristics of other simple and canonic forms of literature, which also tend to be formulaic, repetitive both internally and of each other and therefore prone to variational form. Second, in being simple like other canonic forms of literature, children's fiction remains closer to the roots of fictional narrative in forms of oral storytelling such as fairy tale and traditional epic than do more sophisticated fictions. Both the demand for memorizability in such forms and their obvious faith in the pleasures of repetition also tend to make them repetitive and therefore, again, prone to variational form. As I suggested earlier, the urge to write fiction for children often emerges from adult nostalgia for what are seen as utopian beginnings, simpler times in the Edenic or idyllic past, and texts for children are often modeled on traditional literary forms of earlier times. It is therefore not surprising that children's fiction should replicate the variational patterns found in those simple forms.

But as I also suggested earlier, the nostalgia that leads adults to attempt to replicate something simple and finished in the context of the complex present inevitably brings with it the marks of its origin, and it imports present complexities into the very texts that represent an attempt to escape them. And I suspect it is the paradoxical doubleness inherent in nostalgia, its existence as a sophisticated adult habit of mind that pretends to be simple and childlike—its being a form of pastoral idyll—that best accounts for the variational forms of children's fiction. As a product of nostalgia, children's fiction is not merely simple and formulaic, as I have to assume stories told in oral cultures were. As the product of more complex minds trying to replicate simplicity, it tends always to move restlessly back and forth between the polar oppositions of simple and complex, child and adult, in ways that lead to an obsessive sequential replication of similar elements with variational relationships to each other.

The presence of so much variation in texts for children has obvious pedagogical implications. Variational forms seem like textbook cases of the ways in which information must be constructed in order for it to be communicated. As I suggested in chapter 2, information theorists talk about redundancy as a necessary factor in the communication of new material: we can perceive what we don't know through the repetition of what we are already familiar with. I also described how cognitive psychologists imply a similar idea when they describe how we apply schemata built from previous experiences to new ones in order to make sense of the new ones. In variational forms each succeeding variation offers the redundancy of the previous version as a schema for the new one. If all learning operates in this way, then texts that operate as variations have a particularly rich pedagogical value; and if children's literature is always in some way didactic, as I suggested earlier, then it is no wonder that it should consist so often of variations. I called my article on *Charlotte's Web,* which describes how the plot consists of a simple version of a story followed by a more complex one containing the same basic elements, "text as teacher."[243] Many texts of children's literature act as teachers by virtue of their variations.

That variations create a sequence, an overall structure connecting the individual episodes in a chronological order that relates new information to old, also has important ideological implications. Sequential variation ensures that we understand the present by means of the past. What is being repeated or varied invades the new and thus far unknown and therefore connects the new to the old. In this way sameness absorbs difference; the old accounts for, explains, and therefore dissipates the power of the new. Variation therefore allows the past to infect, shape, and control our understanding of the future. In this sense, at least, variational forms are inherently unprogressive, conservative, repressive.

Raymond Williams speaks of *any* production of a text within a preexisting genre as an act of variation and suggests that "effects of such variations, precisely in their relation to certain expected forms—for example, the conscious variation of rhythm or the departure from an expected ending—still belong to the shared primary process, the effect of the variation depending on recognition both of the expected form and of the change."[244] Williams also says, "Most stable forms, of the kind properly recognizable as collective, belong to social systems which can also be characterized as relatively collective and stable" (189). If my understanding of children's literature is correct, then it doubly exemplifies this stability. In having the expectable characteristics I have been outlining here, it is itself a genre and therefore exists as a series of variations. As this section argues, a main generic marker is its focus on variational forms.

All of this suggests the degree to which children's literature operates as a doggedly conservative force, not only nostalgic for the past but determined to resist change in the present. One of its main purposes is to embed children within their culture, to make them both become like and to perceive themselves as what adults believe they should be. In this light it is interesting how often the final variation in a text of children's literature represents a reversal of patterns established in earlier ones. In the texts I discussed in chapter 1, for instance, Rosamond finally accepts the maternal wisdom she has consistently rejected until the last episode of "The Purple Jar," Peter finally becomes content not to be the big boy he has aspired to be in the final episode of *The Snowy Day,* and Buhlaire decides to stay in the home she has been considering leaving in the final episode of *Plain City.* All of these purport to be happy endings exactly insofar as they represent reverse variations on what preceded them. In effect, the new behavior is explained by and claimed by the patterns established earlier so that what at first seemed unacceptable becomes something to celebrate.

So variation most clearly represents the process by which the past claims the present, the old the new, the adult the child. But merely because the varying continues, there is the implication that the claiming fails—if it succeeded, why the need to try to do it yet again? And as I have asserted in various ways throughout this chapter, writers for children do try to do it again. It is instructive that all but one of the six texts I discussed in chapter 1 have sequels—and that the only exception is the one young-adult novel in the group. Despite what claims they might make as didactic texts for their protagonists' having changed significantly— learned to be better—the other five texts all apparently leave space for a similar story to be told again—for a child or childlike being to err in similar ways again and to learn the same or a similar lesson from it again. As I suggested earlier, the texts operate in ways that allow readers to imagine opposite interpretations to the ones they seem to be publicly espousing; they are so determinedly bipolar that they can never completely desert one pole for the other, never free the childlike from adult perceptions of it or the gaining of adult knowledge and independence from a persistence of childlike ignorance and need for protection, never free the *unheimlich* from the *heimlich.* And that inability to move past the ambivalence leaves room for variation and yet more variation. The infinite progression of endless variation suggests that the childlike, theoretically absorbed into adult conceptions of how the world works, stubbornly remains. The eventually re-pressed returns, in need of being repressed again and again and again.

So far, I have focused on how sequential variation allows the old to infect (or attempt to infect) the new. If the old forms of behavior survive the infection, there is also, clearly, the opposite possibility—that the new can infect and invade the old, that variation might be a means of disrupting and even breaking up repressive schemata. As I suggested earlier, children's literature might be subversive.

In his novel *The Book of Laughter and Forgetting,* Milan Kundera compares his own work to a set of variations by Beethoven:

> You recall Pascal's *pensée* about how man lives between the abyss of the infinitely large and the infinitely small. The journey of the variation form leads to that second

infinity, the infinity of internal variety concealed in all things. . . . The journey to the second infinity is no less adventurous than the journey of the epic, and closely parallels the physicist's descent into the wondrous innards of the atom. With every variation Beethoven moves farther and farther from the original theme, which bears no more resemblance to the final variation than a flower to its image under the microscope.[245]

If variation is a matter of moving ever deeper, developing ever greater understanding of the same basic form, then each new variation is bound to be more complex than the one preceding it. More and more new material is added as the variations progress; and eventually, perhaps, the new material might become more than the old forms can accommodate (as happens, perhaps, in *Plain City*). The final variation might bear no clear resemblance to the original theme. Difference triumphs over sameness, and the apparently closed and repressive schema turns out to contain surprising and freeing possibilities. In Ewers's terms, "written folklore" has been so infected by "literature" that it has become literary.

Furthermore, the mere act of variation implies that the original form or schemata is inadequate—incomplete as a representation of what is or might be. Consider, for instance, the pictures in picture-book versions of fairy tales. The text, which existed independently prior to the making of the pictures, always appeared to be complete, a satisfying and coherent whole. But the making of the pictures reveals gaps in the text: places where an illustrator might add more information to make the story more complete. Similarly, the mere existence of a sequel, planned in the first place or not, denies the adequacy of its predecessor. Consider the extreme case of a book like Ursula Le Guin's *Tehanu*, a fourth book added to a trilogy completed nearly twenty years earlier, which works primarily to subvert and reverse many of the meanings of the earlier Earthsea volumes. Before the sequel came along, the story was over; it was complete, and readers knew everything they needed to know in order to understand it. But now, wait, hold it, it's not over yet, there's yet more to come before it's over—and so on ad infinitum. In denying completeness, variations deny the coherence of old forms—and open the way to new ideas.

(They also, perhaps, reveal something about the infinite possibilities of interpretation and the infinite and insatiable longing that the act of interpretation itself implies. For the mere idea that variations are possible, that an apparently complete text contains gaps for an interpreter to fill with interpretations, is the very fact that makes interpretation possible. An interpretation is a variation on a text, a retelling of the story in different words and with different emphases. And the act of interpreting is the act of making our own variation—claiming the old idea in terms of our own new use of it.)

It is possible that the variational focus of children's literature might suggest ways in which its attempts to repress children fail—in which the variety of the variations ends up exploding the very redundancy they work to reinforce. I can explore that possibility by referring once more to questions of music form. According to Jacques Attali, music, a system of signifiers with no specific signifieds, ultimately signifies merely the shape and structure of societal power, the organizing patterns we give to all aspects of our lives from political systems to gender relationships: "Listening to music is listening to all noise, realizing that its appropriation and control is a reflection of power, that it is essentially political."[246] By transforming unstructured "noise" into coherent preexisting patterns, music closes off the liberating possibilities of the noise that remains outside its particular order—as, perhaps, does the conventional plotting of a characteristic children's text. Attali sees the way out of that closure in a focus on noise itself that paradoxically suggests yet further closure and repression: "The very absence of meaning in pure noise, . . . by unchanneling auditory sensations, frees the listener's imagination. The absence of meaning is in this case the presence of all meanings, absolute ambiguity, a construction outside meaning. The presence of noise makes sense, makes meaning. It makes possible the creation of a new order on another level of organization, of a new code in another network" (33).

Kundera's description of variation as "the infinity of internal variety concealed in all things" suggests that it might well be music's most poignant expression of the paradox Attali suggests: the wish to incorporate everything into a total order, its apparent success, and the paradoxical sadness and liberation of its constant failure. The infinite possibilities of variation represent an infinite ability to incorporate, to perceive unexplored noise and bring it into the patterned structure, to absorb liberating possibilities into its repressive pattern.

As Kundera acknowledges, however, the process never ends: "We all lose in whatever we do, because if it is perfection we are after, we must go to [the] heart of the matter, and *we can never quite reach it*."[247] The mere fact that a variation is possible, that one could hear more noise and go further into that infinity in order to make it part of the music, implies that yet further variations are possible, that there is more to be understood. This signals variation's liberating or frightening eternal failure to be total, to ever be able to absorb all the noise. It announces the eternal presence of unacknowledged noise—absences to be revealed and explored

—in all music. It announces both our sad inability to ever understand anything and our delightful ability to engender and enjoy engendering further possibilities.

Roderick McGillis says that "the folktale form offers a prime example of a textuality that is never complete. A story such as 'The Fisherman and His Wife' is a deconstructionist's delight because of its link to a continuing condition of orality; it is forever being re-created by both artists and translators, and by critics. The meanings of the story can never be closed."[248] Apparently, neither can the meanings of the literature based in part (a significant part) in the fairy tale tradition that engendered "The Fisherman and his Wife"—children's literature.

In any case, variation is paradoxically both repressive and liberating, both satisfyingly or disturbingly ordered and disturbingly or delightfully anarchic. And therefore, it seems, so is children's literature.

A Comprehensive Statement?

I suggested near the beginning of this chapter that my overview of critical commentary on what children's literature is might make me seem more likely to dissent from than to agree with my colleagues. Perhaps it does. But over the course of this chapter, I have rejected only a very few of the large number of statements about children's literature that I have put forward. I have suggested that all the others might be at least part of the whole truth about what characteristically obtains in children's literature, and I have tried to work toward an understanding of how all these various parts might relate to each other to form that whole truth. That ought to put me in a position to produce a comprehensive statement—a summation of what I have been able to accept as characteristically true about texts in the genre. The following represents my attempt to do so:

Children's literature—the literature published specifically for audiences of children and therefore produced in terms of adult ideas about children, is a distinct and definable genre of literature, with characteristics that emerge from enduring adult ideas about childhood and that have consequently remained stable over the stretch of time in which this literature has been produced. Those ideas are inherently *ambivalent;* therefore, the literature is ambivalent. It offers children both what adults think children will like and what adults want them to need, but it does so always in order to satisfy adults' needs in regard to children. It offers what children presumably like by describing characters and telling stories that fulfill theoretically childlike wishes for power and independence. It fulfills real adult needs and children's presumed needs by working to colonize children—imagining a fictional child reader as a model for actual child readers to adopt. But its imagined child reader is divided, both teachable and incorrigible, savage and innocent—eternally ambivalent. It possesses a double vision of childhood, simultaneously celebrating and denigrating both childhood desire and adult knowledge and, therefore, simultaneously protecting children from adult knowledge and working to teach it to them. It is both conservative and subversive, and it subverts both its conservatism and its own subversiveness. It finds its models in literary forms of earlier times, especially the fairy tale and the pastoral idyll—sophisticated versions of less sophisticated forms. Its central characters are children or childlike beings, and its main concern is the meaning and value of being childlike as understood by adults. It implies (or hides) a relationship between an adult narrator and a child narratee. It describes events from what purports to be a childlike point of view in order to teach children to occupy or enact that childlike point of view. It is an apparently simple literature in which adults leave things out—tell children less than the adults know themselves, especially about sexuality. It is a plot-oriented literature that shows rather than tells. But it implies more than it says—sublimates deeper and subtler adult knowledge in an unspoken but clearly present shadow text necessarily available to all its readers, both adults and children. It tends to be utopian in that it imagines childhood innocence as utopian, but its plots tend to place child characters in unchildlike situations that deprive them of their innocence. It is nevertheless hopeful and optimistic in tone and tells stories with what purport to be happy endings, as child or childlike characters purportedly achieve maturity by retreating from adult experience and accepting adult protection and limiting adult ideas about their own childlikeness. Its characters achieve innocence after having experience. It tends to represent visions of childhood pleasing to adults in terms of images and ideas of home, and its happy endings often involve returning to or arriving at what is presented as home. It is binary and oppositional in structure and in theme. Its stories tend to have two main settings, each of which represents one of a pair of central opposites. Its protagonists tend to represent combinations of pairs of characteristics that tend more usually in the world of discourse outside these texts to function separately and in opposition to each other. It is ambivalently unable to dismiss either half of each of its binaries. Its texts are internally repetitive and/or variational in form and content and tend to operate as repetitions and/or variations of other texts in the genre.

By and large, this statement replicates the list I produced at the end of the first chapter. Can the case be made that this complex of qualities does accurately describe texts labeled as children's literature? I believe that it generally does, or that, when specific texts don't match the description, their divergences from it tend to be what is most interesting and most thought-provoking about them. The divergences must either emerge from ideas about childhood and child readers less conventional and less powerful than the ones that have held sway since children's literature has existed, or else they represent new positions being taken within the field. In either case the centrality of the qualities I list above allows them to act as a useful schema in our coming to terms with texts across the genre.

CHAPTER FOUR

The Genre in the Field

Sameness and Difference

By this point in my argument one thing should be clear: children's literature is *not* simple. The most rudimentary of baby books comes to exist and has meaning only within a complex context of assumptions about books, about babies, about books for babies, about language and visual imagery, about education, about pleasure, and about the economy and the marketplace. Children's literature is a field within a field (the field of literary production) and is inextricably intertwined with other fields (particularly the fields of education and librarianship). The characteristic generic markers I have been exploring result from many forces working at once: the history and practice of literature and literary production; the history of ideas about childhood in general and of children's literature in particular; the history and practice of literary criticism and theory both in general and within the field of children's literature; the history and theory of other discourses and disciplines of childhood (developmental psychology, child psychology, and so on); educational theory and practice; the business of publishing and marketing books in general and books for children in particular; the nature of the economy and the ideology of the culture—perhaps even the nature of capital and of modern subjectivity in general.

As I considered various generic markers in the last two chapters, I often found myself suggesting ways in which they might have emerged from aspects of the field and of the forces that shape the field. In this chapter I focus on these matters in a more concerted way. *Why* might children's literature be what it is? How might the nature of the field of children's literature and its relationships with other fields help to account for its characteristics and its stability as a genre? If the field encourages stability, what might account for differences within it, and what kinds of differences might they be?

The Sameness of Children's Literature

The key point of my argument so far has been that the characteristic features I have identified tend to occur in texts of children's literature no matter when or where they were written. If that is true, then what characterizes children's literature remains stable in spite of and possibly even in defiance of history or culture, much the same despite differences in the time or location of its engendering. Yet I have also claimed that these relatively stable qualities emerge from specific moments in history and in specific cultural locations. What might account for this apparent contradiction? How can children's literature be both a product of history and culture and relatively stable across long periods of time and large variations of place?

One possible answer for these questions is clearly inadequate. It cannot be because childhood itself is eternally immutable in ways that transcend history, so that writers in all times and places who correctly understand children inevitably produce literature for children with the same qualities. History teaches that childhood is *not* eternally immutable in that way. If it were, then there would have been texts identifiable as children's literature and recognizable to us now as such produced in the centuries prior to and places different from the ones in which children's literature actually came to be.

Various commentators have attempted to make the case that various texts from earlier times can be identified as children's literature—and have done so on the basis that childhood is immutable. Their arguments tend to operate by imposing current ideas about what children like and need on the earlier texts. For instance, Gillian Adams speaks of clay tablets containing texts produced to train scribes about four thousand years ago in the Sumerian culture in what is now Iraq: "If it can be assumed that the Sumerians believed a story about a young schoolboy was appropriate for use by students of the same age, much as primers today have first- and second-graders as major characters, then it seems likely that this story was written for the use of elementary students and that those students were young. The student's misadventures would be amusing to young children."[1] But there is no evidence that the student scribes were children or even that, as the contemporary developmental assumptions Adams makes here lead her to take for granted, easier texts like this one would have been studied before more complicated ones and, therefore, by younger students. Without evidence that the Sumerians made the same distinctions between children and adults made within Euro-American culture for the past few centuries, there is no reason to believe that this story was intended for a young audience.

In a later article about the possible existence of children's literature in medieval Europe, Adams adopts a somewhat different view: "To assert that only *our* conception of childhood can result in children's literature, a literature that only we are able to judge as literature in terms of its literary value (which for some reason must include 'entertainment'), is the kind of cultural imperialism and ideological colonialism that modern critics, Nodelman among them, often seek to avoid."[2] Adams then argues for the identification as children's literature of a variety of texts: fictional or poetic texts dedicated to children, ones that directly address child readers or portray children as main characters, and ones with language simpler than in other texts by the same author. Speaking of Philippe Ariès's much-disputed view that people of the Middle Ages had no concept of children as significantly different from adults, Adams hopes "that younger scholars who do not suffer from misconceptions about children as unloved and as miniature adults . . . will join me in the exciting search for medieval children's literature."[3] But while medieval adults clearly did not think of children as miniature adults, they did think of them in ways that did not require the production of a specific form of literature, clearly marked off from other literature, for them. What I find most revealing about Adams's comment is that the literature she invites others to find needs to be searched for—that it is not clearly labeled as being literature specifically intended for children and that it is not, at least to begin with, obviously similar to what most people now might recognize as children's literature. It predates the time in which the conditions existed for that sort of literature—the subject of this book—to be produced.

But if the existence of children's literature depends on specific historic and cultural conditions, then it seems logical that it will be different in the different times and places in which it has occurred since it came into existence. What people call children's literature ought to be a variety of quite different texts making different assumptions about child readers dependent on specific local conditions. Zohar Shavit makes this point when she says that "children's libraries in the eighteenth, nineteenth, and twentieth centuries contain the same titles [e.g., fairy tales], but once the books are opened, it becomes quite clear that the contents vary considerably. What really counts is the way childhood is perceived by society, for it is society's perceptions that determine to a large extent what actually lies between the covers."[4] I have no doubt that this is true. I obviously share Shavit's conviction that understanding adult ideas about childhood is the key to understanding what children's literature is, and her assertion that these ideas change in different times and places is incontrovertibly correct. But an exclusive focus on these differences, while a deeply important and even central pursuit of children's literature scholarship, does lead scholars to ignore what I have been outlining here as an equally important underlying sameness, an understanding of which might turn out to be just as important as an understanding of the differences. For this reason I want to accept Shavit's assertion that "it is society's perceptions that determine to a large extent" what children's literature is, but I want to do so in a way she did not intend. I want to identify (and try to account for) what has remained fairly constant in "the way childhood is perceived by society" that could account for the underlying sameness in texts of children's literature produced in different times and places.

I can try to do so by looking at two kinds of literature for children that seem completely opposite to each other: the religious tracts produced by Puritan writers like James Janeway in England in the seventeenth century, which are among the earliest texts that can be clearly identified as being intended exclusively for child readers, and the sumptuously colorful picture books that fill the children's sections of contemporary American libraries and bookstores. The Puritans who wrote the tracts obviously believed that children needed news of the fallen, corrupt nature of the world and themselves, as well as instructions in how to deal with it—primarily by turning away from its supposed pleasures and focusing on salvation. These adults themselves knew and were obligated to provide children with a means of escaping the state of being fallen. Thus, Janeway's *A Token for Children, Being an Exact Account of the Conversion, Holy and Exemplary Lives, and Joyful Deaths of Several Young Children* consists of stories about deeply faithful children who die badly but with their faith wonderfully intact. American adults who produce picture books, however, obviously believe that exactly what children need is access to sensuous and aesthetic experiences, ones that adult artists are capable of and obligated to share with children. Notice what these differing and even contradictory ends and obligations have in common: they both provide access to certain kinds of information or forms of experience that adults already have and children either lack or need more of. Children's literature as people now identify it exists only and always when adults believe that children need something special in what they read that child readers cannot provide for themselves and that adults must therefore provide for them. It is telling that Adams's list of characteristics of potential candidates for medieval children's literature implies exactly this foundational principle—one less likely to be shared by medieval people than simply to be taken for granted by a postmedieval scholar.

All of the distinguishing markers of children's literature that I outlined at the end of the last chapter can be understood to emerge from this basic assumption. Writing in the context of comparative studies of literatures from different countries that focus on reasons for their differences, Emer O'Sullivan asserts that "the features of children's literature . . . that distinguish it from adult literature—its definition as texts assigned by adults to the group of readers comprising children and young people, the asymmetry of communication in children's literature, [i.e., the fact that it is addressed by adults to children], and its belonging to both the literary and the educational realms—can be regarded as universal, as features of all children's literature."[5] Two of these features relate clearly and the third just a little less directly to the idea that children need adults to provide a special literature for them. Until adults made this assumption, there was no children's literature. As long as adults continue to make it, children's literature will possess the underlying samenesses I have been exploring throughout this book. It will imply that children *as* children are different from adults but are also in the process of becoming adults. It will be inherently educational but inherently ambivalent. It will be binary-oppositional; addressed to both children and the adults who select books for children; focalized through combinations of adult and childlike points of view; addressed to divided child readers; both simple and complex, representing both innocence and sublimated experience; both a source of knowledge and a source of pleasure; both subversive and conservative; both utopian and confirmative of normal reality. This is so because these characteristic markers are all variants of and manifestations of the basic opposition between adult and child implied by the very circumstance of adults writing for children.

But the main paradox of children's literature is that the foundational split between child and adult leads to adult narrators characteristically split between adult experience and childlike perceptions and to implied child readers characteristically split between childlike and adult qualities. What seems so firmly oppositional and so based in the absolute separation of child and adult replicates itself in ways that mix the adult and the childlike in both adult authors and child readers and, consequently, undermines itself. Children's literature is, as I have said, always ambivalent.

Furthermore, the ways in which children's literature works to imbricate its readers in ambivalence about the childlike and the adult might well define their future lives as adults—and might emerge from the circumstances that have constructed adult subjectivity in the times and places in which a children's literature has existed. In the literature there is a pull between thoughtless, possibly subversive (and therefore childlike), self-satisfaction on the one hand and communally oriented, conservative (and therefore adult), understanding and the constraint of individual desire it inevitably results in on the other. Feeling that pull is what is demanded of all members in good standing of the contemporary consumer-oriented societies of the modern period in which there has been a children's literature. These societies give their members the freedom to be themselves and please themselves only in return for learning and acting on the knowledge that the freedom takes place within the context of, and is constrained by, the needs of other individuals and of the whole communities to which they belong. It is hard to imagine a society of pure egotists or one that was totally repressive of individual desire developing a form of literature for children so determined both to gratify and to constrain, so unwilling to give up either pole of the bilateral ambivalence that children's literature postulates in the subjects it constructs.

It appears to be no accident that children's literature exists specifically and mainly in the context of consumer-oriented, middle-class culture as it has developed within the last few centuries. "In order to understand the nature of children's literature," John Morganstern says, "we must understand the real, material conditions of bourgeois childhood because the bourgeois child is both the consumer of that literature and the object of its representation."[6] While those material conditions have changed—modern multinational publishing houses in a technological age operate quite differently than did early pioneers like John Newbery—some threads remain unchanged. As I discuss later, it is instructive that the publication of Newbery's *A Little Pretty Pocket Book* (1744), often identified as the first children's book, came with something like the sort of consumer-pleasing tie-ins still popular with children's publishers: the choice of a pincushion or a ball.

Suggesting that the idea of childhood on which the existence of children's literature depends "should . . . be understood as a particularly middle-class inheritance,"[7] Valerie Krips sees it as such specifically in terms of the ideas about women and family that arose with the middle class—the view that women's work should be restricted to the home and that therefore childhood needed to be understood as a state deeply valuable and deeply in need of maternal surveillance and protection. And there can be no doubt that children's literature exists within the context of specific assumptions about motherhood and has always tended to be a field in which women appear to have power. But I suspect that the connections between childhood as people have come to understand it, children's literature, and the rise of a capitalist middle class are more foundational than that—more basic to the structure of middle-class capitalism.

For Morganstern, children's literature developed in the eighteenth century as a sort of by-product of the process by which middle-class adults came to be increasingly literate: "As literacy spread . . . the nature of childhood changed in two ways. First, the social reality of childhood changed as, more and more, childhood became associated with institutionalized schooling in literacy. Second, the nature of adult subjectivity changed as a gap opened between the literacy of adults and children, a gap that children's literature has been invented to fill."[8] Literacy made adults different from people who could not read—including children. But middle-class children were assumed to be in the process of becoming readers, so they needed a literature designed specifically for beginners. That literature, Morganstern suggests, established a childhood subjectivity distinct from that assumed to exist in adults: "The spread of literacy changed social institutions and led to the construction of the child as innocent, which is to say, as a pre-reader. Or, to put it simply, it is not the 'child' that gives rise to children's literature but children's literature that gives rise to the 'child.' "9

While I find Morganstern's theory suggestive, I think it tends to overemphasize the extent to which practical needs drive intellectual agendas; I suspect children's literature could not have given rise to the "child" without an ideological need for the "child" to exist—and to exist as a construct in the culture outside children's literature as innocent in more than just a lack of reading skills. Nevertheless, and revealingly, that innocence is like the lack of reading skills in being conceived of as a temporary state. The "child" typically constructed by children's literature is in the process of ceasing to be a child—not adult, to be sure, but more specifically, not adult *yet*, outside adulthood but on the way in.

This, too, has a close connection with capitalism. In *Empire* Michael Hardt and Antonio Negri argue that "capitalism is an organism that cannot sustain itself without constantly looking beyond its boundaries, feeding off its external environment. Its outside is essential."10 For the production of new capital, workers must earn less than the value of what they produce—and thus are unable to consume all the goods they create; and if the capitalists themselves consumed all the goods, their capital would not grow. There must be a market outside the capitalist system. According to Hardt and Negri, it was the inescapable need for an outside that led the capitalists of the new European middle class to become colonizers—and to engender the rhetoric that insisted there was such a thing as an outside, an other to what the capitalists could then understand themselves to be. To colonize is, inevitably, to view oneself as a colonizer—to understand oneself in colonizing terms. I suspect that this model of subjectivity—an awareness of self built on an understanding of how one differs from what one views as outside and other to oneself—played an important role in the invention of childhood as it is still understood and thus in the childhood of children's literature.

"In the process of capitalization," Hardt and Negri go on to say, "*the outside is internalized*" (226); that is, the outside inevitably becomes part of the capitalist inside as outsider others become constituted as workers inside the system. By the same dynamic, children in this system are understood to be in the process of being created after the image of adults—becoming adults as adults understand their adulthood. Children, as they came to be understood in the age of capitalism, colonizable others, are exactly and most essentially the ambivalent children of capitalism and of the capitalist middle class.

It is instructive that capitalist adults should imagine the childhood of their own children as a form of that which was outside themselves—as a sort of market for their goods (i.e., adult values), as something to conquer and turn into themselves. As such, it comes to parallel other aspects of existence that, as Hardt and Negri suggest, the modern subjectivity founded on capitalism views as outside itself: nature, for instance, or the "primitive" societies of traditional anthropology and colonialism—or, especially, the unconscious of psychoanalytical theory, an outside that is nevertheless inside the human mind and in need of being both acknowledged and conquered in the process of therapy. Furthermore, as Hardt and Negri say, "The process of modernization, in all these varied contexts, is the internalization of the outside, that is, the civilization of nature" (187). That which is out—and which is also already in, already inextricably human because it has the potential to be humanized in spite of its outsiderliness—can be brought in. Childhood as now understood, and as children's literature constructs it, is just one manifestation of a conflicted and ambivalent discourse of inside and outside, human and other, at the heart of the capitalist project.

Not surprisingly, there is a clear connection between the rise of a capitalist middle class and the beginning of the children's literature now recognized as such. According to Harvey Darton, children's literature began "in 1744, when John Newbery, the most authentic founder of this traffic in minor literature, published his first children's book."[11] The book was *A Little Pretty Pocket Book*, "intended for the Instruction and Amusement of Little Master Tommy and Pretty Miss Polly." Darton identifies Newbery's work as foundational because, in addition to instruction, he "deliberately set out to provide amusement, and was not afraid to say so."[12] Note the typically middle-class capitalist ambivalence implied by the presence of those two opposing qualities.

Darton tends to focus on the amusement and downplay the instruction in Newbery's publications. He says of *A Little Pretty Pocket Book* that, "after some preliminary remarks meant for parents, instruction is dragged in only by the scruff" (2). But Peter Hunt insists of Newbery that "even his more light-hearted items had a considerable didactic purpose and amusement was always linked to instruction."[13] Geoffrey Summerfield goes even further in reading *A Little Pretty Pocket Book* as primarily didactic—and specifically as an expression of middle-class values: "It speaks for a mercantile knowingness, keen to initiate children into acceptable social conformity, calculated patterns of conduct, designed to yield a due return of social and business success. . . . It is a sneaky piece of work, and serves only to show how calamitous the didactic book for children could be."[14] Andrew O'Malley offers a more subtle reading: "Newbery astutely observed that a new market for children's books tailored to more modern middle-class sensibilities was flourishing, and the most readily available models for this new children's literature were chapbooks. To make these ancient characters more palatable, he reformed them somewhat and had them espouse the kinds of virtues and ideology middle-class parents were increasingly wanting to hear."[15] As well as pointing to the middle-class connection, what is most instructive about these comments is that they reveal how the same text intended for child readers can be read as all three of the kinds of children's books I mentioned earlier. It can be read as didactic, as utopian, and as an ambivalent combination of each. This presumably foundational text itself expresses the ambivalence of the genre it might well have founded—and of the capitalist childhood subject it helps to construct, the outsider in the process of being brought inside but, also, strangely, kept outside.

Summerfield's comments about "mercantile knowingness" and "business and social success" suggest how closely the text's values relate to subjectivity as constructed by capitalism. It is revealing that Newbery's motto for his publishing business was "Trade and Plumb-cake forever, Huzza!"[16]—a conjunction of profit (the trade) and sensual pleasure (the cake) that might suggest why he and others in his time came to invent children's literature as now understood. It might also suggest some further aspects of the subjectivity constructed by that literature. For middle-class merchants like Newbery to be financially successful, they needed customers willing to buy their products. There had to be people who believed they were entitled to please themselves and entitled therefore to buy the things that might give them pleasure. The children implied as the audience for Newbery's books—and still, I believe, for most children's literature being produced in Europe and North America today—are that kind of good consumers: people who know how to enjoy plumb-cake, who want to and deserve to have their senses pleased. They are in the market for what adults offer them exactly to the extent they are outside adulthood, in terms of standard ideas about the immaturity of indulgence, play, and so on.

The young Puritans who were the audience for books like Janeway's *Token for Children* a century earlier might have been born with an innate capacity for the enjoyment of plumb-cake and other sensual pleasures, but they would have quickly learned from their elders the spiritual danger of indulging in those pleasures. They would have felt guilty about feeling many of the feelings many people now assume children automatically and always feel. A main purpose of most children's stories, poems, and picture books from Newbery's time to now is to encourage and allow children to feel those feelings, indulge in their childlike delight in sensation—in that which is outside adult good sense and self-control.

Childhood as now understood (or invented or allowed) is a decidedly middle-class and mercantile phenomenon.

Even so—and here is where the outsider is urged to come inside—an equally important purpose of children's literature throughout its history has been to foster something suspiciously like Puritan guilt. While the ideal middle-class citizens of a consumer society happily buy things to please themselves, they must also have the skills required to get the money to buy the things. To cease being childish, to be brought in from the outside, children need to learn those skills. One of the skills is deferment—understanding that the hard work that makes money has to precede the rewards that money can buy, that one must feel guilty about not deferring consumption until after the moneymaking labor it will then reward. To be a good consumer is also to be a good producer, to be, as Hardt and Negri suggest, "internalized" into the market. And that means becoming a good, non-self-indulgent acceptor of communal adult values.

Before the age of Newbery, children had been a significant part of the audience for a whole range of popular literary entertainments, ballads, and stories about thieves and heroes available cheaply as broadsheets from street vendors. Since they often bought them for themselves, these texts clearly gave children pleasure, as they did many adults also—albeit mostly adults of low social standing. Indeed, it was the déclassé reputation of this literature that caused many higher-class parents of earlier centuries to disapprove of it as reading for children. In a hierarchy of behavior that clearly mirrored a hierarchy of class assumptions, the pleasure of sensation was lower than and in need of subjection to the regime of reason and restraint. Good middle-class children had to be discouraged from these lower-class tastes lest they, too, end up in the gutter. It was the genius of Newbery and others in his time to see that they could profit from providing children with that pleasure if they engaged it in a war against itself and thus made it respectable—and a spur to trade.

In doing so, they accomplished three important things. First, they found a way of allowing children to indulge in sensuous pleasure—something unacceptable to the Puritans, for instance, but key to current conceptions both of children's literature and of childhood. They allowed consumption. Second, they allowed production, found a way of making money out of doing so, and thus made children's literature—and the child subjects it worked to produce—integral to the continuing health of the economy. And third, the way they did these things made children's entertainment educational and both demanded and undermined pleasurable responses, ensuring that children's literature would construct the ambivalent child readers it required to become a viable source of profit.

Not surprisingly, the texts Newbery published, and the ones still being produced today, imply a child audience with characteristics similar to Newbery's own
declared interest in both plumb-cake *and* trade. What Summerfield identifies as
"a mercantile knowingness"—an ability to get what one wants for oneself by
mastering the communal expectations of those with power—is merely the subjectivity inhabited by all of us, adults or children, who exist in the context of consumer culture. Children's literature continues to have the two main purposes that
underlie its ambivalence: to give children pleasure and to teach them things that
subvert the pleasure. The pleasure is the plumb-cake. The invitation to enjoy
plumb-cake comes at the cost of learning how to be successful in trade—knowing
the right kinds of guilt to feel about indulgence in plumb-cake and the right ways
to defer and manage pleasure and thus keep pleasure in play. The interplay
between these two opposing pulls, toward the outside and the inside, defines not
just children's literature but childhood subjectivity in the time in which children's
literature has existed. That childhood subjectivity remains the essence of the adult
subjectivity it precedes. The continuation of the system demands that everyone
both produce and consume, everyone be both inside and outside and aware of
oneself as both an integrated communal insider and a separate self-indulgent
outsider with a mind and body of one's own. The need to construct such a
subjectivity in those who presumably do not yet possess it accounts for the existence of children's literature—it is usually assumed to be already in operation in
what people identify as literature for adults.

What I find particularly instructive here is how that need to construct clarifies
the absolute didacticism of children's literature—how even the pleasure it offers
and encourages its readers to feel is an important part of what it teaches. From
this point of view children's literature exists to create children—and eventually
adults—who know how to enjoy themselves, how to think about their pleasures in
ways that confirm the values of a consumer-oriented culture by putting the pleasure to the service of both consuming and producing. It allows pleasure in order
to co-opt and control it, and it does so by offering children an adult consciousness
of the significance of their childishness—and an insider's awareness of their own
outsiderliness that controls and contains it even while celebrating it.

But that which is allowed in order to be controlled is still allowed, expressed, in
danger of exceeding or escaping the very efforts to control it that have allowed for
its expression. And the result is, of course, ambivalence: control subverted, but
also subversion subverted by control. All participants in this system are themselves those they colonize and those who resist colonization. The resultant stasis
suggests a further reason why children's literature might remain so much the

same in differing times and places. The pulls in two opposite directions implied in its very being continually thwart each other and thus establish an enduring state of tension between themselves that works to prevent any really radical change within the genre or within adult conceptions of the nature of childhood and of themselves as adults in the consumer culture of middle-class modernity.

In *Empire* Hardt and Negri postulate the recent emergence of a new form of global organization of capital that "establishes no territorial center of power and does not rely on fixed boundaries or barriers."[17] In this new postmodern world, they argue, "there is progressively less distinction between inside and outside" (187). If that is true, if the basic foundational principles and the constructions of subjectivity from which children's literature emerged are changing, then children's literature might be expected to change also. A more fundamental implication of Hardt and Negri's argument, however, is that the world of "hybrid identities, flexible hierarchies, and plural exchanges through modulating networks of command" (xii–xiii) that they postulate is a world without childhood as now understood.

Implicit in what I have been arguing, of course, is that both childhood and adulthood as currently understood are hybrid—that there are hidden adult aspects necessary in the self-understanding of current childhood subjectivity and that adults must retain and be concerned about an uncolonized other within themselves. But both childhood and adult subjectivity as currently defined either demand the hiding of their hybridity or else acknowledge it only as a paradox, and both approaches retain the foundational oppositional nature of the binaries. Without that foundational opposition and that hiding, logic suggests, a literature directed specifically at children cannot exist. In the new regime Hardt and Negri envisage, in which everyone is consciously and happily hybrid, all literature would necessarily have the potential of speaking to all human beings in their full potential for hybridity, not to any specific audience conceived as being other than everybody else.

Meanwhile, however, children's literature still continues to be marketed as such and, I believe, still bears its foundational markers of ambivalence—an ambivalence that does not celebrate its hybridity but hides it. The adult understanding hidden in children's literature remains hidden, in the shadows, necessarily repressed so that both adults and children can continue to understand that childhood is different from and outside adulthood but on the way in. I suggested in chapter 1 that the more complex shadow texts of children's literature have a relationship to their actual simpler texts parallel to the relationship between the pictures and the words in children's picture books. A brief look at the nature of that relationship ought to fill in further details about the nature of the divided subjectivity engendered by such divided texts and suggest further reasons for the continuing sameness of the literature that continues to be divided in these ways.

Merely because picture books express themselves in two different media, their implied audience is inherently divided. Pictures imply a specific sort of viewer merely in being pictures, a viewer unlike the reader implied by the words of a text. Compared to printed words, for instance, pictures directly offer a relatively dense sensuous experience—the kind of experience the words can only imply. Pictures contain textures, colors, shapes, lines—a variety of things for the eye to respond to and be pleased by, for these aspects of pictures are and are meant to be pleasing in and for themselves, without reference to the meanings or objects they have been made to represent. To look at, say, a patch of intense red is sensuously arousing without any reference to the apple or fire truck the patch of red might be representing in a particular picture.

Of course, the colors, lines, and shapes in picture books do represent other things. The red patch is an apple or a fire truck, not just a patch of red. Pictures operate as a system of signs. As I describe in my book *Words about Pictures,* every aspect of them helps to convey specific meanings to knowledgeable viewers. Their implied viewer knows these signs, has a conscious or unconscious awareness of how they allow lines and colors on a flat page to convey ideas of people, places, and things. Such an implied viewer is caught up in and constrained by the cultural understandings that make the visible world meaningful. And as Fredric Jameson suggests, "As sight becomes a separate activity in its own right, it acquires new objects that are themselves the products of a process of abstraction and rationalization which strips the experience of the concrete of such attributes as color, spatial depth, texture and the like."[18] To interpret sensuous information as a sign is to deflect attention from it as purely sensuous experience.

I might, at this point, argue that what is true of the sensuous aspects of pictures is also true of the emotionally satisfying aspects of narrative texts. To interpret exciting events or interesting characters in terms of the meanings that authors inevitably invite us to attach to them—to place them inside narratives with shapes and structures—is to deflect attention from them as purely sensuous experience. Often in characteristic texts of children's literature, the meanings directly undermine and attack the validity of the pleasure, as protagonists like Potter's Peter Rabbit or Sendak's Max of *Where the Wild Things Are* first indulge in and then learn the deficiencies of bodily pleasure. The ways in which pictures engage and co-opt sensuous pleasure stand as a model for the ways in which texts in general hope to act on their audiences.

In picture books, nevertheless, the sensuous information that contains and conveys abstracted and rationalized cultural knowledge remains, and it continues to convey itself while it is conveying the cultural knowledge. The patch of red is still, whatever it represents, a patch of red. It has been brought inside the network of language—but it still retains the essence of its outsiderliness. To understand what the red represents, the implied viewer has no choice but to see it and to respond to it as itself, as well as in terms of what it has come to represent. According to Julia Kristeva, this represents a path to liberation from the constraint of being constructed as a specific kind of subject placed within specific cultural values: "It is through color—colors—that the subject escapes its alienation within a code (representational, ideological, symbolic, and so forth) that it, as a conscious subject, accepts. . . . The chromatic apparatus, like rhythm in language, thus involves a shattering of meaning and its subject into a scale of differences."[19] So, too, it seems, do lines and shapes and textures shatter meanings merely by insisting on being themselves. The act of observing that which contains and conveys meanings therefore undermines the meanings, just as the meanings undermine the pure sensations of the containers in and for themselves. The implied viewer, who can and must both respond to the containers and perceive the meaning they contain, is, once more, pulled in two ways, toward the insiderly meaningful, which is communal and constraining, and toward the outsiderly sensuous, which is pleasurable and unconstrainedly antimeaningful. The implied viewer of picture books is a divided subject and is so, I believe, in ways that help to account for the divided subjectivity invited by texts of children's literature in general. All these texts also inevitably require and invite pleasure in the very process of co-opting and undermining pleasure and thus undermine their own acts of undermining. In moving the inside out—enmeshing children in adult values—they bring the outside in—allow childishness into adult-controlled territory.

In picture books the division in the implied audience is confirmed and reinforced by the fact that the books contain both words and pictures. The viewer they imply knows not only what kind of information to expect from each of these two different media, each requiring a different set of assumptions, but also how to put the information together into a whole. This includes some fairly basic strategies of meaning-making, such as, for instance, assuming that the house one sees in a picture accompanying a text about a house is the house the text mentions—that despite the fact that there are two different signs for it in two different sign systems, there is just one house. Interpreting the picture as intended also requires some more-sophisticated strategies, such as guessing from the appearance of the house in the illustration information about its age, its possible location in time or space as implied by its architectural style, the relative degree of wealth of those who live in it, the possibility of someone being content to live in such a dwelling. The implied reader also knows how to apply all this visual information to the situation outlined by a text—interpret the words and their implications in the light of information provided by a perusal of the pictures. Such a reader knows how to be analytical, how to compare and combine information from different sources, how to infer a complex field of possibilities, how to solve a puzzle (and to enjoy solving it). Children encouraged to become such readers are becoming meaning-makers, actively engaged in solving the puzzles.

I can, once more, argue that the unavoidable doubleness of a text in two media remains a characteristic feature of a text of children's literature in words alone. The shadow texts of contextual information that the text evokes and depends on in order to be at all meaningful operates as an invisible version of the pictures in relation to the words, and it demands more or less the same kind of engagement in acts of interpretation—puzzle solving.

But there is, once more, a paradox and a further division. The mastery that readers develop as puzzle solvers tends to master them, as they increasingly become able to realize solutions to the puzzles that were the ones intended by the author and illustrator, become increasingly aligned with the subject the text intends to construct. This is how texts characteristically work to impose adult images of childhood subjectivity on their child readers, to claim the outsider for the inside.

Meanwhile, the mere act of looking at the words in all texts and both the words and the pictures in picture books in order to make meaning out of them adds yet a further dimension—and division—to the implied reader. People can't make anything like the sense an author might have intended out of words or an illustrator out of a picture with their noses pressed firmly against the books they appear in. To understand both the words and the pictures, people need to position themselves at some distance from them. Marshall McLuhan suggests, "Psychically the printed book, an extension of the visual faculty, intensified perspective and the fixed point of view."[20] If this is true, then pictures, even more intimately connected with the visual faculty than is the printed text, must do something similar. Both require readers to distance themselves from what they observe in order to observe it in a meaningful and accurate manner. Such readers will tend to trust the value and validity of the detached, isolated point of view—and tend to mistrust the value and validity of what they perceive by other means—by touch, for instance.

Younger children who have not yet developed that skill often tend to scan picture books, giving equal attention to all parts of the picture plane—and they often find interesting or unexpected details that more experienced viewers miss completely. Experienced viewers, who know how to stand back and read the information in a picture that suggests perspective and, consequently, a focus on certain objects within it understood to be important—what the picture is "really" about—tend to interpret the discoveries of inexperienced, unfixed scanners as errors. They believe they know the one right way to view. The same is true in terms of texts on their own. Less experienced readers often understand texts in ways different from what adult readers are sure they mean simply because the less experienced readers lack complete knowledge of the repertoire of sublimated knowledge that shadows the texts.

And the "right" meanings, merely in existing and in being right, establish hierarchies, priorities, centers, and margins. The act of looking at a picture and establishing which of the group of visual objects it depicts is actually its focalized subject—the person, or the cat on the person's lap, or the lamp on the table beside the person, or the flower in the drapery in the background—constructs the reader / viewer as conscious of and operating within the context of such hierarchies. So does reading a text and understanding which of the actions or objects it describes are most significant. Such a subject views the world politically, in terms of attributing various degrees of importance to the objects within it. Children who can read and enjoy picture books and other texts of children's literature have become political beings, insiders conscious of and seeking out the inevitably varying dispositions of power and interest and attention in the world around them.

Yet they are also individuals, with a consciousness of their individuality, their separateness from and difference from the world around them. According to Walter J. Ong, oral storytelling, which takes place in the context of shared experience as many listeners become an audience, tends to create communities.[21] Cultures in which oral storytelling predominates imply, and therefore, presumably, tend to consist of, people who think of themselves primarily in terms of their place in the community as a whole and who take less interest in the subtle distinctions that make them unique or just different from others. To read a printed book, however, one must separate oneself from the community, have a private experience in isolation from others. Consequently, cultures with print imply and therefore, presumably, tend to develop individuals conscious of and interested in their separation from and differences from each other—their outsiderliness.

Children's literature obviously does just that—is intended to do just that, can and does offer that isolated and individuality-building sort of experience to solitary readers (and, in terms of picture books, solitary viewers). But texts of children's literature in general—and especially picture books—are often read by adults to children singly or in groups and thus can also support more communal forms of experience and self-perception. Furthermore, the pictures in picture books can be viewed by more than one person at a time, although, of course, all the viewers must be positioned in front of the pictures and at an appropriate distance from them in order to make something like the implied sense out of them. So picture books especially, but texts of children's literature in general, support to some degree the relatively unselfconscious community that Ong as-cribes to oral cultures as well as the self-absorbed isolation of books consisting of nothing but print and that are read privately. This is, once more, a compromise between the self and the communal, possibly even an ambivalent pull in both directions. Is the story just for you alone or for you as a member of a group? Are you most significantly yourself or a part of a community, an outsider or an insider? Once more, the implied reader of these texts must feel both pulls at once, be both inside and outside—possess a divided subjectivity.

The division is confirmed yet again in picture books by the human figures who appear in the pictures and by the relationships those figures imply between themselves and those who view them. Like the actors in a play or a movie, they are there to be looked at. In many picture books they even smile out at us, apparently conscious of and happy about the presence of viewers. Whether they acknowledge their position or not, these figures share in a somewhat less aggressive form the invitation to voyeurism that John Berger discovers in both contemporary pinup photographs and traditional European paintings of nudes. The implied viewer of these pictures is a Peeping Tom with the right to peep, to linger over details, to enjoy and interpret and make judgments about them.[22] He or she is a person of great power in relation to that which he or she views. Once more, the act of looking is a model for the act of reading. Nonpictorial texts are as much an invitation to allowable voyeurism as pictures are.

In the depictions of nude adults Berger talks about, the implied viewer is someone quite different from the person being viewed: a male rather than a female, probably a clothed male rather than a naked one (such clothed males sometimes appear in famous paintings of naked women, looking at the women who look out of the painting at viewers as they view it), and specifically a male with the right to view. As Berger suggests, the person in the picture is defined in a power relationship with the viewer. Men have the right to look, the power to hold what they see in their gaze. Women are primarily that which men have the right to look at, possessions, something whose primary duty is to look good and to be seen. The nude and its implied viewer sum up a power dynamic that defines what was the traditional relationship of men and women in the European civilization that produced such paintings. A sizable feminist discourse based in the psychoanalytical theories of Jacques Lacan talks about women and others becoming "subject to the gaze"—at the mercy of a more powerful being whose power is defined by the right and ability to stand at some distance from them and view them.[23] In learning to become the implied viewer of picture books, the implied outsider/ reader of nonpictorial texts, children simultaneously learn to identify with the powerful gazer and to subject others to their gaze. They learn to be in charge.

In picture books and other texts of children's literature, however, the viewer and the viewee, the gazer and the gazed at, are, in an important sense, the same person. A child views or reads about a child who represents him- or herself, for as I have been suggesting, encouraging child readers to see themselves in terms of the characters represented—to identify with them in order to learn from their stories, to become the children that adults have imagined for them—is a primary characteristic of children's literature. If children are meant to see themselves in these texts, then they must imagine themselves as having the power to gaze at themselves and to see themselves as depicted. On the one hand, they have the power of the gaze. On the other hand, they are subjected to a gaze—which is, strangely, their own gaze.

These books offer a continuing repetition throughout childhood, and possibly even beyond, of the moment Lacan defines as the mirror stage: that moment in infancy in which a child identifies itself with its image in a mirror. At this point the child, who has previously lived in a seamless universe and made no distinction between itself and other things, develops an ego, a sense of self, and does so by realizing that there are things outside it, such as the space around its image in the mirror. The child perceives that it exists as a separate self, only inside a context that is larger than itself, and this context makes the child feel small in relation to it. Once people identify themselves with the smaller versions of themselves they see in the mirror, therefore, they are always conscious of themselves as diminished, lacking a wholeness they once had, eternally striving for it and never achieving it. The image constrains and constricts them—as smaller-than-life representations of children in picture books construct child viewers who identify with them, as the safely contained representations of subversive anarchy in children's books in general contain children within adults' ideas of the childlike.

To be conscious of oneself in terms of the imagery of mirrors is to be inevitably divided. Lacan speaks of "the very bipolar nature of all subjectivity."[24] A self is both that which thinks or views, the separate detached consciousness, and that which is being viewed or thought about. I am that which sees myself as this. In demanding and therefore confirming this relationship in the number of ways I have been describing, picture books play their part in establishing what Lacan calls "an alienating identity" built on what is only an "illusion of autonomy."[25] Viewers are what the pictures have encouraged them to believe themselves to be. But merely by being enough outside of that constructed self to observe it, they inevitably sense how incomplete and illusory that self is. Viewers are also, therefore, that which senses the incompleteness of what they now call themselves. They are free and not free, autonomous and constrained, isolated and enmeshed. They are divided.

I suggested earlier that impositions of meaning on the basic sensations of color and shape and line still leave the sensations operating outside the system. Here, similarly, the imposition of adults' ideas of children on children still leave that which the ideas do not contain, an unconscious or just an unacknowledged presence, operating outside them. In both cases there is something of the outside left inside the inside. Both the texts that the system produces and the subjectivity that those texts work to construct are divided in terms of being both colonized and uncolonized—adult and not adult.

But if Lacan is in any way right to postulate the mirror stage, then the division is inherent and unavoidable. It is not a distinct description of the subjectivity invited and implied by children's literature, specifically, but merely a description of one stage of human development—a stage that leads to and underpins the nature of all human consciousness, not just that of children. Similarly, if Mc-Luhan and Ong are in any way right about the effects of reading on readers, then the detachment I have described is also inherent and unavoidable. It is not a distinct description of the subjectivity invited and implied in child readers specifically, but merely a description of all readers. Human beings are all either children with adults operating inside them or adults with children hidden inside them.

It is true, of course, that some human beings are excluded from these general descriptions—for instance, those from cultures prior to the invention of the printing press in which most people did not read. And while Lacanians and other adherents of psychoanalysis might object, it seems safe to postulate that the dynamics of subjectivity Lacan described are also based in culture—how subjectivity works in the consciousness engendered by specific historical forces. It might be no accident that literacy and middle-class values begin at more or less the same time and place, and have such an interconnected history, or that critiques of psychoanalysis often focus on its specific application to middle-class Europeans of a particular time and place. The various theories of divided subjectivity that I have been exploring have clear connections with each other and

represent ways of understanding different facets of the same entity: consciousness as it developed over the last half a millennium or so from an origin in
Europe.

In these circumstances my arguments about the sameness of children's literature are true but possibly pointless. It seems that texts of children's literature
remain the same as each other across time and place merely because they share
the features of *all* texts produced by human beings in that half-millennium. These
particular explanations of sameness actually undermine the possibility that children's literature is a distinct genre.

To some degree, I think, they do. All texts inevitably must have shadow texts,
and all readers must be aware of them. Most texts in the history of European
writing—all but what Roland Barthes identifies as the "writerly" ones that readers
more or less make meaningful for themselves[26]—invite their readers both to adopt
an author's way of thinking about the world and themselves *and* be conscious of
themselves doing so, be outsiders being brought in but also, simultaneously, being
left out. As a result, most texts invite a bipolar, ambivalent subjectivity and an
enactment of consciously inauthentic selfhood. But texts of children's literature do
so in a particularly direct, particularly pure, particularly intense, and particularly
deliberate way.

They do so, once more, because of the basic condition of their existence: an
author who knows more producing literature for an audience that knows less and
cannot produce literature for itself. In a sense all literature is produced under
these conditions. Writers know more of what they think and imagine than their
potential readers do, and they operate with the assumption that those readers
cannot imagine and think for themselves as the writers do. If they could, there
would be no need for the literature to exist. The fact is that adults' conceptions of
themselves as adults and of young people as childlike (i.e., lacking something
adults have) represent intense, extreme, and highly conscious versions of all
writers' conceptions of themselves and of their audiences. Thus, children's literature is characterized by its intense, extreme, and highly conscious expression of
that relationship.

I might put this in a slightly different way. Childhood, as understood in the
time in which children's literature has existed, is inexplicable without its implied
comparison to adulthood. Children can be perceived as lacking only in terms of
what adults have, as simple in their thinking only in relation to more complex
adult thought, and so on. Childhood is outside only in relation to adulthood as
inside. Inevitably, then, children's literature bears the marks of that comparison.
It exists oppositionally. It is not merely simple but simpler and less complete than

adult literature. It must, therefore, be inherently oppositional, imply what it purports to exclude. As I suggested in the last chapter, deconstructionists like Jacques Derrida argue that the characteristic of implying that which is different and other is an inherent quality of all uses of language, which operates by allowing us to understand things and concepts exactly in terms of how they differ from what they are not and that, consequently, always carry within themselves the very meanings they exclude. From this point of view, the ways in which childhood inevitably implies its opposite and in which children's literature is best characterized by its hidden adult content, is merely a special—and again, I believe, a fairly deliberate and especially intense—example of how language in general and human thought in general operate, at least insofar as they have been understood by writers and thinkers in the modern era. Its business of inviting children to think of themselves in terms of shared adult understandings of childhood is merely its most characteristic expression of an overall and unavoidable function—a function of all communication in recent centuries: to place people inside of and see themselves in terms of and yet at odds with the system of meanings and constraints and differences that language itself is.

Children's literature does this in its characteristic especially intense way for a variety of reasons. First, it insists on defining itself as lack or absence and therefore inevitably evokes that which it lacks and makes absent. Second, it works to efface its shadow—to be simple, childlike, and so on—and thus implies particularly marked contrasts between its surface and its shadows. Third, it assumes that the double subjectivity it supports is in the process of being created, as not yet in place, and therefore it addresses its implied readers as in the process of becoming the subjects it seeks. It is inherently didactic.

Different Children's Literatures: The Effects of Personality and History

I suggested earlier that there could be no question but that, despite its underlying sameness, children's literature produced in different times and places was bound to be different. Now I would like to explore the nature of those differences a little further. My intention is not to offer a survey of the history of the genre. That is a monumental project deserving of at least another book or two—and, ideally, not by me. I want here merely to identify some specific forces that might lead to differences and to consider the mechanisms that might account for what does change and especially, since this is my main purpose in this book, what doesn't change.

Beyond individual details not affected by the fact that the texts are intended for children, the most obvious—to my mind, the only obvious—reason for differences in texts of children's literature must be differences in the adult ideas about childhood that lead adults to write for children. How adults imagine childhood determines why and how they address child readers—and different adults have imagined it differently, both on an individual basis and more generally, in different times and places.

The key defining markers of children's literature—simplicity, adherence to conventional story patterns, focalization from a childlike point of view—all work to make texts for children more like each other than not. Despite the recent "metafictional" texts I discuss later in this chapter, most adults have a hard time accepting a text identified as being for children that varies much from these qualities—one that is noticeably complex or that presents events in an unusual narrative sequence—as a text for children at all. As a consequence, individual difference, the qualities that distinguish one author's writing from another's even when the two writers write in the same place at the same time, is less pronounced in even the most literary texts of children's literature than it tends to be in serious adult literature. As Maria Nikolajeva suggests, children's literature is a "canonic" literature—one that sticks to its formulas and archetypes.[27] Lois Kuznets has shown how respected children's novels by Lois Lenski and Noel Streatfeild contain the underlying formulas of popular fiction that the theorist John G. Cawelti has outlined: "Both seem to have produced only a layer of realism imposed upon a stereotypical structure, which in turn rested upon an archetypal base."[28] Kuznets suggests that these books and many other "good" children's novels are "individualized formulaic narratives," as distinguished from more complex children's novels. But as I have argued throughout this book, even more complex texts of children's literature tend to have more in common with works of popular fiction than do literary texts for adults. As my interpretations in chapter 1 suggest, relatively complex texts like *Alice's Adventures in Wonderland* or *Plain City* can also be read as individualized formulaic narratives, their distinct surfaces resting on conventional story patterns. I have no doubt that those patterns can be seen to rest on archetypal bases—that, for instance, Alice and Buhlaire fulfill the roles of questing heroes.

This is not to say that these texts are not individualized, that individual differences between texts don't exist, or that individual texts of children's literature are not expressive of an adult author's complex and distinct adult personality. They obviously are. Sendak's *Where the Wild Things Are* and Keats's *The Snowy Day* were produced within a year of each other in the same city. Both use similarly simple language, a child's focalization, and the same story pattern, a trip away from and back to a restraining but safe home presided over by the protagonist's mother. More generally, both follow the rigid conventions of picture books produced in the United States in their time (and still in ours): a set number of pages, a recognizable shape and size, very short texts surrounded by a lot of white space, one relatively complex color picture on every double-paged spread. Even so, each of these books has a distinct tone, creates a distinct atmosphere, and conveys a distinct sense of what it feels like to be human and alive. It is highly unlikely that anyone not knowing who produced these books would imagine that they were by the same author. Both of them have a quality that adult readers tend to identify with literary excellence: they seem to possess and convey something unique—presumably, something that emerges from their authors' distinct personalities.

Still, Sendak's and Keats's expression of their distinct selves is seriously constrained by the fact that the texts they have produced aspire—and aspire successfully—to be children's literature; they are positions taken in a preexisting and complex field. They must express their distinct adult voices in terms of the forms of address conventionally used for their implied audience; they must speak (and also draw) less distinctively than they would most likely have the freedom to do were they producing equivalently literary texts for adults. Kuznets's discovery even in quality children's novels of Cawelti's markers for popular literature—a veneer of specific realism over a stereotypical structure based on an archetypal formula—points the way to an understanding of the combination of formula and distinctness characteristic of children's literature. Unlike a lot of popular literature for adults, these texts do tend to have distinct flavors or personalities. But unlike serious literature for adults, that distinctness is noticeably constrained by the assumptions about lacks in children that underlie the genre. "Quality" children's literature—that which adult critics recommend and admire and that is not itself just formula fiction—represents a balancing point where the required sameness of formula fiction and the required difference of serious literature for adults meet and balance each other.

Beyond the distinctions between individual texts, children's literature in general might well be different at different points in history. As societies change in response to the passage of time and the pressure of disruptive events and economic forces, their ideas about children—and therefore, the texts they produce for children—are as likely to change as much as anything else does. And they obviously have changed. What continues to interest me is what I have focused on in this book: the less obvious sameness underlying these obvious differences in the time in which adults have produced children's literature.

Let me return for a moment to James Janeway. Earlier in this chapter I made two possibly contradictory assertions about his writing for children. First, I suggested that there was an underlying similarity between *A Token for Children* and picture books of our own time that could be accounted for as the inevitable consequences of adults deciding to write for children. Second, though, I suggested that the audience implied by children's literature since Newbery is different from Janeway's audience in being allowed the delights of sensual pleasure. I have said that *A Token for Children* is both fundamentally the same as and decidedly different from the children's literature that followed it. How can both be true?

The answer cannot be simply that Janeway is an individual writer like Sendak or, for that matter, Newbery, whose variations from generic markers can be accounted for in terms of his distinct personality. His texts vary from all those written later in much the same way as do other texts written by others in his place and time, and they do so almost exactly because of the ways in which the Puritan values of these writers are at odds with those of the consumer culture that has been the source of most children's literature since. There is, however, a connection between those cultures that can account for the underlying similarity in the texts they produce for children. They were both capitalist cultures.

According to the time-honored thesis of the sociologist Max Weber, it was Protestant ideas about salvation that led to bourgeois capitalism and its focus on success in the marketplace.[29] God in his omniscience had elected those destined for eternal life prior to their birth and revealed their status to them and others by rewarding them here on the earth. Therefore, those who made (and could spend) the most money could be most convinced of their state of grace: the antimaterial spirituality of Protestantism then led inevitably to the materialism of capitalism. Although sociologists have been challenging Weber's ideas for decades, the ideas do suggest an important link between the thinking of Puritans like Janeway and merchants like Newbery—a link that might help account for the sameness that underpins their quite different writing for children.

The possibility of that link points a way toward the possibility that the differences might merely be different forms of the same thing. The major difference is Newbery's focus on plum-cake—on offering pleasure as a positive thing. It is hard for adults now to imagine that children in Janeway's time might actually have enjoyed his hair-raising horror stories about deeply faithful children who die badly but with their faith wonderfully intact. But I think that is exactly what the adults who produced them did imagine. As Harvey Darton says, "They *were* meant to give pleasure: the highest pleasure, that of studying and enjoying the Will of God."[30] I would wager, furthermore, that they did give pleasure to the children for whom they were intended, for those children would have been immersed in their parents' spiritual values. These texts might well operate as a sort of wish-fulfillment fantasy for the child readers they imply, who are themselves in need of reading about and learning from ideally faithful children exactly because they are not (or at least not yet) so perfect themselves. In these years prior to Newbery, in this community so different from the mainstream twenty-first-century one, what offered pleasure was different from what people now assume is pleasurable. But the ambivalent wish to both instruct children and please them was already in place, and the stories in *A Token for Children* express many of the qualities I arrived at as generic markers at the end of chapter 3.

Consider, for instance, Janeway's "Of a notorious wicked child, who was taken up from begging, and admirably converted; with an account of his holy Life and joyful Death, when he was nine years old." Like many later stories for children—and including recent Newbery medal winners like Christopher Curtis's *Bud Not Buddy* and Linda Sue Park's *A Single Shard*—this story concerns an orphaned child who experiences the dangerous complexities of the adult world outside before achieving an appropriately safe and childlike home. As in many children's stories, this child is first "a very Monster of wickedness . . . old in naughtiness when he was young in years," and then presumably "young" in lack of naughtiness as he gets older: "such a strange alteration was wrought in the child, that all the parish that rung of his villainy before, was now ready to talk of his reformation . . . and he is like another creature."[31] Like the children in many later stories, he achieves this successful otherness by adopting an adult conception of his childish self: "The child grew exceedingly in knowledge, experiences, patience, humility, and self-abhorrency, and he thought he could never speak bad enough of himself; the Name that he would call himself by, was a Toad" (52). Finally, and to my mind, ambivalently, his self-abhorrence brings him self-acceptance and a happy ending, as "he snapt his fingers and thumb together with abundance of joy," accepts Christ's will, and dies "in full joy and assurance of Gods love" (53). He is an outsider successfully brought inside enough to be able to express in safety an outsiderly sort of joyous exuberance. He can be safely joyful because he now has an insider's guilty understanding of what his own outsiderly joy means.

If Puritan children's literature can be read as a variation on the children's literature that emerged later, so, too, can texts written in later periods be read as variations of Newbery's and of each other. There are a number of points in the last few centuries at which the nature of children's literature as a whole changed direction and became different from what preceded it and yet, more remarkably, remained the same.

Consider, for instance, Andrew O'Malley's idea that the texts published by Newbery and others often identified as the first children's literature represent an imposition of new meanings on already existing texts—the chapbook stories of giants, heroes, and criminals. O'Malley's description of the way these texts retain a residue of their sources in the context of new didactic purposes—"the cohabitation of . . . middle-class sentiments in the same text with episodes of a decidedly fantastic, fairy-tale quality"[32]—makes them sound like the perfect representatives of the ambivalent balance between pleasure and learning that I have been suggesting is most centrally characteristic of children's literature.

As becomes clear in a consideration of Newbery's precursors, earlier texts written for or read by children seemed to represent one or the other of these qualities but rarely, in any noticeable way, both. As O'Malley suggests, the popular chapbooks he discusses, not intended specifically for an audience of children, were relatively devoid of didactic content and marked by a fairy-tale quality. They emerge from the tradition of oral tales that later came to be written down as what we now call fairy tales, produced specifically for audiences of children. Texts like Janeway's, however, intended for children and not obviously similar to fairy tales, have their roots in a tradition of didactic literature going back to Aesop's fables and the parables of the New Testament. Children's literature as we know it thus emerged as a combination of these two different and even opposite forms of story, implying two different and opposite needs in their readers.

Fables are anti-wish-fulfillment. They tell those who read or listen to them that they won't get what they want unless they learn the socially acceptable values being promoted. Fairy tales are antididactic. They tell those who read or listen to them that they don't have to change to get what they want. (Traditional popular fairy tales such as Perrault's "Cinderella" insist that people get what they want exactly be being childlike—powerless, innocent, rather stupid—and chapbook tales often describe triumphantly successful thieves and tricksters.) As a blend or a balancing of these two kinds of text with opposing views of the world and of how and why things happen to people in it, children's literature since Newbery has had no choice but to be ambivalent—as ambivalent as the childhood subjectivity it works to construct. As I suggested earlier, it seems to have been the urge to construct such a subjectivity that led to the blending of these two kinds of texts.

But O'Malley argues that texts like Newbery's are not just balanced but transitional—that the balance is between an earlier primarily pleasurable chapbook experience and "the predominantly didactic form of the children's book characteristic of the rational and evangelical writing movements of the late eighteenth century."[33] The implication is that children's literature does change—diverges from its most characteristic form even a few years after the first appearance of its foundational texts. Clearly it does. But as I argued in chapter 1, even a "predominantly didactic" text like "The Purple Jar," written only shortly after the late eighteenth-century texts O'Malley so characterizes, still allows for, even insists on, some ambivalence about the value of childishness. I might suggest, then, that children's literature changes by changing the balance of its two poles of the didactic and the pleasurable in response to current pressures but that it remains the same by always representing *some* balance of the two poles.

This becomes clearer in the next widely different form of children's literature to develop, in the texts produced in England and America later in the nineteenth century. Victorians developed an interest in childhood that led them to treasure its irrational innocence and vulnerable need for adult care in ways quite at odds with Edgeworth's declared focus on making children more reasonable and self-reliant. As Alan Richardson says, "Nineteenth century children's literature, both in Britain and America, is pervasively indebted to canonical Romanticism. . . . The 'Immortality' ode alone had an extensive influence."[34] Julia Dusinberre agrees, claiming that Wordsworth's "Intimations" ode "must be almost the most quoted text of the nineteenth century, appearing with wearisome regularity every time children are mentioned," and Barbara Garlitz adds that "the Ode was to the first half of the nineteenth century what *The Origin of Species* was to the last half. In fact, the Ode had as powerful an influence on nineteenth-century ideas of childhood as Freud has had on present-day ones."[35]

Yet a Victorian text like *Alice's Adventures in Wonderland* is as ambivalent about the value of Alice's innocence as Edgeworth is about Rosamond's capacity for mature reason. Speaking of Victorian fantasy writers for children, U. C. Knoepflmacher says, "Torn between the opposing demands of innocence and experience, the author who resorts to the wishful, magical thinking of the child nonetheless feels compelled, in varying degrees, to hold on to the grown-up's circumscribed notions about reality."[36] Indeed, as Knoepflmacher says in his book *Ventures into Childland*, "Authors who write (and illustrate) books for children inevitably depict a traffic between childhood and maturity."[37] The ambivalence of that traffic is there, in variant forms, across the periods and is exactly what leads to the variations, as one side or the other of the various oppositions inherent in adult thinking about childhood perform their continuing dance of excluding and insisting on each other. A comment by Alan Richardson is instructive here: "The Romantic emphasis on growth and on the self as a 'mind that grows' participated in a larger cultural enterprise to place individuals within developmental schemes subject to internalized observation and self-regulation. . . . Thus the Romantic cult of childhood can be linked to its apparent contrary, the rationalist and progressive child-centred discourse which insures the reproduction of 'self-regulated, rational and autonomous subjects' required for the self-perpetuation of modern capitalist economies."[38]

As a precursor of modern capitalist economies, the Victorian age was the time when the empires of European countries were at their most powerful, so it is not surprising that the texts it produced for children show signs of imperial thinking and work to construct a specifically imperial subjectivity. According to Daphne Kutzer, "empire is everywhere in classic children's texts of the later nineteenth century, and its presence continues well into the twentieth."[39] Peter Hunt and Karen Sands agree: "Just as the concept of 'empire' saturated British culture, so virtually all (English-language) histories of children's literature agree that children's books, always fundamentally involved in reflecting and transmitting culture, were the witting or unwitting agents of the empire builders."[40]

Perhaps they were. As I suggested in chapter 3, however, children's literature generally constructs subjectivities in ways that seem colonial—that make it seem something like an imperial project of adult needs. So perhaps the specific childhood subjectivity of Victorian empire builders merely replicates the childhood subjectivity typical not only during but also before and after the Victorian period. Hunt and Sand ask, "Is colonialism now an ineradicable virus in the British psyche, or was, for example, the adventure story of exploration a mode predating and appropriated by empire, which can re-emerge unscathed from its shadow?"[41] I suspect the answer is both. Empire might well have appropriated already-existing forms of children's literature for its own imperial purposes—forms that represent not so much a specifically imperial virus in the British psyche as a more generally colonial virus in the mainstream adult psyche. Post-empire, the children's adventure story might well emerge from the shadow of empire—but, paradoxically, it is likely to still be colonial.

Even so, as Jo-Ann Wallace says, it is "no accident that the 'golden age' of English children's literature peaked . . . during the high noon . . . of Empire.'"[42] The imperialism of empire seems to have concentrated the colonialism inherent in children's literature and, therefore, helped to establish conventions that might well still operate in children's literature now, perhaps exemplifying the ideology of form that Jameson views as a text's "political unconscious."[43] Speaking of Edward Said's question, "How does Orientalism transmit or reproduce itself from one epoch to another?" Mavis Reimer says, "Imperialist children's literature in general seems to me one of the important sites for investigating Said's question of reproduction, since it is the literature of the last half of the nineteenth century that has set many of the narrative paradigms and practices of what we continue to recognize as children's texts."[44] The specific characteristics of children's literature of one time might turn out to have become the characteristics of children's literature generally.

As well as continuing to reflect empire in ways that began earlier in the Victorian period, the last decades of the nineteenth century and the first ones of the twentieth seem a particularly important turning point for children's literature, at least in England. Wallace is not alone in identifying this time as a "Golden Age." Humphrey Carpenter says, "The expression 'Golden Age' is often applied to the period of English children's books from Carroll to Milne."[45] This was certainly a time of change in the culture as a whole and, consequently, a time of change in writing for adults.

Although not intended for children, that writing had a lot to say about childhood—especially the idyllic childhood viewed through the lens of nostalgia. As Kimberley Reynolds suggests, later Victorian writers like Pater, Morris, and Ruskin "thought of the past generally as superior to the present, and since childhood could be understood to represent the past in a number of ways (for instance, in the past all adults were children, children were thought to be more primitive than adults and so more closely linked to the past, etc.), it came to have considerable metaphoric value in late-Victorian Britain."[46] Not surprisingly, ideas of a utopian past and ideas about a utopian childhood came together in texts written specifically for children: "Quite apart from the sheer quality of the books," Carpenter says, "one observes that many of them seem to be set in a distant era when things were better than they are now. And childhood itself seemed a Golden Age to many of these writers, as they set out to recapture its sensations."[47]

But the idyll was not an untroubled or uncomplicated world of innocence. Other cultural factors were also at work. "The 1880s and 1890s," says Elaine Showalter, "in the words of the novelist George Gissing, were decades of 'sexual anarchy,' when all the laws that governed sexual identity and behavior seemed to be breaking down. . . . During this period both the words 'feminism' and 'homosexuality' first came into use."[48] It seems logical that the cultural forces that led to such changes would also change ideas about childhood, particularly since, as I suggested in the last chapter, ideas about childhood tend almost always to be intimately connected with assumptions about gender and sexuality, and ideas about gender have tended to be a significant component of ideas about childhood ever since children's literature came into existence.

According to Showalter, "Women's social or cultural marginality seems to place them on the borderlines of the symbolic order, both the 'frontier between men and chaos,' and dangerously part of chaos itself, inhabitants of a mysterious and frightening wild zone outside of patriarchal culture."[49] Equally marginal, children occupy the same border position between the inside and the outside, and traditionally, as my earlier discussions of colonization reveal, need to be policed and constrained for the same reasons. Showalter shows how women's demands for power toward the end of the nineteenth century came to be represented as a dangerous but attractive intrusion of anarchy. The same could be said for childhood as envisaged by children's writers of this period.

In earlier times children's literature seemed to represent children as either pure innocents, and therefore good and admirable, or as uncivilized anarchists, and therefore bad and in need of education. I have argued that read more closely, a text like "The Purple Jar" troubles that view. "Golden Age" writers like James Barrie, E. Nesbit, Kenneth Grahame, and Rudyard Kipling confuse the categories in a much more obvious fashion. They imagine children like Barrie's Peter Pan or Nesbit's Oswald of *The Story of the Treasure Seekers* or Kipling's Stalky of *Stalky and Co.*, or childlike creatures like Grahame's Toad in *The Wind in the Willows,* as uncivilized anarchists and therefore, paradoxically, good and admirable: the idyllic is anticivilized. It is at this point, I suspect, that childhood begins to function as subversive—as a way for adults to attack commonly held adult values. It is instructive that many of these books contain references to Pan *(Peter Pan)* or Pan-figures *(The Wind in the Willows)* or other tricksters (Stalky, Nesbit's Psammead)—representations of a joyfully antisocial and antirational spirit of disorder and anarchy.

According to Julia Dusinberre,

> When the late nineteenth century found that its researches into origin and development focused attention on the child, it simultaneously produced for those children a literature which revealed as clearly as possible adult hopes for the new generation. This will always be the case because children do not write their own books and their books are bought for them by teachers and parents. But it also means that in times of great change some of the most radical ideas about what the future ought to be like will be located in the books which are written for the new generation.[50]

Dusinberre finds an "attack on Victorian stuffiness, humbug, self-importance, moral earnestness, utilitarianism and middle-class complacency" in Carroll's *Alice* books and suggests that "the children's writers who followed Carroll . . . anticipated in different ways the radical experiments not only of [Virginia] Woolf's later novels but also of *The Voyage Out, Night and Day* and *Jacob's Room*" (74).

Significantly, however, that radical anarchy in these texts for children does not extend to the free expression of bodily desire. Childhood is understood as asexual and tends to function as an escape from adult sexuality. In many texts of this period there is a nostalgia for childhood as a place before or beyond sexual desire. In *Epistemology of the Closet* Eve Kosofsky Sedgwick speaks of the eponymous hero of Barrie's novel for adults, *Sentimental Tommy*, "as a man with a specific, crippling moral and psychological defect [he cannot feel desire for a woman] and as the very type of the great creative artist."[51] Peter Pan is a child version of the same combination—he has what Barrie identifies as a specifically childlike inability to care about others, and—as a result, it seems—a profoundly childlike playfulness and imagination. And he refuses ever to grow up—that is, to constrain his own exuberant creativity and self-indulgence in terms of the perceptions and needs of others. He can be whatever he imagines, get whatever he desires, as long as what he desires is purely self-centered, self-indulgent, not connected to a need for or interest in or love of or perhaps even lust for others.

It is no accident that Jacqueline Rose identifies Peter Pan as *the* archetypal novel for children. For writers like Barrie—and increasingly as the twentieth century progressed—childhood becomes identified exactly as this peculiar form of appropriately gratifiable desire without real human objects (except oneself?)—sexless (or at least onanistic) and therefore utopian and fulfillable passion—pure self-indulgence beyond societal restrictions, which seems to move out of childhood and on up as the image of an ideal adulthood—that is, an eternal childhood. This form of childhood is seen as desirable in children's literature exactly to the degree to which it represents freedom from adult obligations, from conventional values, from sexuality in general. It is instructive that this better place should be conceived of as better exactly to the extent to which it opposes adulthood—and specifically, I am assuming, adult sexuality. Kimberley Reynolds speaks of "the way real children and real children's bodies were made to disappear in children's literature and were replaced by more spiritualized, ethereal, and idealized images."[52]

There might be another way of understanding the patterns I have been exploring here. I have been assuming that the nostalgia for childhood characteristic of golden age children's literature represents distaste for adult sexuality in general—but it might just as well be read as representing distaste for heterosexuality in particular. Peter Pan and Grahame's animals find happiness in a life lived apart from females and with a group of male friends—so, for that matter, does Robert Louis Stevenson's Jim Hawkins in *Treasure Island* and the protagonists of Rudyard Kipling's *Kim* and *Stalky and Co.* As I suggested in chapter 1, there is a similar pattern in the somewhat later *Dr. Doolittle*, in which the doctor finds happiness away from females amid animals and, perhaps tellingly, one young boy. It might well be possible to read these stories of utopian adventures away from women as specifically antifemale and even, perhaps, as closeted gay texts. There is no question but that Jim Hawkins's most ardent relationship is with Long John Silver, Grahame's Mole with his male friend Ratty, and so on. To make such a reading, of course, I would have to eliminate texts by female writers like E. Nesbit—or perhaps read them, too, as expressions of a female desire for freedom from heteronormative sexuality. But it is certainly possible that the sexlessness of childhood as we have come to know it since the 1880s might well leave space for the closeting of gay desire in texts of children's literature. And that might be the case especially because these texts, for all their apparent exclusion of sexuality, tend to put so much emphasis on the significance of gender. It is no accident that all of Peter Pan's gang except the maternal Wendy are boys, that all of Mole's riverbank friends in *The Wind in the Willows* are male animals. If there really is no sexual intent, then why is not just the absence of females but also the presence of somewhat childlike males so necessarily part of what is utopian? And why are so many of the significant female figures of texts of the 1880s and beyond—*Peter Pan*'s Wendy, *Charlotte's Web*'s Charlotte, Ida in Sendak's *Outside over There*—substitute mothers, female, apparently, in the only way acceptably accessible to childhood?

In any case, the children's literature of the golden age clearly varies from texts written earlier—and it does so for many of the same reasons that Showalter identifies as causing parallel changes in adult texts about gender and sexuality. Once more, it is clear that trends in the culture as a whole find expression in children's literature and mark that literature as different from children's literature of other times. And yet, once more, they do so in texts that still remain recognizable as children's literature and that therefore retain their similarities with children's literature of other times. Thus, for all its utopian nostalgia, *The Wind in the Willows* still operates as a series of home and away stories, as childlike animals lust for adventure and learn about the comforts of home; still explores binaries customary in children's literature; still undermines the conservatism of the riverbank creatures with the subversive self-indulgence of Toad and then subverts Toad's subversiveness; and so on. I arrive once more at the same conclusion: the balance between difference and sameness in texts that belong to the genre of children's literature mark them as neither completely different nor completely the same. They are, instead, variations on each other and best understood as such.

At least two significant theorists postulate that the changes children's literature undergoes with the passing of time are evolutionary. Both Eliza Dresang and

Maria Nikolajeva focus on texts produced in the past few years as most different from—and more complex and more sophisticated than—earlier texts.

For Eliza Dresang many children's books of the recent past represent what she calls "radical change": "Fundamental change, departing from the usual or traditional in literature for youth, although still related to it."[53] Dresang sees this change as emerging from and related to new technologies and the ways in which they process and shape information: "Three digital age concepts underpin and permeate all the radical changes that are taking place in literature for youth: connectivity, interactivity, and access" (12). The texts Dresang focuses on as representing radical change are book-based texts with the hypertextuality, multiple focalization, and openness to random access of information as presented online. They tend to represent previously unheard voices and deal with previously forbidden topics. Dresang believes that texts with these qualities emerge from accurate observations by perceptive adults of changes in the intellectual habits of contemporary young people: "Society is changing, and so are perceptions of youth. This represents a radical change in culture for young readers—not for all readers, but certainly for many readers, some of the time. They are growing up differently, in a digital world" (57).

Dresang marshals an impressive collection of texts written in the years immediately prior to the publication of her book to support her thesis. There is no question that these texts possess many of the qualities she focuses on as innovative in recent children's literature. What is less clear is whether they actually represent a radical departure from the conventional markers of children's literature that I have been outlining in this book. Dresang herself isn't particularly sure: "It is important to keep in mind that *radical* describes 'fundamental' change but does not have to imply an abrupt or sudden departure from the past" (29). Indeed, she finds evidence of "radical change" in books as old as *Alice's Adventures in Wonderland,* which she says develops hypertextually, and Louisa May Alcott's *Little Women* (1868), which was written from a marginalized feminist perspective. That such books can be viewed as possessing qualities not only prevalent at a much later time but understood as emerging specifically from new factors in the culture of that later time seems like a clear example of new developments in the present leading to reinventions of the past. Furthermore, these books are canonic texts, clearly recognizable as children's literature by generations of readers. I proposed in chapter 1 that *Alice* shared the markers of the genre. I believe I could easily make a case for *Little Women* doing so also—it too is about the joys of home, the wonderfulness of being childlike, the pull between imaginative childlike indulgence and rational adult duty, and so on. It, too, allows its protagonists to grow up without growing up. If these texts of the past can be read as both representing radical change and possessing the generic characteristics of children's literature, then I suspect that the contemporary texts Dresang discusses can also.

In order to test this, let me look at two texts to which Dresang pays special attention, David Macaulay's picture book *Black and White* and Virginia Walter's novel *Making Up Megaboy,* illustrated by Katrina Roeckelein. *Black and White* tells what appear to be four different stories at the same time on page spreads divided into four separate sections. *Making Up Megaboy* makes much use of pictures and graphics to tell from a variety of different perspectives about how a boy shoots a Korean shopkeeper. Both stories appear to demand the reader's participation in determining how to fit the information together and give the reader scope to interpret the story in a variety of ways. They seem to exemplify what Roland Barthes identifies as "writerly"—an openness to being read as the reader wishes, an openness that theorists like George Landow equate with the hypertextuality of computer-based information and that marks many complex literary texts for adults in the postmodern era.

But are these texts really that open? A closer look at *Black and White* reveals that its stories connect to each other in exceedingly complex and cohesive ways— that underlying the innovative technique is a very conventional chain of cause and effect. Dresang herself says of *Making Up Megaboy* that, "because of the way Walter tells the story and the way Roeckelein illustrates it, the careful reader can understand exactly why this thirteen-year-old boy would take a gun and shoot a shopkeeper."[54] In terms of allowing readers freedom, these texts are more typical than they at first appear. I recall Roderick McGillis's questions about books like *The Stinky Cheese Man,* which Dresang identifies as another text representing radical change: "Are these books in any political sense radical, or do they too put to rest the transgressive instincts of their readers?"[55] They might even be viewed as co-opting the very freedom they purport to allow by appearing to be open and then working to move readers toward conventional understandings and assumptions. And if they are conservative in this way, they might well turn out to be conventional in other ways also. In fact, both books represent versions and variations of the markers of children's literature I have been discussing throughout this book.

Making Up Megaboy explores how and why Robbie Jones, an apparently innocent child, shoots and kills a shopkeeper. The story shares the main concern of children's literature I identified earlier: the meaning and value of being childlike as understood by adults. It does so by offering a variety of ideas about the subject.

The shopkeeper, a Korean immigrant, sets events in motion by telling a girl who the main character has a crush on, "No cigarettes! Too young."[56] Since the events take place in what a TV reporter calls "a quaint, old fashioned town with nice homes and shady trees and a Main Street that looks like it did in the 1950's" (19), the shooting is an intrusion of the contemporary world into a nostalgic idyll much like the worlds of Henry Huggins or Encyclopedia Brown—of presumably adult matters into an admirably childlike place.

Underlying the childlike appearance, however, is a hidden adulthood. The girls do smoke in spite of being "too young," and Robbie's father keeps a gun in the house. Robbie's life as a typical protagonist of a young-adult novel, a powerless outsider wanting power, signals the inner turmoil and the complex fantasy life underlying his apparently idyllic childhood that lead him to use the gun. The hollowness of the idyll is implied by Robbie's principal, who responds to the shooting by saying, "This is a good community. We believe in family values. Our children don't get into this kind of trouble. . . . We need to rebuild our image" (42). The shopkeeper's wife adds another dimension to the discussion of what childhood is or should be by saying, "Children do not have guns in Korea. What kind of country is this?" (37).

I argued in chapter 1 that, since innocence is a central feature of our constructions of childhood, texts of children's literature typically present innocence and knowledge in oppositional terms and explore the merits of knowing and not knowing. *Making Up Megaboy* offers such an exploration not just in terms of its focus on the disruption of what claims to be childlike and idyllic but also in terms of the meaning of Robbie's shooting. On the one hand, it represents his access to and willingness to act on adult knowledge and experience. It is tragic because it is not childlike. On the other hand, however, it is an act of innocence, tragic because it *is* childlike. It becomes clear that Robbie shoots the shopkeeper as a response to the superhero comic books he reads, imagining a scenario in which he protects the girl he loves from evil forces. It also seems that he has confused the fantasy of Megaboy with his father's presumably manly need for a gun and his urging for Robbie to stop being a sissy (thus making the book another example of the ongoing concern in children's literature with constructions of gender). The gulf between what Robbie does and what he has imagined it to mean implies Robbie's dangerously childlike ignorance about the implications of his actions. Is Robbie too childlike or not childlike enough? Does the shooting represent his unfortunate submission to childlike desire or to adult knowledge? *Making Up Megaboy* is as ambivalent about these matters as many of the most characteristic of texts of children's literature are.

Paradoxically, *Making Up Megaboy* amplifies its explorations of questions of knowledge in terms of the characteristic that most clearly allows writers like Dresang to identify it as unlike mainstream children's literature. I have suggested that children's literature characteristically describes events from what purports to be a childlike point of view. *Making Up Megaboy* does not consistently do that—it presents events as viewed by a variety of different characters, including many adults. In doing so, however, it reveals to readers a wider and more complex story than any of the individual narrators can understand. As a result, it makes each of the narrators childlike as commonly understood: innocent of at least part of the whole truth.

In this way *Making Up Megaboy* seems to represent a more obvious version of the situation that Mikhail Bakhtin says holds in all fiction—that "diversity of voices and heteroglossia [the ways in which all utterances depend on their inter-textual relationships with others] enter the novel and organize themselves within it into a structured artistic system." For Bakhtin, "This constitutes the distin-guishing feature of the novel as a genre."[57] As I have described them in this book, most children's novels tend to disguise and even subvert their potential for po-lyphony—to foreground one voice representing one point of view as viewed through and understood by means of the controlling narrative of one authorial narrator. While it is possible for readers to become aware of multivocality in *Dr. Dolittle* or *Henry Huggins* and read them in ways that compete with the more obvious thematic concerns I discussed earlier or simply celebrate the polyphony, the novels themselves imply and invite a reader uninterested in doing so. What interests me here is that, despite its representation of many different voices, *Making Up Megaboy* seems to share that generic resistance to multivocality.

Bakhtin describes the multivocal novel as "a whole formed by the interaction of several consciousnesses, none of which entirely becomes an object for the other."[58] But as *Making Up Megaboy* presents each voice in turn, the novel offers its readers an increasingly more complex shadow text for each of the narrations. Memories of all the other voices already experienced offer a way to see through and beyond each one that turns the narrations into variations of each other (another way in which the novel represents the main generic markers of chil-dren's literature).

As a whole, the narrations all imply the presence of a hidden adult narrator in control of what readers get to hear when and finally, also, of what the truth actually is. All the characters become understood by, and objects to, this control-ling narrator. In this way the novel confirms Robyn McCallum's contention that even when offering multiple voices, "a substantial proportion of children's fiction

. . . attempts to construct and impose a unified (monologic) world view upon readers, and in doing so represses the dialogic potential of the novel genre."[59]

That controlling truth expressed in *Making Up Megaboy*, declared by an adult, concerns the failure of adults either to keep children safe from themselves or to impose adult visions of a safely idyllic childhood on children. Underneath the ironies surrounding the adult discourse about how idyllic the community is lies a clear sense that it ought to be exactly as idyllic as it fails to be. It is obvious that readers should view the girl's desire to act adult as "wild," Robbie's mother's intolerance and his father's need for guns and machismo as close-minded, the minister's reading of the situation as a falling away from the teachings of his church as self-serving. These people ought to be kinder, more accepting—more childlike. Even though I personally tend to agree with these conclusions, I can't avoid noticing that, for all its apparent experimentation, *Making Up Megaboy* represents exactly the same nurturing and tolerant liberal humanist ideology that has conventionally marked children's literature. I feel safe, therefore, in concluding that *Making Up Megaboy* is more like other children's books than not. What appears to be a divergence from the norm of children's literature is actually a variation on it—an amplification of some of its most fundamental effects.

Making Up Megaboy also operates as a variation on key characteristics of children's literature in another way. It represents many of them in Robbie's fantasies about Megaboy, in ways that make the book a commentary on conventions of children's literature, as well as an example of them. Not only does Megaboy represent a familiar fulfillment of childlike wishes for power, but he does so in terms of a thoroughly recognizable orphan story. As a result, the desires fulfilled include both the freedom of a separation from parents and the knowledge that one's supposed parents are part of what Robbie calls "the forces of evil who oppress children on this planet."[60] Readers' perceptions of both the distance and the relationship between the fantasy and Robbie's real circumstances allow both a critique of and a desire for the safe but constricting homes often postulated by texts of children's literature. Robbie's fantasy reveals the extent to which his home—and even his community, which his mother views as "a safe place" (9)—is actually oppressively closed to good things that it pushes outside (like Robbie's friend Ruben, whom his mother views as a "bad" friend because he is Mexican) and dangerously infected by the bad things (like the gun) that it hides inside. The novel thus mirrors the dialogue about the meaning of home that is key to children's literature.

Like *Making Up Megaboy*, *Black and White* operates as a variation on conven-

tional texts of children's literature by retaining but multiplying and thus intensify-
ing central characteristics. Instead of one story, there are four, and together they
add up to a fifth. Deborah Kaplan suggests there are even more stories in it.
Rather than being what many similarly complex and apparently disrupted and
open-ended narratives are, an invitation to question whether anything is ever
certain, "*Black and White* is not unclosed, but hyper-closed, encouraging its readers to find one closed story, and then another, and then another. . . . *Black and
White* encourages its readers to find the possible validity of any narrative and
invites delight."[61] It then offers a concentrated version of a key aspect of storytelling for children: the satisfaction in perceiving an appropriately complete closure
that underlies the "happy endings" we expect of texts for children.

The various stories in *Black and White* are tied together (and invite a sense of
closure) primarily because details in one story answer questions left unanswered
by the others. Thus, both the mysterious moving rocks a boy sees blocking the
tracks in "Seeing Things" and the reason for the train's delay in "A Waiting
Game" turn out in "Udder Chaos" to be cows that an escaped convict has released
from their field. I am assuming, of course, that the train that appears in all three
stories is the same train in the same place at the same time, an assumption I make
both because of Macaulay's note saying that the book "may contain only one
story" and because my understanding of literary convention has trained me to
expect and look for unity in narrative situations. Having looked for and found that
one story, I have no choice but to conclude, as I did about *Making Up Megaboy*, that
the characters in the individual stories who know less than I do occupy innocent
and therefore childlike points of view.

Like *Megaboy*, and like many other children's books, *Black and White* is about
the relative value of innocence and experience, knowledge and lack of knowledge.
Also as in *Megaboy*, there is ambivalence about what the value is. The events the
boy mistakenly imagines in "Seeing Things"—moving rocks, strange creatures
singing amid clouds of snowflakes with words on them—are no less delightful
than the strange truth turns out to be. It's not necessarily bad to view the world
without total knowledge of it; what innocence sees is at least as good as the truth.

Black and White celebrates childlikeness in other ways also. Each of its individual stories, and consequently its overriding one story, concerns an unexpected
outbreak of irrationality, disorder—anarchy. As in much children's literature,
from nursery rhymes to young-adult fiction, order, reason, good sense, and normalcy are clearly identified with the world as constructed and legislated by adults,
the world of fences and train schedules and prisons for lawbreakers. As a result,
anarchy is understood to be appealing to children as a freeing defiance of adult

oppression and, therefore, as essentially childlike. The four stories of *Black and White* explore all the positive aspects of anarchy on which children's literature typically focuses: as delightfully mysterious strangeness (the moving rocks), as playful defiance of norms (the adults waiting for the train dressing up in their newspapers and singing), as creative imagining of new uses for things (newspapers as hats), as masquerade (the convict as an old lady in a choir gown), as, above all, empowering freedom from oppression, constriction, and conformity (cows, convicts, and everyone else escaping). The book represents its disorderly events as a version of Bakhtin's carnivalesque.

As Bakhtin suggests, however, the carnivalesque is a "temporary suspension of all hierarchic distinctions and barriers among men and of . . . prohibitions of usual life," an allowance of disorder that purges disorder and thus maintains the orderly system as it is.[62] It is revealing that it is primarily the adults in *Black and White*—parents and convicts—who indulge in disorderly behavior, whereas the children observe and are invited to join their adult enactment of the childlike. The focalizing child character of "Problem Parents" is deeply distressed by her parents' unusual childlikeness and, after they talk her into joining them in their horseplay, only grudgingly admits that "it was kind of fun in the end" (not paginated). Both by showing these parents acting in this way and by telling this story about parents acting in this way in order to encourage child readers to accept their wisdom, *Black and White* reiterates the fundamental thrust of much children's literature: adults teaching children how to be childlike. In doing so, it represents an imposition of a specific version of childlikeness on child readers—a reining in of the freeing aspects of carnivalesque in the name of one particular—and therefore, I must assume, particularly nonthreatening—version of it.

That the anarchy in *Black and White* is essentially safe is revealed by the fact that it is over before the book ends. As usual, the carnival ends and order is restored, more or less as it was. There is, however, one key difference: the convict, who turns out to have created all the anarchy, remains free as a result of it. The purpose of the disruptions turns out to have been not an end to the original order but a rejuggling and reestablishment of it that empowers someone previously marginalized by it. According to Northrop Frye, this is the basic plot pattern of traditional comedy—a pattern that works to enforce the very order it violates.[63] It also appears in much writing for children, which often works to assure readers that happy endings involve the safe integration of bored or threatened or otherwise marginalized characters into a society that previously constricted and oppressed them.

In describing order restored in a way that changes it, *Black and White* mirrors a recurring plot pattern of children's literature—the story of a safely normal "home" safely invaded by that which it exists to keep outside itself. Like many children's stories, each of the four stories in *Black and White* starts and ends with a safe and apparently boring normalcy in a way that allows it to focus on the unsettling and delightful dangers that invade it in between. The stories thus operate not only as variations on central story patterns of children's literature but also as variations on each other.

In doing so, they seem to represent the quality of variation Kundera identifies when he speaks of it as a journey to a "second infinity."[64] If I read the four stories in the usual order, from top to bottom of each page and then from the left page to the right page of each double-page spread, each successive story moves deeper into anarchy and becomes more complex—and more unsettling, thus eventually integrating and dissipating ever more threatening challenges to the norm. What is merely a vague and fairly insignificant mystery confronted by a sleepy child in the first story becomes an unsettling vision of manic parents for the focalized child in the second story. Having been invited to accept the harmless fun of the first story, readers are primed to accept as equally fun the more unsettling events of the second. The third and fourth stories vary the first two by placing viewers themselves, as observers of otherwise unfocalized anarchic events, in the position of the children in the first two. Thus, viewers also become implicated in the accepting attitudes that the children in the second story are invited to accept. Then, just as the second story reveals what was unsettling about what seems easy to accept in the first, the fourth story reveals what is unsettling about what seems like fairly harmless fun in the third. An actual adult convict escaping the law replaces playful adult commuters, revealing and amplifying the lawlessness inherent in the playfulness. At the heart of all the fun, it turns out, is a criminal who disrupts every social constraint and breaks every social category. He lets the cows out, confuses cows with choir members and himself with both the choir and the cows, and is a man who dresses as a woman. And then he restores everything but himself to the way it was—and he himself becomes part of the normal order. In telling a series of ever more dangerous versions of what is basically the same story, and in dissolving the threat, *Black and White* replicates both a structure common in many children's stories and the chronological sequencing constructed for presumably developing child readers by children's literature as a whole. In this way, too, *Black and White* becomes distinctive merely by operating as an intense and concentrated variation on characteristic generic markers of children's literature.

These apparently postmodern, radically changed texts, I conclude, can continue to be considered children's literature not just because, as Dresang herself says, they represent new growth from the roots of conventional children's literature. They also continue, inevitably, to bear the weight of adult perceptions of lack in children and young adults, and of adult educational intentions toward child readers in order to dissipate that lack, so that the sophisticated freedom they offer is tempered and constrained. While their use of hypertextual techniques and multiple perspectives marks them as postmodern, they represent a form of postmodernity peculiar to children's literature—and still expressive of its major obsessions and values. What is the same as conventional children's literature in these texts remains as important as what is different in them.

Maria Nikolajeva's views of evolution in children's literature differ from Dresang's in downplaying the significance of forces outside the field of children's literature itself—downplaying, even the significance of extratextual sources within the field. She does acknowledge that what she calls the "semiosphere" of children's literature—a discreet but evolving collection of codes that define it—is influenced by events outside itself: "In our time, impulses from film, TV, video, teenage fashion, rock texts, the toy industry, advertisements, cartoons and entertainment are important in the evolution of children's literature."[65] But for Nikolajeva it is less changes in culture or technology that cause change in children's literature than it is the pressure of the genre itself, the increasing weight of already-existing texts that new writers must position themselves in relation to: "Since in any semiosphere it is the borderline that is active, while its centre is passive, the borderline texts move successively towards the centre. . . . As the central code is forced aside, it becomes less and less effective and is 'desemiotized.' Through centripetal movement the peripheral code acquires the central position" (ibid., 62–63).

Nikolajeva goes on to explain why the center of a semiosphere is passive. Once a literary code has become established, it becomes standardized, defined by rules and prescriptions and, therefore, resistant to change and prone to dullness: "The longer a code has been central, the greater the risk that it will become petrified and lose its appeal to readers. At this point, peripheral and therefore more flexible codes come and take its place" (ibid., 63). In traditional children's literature, simple, straightforward plots ending with a return home have been central; inevitably, then, these characteristics are being replaced in our time by what they marginalize: greater complexity, greater uncertainty, open endings that question the value of a return home. In this way Nikolajeva complicates Dresang's explanations for innovation in contemporary children's literature by adding another factor to account for it.

There is no question but that the establishment of a fixed code invites subversions of it. I question, however, whether the evolutionary model for literary change that Nikolajeva borrows from semioticians who concentrate on literature for adults works so well with children's literature. As usual, the complicating and extraordinary factor is the matter of adults, who know more, writing for children, who know less. Children's literature can evolve and in doing so become more sophisticated; but if it becomes *too* sophisticated, then it is in danger of losing exactly that which distinguishes it as a type of literature: its lack of sophistication. As Nikolajeva herself suggests in an article called "Exit Children's Literature," "an ever-growing segment of contemporary children's literature is transgressing its own boundaries, coming closer to mainstream literature."[66] She concludes that "sooner or later, children's literature will be integrated into the mainstream and disappear" (233).

In fact, and despite their sophistication in relation to more conventional texts of children's literature of both the past and the present, all the texts that Dresang and Nikolajeva single out as examples of significant change in recent children's literature are still less complex, less sophisticated, less radical, less evolved than the equivalently radical or innovative texts of adult literature. They *must* be so. A defining quality of children's literature is that, no matter how complex it is, it tends to be understood as simpler than adult texts of the equivalent kind. It may contain hidden depths—indeed, I have argued it almost always does. But it announces itself as simple, and simpler than what is offered adults. Why, otherwise, identify it as a text for children? As long as cultural concepts of childhood focus on it as simpler than the adulthood it derives its meaning in relation to and opposition from, the centrality of that opposition will continue.

Furthermore, it does so because it has always done so. Children's texts have the power of tradition, of the way things always have been and must therefore, most obviously, continue to be. Like Dresang, Nikolajeva ignores the many texts that don't innovate; according to Emer O'Sullivan, Nikolajeva's evolutionary model, which sees children's literature "in terms of stages of development to be overcome, of didactic and formulaic texts being cast off to make way for the exclusively elaborate . . . is deterministic and ultimately impoverishing."[67] Such a view specifically underplays the power of convention to defang and absorb that which works to subvert it, as in both *Making Up Megaboy* and *Black and White*.

There is truth, however, in Dresang's and Nikolajeva's perception that both forces outside the field of children's literature and the characteristic behavior of literary genres in general do work to promote change and innovation. What becomes most interesting is how the field works to allow that change without actually disrupting it or dispersing it or in any significant way changing its main thrust and purpose. In *Masculine Domination* Bourdieu highlights this sort of resistance to change in culture generally: "I have always been astonished by what might be called the *paradox of doxa*—the fact that the order of the world as we find it, with its one-way streets and its no-entry signs, whether literal or figurative, its obligations and its penalties, is broadly respected; that there are not more transgressions and subversions, contraventions and 'follies' . . . or, still more surprisingly, that the established order, with its relations of domination, of rights and prerogatives, privileges and injustices, ultimately perpetuates itself so easily."[68] In terms of generic considerations—the field as inscribed specifically in the texts it produces—a focus on this sort of resistance translates into a question of how apparently innovative texts maintain the characteristic markers I have been outlining and do so in ways that allow childhood to continue in more or less the same traditional terms that have obtained for the past few centuries.

Earlier in this book I discussed Fredric Jameson's argument that the formal characteristics by which we identify texts as belonging to genres are "sedimented content"[69] that carries its own ideological messages distinct from the apparent messages of the texts. Theoretically, I should be able to explore recent innovative texts of children's literature in the expectation of finding generic messages representative of earlier times and less innovative or radical values. My analyses of *Black and White* and *Making Up Megaboy* represent exactly that sort of exploration. Merely in being conceived as being children's literature, I conclude, a text sublimates its author's knowledge of the genre—drags it along as a specific and unavoidable part of the adult knowledge that texts of children's literature always drag along as sublimated content. Present in its apparent absence, this genre knowledge tends to have two effects. First, it undermines apparent innovation, holds back change. Second, however, it reinscribes binary ambivalence by reinserting the opposite of what is radical in a way that allows the radical. That which appears to defang, then allows its opposite, allows the fangs. Children's literature subverts its subversiveness but also possibly subverts the subversions of its subversiveness. In all these ways, in any case, the generic markers of children's literature remain consistent—even and perhaps especially in terms of the presence of radical, innovative, potentially subversive content.

Different Children's Literatures: The Effects of Nationality

Writing in the context of translations of *Alice's Adventures in Wonderland* into German, Emer O'Sullivan recalls Paul Hazard's assertion that underlying apparent cultural differences there is a "world republic of childhood": "Even today, children's literature—especially its classics—is frequently regarded and referred to as the product of an international culture of childhood, monolingual, monocultural, in which international understanding is the order of the day. To speak in this nice, rather cosy and certainly very idealistic way about children's literature is to ignore both the conditions influencing its production and those underlining its cultural transfer."[70] According to Maria Nikolajeva, similarly, "The notion that there is a 'common' children's literature in all countries in the world is a misunderstanding. . . . With very few exceptions, children's literature in different countries has little in common."[71] Nikolajeva presents persuasive evidence to support this argument. She points out that Sendak's matter-of-fact acceptance of the fact that Max has a room on his own in *Where the Wild Things Are* seems strangely exotic to readers of Russian children's literature, which accurately depict Russian children sharing spaces. She also points out that topics such as masturbation, taboo in American books for very young children, are common in Swedish ones.

At the same time, though, Nikolajeva insists that the development of these differing children's literatures *always* goes through the same four stages of development: first, adaptations of existing adult literature and folklore, then didactic stories, then a period of "canonic" classics, and finally, innovative modern texts. If all national literatures inevitably follow this same evolutionary pattern, why do they turn out different from each other and, as Nikolajeva asserts, become ever "more and more national and isolated?"[72] Her answer is that each is a different semiosphere, with different adult texts and texts of folklore to adapt in the first stage, leading to the presence of different defining qualities in the canonic classics and thus different central codes to be invaded by different marginalized qualities in the last stage.

As O'Sullivan suggests in *Comparative Children's Literature,* Nikolajeva's analysis ignores how significant differences in national histories make their literature different: "Developments in postcolonial Africa and Ireland, different as they may be in respect of questions of literacy, linguistic diversity and economic factors, have in common the fact that they followed a different course from children's literatures in certain Western industrialized nations, for whose development universality has been claimed."[73] Nikolajeva also ignores, however, the degree to which national semiospheres are penetrated and thus affected by materials from elsewhere—particularly, in our current world, by books written in English and by American movies internationally. Speaking of translation, for instance, Sullivan reports that "those countries that export the most also import the least,"[74] so British and American books and films are available in translation for children internationally, but American and British children have little access to books and films first produced in other languages. So the universal developmental pattern Nikolajeva postulates downplays both differences in the history of different children's literatures that makes them different and their diachronic connections with each other that make them similar at different points in their development.

Nevertheless, Nikolajeva's conviction that national literatures develop in the same way in the process of becoming different does imply a suggestive balance between what changes and what remains the same. John Stephens implies a similar balance of opposing forces when, speaking specifically of Australian children's literature, he says, "Insofar as children's texts seek to shape, impact on, or intervene in, culture, it is to be expected that representations of the common themes of children's literature—personal growth and development of a sense of one's place in the world; conflict with family, peers and community—will be nuanced in particularly local ways in response to this changing society."[75] There *are* common themes—and, I would add, common structures and patterns; they get expressed differently in different national contexts.

To find the sameness she believes underlies the very real differences, Nikolajeva asserts that "the only feasible thing is to attempt to sketch the historical poetics of children's literature as such, to ignore details, concrete works and authors, and instead look for tendencies, recurrent phenomena, typological similarities, and possible paths of evolution."[76] The list of what Nikolajeva wants to ignore seems like an invitation to miss almost everything that really matters, but it also suggests a specific way of understanding how literatures that are quite unlike each other might yet be similar. They might represent variations of the same basic patterns— perhaps even variations of each other. While I have different reasons for doing so, I can similarly argue that the differences between national children's literatures allow them to be read as variations of each other in another, equally important, way. I can view them as rejugglings of the same basic and, I believe, international generic markers—markers that include the themes Stephens mentions. O'Sullivan also suggests something much like this when she suggests that a comparative children's literature would focus on "what is characteristic, distinctive and exclusive to individual children's literatures, which emerges, as do their commonalties, only when different traditions are contrasted with each other."[77] That the commonalties remain reinforces what the genre theorist David Fishelov asserts: "The fact that a genre can retain its identity in the face of sometimes radical changes in its linguistic and cultural environment illustrates the flexibility of the genre's rule and its ability to absorb 'culture shock.'"[78]

Let me use the children's literature of my own country as an example of that combination of identity and variation—or, at least, that part of it written and published in English. The French-language children's literature produced primarily in Quebec represents an entirely separate field of production—and thus a separate and different semiosphere, substantially isolated not just from English-language children's literature but also quite substantially from other French-language literatures. What most marks English-language Canadian children's literature, though, is its *lack* of isolation from other English-language children's literature—a lack that might, paradoxically, point to what has been and might remain unique about it. It is instructive that, according to its editor, William Toye, the title of the first major guide to English-language Canadian children's literature, Sheila Egoff's *Republic of Childhood,* "was suggested by Paul Hazard's statement about the international reach of children's books."[79] Ironically, this effort to assert affiliation with the international republic—a claim that Canadian children's literature is like all other children's literature—may have implied its opposite. As Egoff acknowledges when she says that her study "pays a good deal of attention to some obviously poor books,"[80] the claim reveals a need to justify what Egoff and others until quite recently have often viewed as defined by its inferiority and inadequacy—its unfortunate difference. The claim of belonging in the republic paradoxically establishes a clear sense of not belonging—of being outside it and different from it, at best a poor relation to it.

The history of children's literature in Canada shows why. For many decades after the founding of the country in 1867, the literary needs of English-speaking Canadian children were filled primarily by books from outside the country. There was no Canadian children's publishing industry of any substance before about 1975. In their sequel to Egoff's guide, *The New Republic of Childhood,* Egoff and Judith Saltman report, "From records extant it would appear that only ten children's books were published between 1921 and 1923, and until 1950 there were only about nine or ten each year. There was a slow increase until the 1960s and early 1970s, when about fifty or sixty were published annually."[81] The one universally regarded classic of Canadian children's literature, L. M. Montgomery's *Anne of Green Gables,* was first published in Boston and thus had to be imported back to its author's and characters' country, along with many books by American authors. When a Canadian children's publishing industry did come into existence in the mid-1970s, primarily as a result of efforts by government funding agencies, its products continued to appear in bookstores and libraries surrounded by a much larger number of British and American books. They still do so, today, although, since the North American Free Trade Agreement of the early 1990s, there are increasingly fewer British ones and an almost universal availability of American ones.

These circumstances help account for ways in which Canadian children's literature has differed from the American and British writing for children in the midst of which it has existed. American and British books were and still are often cheaper than their Canadian equivalents. They are produced to be profitable in terms of wide sales in larger markets, only marginally including Canada, whereas the Canadian books—rarely of widespread interest to purchasers outside the country—have traditionally needed to make their profits in a much smaller domestic market. To justify higher costs, Canadian publishers tended traditionally not to produce books with American or British competitors. Instead, they focused on ones that might be viewed as distinctly Canadian enough to warrant purchasing, both inside and outside of Canada, not instead of the less expensive and more renowned foreign books but in addition to them. Canadian books thus traditionally tended to represent something not simply Canadian but *distinctly* so. For instance, most had distinctly Canadian settings—the northern tundra or the wild forest or the pastoral idyll of Anne's Green Gables—rather than the urban places most Canadian children actually have lived in throughout much of Canadian history. There were also many versions of Canadian aboriginal tales and almost none representing the European and other backgrounds of the majority of Canadian children.

Works of French or Finnish children's literature tend to focus on the ordinary lives of mainstream French or Finnish children—characters a lot of French or Finnish children can identify with. Traditionally, Canadian children's literature did *not* try to do that. It was left for books from elsewhere—ones representing the international republic of childhood that, presumably, included mainstream Canadian childhood. Since descriptions of ordinary life were imported, normalcy came from elsewhere, much as "normal" Europeans had come to Canada from elsewhere and brought their culture with them. The "Canadian" life actually described in Canadian children's literature was marked by its exoticism and thus by its distance from the lives of most of its readers, including Canadians.

It seems unlikely, for instance, that even those Canadian readers who actually lived on Prince Edward Island would have already been prone to view their ordinary surroundings in terms of the magic L. M. Montgomery ascribed to then in *Anne of Green Gables*—or to view Anne, the magically wonderful living spirit of that exoticized landscape, as an immediately recognizable version of themselves. For most Canadian child readers, the "Canada" and "Canadians" of most Canadian children's books were likely to be as distant from their own experience of their place and themselves as it would have been for non-Canadians. "Canada" was somewhere other—and more interesting—than where they actually lived, much in the same way that Carroll's Wonderland was different from England. In representing the real places of their target audience as something like fantasy ones, Canadian books were, for the most part, clearly different from international English-language children's literature.

The establishment of a more substantial Canadian children's publishing industry in the 1970s changed these tendencies. As Robert Lecker suggests, the Canadian publishing industry generally "had its origins in the post-Massey Commission emphasis on the importance of developing an indigenous publishing culture that could support and disseminate national value,"[82] and a viable children's publishing industry came into being in Canada as a result in large part of funding programs developed both by the federal government and the governments of the provinces to support writers in their writing, publishers in their publishing, and libraries and other institutional purchasers in their purchasing. These programs were designed primarily to foster the development of Canadian culture and thus Canadian self-perception and national feeling. The new publishers, like Kids Can, Annick, and Groundwood, that came to exist in the 1970s as a result of these government initiatives understood their mandate to be the production of books that mirrored and thus helped to construct the lives and identities of real Canadian children.

Paradoxically, however, the more accurately they did so, the less distinctive the books became. The reason for this is simply that in Canada what is recognizably normal is, primarily, what is American. It was for that reason that Canadian governments felt an interest in developing a distinctly Canadian—that is, most significantly, a non-American—culture. Through much of Canada's history, and increasingly since the North American Free Trade Agreement, most aspects of Canadian life have originated in the United States. Canadians wear American-style clothing, often produced by American companies and purchased in Canadian branches of American stores. Canadians eat at local branches of American fast-food chains or prepare at home the same brands of prepackaged food that are available in the United States. Most of the movies shown in Canadian theaters are American, most of the television shown on Canadian stations is American, most of the music played on Canadian radio stations is American. Most of the teams in the Canadian "National" Hockey league are located in American cities, and there are or have been baseball teams in both the "American" and the "National" (i.e., American national) league located in Canadian cities. Canadian educators, social workers, child psychologists, sports coaches, and children's literature specialists attend American conferences in their fields and often take it for granted that what they learn there applies equally to Canadian children. As a result Canadian children have their lives constructed by schools and institutions heavily affected by American trends and interests.

In discussing the Englishness of English children's books, Margaret Meek says, "English life and literature haunts the picture books that English children are at home with. The deliberately polysemic texture devised by book artists comes from the visual semiotics of children's lives, localised as TV and advertising."[83] In working to present an equivalent Canadianness in the 1970s and 1980s and beyond, Canadian children's writers, illustrators, and publishers inevitably ended up producing books almost indistinguishable from those produced in the United States.

Almost—but not quite. The books did make a point of using Canadian place-names, for instance, and of offering specific descriptions of Canadian places. They also often managed to create a sense of a specific Canadian place, a farm on the prairies or a school in Toronto, as a distinctive variation of the homogenized North American culture. Thus, for instance, Diana Wieler and Kevin Major represent their teenage characters as typical North American adolescents confronting typical North American adolescent problems as North American adolescents usually do in American novels for young adults. But in *Bad Boy,* for instance, Wieler also offers a convincingly detailed sense of the cultural significance of hockey in a small town on the Canadian prairies. Many of Major's novels place their characters quite specifically in their Newfoundland settings both in terms of how they talk and understand each other and how their geographic and economic circumstances affect them. Meanwhile, writers as diverse as Janet Lunn and Brian Doyle offer very specific senses of what it might feel like to have lived in distinctly Canadian communities in particular and convincingly particularized moments of the past.

Since the North American Free Trade Agreement, that has happened less often. There is an almost universal availability in Canada of all the books published in the United States—not only in Canadian bookstores but through the Internet from American firms like Amazon (which operates Amazon.ca for Canadians), and not only books by American authors but even the American editions of books by Canadian writers with separate Canadian publishers and therefore theoretically not to be sold in Canada. Canadian publishing has become more precarious for other reasons also. One large bookstore chain, Chapters Indigo, controls a sizable proportion of the sales of books in the country and can demand substantial discounts from publishers that lessen profit margins, and enforce return policies that wreak havoc on publishers' cash flow. Cost-conscious governments across the country have cut funding both for programs that support publication and for institutions like schools and libraries that purchase books. According to Rowland Lorimer, for instance, "In two years, 1997 and 1998, the publishing industry lost half its federal grants—cuts everywhere were the order of the day—and, the only credible political alternative[s] were deeper cuts promised by Preston Manning [of the opposition Reform party] and put in place by various provincial governments, Ontario and Alberta in particular."[84] The significant decline in this sort of funding by all levels of government in recent years has had as serious a negative impact on Canadian children's literature as it earlier had a positive one. Meanwhile, American interests have, sometimes successfully, attacked initiatives that protect and foster Canadian culture as unfair trade practices. In response to a growing interconnectedness with and dependence on the American economy, Canadian nationalism has become far less fashionable for Canadian governments and for many Canadians, who see no real need for Canadian books that can't survive without government support.

Meanwhile, North American culture in general has become increasingly less literate. As children read less, it becomes feasible to produce only those books most likely to interest them—the kinds of American movie tie-ins and series fiction that Canadian publishers have always had to leave to American publishers. Thus, even those children who do still read tend to read mostly American materials.

As a result of these factors, it is increasingly difficult for Canadian publishers to profit from books published exclusively for the Canadian market. Fewer publishers try at all. Those who do then try to market their Canadian books in the United States, as well as Canada, or, in the case of books by Canadian writers with American publishers for the U.S. market, make arrangements to share production and printing costs.

At this point the insularity of American culture becomes an issue. To be economically viable in a country where translations of children's books from other countries and cultures are increasingly rare, and where even English-language books like the British Harry Potter series need to be "translated" into American English,[85] books written and produced by Canadians must be divested of anything distinctly Canadian. There can be no Canadian spellings, for instance, and no descriptions of specifically Canadian places or objects or accents that might alienate American child readers by preventing them from identifying with the characters. Increasingly, Canadian writers for children and young adults actually set their books in American locations, understanding that Canadian children, unlike American ones, are used to reading books and seeing movies about places not their own as descriptions of themselves.[86] Canadian children are being encouraged to understand themselves as ordinary Americans who happen to live outside the United States, not just by the American books they usually read but by Canadian books that are increasingly and normatively "American."

In these circumstances it seems easy to suspect that there remains little if anything distinctive about Canadian children's literature. Once insecurely and then proudly outside American children's literature, it has come inside enough to seem indistinguishable from it—if not part of the international republic of childhood, then certainly part of the American one.

It is telling, however, that most Canadians would be likely to object to my making this assertion. Canadians generally prefer to think of themselves as not American, of Canadian books as not American. Indeed, that is quite literally the case. When I have asked university students to explore what might be Canadian about Canadian children's literature, they inevitably respond first by suggesting how Canada is different from (and usually opposite to) the United States and how Canadians are different from (and usually opposite to) Americans. Canadians, they tell me, are courteous, unlike Americans, or refreshingly free of flamboyant patriotism, unlike Americans; or they speak of the multicultural Canadian mosaic as opposite to the American melting pot. Just as children's literature specialists often assume that the best way to understand children's literature is to pinpoint how it is different from adult literature, Canadians tend to assume that the best way to define being Canadian is to pinpoint how it is different from being American. According to Eva Mackey, "The constant attempt to construct an authentic, differentiated, and bounded identity has been central to the project of Canadian nation-building, and is often shaped through comparison with, and demonisation of, the United States."[87]

That suggests two important things, I think. First, Canadians' constructions of their own identity require and thus institute a sense of the American identity in order to define a difference from it. The imagining of one requires the imagining of the other it will then differ from. Canada is the opposite of that which it imagines the United States to be (and paradoxically, knows itself more obviously to actually be). Second, the identity is something that *must* be imagined and, furthermore, remains in the process of being imagined.

According to Benedict Anderson, all nations are imagined; a nation is "an imagined political community," and "communities are to be distinguished, not by their falsity/genuineness, but by the style in which they are imagined."[88] So if the Canadian nation is unlike others, it is not because it is imagined but because it is in the process of being imagined, in dispute and under construction—and thus is more clearly imaginary than are, for instance, the already generously imagined nations like the United States or those in Europe. Its style is the ongoing development of a style. As Allor, Juteau, and Shepherd say, speaking of culture and identity in Canada "is to speak not only of a terrain that is fractured and contested, but of a terrain whose identity as Canadian is in dispute."[89] In this way Canada is somewhat like other relatively new settler societies. According to Bennett, Turner, and Volkerling, "Unlike the 'traditional' European nations, the new settler societies have had to undertake the process of nation formation urgently, visibly, defensively, and are always being caught in the act, embarrassed by the process of construction."[90] What most distinguishes the styles of these nationalisms is the visibility of their imaginary quality.

This is not to say that these nations do not exist. When Canadians imagine for themselves a difference from Americans that might seem all but invisible to non-Canadians, the imaginary difference has real effects. It changes the ways in which people see themselves and others. What is imagined becomes true for those who believe it to be true. Canadians who imagine themselves different from Americans, even as they live almost exactly the same lives, *are* different, just as children who accept adult constructions of childhood that promote their difference from adults do become different from adults, more or less in the ways imagined. Furthermore, being perennially "caught in the act" of imagining identity is itself a distinct form of identity and has real effects on the lives of those so caught.

I emphasize these matters simply because they reinforce the possibility that Canadian children's literature might, despite its apparent sameness, be different from American children's literature—and might be different in ways to relate to the ways in which Canadians have imagined, continue to imagine, and continue to be caught in the act of imagining their Canadianness. Consider, for instance, the matter of Canadians being Americans who are *not* American, a people who act like Americans but who are outside the borders of the United States. Canadian discourse often refers to the fact that Canadians and Americans share the world's longest undefended border. An Internet search using Google on June 18, 2007, brought up about twenty thousand references to the phrase "longest undefended border," in contexts varying from tourism to trade to the National Library of Canada's explanation of how Canadian confederation happened. On the other side of a border that, although undefended is still a border, Canadians are in the position of being insiders on the outside—or perhaps outsiders on the inside. One way or the other, they are inherently divided, separate in a significant way from that which they in fact are. In other words, Canadians tend to imagine themselves as being much like the children of conventional constructions of childhood as I described them earlier in this chapter. It would not be surprising if Canadian books for children represented the marks of this division—represented, as all children's literature tends to do, children ambivalently childlike and adultlike, perhaps in terms of being ambivalently both Canadian and American.

Insiderly outsiderliness seems to have other effects on Canadian writing, both for children and for adults. Canadians often claim distance from the American lifestyle they more or less share, to be critical about what they know so well from lived experience but also understand to be someone else's values they have acceded to but do not wish to claim as their own. Canada's most successful writers for adults, both inside and outside of Canada, tend to be critics like Northrop Frye and Marshall McLuhan or satirists like Margaret Atwood and Mordecai Richler. Canadian children's writers like Brian Doyle *(Mary Ann Alice)*, Robert Munsch *(Smelly Socks)*, and, once more, Richler *(Jacob Two-Two Meets the Hooded Fang)* often work with satiric points of view. Others, like Kevin Major *(Hold Fast)*, Carol Matas *(Daniel's Story)*, Diana Wieler *(Bad Boy)*, and others, explore outsider anticonventional positions—rebellious adolescents, members of marginalized groups at odds with but also somehow connected to those in power. Often they do so with a strong sense of what it feels like to be somehow both inside and outside not always evident in children's and young-adult books about equivalent subjects published elsewhere.

As well as focusing generally on Canada as *not* the United States, Canadian discourse about Canadian identity has imagined a variety of explanations for Canadian difference, each suggesting ways in which Canadian writing for children might be distinct from children's literature generally. A lot of discussion has focused on what Jean Webb has suggested is a first phase of development in such discussions in colonial and then postcolonial cultures: "suppressed cultures establish separation and identity by reflecting on landscape and a sense of cultural self."[91] Speaking of depictions of landscapes in Australian picture books, John Stephens suggests that "the social and ideological force of such landscapes lies precisely in their apparent depiction of an ordinary reality. An audience may then be induced to see therein a mirroring of its own being and identity."[92] What, then, are the ordinary realities of the Canadian landscape?

Canada is a big, often cold, often empty country. When there are trees, the trees go on for thousands of miles. Where there are prairies, the prairies go on for thousands of miles. Speaking in *The Bush Garden* of the absence in Canada of an Atlantic seaboard, Northrop Frye says that "to enter Canada is a matter of being silently swallowed by an alien continent."[93] As Mackey suggests, this sort of demonization of the landscape "assumes and generalises a male settler's point of view. . . . The settlers are uncomfortable because *they* don't *penetrate* and control the (natural/female) foreign space; nature *engulfs* them and swallows *them*."[94]

Not surprisingly, Frye sees this attitude as significantly *not* American. Americans see an empty natural space as something to conquer and build on, something that allows them to enlarge themselves. But in response to the vast emptiness that threatens to engulf them, Canadians have developed what Frye calls a "garrison mentality."[95] They are so frightened by the landscape—so afraid that they will be eaten up by it and disappear within it—that they build walls against it and hide behind the walls. Most Canadians live together in cities, huddled together in tightly packed places dropped down in the middle of the emptiness, trying to keep warm together (and consequently, perhaps, denying the ways in which they themselves are not American?).

Canadian children's literature has often seemed to represent attitudes of this sort. In both Janet Lunn's *Shadow in Hawthorn Bay* and Monica Hughes's *Hunter in the Dark,* for instance, young people fear the wilderness as a monstrous and oppressive enemy that engulfs them and must learn to accept it. But it may be instructive that Lunn's main character is herself a settler in earlier times and that both Lunn and Hughes are themselves settlers in this land, immigrants from elsewhere. While native Canadian writers of recent times often describe Canadian landscapes as potentially dangerous, they are less prone to describe them as purely monstrous. Instead, they tend to describe the enclosed places characters call home and the open spaces away from those homes with as much ambivalence as does children's literature produced elsewhere. In their survey of award-winning Canadian books in both French and English, Mavis Reimer and Anne Rusnak conclude: "home is not boring or calm; it is not a place safely fenced from danger or hedged against anarchy; it is not a stable location that secures an inside by holding in place an outside. In fact, in a variety of ways, home itself is the greatest adventure in award-winning Canadian children's literature."[96]

What may be most interesting about Frye's theories considered in relation to children's literature is simply the extent to which his descriptions of Canadians responding to the Canadian landscape parallel the descriptions of children responding to the adult world generally characteristic of children's literature. Like the adults who write children's books that reinforce the inadequacy and need for protection of children, Canadians see themselves as inadequate and in need of a garrison—childlike. It is possible that not just Canadian children's literature but Canadian literature in general shares the common characteristics of international children's literature, so that Canadian children's literature, simply in being Canadian, does not significantly vary from children's literature elsewhere.

In her analysis of the development of postcolonial cultures, Webb suggests that a second stage in the development of identity occurs when "suppressed cultures force through the dominant culture by constructing and reconstructing myth."[97] In *Survival*, her 1972 guide to the Canadianness of Canadian literature, the novelist Margaret Atwood either unveiled such a myth in earlier writing or, simply, constructed one herself. For Atwood the essence of being Canadian is the perception of oneself as a victim. Canadians internalize the garrison mentality, see themselves as little and powerless and in the control of vast forces, and believe that everyone and everything is out to get them. They tend to be depressed about it all, convinced of their general inability to control anything or anyone. As a result, they never get to the last of the victim stages Atwood outlines: to refuse to become victims and become creative nonvictims.

Once more, Atwood's descriptions of classical texts of Canadian literature for adults make them sound a lot like children's books—or, more precisely, young-adult books, albeit without the requisite happy ending in which the victims either cease to be victims or come to their senses and cease to feel victimized. In the first version of "Canada: Case History," a poem frequently reprinted over the decades in Canadian school anthologies, the Canadian poet Earle Birney directly connects Canadians with adolescence:

> This is the case of a high-school land,
> deadset in adolescence
>
> . . . .
>
> Parents unmarried and living abroad,
> relatives keen to bag the estate,
> schizophrenia not excluded,
> will he learn to grow up before it's too late?[98]

If Birney's characterization is now or ever was apt, then we might expect Canadian books for children of all ages to exhibit the angst and depression supposedly characteristic of all Canadians but commonly featured internationally only in books for older children and young adults. But Canadian picture books for younger children are not noticeably more anguished or less optimistic than books from elsewhere—and the unhappy situations in them almost inevitably end happily. In this key way, prevailing international assumptions about the need to preserve childhood innocence, and thus the necessary absence of theoretically painful adult matters from children's literature, overcome the expression of what claims to be a national habit of mind. Even for Canadians, it seems, Canadian children's literature can remain children's literature only by *not* being what presumes to be distinctly Canadian.

There is another way in which self-perceptions of victimhood make themselves apparent in Canadian life—and, perhaps therefore, in Canadian children's literature. Feeling powerless, insecure, unable to have much effect on the world, victims tend to feel sympathy with other victims. When asked to discuss these matters, the university students I teach in Canadian children's literature courses express an intense conviction that Canadians are kinder than Americans, that Canadian society is more civil, more polite, more communal, more charitable. Politically, traditionally, Canadian governments have occupied a position to the left of mainstream American ones, and Canadians generally have felt much more comfortable with, for instance, government health care and gun control laws than do many Americans.

As a result, we might expect the characters in Canadian children's books to be kinder, humbler, less aggressive than their American equivalents. But I don't think they are, simply because the characters in American books for children tend to be kinder, humbler, less aggressive than American stereotypes and even the values of many American adults might suggest. In the United States, as elsewhere, the field of children's literature tends to represent nurturing, communal values approved by a still surprisingly maternal educational system as appropriate for children even when they are not necessarily operative for adults. As I will show later in this chapter, popular series like the Goosebumps books can achieve success only by concealing their divergences from these kinder values. In representing what might be characteristically Canadian communal and charitable values, Canadian children's books do not become distinct from American ones.

In the decades since Frye and Atwood proposed their models for a distinctly Canadian sensibility, theorists in Canada and elsewhere have become suspicious of this brand of totalizing mythology. The idea that a community has a mythology tends inevitably to silence the differing views of individuals or marginalized groups. Susan Rudy Dorscht suggests that " 'Canadian' is a problematic term that continues, despite the rhetoric of multiculturalism, to signify white and middle class when . . . Canadians are already hyphenated."[99] Similarly, in a book called *What Is a Canadian Literature?* John Metcalf asserts that "the only thing most of our critics have in common is the desire to exclude. . . . Nearly all the visions of our literature are nationalistic, chauvinistic, smug, and amazingly *white*."[100] It is clear, for instance, that both Frye's and Atwood's representations of a Canadian identity based on fear of the wild represent a European settler view that works to identify Canadian aboriginals with wildness and, thus, danger. This imperialist view ignores a quite different view of the same landscapes in traditional and contemporary aboriginal cultures.

Exploring the kinds of communities Canadians have imagined themselves to belong in, then, might be less revealing of their accuracy than they are of how the imaginings work to disperse and manage power among Canadians. Speaking of a different country with a somewhat similar colonial past, Ien Ang and Jon Stratton distinguish "Australia, the geographically specific and spatially bounded nation-state, from 'Australia,' the discursive nomination articulated by an open-ended proliferation of a range of diverse, sometimes incompatible, discourses. The relation between the two is not static, but subject to change and contestation. There is, in other words, a constant struggle over the representation of 'Australia,' whose equivalence with the nation-state bearing that name cannot be taken as given, but is always actively constructed and reconstructed."[101] Rather than promote any one of the contesting discourses, more recent discussions of Canadian identity have centered on the multiplicity of the discourses and have read that multiplicity as being, in itself, the Canadian identity. For instance, W. H. New says that "Canadian cultural practice . . . has repeatedly been preoccupied with multiple possibilities," and he adds, "The principle of cultural flexibility has led some commentators to assume that Canada has no 'identity' at all. They thus miss the point."[102] Similarly, E. D. Blodgett asserts that Canada "is a place of plurality that at once constrains and liberates. . . . Canada is to be defined as a crisis. Crisis, no matter how intense, is the intersection of competing arguments."[103] In comments like these, multiplicity itself is totalized and viewed as a universally Canadian myth—one also likely to be expressed in Canadian children's literature. This happens in at least three different ways.

First, as Dorscht and New suggest, Canadians speak frequently of Canada as a multicultural country, and government initiatives and educational policies have encouraged publishers to focus on books about children constituting a rainbow of cultural backgrounds for more than three decades. For a long time this multicultural focus did clearly distinguish Canadian children's literature from its American counterpart—although probably with a smaller proportion of books about multicultural children being published than the theories would suggest. Since the early 1990s, however, American educational policies mirroring Canadian ones have encouraged an intense focus on multicultural children's literature. As I suggested earlier, these policies have resulted in fewer books about multicultural children than might be desirable;[104] and in this way, I believe, Canadian books are once more indistinguishable from American ones. In both countries, also, children of what are represented as being different cultural backgrounds most often turn out to be "normal" children with shared mainstream middle-class values. In mainstream publishing, at least, the connections between children's literature and middle-class values turn out to be more significant and more universalizing than efforts to represent cultural difference.

A second way to foreground Canadian multiplicity is to focus on regionalism. Canadian geography and culture as a whole may lack unity—but perhaps the prairie landscape helps to create a prairie sensibility, and perhaps the specific ethnic mixes in specific parts of the country help to do so also. If specialists in Canadian literature are willing to generalize about the shared characteristics of texts, they do so only in terms of regional literatures—texts produced in southern Ontario or on the prairies, for example. There might, then, be distinct regional Canadian children's literatures.

So far in this section, I have been looking at texts of Canadian children's literature in terms of how they represent an intersection of two different paradigms, children's literature and Canadian literature. Since books from any particular region are still Canadian, and thus still affected by national economic factors and political influences, a consideration of regionalism adds a third paradigm. Simply by offering more complicated ways of approaching a text, a multiplication of paradigms does seem almost automatically to imply more complexity in the text and, thus, variation from any one of the inevitably simpler paradigms.

The texts for children produced by Canadian regional publishers seem to be different from those produced by Canadian mainstream publishers in two main ways. First, as might be expected, they tend to offer descriptions of childhood as experienced in the region. British Columbian publishers tend to produce books set in British Columbia such as Sheryl McFarlane's *Waiting for the Whales,* published in Vancouver by Orca. Second, regional books often vary from mainstream books by being more willing to treat subjects that children's literature often minimizes or remains silent about. Beatrice Culleton's *In Search of April Raintree,* first published by a small aboriginal press in Manitoba, describes the depressing history of an aboriginal child's life in loveless foster homes with an honesty absent from much young-adult literature, and Cherilyn Stacey's *How Do You Spell Abducted?* first published by a small press in Alberta, is surprisingly honest about a potentially abusive father stealing his children.

Economic circumstances, however, and especially the powerful generic demands that make those books most recognizably like mainstream books likely to be profitable, work to counter both these differences. Just as the multicultural children of mainstream books tend to be acceptably mainstream in their values and lifestyles, so, too, do the regional children of regional books. If the books diverge too far from mainstream assumptions about childhood, either in depic-

tions of characters or in inclusions of matters usually left out of children's literature, they tend to be less sellable beyond or even in the region. Thus, *April
Raintree* can remain economically viable as a school text in the province of Manitoba only in a special edition that leaves out some of the more graphic details of a
rape scene. As successful regional publishers for children become more knowledgeable and more shrewd, regional books have become more like mainstream
ones—just as mainstream Canadian books have become increasingly like their
American counterparts.

A third way of foregrounding multiplicity is suggested by W. H. New, himself a
prominent scholar of Canadian studies:

> I propose that the various Canadas that "Canadian Studies" discuss in large part
> *derive from*—not just "use"—various forms of boundary rhetoric. What does this
> mean? It acknowledges, simply, that boundaries function both as descriptions of
> concrete agreements *and* as metaphors of relationship and organization. . . . I want
> to argue that the paradigms of boundary rhetoric variously construct Canada as a
> place that *includes,* a place that *excludes,* as a place *divided,* as a place that *distributes*
> resources and power, and as a place that embraces some ongoing principle of *bound-
> ary negotiation.*[105]

If there is validity in what New suggests, then it seems logical to suspect that texts of
Canadian literature—including those intended for children—would represent these
constructions. The texts might be read in terms of the boundaries they negotiate.

And indeed they might—but not necessarily because they are distinctly Canadian. As I have suggested throughout this book using somewhat different termi-
nology, discourse on children's literature everywhere focuses almost totally on
boundary issues as New describes them. The literature concerns itself centrally
with the boundaries between children and adults, between what adults know and
children are able or allowed to hear. It focuses on the boundaries between what
can be spoken and what must be censored or *excluded,* and between what is
didactic and what is pleasurable. Theorists often view children's literature as a
literature *divided*—between what texts offer implied child readers and implied
adult readers (a double readership presumably claiming the same texts in different ways); between how texts socialize and how they inculcate bad behavior
(and thus *distribute* power); between their view of inexperience as innocence or
ignorance and of experience as maturity or destructive repression; between the
different and opposing values implied by their focus on ideas of home and being
away from home. And certainly, texts of children's literature represent *negotiations* of all the things they oppose—ways of crossing the boundaries they establish.

This means that children's literature generally is inherently ambivalent—double and divided. It is literature written across a boundary, by adults but for children perceived as different enough from the adults who write for them to need to be written for differently. It almost always therefore deals with contrasts, conflicts, and negotiations between the adult and the childlike.

In being both Canadian and for children, Canadian children's literature seems to represent a particularly intense version of this state of affairs. It represents its country best by being divided—not just in terms of its being set off from the North American and other children's literature it forms part of in bookstores and libraries, and not just in terms of the proclaimed differences of its various subliteratures, from Manitoban children's literature to aboriginal writing for children. Its texts also seem to deal *internally* in divisions and doubles and negotiations between them and to do so in particularly intense and obvious ways.

Like most texts of children's literature, Canadian ones tend to focus on questions of home and away—but as the work by Mavis Reimer and Anne Rusnak reveals, they tend to do so in terms that end up bringing away back home and vice versa or, as the work by scholars in *Home Words* reveals, by troubling conventional ideas of home in other ways.[106] In parallel with ideas about Canadian identity, the idea of home as a clearly defined space is in question. Furthermore, many texts of Canadian children's literature—proportionately more than seem to be produced in other countries—have double focalizations. They *include* and are *divided* between two different narrators, sometimes in two different times, telling their interconnected stories in turn. In many of these texts, two characters who represent different cultural groups occupy the same territory, disagree about to whom it belongs, and must *negotiate:* Welwyn Katz's *False Face* and *Out of the Dark,* Martha Brooks's *Bone Dance,* Kevin Major's *Blood Red Ochre,* Joan Clark's *The Dream Carvers* (and, to some extent, *The Hand of Robin Squires*), Jim Heneghan's *Promises to Come,* and Monica Hughes's *Log Jam.* The resultant agreements represent *distributions* of power. Something similar but less obviously related to ethnicity happens in other double-focalized books such as Katz's *Time Ghost* and *Come like Shadows,* Diana Wieler's *Bad Boy,* Karen Rivers's *Dream Water,* and Paul Kropp's *Moonkid and Liberty;* and contested homes also appear in books without double focalizations, such as Tim Wynne-Jones's *The Maestro* and Janet Lunn's *The Root Cellar* and *Shadow in Hawthorn Bay.* These books often end with an agreement by two or more different people to own and occupy the same place, to belong there together.[107]

So texts of Canadian children's literature often replicate in their themes and structures the disputes and negotiations over borders that exist in both the cultural field that produces them—Canada—and the literary genre to which they belong—children's literature. These texts mirror internally their position as children's literature in relation to adult literature or literature in general, as Canadian literature in relation to U.S. and/or North American literature and/or global literature, and as regional Canadian literature in relation to general Canadian literature. In this way, by offering intense versions of the problematics of Canadian identity and children's literature in general, Canadian children's literature represents a particularly instructive variation that both represents and differs from the generic markers of children's literature as a whole.

The Genre in the Field

As I suggested earlier, Maria Nikolajeva's version of the semiosphere of children's literature seems incomplete because she downplays the power of the many cultural and economic forces that impinge on the literature. In *Sticks and Stones: The Troublesome Success of Children's Literature from Slovenly Peter to Harry Potter,* Jack Zipes focuses more persuasively on what he calls "the institution of children's literature governed by market conditions and educational systems"[108]—on children's literature as a field of production. Zipes rightly says that "it was not possible for a broad range of books to be approved and to reach children in specific ways until the system of production, distribution, and reception was instituted and became focused on how to socialize children through reading. . . . It was and still is the need of the socioeconomic order that dictates how children will be formed and what forms are or are not acceptable" (46).

Zipes goes on to argue that this need has changed recently, that "the book for children in today's highly commercialized and computerized world of learning has an entirely different function from only a few decades ago" (47). Intriguingly, however, the books Zipes focuses on in order to make his case are not the innovative ones that Nikolajeva and Dresang point to as signs of a different children's literature. His concern is the exact opposite kind of books, those that are "formulaic and banal, distinguishable from [one] another only by their brand labels" (7). Zipes sees such books as predominating in the current field so that the change is away from innovation, not, as Dresang and Nikolajeva would have it, toward it.

Taken together, Zipes's arguments and those of Nikolajeva and Dresang undermine each other. They suggest that children's literature is getting both more innovative and more formulaic, more subversive and more conservative, more liberating and more repressive. In other words, the literature changes by providing yet more versions of what it already was, presumably because central factors of the "socioeconomic order" that engender it have remained fairly stable over the centuries and in the variety of countries in which it has been produced. I would like now to do a quick survey of some of those factors and the ways in which they leave their marks in texts—those marks being the characteristic markers of a text of children's literature.

First, and most obviously, ideas about children and the nature of childhood account for most of the recurring characteristics of children's books—their simplicity, their utopianism, their didacticism, their ambivalence about some elemental binaries. These characteristics emerge from and are mandated by a history of ideas about the value or danger of childhood lack that begin to be significant in the work of philosophers like Locke and Rousseau and continue, complicated but basically unchanged, in contemporary developmental theory as constructed by Jean Piaget and his followers.

As I have described earlier in this book, for instance, one primary theme running through the discourse of childhood in the last few centuries views that lack as utopian innocence and marks childhood as symbolic of a state of perfection that adults have moved away from and need to rediscover. In *Constructing the Canon of Children's Literature,* Anne Lundin describes how the development of children's librarianship in America in the first half of the twentieth century shaped children's literature in terms of specific ideals: "Children's librarians created a dominant ideology that privileged certain texts within a romanticized construction of the literature of childhood."[109] Texts expressing these views were more likely to achieve acclaim and sales; thus, says Lundin, "the connection between the rhetoric and regimen of children's librarians and the consequent supply of books created and produced and distributed to children in the twentieth century exemplifies how literature is cultural capital: the confluence of art and commerce, of morality and materialism, of creation and production" (30). While texts possessing cultural capital in other times and places might well represent different views, Lundin also points out how the ideology of librarianship she describes found its roots in earlier romantic concepts of childhood and privileged certain "classic" texts for children as models for new writing; and as I have shown, those concepts can still be found even in the most radical of texts still identifiable as children's literature. Despite variations in how cultural capital is distributed in different times and places, there is an underlying continuity of concern with the utopian nature of innocence.

A second major theme underlying the discourse of childhood across the centuries is a contradictory focus, not on how lack is desirable but on how it must be and is gradually eliminated through processes of education and development. As well as convincing adults that they know what behaviors to expect of individual children of a given age or stage, developmental assumptions mandate an educational system firmly attached to a structure of grades tied to specific ages. The field of children's literature is shaped by the demand for books that can successfully represent the varying levels of sophistication represented by the grades and stages adult purchasers believe in and thus enforce. Consequently, books that make greater or lesser demands of readers than publishers or educators assume is typical of a specific age or stage, or whose characters vary significantly from the very specific kinds of childhood developmental psychology constructs, are difficult to get into print or to sell.

In recent decades the fundamental assumptions of developmental theory have come under attack from a number of perspectives—even from many developmental psychologists, who have so challenged, transformed, and diverged from Piaget's ideas that, according to the psychologist William Kessen, "we are in a post-Piagetian world."[110] As currently understood, development does not suggest any sort of lockstep progress through a progressive series of stages. Children not only develop at different rates from each other but also, as individuals, develop differently in different aspects of their being so that any one child (or adult) tends to have a supposedly adult grasp of some things intermixed with an infantile grasp of others. Real people are more hybrid than constructions of development— and the children's literature that supports them—might suggest. Furthermore, current understanding of the strategies of development, building on theories like those of L. S. Vygotsky, suggest that limiting the information to which we give children access is counterproductive—that people always need access to more than they understand already in order to learn how to understand more. From that perspective the entire enterprise of children's literature as that which aspires not to say more or show more might seem suspect.

In the context of adults writing for children, the most telling critiques of Piagetian thinking focus on the ways in which developmental assumptions create the truths they describe. Questioning the universality of development, Erica Burman says, "What we have here are features of white middle-class US society mapped onto models of development which are then treated as universal."[111] According to Rex and Wendy Stainton Rogers, moreover, even those features of white middle-class American society are constructed culturally: "the process of socialisation as promoted under developmentalism *is* no more than a story [i.e., a narrative human beings invent about themselves]. However, it has become a story with such compelling plausibility it has overwhelmingly acquired the seeming status of incontrovertible truth—this is the way things *really are*."[112] Keeping it "the way things *really are*" ensures, even requires, the continuing existence of a children's literature that describes it as if it already really exists and thus helps to bring it into existence as a construction children learn to occupy or at least pretend to occupy.

If ideas about childhood remain fairly stable, then the literature that emerges from them will remain stable also. Contrary to Dresang and Nikolajeva, Jill May sees even highly acclaimed and relatively distinctive texts of children's literature as remarkably noninnovative:

> When authors in children's literature deal with controversial issues, they are usually dealing with issues society has already begun to discuss. Traditionally, children's literature has fit so well into the fabric of American society that it will not cause loud outcries of concern about story pattern, tone, or dialect. Critics argue that "inferior" children's literature will not fit "the patterns of good literature" and they often place books with diverse literary patterns outside the winning circles. While award-winning children's literature is well written, the books selected generally reflect the state-of-the-art in children's writing instead of innovative or divergent writing.[113]

A number of aspects of the marketplace work to encourage this replication of traditionally characteristic features in the new texts being published.

The most obvious of these is the extent to which the market is controlled by people committed to accepted constructions of childhood. The purchasers of almost all children's books are adults—specifically, adults with strong reasons to believe they know what children are, what they like, and what they need. These consumers have traditionally most often been teachers and librarians, people educated and certified by professional institutions that, like all such institutions, tend to be committed to transmitting the accepted wisdom they give power to and that thus gives them their power—like, for instance, the assumptions of developmental psychology. Most parents have been brought up on and believe in such assumptions—and so do many children. The producers of children's literature, also adults, can achieve success only by producing books that represent the kinds of childhood purchasers approve of.

They must also produce books that fit into the categories available in the marketplace. If bookstores did not have children's sections, there would be no need for children's books designed to take their places on the shelves of such sections. On another level, also, writers and publishers produce only certain kinds of children's books: picture books, "chapter books" for relatively new readers, young-adult novels, and so forth. A book that does not fit into a recognizable niche may not occupy any available slot in a publisher's catalogue, a bookstore, or a library and might therefore be difficult if not impossible to market.

There are other structural aspects of the marketplace that constrain what gets produced. In recent years in North America, for instance, the primary market for hardcover children's fiction has been educational. The teachers and librarians who have done the bulk of the buying have focused their purchases on what has been used most—which has meant, primarily, the kinds of books that official curricula have identified as important components of what children must read. Since whole language programs have mandated a study of history that involves the reading of historic fiction, there has been a market for historical fiction—and writers and publishers with a feel for the game have produced it. Since, as has recently been the case in the United States, the curricula of many states required compulsory study of the Holocaust, there has been a market for novels about the Holocaust. Since, on the other hand, the history of Italy in the Renaissance hasn't appeared on many curricula, there has been no specific market for novels on that subject. No matter how passionately novelists might have felt about the subject or how interestingly they might have been able to write about it, few such novels have been published.

In the past few years, however, the American education system has been moving toward practices that make less use of the texts of children's literature produced by mainstream noneducational publishers that have, until recently, been so important. As a result, those publishers have been refocusing their offerings and producing more formulaic and less educational books that they believe will satisfy the buyers of children's books in commercial book stores. As Zipes suggests, therefore, the individuality of writers "is quite often bracketed and categorized by the demands and needs of the publishers. What appears at first to be diverse is sooner or later homogenized or suppressed if it does not accommodate itself to publishing and the institutions of education."[114]

The field of children's literature as it has come to be constituted is a powerful institution, controlled by powerful economic forces—most publishing houses have become branches of large multinational corporations. As I suggested earlier, those who have power within this field and derive income from it do so because they know how to operate successfully within it. They are unlikely to make decisions that would in any serious way upset the system in which they theoretically have the power to do so. Should they try to do so, Bourdieu's theories suggest, the field would tend to operate to maintain itself by depriving them of their power within it.

What gives power? The answer is paradoxical. In all fields participants win distinction through their ability to manipulate the habitus—play the game well enough to win over others in an ongoing struggle for power. In terms of the field of children's literature, those with the most power are those whose books are most distinct—noteworthy enough to stand out from other books and to win awards and/or wide audiences. The implication appears to be that power should accrue to the producers of innovative texts, ones that become key parts of the habitus for others to emulate and distinguish themselves from, so that the field constantly undergoes transformation as innovations are absorbed and in turn undergo innovation. But, Bourdieu asserts, "It is one of the generic properties of fields that the struggle for specific stakes masks the objective collusion concerning the principles underlying the game. More precisely, the struggle tends constantly to produce and reproduce the game and its stakes by reproducing, primarily in those who are directly involved, but not in them alone, the practical commitment to the value of the game and its stakes which defines the recognition of legitimacy."[115] In the field of children's literature this commitment to the game and its stakes works in a variety of ways.

Most basically, the mere existence of the field depends on the existence of its implied audience: children who are different from adults in ways that require adults to produce books for them. Without the idea that such children exist, there is no reason for writers to write, publishers to publish, librarians to purchase. Consequently, a whole and fairly sizable segment of the economy and the livelihoods of many people depend on the creation and maintenance of the childhood defined by the lacks that children's literature then must inevitably continue to describe and construct.

What is generally true must then be true of specifics—of specific kinds of books and of specific characteristics in those books. Underlying the apparent distinctness of powerfully innovative texts for children must be an accordance with the established habitus of the field of children's literature. Such texts can be distinct or unique only in ways that offer no real challenge to the basic structure and values of the field as it already is.

Consider, for instance, the novels that win the Newbery Medal as the "the most distinguished contribution to American literature for children published in English in the United States during the preceding year."[116] Producing the most distinguished book clearly brings distinction to practitioners in the field, both economically and in terms of literary status. Just about every library housing children's literature feels obligated to purchase a Newbery winner. The books remain in print long after others produced at the same time and, being widely available and widely considered significant, continue to attract the attention of scholars and others who discuss and recommend children's books. In the light of widely accepted ideas about what makes for literary merit, we might assume that such distinction can accrue only to the most notable books—the most innovative and imaginative. But, as Jill May's comments about the lack of innovation suggest, that is not the case. According to Martha Parravano, "Even the most cursory glance back through Newbery history reveals that there is indeed such a thing as a quintessential Newbery book. Call it the *ur*-Newbery."[117] Parravano describes the ur-Newbery in these terms:

> It's fiction, with an older (twelve-ish) protagonist who is nevertheless not an adolescent (not preoccupied with adolescent concerns). The main character can be either male or female, but most often male. . . . He (or she) must face some adversity, must struggle against himself, or someone close to him, or with some idea or stricture, to find the right form of self-expression, the best way to be human; and if along the way he can have adventures that occur against a background of sweeping events and perhaps even face a threat to his own or his family's survival, all the better. (436–437)

What interests me most about these traits is that they seem to represent a particularly powerful version of the distinguishing characteristics of children's literature as I identified them in earlier chapters. They combine the fairy tale of triumphant adventure with the lessons learned of didactic fable. They primarily concern questions of knowledge, as a childish innocence confronts the world of adult experience, and questions of safety and danger, freedom and repression, desire and the dangers of desire. Although Parravano doesn't say so, these books tend to offer ambivalent answers to all these questions. The choice of a twelve-year-old-but-still-childlike protagonist represents this ambivalence: the books focus on the border between childhood and adolescence, between the joys and limitations of childhood and the demands and benefits of adulthood. They tend to both celebrate anarchy and applaud its repression. They tend to indulge both in nostalgia for childhood and hope for a mature adult future.

All of these features confirm the construction of childhood that the field of children's literature most often confirms and works to produce. Furthermore, each of the features of that construction can be understood specifically in terms of how it acts to confirm the need for the literature as it is and, consequently, for the field that produces it as it is. Parravano's twelve-year-old protagonist, innocent, in need of adult wisdom and protection in the face of danger yet willing, eventually, to accept that adult wisdom, acting on it and thus becoming adult, represents a perfect reader for the kind of book he or she appears in. The field replicates this sort of book, describing this sort of child and helping to construct this sort of child subjectivity as a means of replicating itself.

What makes Newbery winners winners, then, is the extent to which their apparent distinctness actually reproduces the game and its stakes. In "Prizing Children's Literature" Kenneth Kidd offers a perceptive analysis of how and why the Newbery came into existence and how it helped establish "a middlebrow tradition of children's literature" and perhaps also positioned children's literature "as a middlebrow formulation more generally,"[118] as being neither as sophisticated as adult literary fiction nor as superficial and lacking in artistry as popular literature—how, in other words, the Newbery emerged from and continues to shape the field the winners then represent. In the next section I will return to this theme and consider how a canonical text of children's literature embeds and encapsulates the field as a whole and argue that its doing so is the operative condition for its canonicity.

But what about noncanonical texts? My overall purpose here has been to describe how similarities underlie the differences of different texts of children's literature. In arguing that highly valued texts like Newbery winners embed and encapsulate the field, I might be contradicting my own argument by implying that they do differ from less canonical texts. As many teachers and librarians have told me, Newbery winners are notoriously unpopular with young readers—their cultural capital as must-buy texts for children's librarians doesn't necessarily translate into cultural capital for child readers. Less canonical texts, usually those that more obviously repeat common patterns, clearly work to maintain and thus reproduce the game and its stakes. But do they do so in ways different from more admired texts?

Let me look at some texts that represent another form of distinction—financial success. For some years in the mid-1990s, R. L. Stine's Goosebumps series was wildly successful—the best-selling children's books produced up to that point. But if a vast spectrum of teachers, librarians, reviewers, and experts in children's literature were right, these books possess little else in the way of distinction. They have been almost universally reviled by adults with power in the field as formulaic, repetitive texts with no obvious literary merit—with none of the sort of artistic distinction that leads to Newbery medals. In discussing the series, Jack Zipes takes the obvious banality of its contents so much for granted that he dismisses its significance in the project that most concerns him—the ways in which the sophisticated marketing surrounding the books works to turn readers of the series into uncritical consumers: "What is offensive about such books as the *Goosebumps* series is not their horrific content but that the purchase and reading of such books can lead to an addiction whereby the young, curious reader is transformed into a homogenized reader, dependent on certain expectations and codes that make it appear the world is manageable and comforting."[119]

There can be no doubt that the success of Goosebumps had much to do with the cleverness of their marketing—a masterful use of tactics developed long ago but increasingly widespread in children's publishing. There are the collecting appeal of a numbered, similarly formatted series, the challenging incitement to machismo in often reiterated dares in jacket copy and in advertising to undergo the terror the books purport to offer, and the proliferation of toys, games, and TV tie-ins. But in addition, and central to the popularity of the series, I believe, is what Zipes slides over: what happens within the books themselves.

Each of them describes one or two middle-class, usually white, usually suburban children, represented as indistinguishably "normal" enough for a vast spectrum of readers to identify with. These characters are self-centered and acquisitive. They have a profound need to compete and a profound conviction that not giving in to fear in fearful circumstances—an insensitivity to horror that allows them to act horribly toward others and thus triumph over them—is the best way to win. The books are silent about the moral or ethical implications of this behavior. In an interview for *People* magazine, Stine truthfully says, "I have no crying, no hugging, and the kids never learn anything about themselves."[120]

In each book of the Goosebumps series this "normal" world is invaded by something defined as horrible and frightening—something monstrous: a werewolf, a murderous ventriloquist's dummy, a giant worm. In spite or because of their monstrosity, however, these monsters merely echo the characteristics of the supposedly nonmonstrous normal children with whom they interact. They are frighteningly self-indulgent and antisocial, able to triumph over weaker beings exactly to the extent that they can and do engender fear. Even more oddly, these monsters sometimes do actually triumph over human children—turn out to be more powerful—or some of the child protagonists actually turn into monsters. As in the normal world of consumer culture, desert in these texts is defined not by the inherent rightness or essential goodness of some of the combatants but by who actually wins. Values are nothing. Winning is everything; therefore, what is valued is what allows one to win: fearful monstrosity.[121]

What Stine depicts purports to be simply the way things are—presumably, the only way things can be. In this way the books work to confirm and thus construct a consumer subjectivity in their readers that supports and amplifies the merchandising system in general. I might conclude that these books differ from those that achieve literary distinction in presenting a one-sided and thus nonambivalent view of the standard binaries of children's literature. Stine's comment suggests that he offers no didacticism to balance the wish-fulfillment. His books celebrate indulgence over repression, self-interest over communal concern—in terms of the foundational binary of children's literature, the childlike over the adult. In doing so, they reveal the extent to which the most appropriate subjectivity for both children and adults in consumer culture is what has been traditionally understood as childlike.

But that is not exactly the case, simply because of the uncertain status of monstrosity here. In more conventional horror fiction—in many of the novels of Stephen King for instance—something horrid enters the normal world as a dangerous aberration and is then expelled as the book ends happily. The monstrous is clearly bad, clearly at odds with normalcy. In the Goosebumps books, however, the monstrous is both monstrous and, as a fantasy version of the supposedly normal reality it invades, normal. Why should it be depicted as monstrous at all?

The answer, I think, is an unease about the simple and nonambivalent statement of approval for the values these books support. In a culture that often hypocritically claims faith in the value of fellow feeling, charity, and communal involvement, it is inappropriate to be too baldly at odds with these values. It is particularly inappropriate in the context of children's literature, the defining characteristic of which is its ambivalence about the relative value of the childlike and the adult. In representing what they actually support as monstrous, the Goosebumps books separate their typical and therefore nonmonstrous child protagonists from what they have desired and thus seem to make its supposedly antisocial danger clear. In this way they appear to operate as do more characteristic texts of children's literature. But this separation also makes the monstrous fantastic, a clear intrusion of the imaginary into normal reality that divests it of its relevance as a real concern in terms of a reader's own desire or behaviors. If the monstrous is, after all, only a fantasy, it is not something to really be concerned about in one's own life. Having thus been divested of dangerous relevance, the fearful power of the Goosebumps monsters can be enjoyed by readers without any conscious (or acknowledged) awareness of the implications of the various triumphs of unhampered monstrosity. Readers who respond as Goosebumps invite them to respond both desire that which is theoretically monstrous and fearful and are not aware of that desire. In other words, these books are able to vary from the ambivalence characteristic of children's literature exactly and, I suspect, only by appearing not to vary from it—by seeming to be typical. In evoking the appearance of the typical, they confirm their place in the genre even as they diverge from its norms. In Goosebumps books, as well as in Newbery winners, the specific characteristics of characters, plots, themes, and structures all work to echo, support, and maintain the field as it is. What is generic in children's literature is what the field mandates in its constant efforts to maintain itself.

Distinctive Texts in the Genre

In the previous section I argued that Newbery Award winners maintain the conventions of the field just as much as do widely popular series books. But surely *some* texts of children's literature must be genuinely different. Books that are read and reread by generations of readers—"classics" like *Alice's Adventures in Wonderland*, Beatrix Potter's *Tale of Peter Rabbit*, or Maurice Sendak's *Where the Wild Things Are*, for instance—must surely do something more than or different from simply replicating the generic characteristics I have focused on throughout this book, mustn't they? So, too, for that matter, must the novels in J. K. Rowling's uniquely successful Harry Potter series, texts of children's literature that have captured more public attention and more readers than any other children's literature ever. I have suggested that *Where the Wild Things Are* achieved success by taking a powerfully cagey position within the field of children's literature and that *Alice's Adventures in Wonderland* might stand apart from the other six texts I looked at in chapter 1 in having a metafictional relationship with the conventions of the field. Now I would like to build on these suggestions about distinctiveness by considering what makes special texts special yet allows them to still remain recognizably representative of their genre. I do so by looking at two examples that represent different forms of being special: first *The Tale of Peter Rabbit*, as a representative of the canonic classic, and then the Harry Potter series.

Peter Rabbit is clearly a classic. It is, for instance, included in a recent anthology called *Classics of Children's Literature*.[122] But as that title asserts, it is very specifically a classic of *children's* literature—not a classic generally. While many people refer to specific texts for children as "classic," those texts rarely figure in the lists of texts considered to be classics of literature generally, and they are rarely discussed by literary scholars outside of the journals devoted specifically to the study of children's literature. But while no text of children's literature (with the possible exception of Carroll's *Alice*) appears in the mainstream canon of literature respected and studied by those with power in the larger field of literary study, there *is* a canon within the narrower field of children's literature studies. There *are* classics. It is possible that theoretical discussion of what makes classics classic might help explain what makes children's classics classic—with, of course, the proviso that this paradoxical state of being classic only within the confines of this one specific corner of the larger field of literature as a whole will need to be accounted for.

In *What Is a Classic?* T. S. Eliot argues for the inherent superiority of classics, based on their intrinsic qualities of "maturity," "comprehensiveness," and "universality."[123] Merely in being written for an immature and specifically defined audience, texts of children's literature would seem to be disqualified. Or are they? The supposedly intrinsic qualities Eliot names can exist only in relation to extrinsic forces—to the less mature texts they surpass and to the main characteristics and values of the language and society that they comprehend. For Eliot it is consciousness of these relationships that allows readers to use a text like Virgil's *Aeneid* (which he identifies as "the unique classic") as a "critical criterion"[124] for texts still being written today—even, therefore, texts of children's literature, some of which, as contradictory as it may seem, can be viewed as being relatively more "mature" and universal than others. *Peter Rabbit* might be one of those. Possibly the Harry Potter books are, too.

But Eliot's argument depends on his belief that certain values are inherently correct, so that the most comprehensive expression of them represents the greatest maturity—and I doubt that *Peter Rabbit* has been beloved for so long or Harry Potter so widely because they represent inherently correct values. Although Frank Kermode bases his views on Eliot's, he offers an elegant variation on Eliot's comprehensiveness that avoids the question of correctness: the idea that classics have "an openness to accommodation which keeps them alive under endlessly varying dispositions."[125] This "openness" is less a mature totality than a yielding flexibility—less the transcending ability to include a wide range of possibilities than the adaptive ability to change in relation to them. For Kermode, "the only works we value enough to call classic are those which, and they demonstrate by surviving, are complex and indeterminate enough to allow us our necessary pluralities" (44). These texts allow different readers to read them and make use of them in various ways. Consider how Harry Potter is read and used differently by audiences of different ages—as, for that matter, is *Peter Rabbit:* consider its appeal to nostalgic adult collectors of china figurines. Consider also the surprisingly large number of critical interpretations of *Peter Rabbit* that adult critics of children's literature have produced over the decades and the even more surprising number produced of Harry Potter in the relatively short time the Potter series has existed.

Bourdieu also refers to this ability of texts to be read differently as significantly operative in the field of literature, and he offers a cynical explanation for it: "The ideology of the inexhaustible work of art, or of 'reading' as re-creation masks—through the quasi-exposure which is often seen in matters of faith—the fact that the work is indeed made not twice, but a hundred times, by all those who are interested in it, who find a material or symbolic profit in reading it, classifying it, deciphering it, commenting on it, combating it, knowing it, possessing it."[126] It is not so much that a text is open to different readings that gives it the power of a "classic" as that those seeking power know how to use it that way.

The Harry Potter books offer a particularly telling example. In a *New York Times* article published at the height of their celebrity, Robert H. Frank says, "An important element of reading a book or seeing a movie is the ability to discuss the experience with friends. Indeed, once the popularity of a cultural experience reaches a certain threshold, failure to consume it may entail significant social costs. For instance, this past winter [1999–2000] many people simply could not participate in office conversations on Mondays if they had failed to watch 'The Sopranos' the night before. Current sales levels suggest that children who haven't read the latest Potter novel may pay a similar social price."[127] At the point when the Potter novels became the most widely read and discussed children's books ever, knowledge of them became an important form of what Bourdieu calls "culture capital"—and not just for children. Whether children or adults, readers of best sellers or theorists of cultural studies or children's literature, those who had not read Harry Potter declared themselves to be outsiders unworthy of the respect of those with power in a variety of different fields.

There is no question that part of what makes such texts matter is the sheer weight of fame or of history, the inertia of established status—their mere possession of culture capital. But while that is certainly the case with *Peter Rabbit* and the Harry Potter series, I am not prepared to conclude that it is merely their reputations that distinguishes them from other texts. I want first to explore the possibility that there is something about texts like these that has allowed them to develop their reputations in the first place, an inherent quality that makes them a focus of attention and a locus for the expression of interpretive power.

Kermode suggests that the classic's "openness to accommodation" is itself this quality: "the survival of the classic must therefore depend upon its possession of a surplus of signifier"[128]—that which allows readers to find a variety of significations. But he argues the existence of that surplus only from the fact of many interpretations, and he gives no clear idea of how its presence in a text might be recognized in any way but by its effects. Since a classic can be defined only by hindsight, there is no reason to conclude that classics do contain a special sort of surplus of signifier. Presumably *any* literary text might be reinterpreted, if some new development in history or culture made people feel the need to do so or if someone with a strong habitus for the field worked to make it happen, and the new interpretation would then imply an original surplus of signifier. Let us assume for a moment that another children's series about apprentice wizards— Ursula K. Le Guin's Earthsea books, say, or Diana Wynne Jones's Chrestomanci books—had developed massive fame and readership instead of Harry Potter. It seems likely that they would then be the subjects of many and more diverse critical readings than they have currently attracted. Kermode's argument offers no reason for not simply assuming that it is merely the forces of chance and history that have caused certain texts to be singled out as those that require reinterpretation and therefore to seem to have some special surplus of signifier.

Kermode asserts that possibility more explicitly in a later book, *The Genesis of Secrecy,* when he says, "Whatever is preserved grows enigmatic; time, and the pressures of interpretation, which are the agents of preservation, will see to that."[129] Thus, the many extant readings of *Peter Rabbit* imply a mysterious ambiguity in the text itself that invites further interpretation. Still later, in *Forms of Attention,* Kermode makes it even clearer that the existence in a text of a special sort of surplus of signifier may be less a fact than a faith imposed by the accidents of history that have made that text canonical—an important text worthy of attention: "To be inside the canon is . . . to be credited with indefinitely large numbers of possible internal relations and secrets";[130] if the surplus of signifier is merely "credited," then there is no need to believe in its actual presence. More recently, Kermode has moved closer to Bourdieu's view and explicitly asserted that it is the interpretive acts of practitioners that create the meanings that allow classics to continue to be classic: "My view is that nobody will have any true contact with a work of art if it isn't modern; I mean that if it isn't modern it has to be made so, and it's made so largely by commentary."[131]

But while all texts might be viewed as possessing a potential surplus of signifier, not all texts can be "made modern," nor is the "modernity" Kermode speaks of here necessarily the same modernity as that possessed by actual recent modern —or postmodern—texts. Speaking of Kermode's "surplus of signifier," Oliver Taplin asserts that "this is too easy; and it evades any form of literary discrimination. On this criterion any vague, directionless text will be a classic; in fact the looser and more confused the better."[132] Many of what are identified as "postmodern" texts achieve power by deliberately recreating the interpretable effect of the classic as Kermode describes it—by being vague and directionless in ways that invite and allow a variety of readings. In ascribing openness to classics, Kermode acknowledges a debt to Roland Barthes' famous distinction between the *lisible* and the *scriptible,* the readerly and the writerly. For Barthes the readerly classic is a closed text, totally caught up in the system that produced it, while the writerly text deliberately defies closure and demands a variety of interpretations or new "writings"; Kermode says, "In fact what Barthes calls 'modern' is very close to what I am calling 'classic,' and what he calls 'classic' is very close to what I call 'dead.' "[133]

As often happens, texts written for children reveal, in their difference from other literature, what is wrong with Kermode's conclusion here. As I suggested earlier, even those texts of children's literature that claim to be postmodern are rarely loose and directionless. As a genre based in simplicity and adherence to established formulas, children's literature resists this sort of modernity. Despite claims like those made by theorists of "childness" or the "childist" about the extent to which children make the texts they read their own, it is not obviously a "writerly" literature, depending on readers to give it its meanings. Nevertheless, the many published interpretations—or "writings"—of texts like *Peter Rabbit* and the Potter books reveal that at least some texts of children's literature do express a form of writerliness—a form *not* resulting from or dependent on looseness and lack of direction. Perhaps the same is true of the other texts that Kermode identifies as classics also.

While Barthes' "modern" may be close to Kermode's "classic," there is one important difference: Kermode's classic was not written *deliberately* to encourage multifaceted responses. It does allow a writerly response—the effect in readers that they *can* make their own sense of it in ways different from other (usually earlier) readers; but unlike postmodern fiction, the sense readers make of a classic *satisfies* them. Readers don't usually see their interpretations of classics as just one of many possible ways of reading them but with a sense that they have seen something important and complete. While they might pay lip service to the idea that different people read differently, each of the writers of the published interpretations of *Peter Rabbit* and the Potter books clearly believes that he or she has arrived at the key, essential truth—the one most right or most important way of reading the text in question. Even though they know others have reached different conclusions and may even suspect that still others will reach further ones, they are less impressed with the multifaceted potential of the text than with their own particular use of that potential.

While Kermode never says so, I suspect it is this difference in the nature of readers' responses that separates his classics from deliberately writerly texts and that suggests the specific nature of their surplus of signifier. Kermode's focus on the openness of classics causes him to slide over the significance of his own comments on "the coexistence in a single text of a plurality of significances from which, in the nature of human attentiveness, every reader misses some—and, in the nature of human individuality, prefers one."[134] Perhaps it is not a question of human individuality but an effect specific to such texts—an intrinsic quality they possess, or at least appear to possess, for those with a habitus in the fields of reading literature and literary study.

But saying that these texts allow many different readings, each of which strikes its reader as the best one, does not explain *how* they do so. I can best explore that by looking at some readings of a specific text. *Peter Rabbit* is so simple that those unfamiliar with the criticism of children's literature might be surprised by the frequency with which it has been interpreted. How is it that so many people have so much to say about an apparently straightforward cautionary tale about a rabbit who disobeys his mother, raids a vegetable garden, and escapes with his life after a series of narrow escapes from an angry farmer?

Many readers do read this story as exactly that straightforward cautionary tale, and for good reason. As my discussion of definitions in chapter 3 reveals, it is a common assumption that all children's literature is primarily educational, and this story about an animal who dresses and thinks like a human has clear relationships with the tradition of cautionary fables that begins with Aesop. Peter is given an obvious warning by his mother, who not only says, "Don't go into Mr. McGregor's garden," but who also offers a highly persuasive justification for her warning: "Your Father had an accident there; he was put in a pie by Mrs. McGregor." The narrator then calls Peter "very naughty" for disregarding this sound advice and goes to great lengths to show how intensely he suffers as a consequence.

Donna Norton confirms that *Peter Rabbit* is a cautionary moral tale when she suggests that Peter "wants to go to the garden so badly that he disobeys his mother. . . . Children know that such behavior cannot go unpunished. Peter must take a dose of camomile tea to compensate for a stomach-ache; his sisters feast on milk and blackberries."[135] Similarly focusing on food, Scott Pollard and Kara Keeling suggest somewhat more subtly that whereas "Peter's mother and sisters dedicate themselves to using the food they gather, prepare and eat as the signifying center of the family's civilizing culture," Peter himself foolishly "dares becoming food for someone else's table" by venturing into Mr. McGregor's garden in search of forbidden food, so he must suffer: "for Beatrix Potter, solitary, wild, uncontrolled eating is unacceptable, and a price must be paid for such excessive and abnormal behavior."[136] Rebecca J. Lukens, who denies that the book makes a specific statement about disobedience, suggests that "it seems likely that an implied theme—'Even when you're naughty, mother loves you and accepts you'—has kept it a much-loved story."[137] William T. Moynihan calls Potter "an Aesop for her time" and, although he doesn't specify any particular moral, says, "All the charm of Potter's language and illustrations cannot obscure the fact that hers is a cautionary art."[138]

But is it only that? Jill May suggests that there is more—that like all of Potter's work *Peter Rabbit* is "both a morally instructive tale and an adventurous tale about animals in human situations."[139] And a closer look reveals details and possibilities that a focus merely on moral instruction does not account for. These details undercut the significance of the supposed moral by dwelling on the oddity of what most moral fables take for granted—that within the world they describe animals act like human beings.

Potter first raises the peculiarity of these quasi-human rabbits in the marked contrast of the pictures accompanying the first two pages of text. While the second shows the rabbit family dressed as humans and Mrs. Rabbit passing a basket to her daughters, the first shows the rabbits undressed and outside the sandbank "underneath the root of a very big fir-tree"[140] that is their home—very much creatures of the wild. Viewed in the context of this first picture, the second picture seems (to me) to invite viewers' attention to the strangeness of the clothing. It is not surprising that the next picture focuses on Peter's marked discomfort as his mother buttons the constricting collar of his jacket.

Peter's human clothing causes him problems throughout the adventure that follows. As he flees Mr. McGregor, his shoes hold him back. "After losing them," says Potter, "he ran on four legs and went faster, so that I think he might have got away altogether, if he had not unfortunately run into a gooseberry net, and got caught by the large buttons of his jacket" (30). Once rid of the jacket and able to act like a natural rabbit, he can finally escape the garden.

If readers notice that the human clothing that Peter's mother forces him to wear is as much to blame for his problems as his act of defying her, they may also realize that Peter is merely doing what real rabbits do, and even should do: forage in a garden for appropriate food. The clothing seems to represent the same repressive attitude toward acting on one's primal urges as that implied by the assumption that the book is a fable about obedience and the virtues of safety. That fable is most clearly undermined when the text explains that Peter's mother was particularly angry because "it was the second little jacket and pair of shoes that Peter had lost in a fortnight" (54). Apparently Peter has not learned anything about acting obediently and safely from his own previous experience, so why should those who hear his tale assume that there is a lesson to be learned from it?

Furthermore, Peter is not really punished for his behavior; he goes to bed because he is ill, not because he has been sent there. It seems likely that for many readers much of the pleasure the book offers emerges from Peter's ability both to cope with danger and to survive it relatively unscathed. A minor illness and some camomile tea may seem a small price to pay for all that excitement (and all those vegetables). Instead of being a story about a human child who gets into trouble when he acts like an animal, *Peter Rabbit* may be the story of an animal forced to act like a human child who triumphs when he acts like his natural animal self.

Many interpretations focus on details like the ones I have just discussed and deny the cautionary nature of the tale. Contrary to Pollard and Keeling's insistence that Potter was essentially "a repressed Victorian" for whom "all pleasures have their price," Humphrey Carpenter says that "the voice we hear again and again in her stories is not that of the late Victorian spinster decorously instructing her nieces and child-friends in acceptable social behaviour, but of a rebel, albeit a covert one, demonstrating the rewards of nonconformity, and exhorting her young readers to question the social system into which they found themselves born."[141] As I suggested earlier, Alison Lurie speaks of the "concealed moral" of *Peter Rabbit*: "that disobedience and exploration are more fun than good behavior, and not really all that dangerous, whatever Mother may say."[142] For Ruth MacDonald, similarly, "Peter is not simply, irrationally willful in his violation of the sanction; he is also imperilled and daring"; she claims that "most readers find Peter's transgressions utterly engaging, and are not prepared to shift their approbation from son to mother."[143] June Cummins reads *Peter Rabbit* as a version of the Adam and Eve story in which the transgressive rebel enjoys the forbidden food he eats and, although expelled from the garden, is not punished: "Potter has written a *pro-child* story."[144] Comparing the published *Peter Rabbit* to an earlier manuscript version, Roger Sale asserts that "a tossed-off cautionary tale is transformed into a story of sad adventure that has no moral but does have a complicated moral tone."[145] That tone derives from the ambiguity of Peter's animality: "Short as *Peter Rabbit* is, it would not be easy to list all the effects its words and pictures conceive concerning the animalness of people, the peopleness of animals."[146]

Similarly, Carole Scott speaks of "the delicate interaction between animal nature and civilized behavior" in Potter's books generally and finds that "the major conflict" in *Peter Rabbit* is "between the fixed order of society and the forces that seek to undermine it, . . . between human civilization and animal nature." She suggests that for Potter, clothes represent social expectations ambivalently, both as constraining personal freedom and as providing "the opportunity for joyful relationships and for personal growth and fulfillment." In a later article she adds that "for Potter, clothes are what people must learn to wear as they grow up and go out into the world."[147]

Charles Frey, who also focuses on the ambiguity of the book, speaks of the mix in Potter's work "between homiletic hominess and more savage celebrations."[148] Using different but similar binaries and implying the same dynamics, Daphne Kutzer suggests that in Potter's work generally "there is at the very least an ambiguous tension regarding the pleasures of home, and at times home itself becomes as perilous as the wilderness. Wildness and wilderness . . . threaten to burst out of seemingly safe domestic spaces (as in *Peter Rabbit*)."[149] And while many readers follow Kutzer and identify Peter's home under the tree as primarily a safely civilized place that he deserts for the wild adventures of the garden and then returns to, Margery Hourihan reverses the binaries, seeing the garden as representative of a dangerously civilized human world: "So our neat, civilized world is perceived as dangerous and antithetical to nature and thus to life and joy."[150] In a somewhat similar formulation, Fred Inglis says, "The imagery of Beatrix Potter's world balances a colonized, accomplished horticulture and agriculture, and the stable but mysterious Nature which lies untamed beyond the garden wall."[151]

W. Nikola-Lisa speaks of a similar but different set of binaries: a "tension" in Potter's work between convention and independence" that Nikola-Lisa sees as representative of a woman's role in Potter's time: "Peter Rabbit *is* the projection of this inner state of tension indicative of women caught between the confines of the home and the lure of freedom" and represents a longing for independence but insists on "the inevitability of social bondage."[152] Thus the story remains suspended between the two poles. Frey, however, identifies Peter's "savage celebrations" as an expression of maleness and sees the book as doubly ambivalent. First, it only seems to disapprove of Peter's challenging authority "through selfish and somewhat atavistic behavior," and it less obviously invites us to applaud his daring; but underlying that applause, the story is "deeply cautionary: the expression of all that boyish energy and challenge rouses a violently retributive response from male power in the world."[153] Or does it? Speaking of the book as an expression of "male resistance to the civilizing influence of family," Pollard and Keeling claim, "Potter seems to be walking a thin line here, preferring obedience but admitting in a subtle and backhanded way that the idyllic existence that obedience might make possible is not possible at all."[154]

So *Peter Rabbit* is either a celebration of wildness and self-determination that appears to condemn them or a condemnation of wildness and self-determination that appears to praise them. Some interpreters simply suggest that it combines the two. Peter Hollindale sees it as evidence of "the war in Potter between subversion and conformity," and Alice Byrnes says, "Because Peter Rabbit is presented as a composite of animal instincts and human behavior, we tend to apply a dual set of standards to his harebrained activity. . . . Inwardly, we delight in Peter's impetuous nature and his ability to survive."[155] When Suzanne Rahn says that Potter's *Tale of Two Bad Mice* "satisfies the young child's strong and complementary needs for adventure and for security," she adds, "It is rather like *Peter Rabbit* in that respect";[156] and Jackie Eastman calls Peter "childlike and heroic," saying, "Despite his vulnerability . . . , Peter manages to overcome *by himself* the danger presented by a far more powerful enemy."[157] For Margaret Mackey this implies a key ambiguity in Potter's view of Peter: "The detached tone with which Potter describes Peter's disobedience actually functions to raise the question of just whose side she is on. . . . The overwhelming achievement of the book is its ultimate ambiguity on this topic."[158] Eliza Dresang agrees: "Potter is ambiguous on the subject of 'being good.' . . . Peter disobeys and still he is clearly the hero of the tale."[159] So does Hollindale: "Balancing humanized domesticity against wild rabbit foraging, Potter subverted parental authority and its built-in hypocrisy while also, in a minor key, endorsing prudence and property rights."[160] As Frey says, "*The Tale of Peter Rabbit* leaves us with a good many open questions concerning its intention."[161] It is less straightforward than it first seems, and like the classics of adult literature that Kermode discusses, it can be interpreted in a variety of ways.

But those ways seem to center on the relative significance of Peter's rabbitness and his humanity—and perhaps surprisingly so, for almost none of the commentators I have mentioned make any reference to each other's work. They appear to have arrived at their similar concerns quite independently of each other. Furthermore, anyone familiar with even a few of the texts written for children in the last hundred years or so will realize that the tension between animality and humanness is one of the aspects of *Peter Rabbit* that most clearly identifies it as children's literature. Many children's stories are about animals like Peter who act like humans, and many others deal with human children whose "bad" behavior is considered to be dangerously "wild" by adults. As I discussed in chapter 3, animal and human, wildness and civilization are central pairs of the binary opposites characteristic of texts for children.

Because this concern with the animal and the human is so widespread in children's literature, its mere presence does not make *Peter Rabbit* into a canonical text. That must depend on the particular way in which it expresses that concern. My discussion of it thus far suggests what that way might be by revealing two apparently contradictory facts about it. First, since it has been singled out for special attention, it must be special, unusual, even unique. But second, it has enough in common with many other texts for children that it can be said to express the most common characteristics of the genre as a whole. *Peter Rabbit* represents an impossible combination: at one and the same time, it is both unique and representative.

In *The Classic* Kermode suggests a way of understanding this unique sort of representativeness. Discussing the relationship between historical conceptions of classics and the history of the idea of types, he quotes the nineteenth-century biologist Louis Agassiz: "It is common to speak of the animal which embodies most fully the character of a group, as the type of that group."[162] This unsatisfactory view of animals is nevertheless highly evocative of the special nature of canonical texts: like Agassiz's types, they are those texts that uniquely possess the character of a whole group of literature as those characteristics are understood by those who are in the process of defining the group. They are paradigmatic examples, and as David Fishelov asserts, "In every generic category we witness an intimate, hermeneutical relation between paradigmatic instances and the associated rules: generic rules are drawn from, and exemplified by, those representative cases."[163]

The Tale of Peter Rabbit is a "type" or paradigmatic example in something like this way. As the unusual details that interpreters concentrate on suggest, it is too distinctive to be considered what we usually call "typical"—that is, a mere member of a class, a lowest common denominator expression of the most obvious characteristics of the genre. But part of its distinctiveness is that it implies and contains the defining characteristics of many other texts of children's literature, many of them different from each other. As Jill May suggests, Potter "melded two genres—fantasy and realism—in a single plot"; and Maurice Sendak speaks of the "imaginative blend of fact and fantasy, integrated and working together harmoniously, that creates for me the aliveness of *Peter Rabbit*."[164] Indeed, the distinctiveness of *Peter Rabbit* is that it "embodies most fully the character of a group"—the group being the genre of children's literature as we understand it as a whole.

Earlier I suggested that children's literature as it now exists emerged as a combination of the didactic fable and the wish-fulfilling fairy tale. Most fiction for children falls somewhere on the spectrum between fables that are aggressive adult propaganda and fairy tales or adventures that are pure wish-fulfillment fantasy. But the readings of *Peter Rabbit* I have described tend to consider it as either one or the other, as either a fable or a fairy tale—or a combination of the two. For every William T. Moynihan who insists that Potter's is "a cautionary art," there is a Humphrey Carpenter who argues that "the theme she had chosen to tackle in her earliest story, *The Tale of Peter Rabbit,* is one that recurs throughout her work: . . . Jack in the Giant's castle, the little fellow, the folktale hero who has nothing but his courage and his wits, struggling against an opponent of far superior physical strength."[165] For every Gillian Avery who focuses on Peter's tears in the garden and says, "By the end of *The Tale of Peter Rabbit* we know Peter is a wimp, certainly not the sort of person to whom we would care to trust our destinies," there is a Ruth MacDonald who insists that the tale replays the most basic sort of wish-fulfillment fantasy, "the outwitting of the large and powerful by the small and cunning."[166] That it can be read in both these contradictory ways makes it unlike more "typical" children's books, which tend to be clearly either fairy tales or fables, but not both at the same time, and more prototypical—representative of the scope of the genre of children's literature as a whole.

Peter Rabbit can be read as a fable, but to do so is to ignore details that undercut the fable's message. Or to put it another way: while it can be read as a wish-fulfillment fantasy, to do so is to ignore details that undercut the triumph of the fantasy. The story possesses a specific sort of surplus of signifier because that which remains as surplus after an interpretation has been accomplished contradicts the implications of that interpretation. It has what Kermode identifies as "a plurality of significances from which, in the nature of human attentiveness, every reader misses some—and, in the nature of human individuality, prefers one."

Furthermore, the contradictory surplus is not merely contradictory: it specifically represents the other pole of a binary central to the genre of children's literature—central to discourse about and to children in the last few centuries. As I have argued throughout, texts for children act to construct childhood in opposition to adulthood, as inferior or superior to adulthood, as fortunately or unfortunately less repressed, more animal-like, wilder. The field in which adults discuss and address children as a whole involves contradictory attitudes toward these concerns. The most powerful positions taken within that field transcend tenacious adherence to a one-sided view and blindness to contradictory ones, and they reveal an awareness of and account for the entire spectrum of contradictory possibilities—not just blind praise for the idyllic nature of childhood or panicky concern for the inadequacy of childlike ignorance but awareness of the ignorance of innocence and the innocence of ignorance. The most powerful texts of children's literature, like *Peter Rabbit,* mirror that comprehensive ability to imply the scope and the subtleties of children's literature as a whole. The status of Potter's story as a classic relates to the uniquely comprehensive position it takes, which makes it a prototypical expression of the characteristics of the genre to which it belongs. It attracts readers and interpretations as an intense (and therefore powerful) expression of the same characteristics and concerns that draw readers, adults or children, to the reading of children's literature generally.

The same is true, I believe, of the Harry Potter books.[167] Pointing especially to the similarity of heroes who are "neither saint nor sinner" and a shared surface simplicity that hides complexity, Eliza Dresang says, "I suspect that some of the enduring popularity of *Peter Rabbit* explains the immediate popularity of *Harry Potter*."[168] Amanda Cockrell also argues for a similarity: "*Peter Rabbit* is about life and death, about the monster in the beautiful garden and the possibility of ending up as stew. *Harry Potter* is about the monsters within and without the self."[169] These connections with *Peter Rabbit* suggest how the Harry Potter books also represent a powerful position taken in the field of children's literature by encapsulating their genre.

And encapsulating it in very similar ways. While one text is a very short story with pictures and the other a multivolume set of novels, both describe how a young male, repressed at home, goes off to a place those at home define as dangerous and wild. There he has triumphant adventures, mostly by doing what both those at home and those in the dangerous place define as "bad"—by breaking the rules and defying the power of those who control the theoretically wild place that is nevertheless orderly (in one case a seminatural garden, in the other a place of magical anarchy rigorously controlled by a bureaucracy). Much as Peter triumphs over a powerful enemy to whom his father fell prey, Harry wins out over his father's enemy and murderer, Voldemort, in book after book in the series. Both *Peter Rabbit* and the Potter books suggest that the supposedly wild place away from home might be the boy's true home, where he really belongs—but at the end of *Peter Rabbit* and of each of the Potter novels except the last, he returns, for a while at least, to his original repressive dwelling. A rabbit in and out of human clothing, a boy half wizard and half typical human, he truly belongs in both places or in neither.

Both texts thus offer complicated versions of the formulaic home/away/home story so characteristic of children's literature. And in doing so, both concern themselves ambivalently with binary oppositions that relate to ideas of home and away: normalcy and aberrance, order and anarchy, repression and wildness—binaries that are fundamental to children's literature generally. What distinguishes the Potter series is not just that it engages these common binaries. It is the ambivalence. Like *Peter Rabbit* it includes in itself the variety of ways that a range of texts within the genre deals with them. As its strange insistence on the bureaucratic nature of its supposedly anarchic wizard world suggests, it is inherently ambiguous. In offering ambivalent or paradoxical combinations of things often kept separate elsewhere, it operates as a macrocosm of children's literature, a type of the genre as a whole.

The characters that inhabit the world of Harry Potter are themselves ambivalent. On the one hand, they fulfill conventional roles in the formulaic story they appear in. Harry is always understood to be good—and perhaps even more important, nice, the typical kind of boy everyone ought to like—as his role of hero demands. Similarly, his enemies are suitably malevolent. On the other hand, however, Rowling manages to maintain Harry's ordinary likeability while simultaneously conveying his exceptionalness, not merely as the Chosen One, as he is often called in later books in the series, but also in terms of his amazing skills at quidditch and mastering complex forms of magic such as the production of a protective patronus. Nor does she ever clarify whether Harry is the protagonist of her stories because he possesses these heroic skills or merely because, being born to the right parents at the right time, fate put him in the right position—whether it is birth or character that makes him special; she somehow suggests it is both. She also manages simultaneously to report his almost effortless series of triumphs and his ability to maintain his position as a theoretically fragile underdog; despite his previous victories, each succeeding novel reconfirms the unlikelihood of someone so weak defeating enemies so powerful. And while Harry does many things that might be understood to be cruel or thoughtless—he rarely shares his vast financial resources with his poorer friends, for instance—the texts continue to invite us to think of him as likeable, even as he angrily submerges himself in adolescent self-pity in *Harry Potter and the Order of the Phoenix*.

Other characters fill equally formulaic roles and yet are equally ambivalent. The ineffably wise and respectable wizard Dumbledore makes childish jokes and is childishly fond of candy. Speaking of "explicit shifts of archetypal imagery between characters" that allow both Harry and Voldemort to fill, at times, the Jungian role of the powerless Child or both Voldemort and the Weasley twins to operate as tricksters, Alice Mills says, "This pattern in the Harry Potter books renders them trickster texts; they are far from simplistic in their treatment of (generally) formulaic material."[170]

The plots of the novels confirm this conclusion. Each novel in the series offers a variation on the same basic plot pattern—not just a generally archetypal underdog story but a quite specific version of it: Harry suffers at the hands of his relatives until he is magically wrested from them, arrives at school, breaks rules and gets away with it, confronts a mystery that threatens him or his adherents, suspects an apparently bad teacher who usually turns out to be on his side, tends to admire an apparently good teacher who often turns out to be an enemy, solves the mystery with the help of his friends, and then ends up in trouble in a dark place, often underground, where he confronts the evil Voldemort or his followers and triumphs over him or them, often with the help of adult supporters. In each case Harry learns more about what happened in the past, specifically to his parents and their friends and their earlier engagement in the battle to save the world from Voldemort—the plot overall is a series of carefully orchestrated revelations about events that happened in the past and that continue to influence Harry in the present, events that Harry comes to understand more subtly and in more detail in each succeeding book. But despite being so formulaic and so determined to reiterate the pleasures of rehearsing expected events in expected ways, the novels are surprisingly loose in their plotting. By and large, little exciting happens in any of the novels in terms of events that move their plots forward for much of the way through. The novels each raise the key problem they deal with fairly early on, and events do occasionally remind readers of them; but as Maria Nikolajeva suggests, "It is the never-ending chain of everyday episodes, albeit generously seasoned with magic, that the bulk of the *Harry Potter* volumes contain."[171] They actually focus most of the time on matters not directly related to their main plots—on descriptions of quidditch matches and strange beasts and stranger candies, on magical people and magical shops and magical objects, on all the wonderfully wild anarchy of the world of wizards. As Nicholas Tucker says, "Where Rowling has . . . excelled beyond argument is in her extraordinary powers of invention. There have been many ingeniously inventive children's authors before, but seldom one with an imagination so endlessly fertile."[172] That inventiveness allows her to get away with not focusing on the key events of the plot throughout most of her novels and therefore to tell formulaic stories that seem decidedly nonformulaic.

Rowling's focus on the anarchy of the wizard world allows her other ambivalences that represent the ambiguous coming together of things often found separately in other, simpler texts for children and confirm the series as a type of the genre. A main source of enjoyment for readers is the wonderful and wonderfully detailed imaginativeness of her version of wizardry. This wild abundance of wizardly things is freeing, exhilarating, and it is not surprising that Harry almost always wins as a result of being as defiantly dismissive of order as the magic is, trusting himself rather than his adult protectors, breaking rules and acting wildly, just as Peter Rabbit wins when he ditches his restraining parent-imposed clothing. But Harry's enemies are understood to be truly evil because they are the ultimate anarchists who engage in the most serious anarchy—the destruction of the orderly structures of wizard society in favor of their own private views and needs. It is only the presumably less evil (or less good?) people, like the loathsomely bureaucratic Miss Umbridge of the Ministry of Magic in *Harry Potter and the Order of the Phoenix*, who privilege rules, order, and the established hierarchies. As Harry's enemies often point out, even Dumbledore often breaks the rules of the school he administers in Harry's favor. It sometimes seems as if this small-minded holding to rules and refusal to indulge in anything wildly magical and exuberant is the true enemy. As the series proceeds, there is an increasing connection between Harry and Voldemort: both are slight, dark-haired boys with a charismatic gift for leadership and a loyal cohort of devoted followers, both have one wizard and one nonwizard parent, both are orphans raised by those who don't care for them, both are rule breakers with vast magical resources they need to confront and learn to deal with. It is as if Peter Rabbit and the rabbit slayer, Mr. McGregor, were versions of the same character (as perhaps, looking back from the vantage point of the Potter books, they are). The story in the Harry Potter books, as in *Peter Rabbit* and in Sendak's *Where the Wild Things Are*, is about a boy who remains unregeneratively wild, still childish despite attempts to constrain and civilize him, who goes where the wild things are and triumphs over them (i.e., diminishes wildness) by being the wildest one of all—and who then childishly seeks the comforts of home, where he is allowed to be relatively wild, safely constrained. The series has it both ways: the orderly society that Umbridge so rigorously represents is both a good thing and a repressive one, and the freeing lack of constraint of a Voldemort is not only pure evil and purely dangerous but also freeing and lots of fun. These books are sententious fables that offer the pleasures of wish-fulfillment fantasy and pleasurable wish-fulfillment fantasies that (increasingly in the later books in the series) offer the thoughtful didacticism of fable.

Voldemort is not the only character who resembles Harry in some key way. There are many orphan outsiders, not just Harry and Voldemort, but also Hagrid and Neville Longbottom. Neville, born at the same time as Harry and, like him, orphaned by Voldemort's rebellion, might, the novel suggests, also be the boy destined to defeat Voldemort; and, like Harry, when confronted by his parent's killers, he rises to the task. The nasty Draco Malfoy also shares Harry's body type and his quidditch position, and his cohort of supporters echoes Harry's cohort. Harry's close group of friends use their various abilities to aid him, an echo of his father's close group of friends who similarly have a range of differing skills they used to help Harry's father in the past. There are a range of characters who at various times act as father to Harry: Dumbledore, his friend Ron's father, various teachers at various times, Sirius Black. Harry's position as a celebrity of interest to the media is echoed by Gilderoy Lockhart.

But Lockhart is clearly foolish, a seeker after fame, unlike Harry, who flees it; and despite the similarities I have mentioned, the usually incompetent Neville seems like Harry's opposite in one way, as does the decidedly nasty Draco Malfoy in another. The similarities also draw attention to differences, and they suggest another significant aspect of Rowling's depictions of magical anarchy: for all the fecund, anarchic detail, there is order, an order created by the ways so many aspects of the text act as variations of each other. The similar-but-different nature of the characters is just one thread of a complex network of variations.

First, the fantasy of wizardry operates as a variation of the world readers already inhabit. The ways in which mail is delivered or newspapers report gossip or quidditch is marketed and played all have less-magical real-life equivalents readers can recognize, so the pleasure they offer is not merely their imaginativeness but also the recognition of how they imaginatively vary from what readers normally think of as real—and often, also, an awareness of the satirical implications of the similarity. As Kate Behr says, "The wizard world exists only in relation to the 'real' world, echoing/mirroring all its customs and discourse, and thus reflects our Muggle world back to us, the Muggle readers—the same yet different."[173]

Each of the novels in the series—and it is instructive that they should be a series and thus replicate the tendency of the genre to tell new stories about the same characters—acts as books in series do. As different versions of the same basic material, they operate as variations of the others in the series. As I suggested earlier, their plots each follow more or less the same pattern. Indeed, they are doubly patterned, as the series of repetitive events that make up the plots take place over the course of and follow the repetitive rituals of a school year. But despite all this repetition, each book includes surprisingly different (and very imaginatively innovative) events, characters, and other details. Furthermore, each succeeding novel furthers the plot of the story as a whole, answering some of the key questions readers have been invited to ask but also leaving others unanswered and introducing important new questions; meanwhile, each succeeding confrontation with Voldemort and his henchmen takes Harry a step closer to the final confrontation at the end of the seventh volume.

The series as a whole gradually changes in tone. The later volumes offer a more complex description of the wizard world and a greater sense of how Hogwarts is situated in relation to readers' expanding knowledge of wizardry internationally. Readers not only learn more new information but also more details about aspects of the wizard world of which they were already aware. As Behr says, "Core facts remain the same from first to last, but the reader's perceptions change as the stories and characters grow in complexity and acquire a history. Our understanding moves in a hermeneutic circle, as clues or references planted by Rowling in earlier books are only appreciated in the light of later events, usually moving from a mood of comic relief to one of tragic intensity."[174]

The later books are darker than the earlier ones and more concerned with drawing readers' attention to the ambivalences and moral ambiguities that have been present, though less obtrusive, from the beginning. In *Harry Potter and the Order of the Phoenix,* for instance, Harry's earlier sense of his father's perfection is challenged when he enters his hated teacher Snape's memory of how James Potter once viciously bullied him for the sheer fun of it, knowledge that explicitly confirms the sense implied early on in the series that things are rarely as simple as people might like. That Snape then loses any sympathy Harry might have developed for him here by entrapping Dumbledore in the next book, *Harry Potter and the Half-Blood Prince,* adds further layers to the complexity—as does Snape's emergence as a hero in the final book.

While the first few books in the series seem the ones most typical of children's novels, the later ones describing Harry's voyage into adolescent angst might be read as more typical of young-adult fiction. Roberta Trites suggests that the series as a whole *is* young-adult fiction: "As a series, the Harry Potter books provide us with the opportunity to interrogate what constitutes adolescent literature."[175] What I find especially interesting here is that the same basic plot, reiterated in each book and, in a way, in the story of the series as a whole, has the potential to be told as both forms of literature for younger people, as children's fiction and as young-adult fiction—forms usually considered to have significantly different characteristics. The novels thus encapsulate the genre in a very real sense. Not only do they include these two different but similar forms in their usual chronological order, allowing readers of the series to replicate the patterns of their reading as young people generally, but they do so in a way that allows the series to reveal the "adult" matter hidden within the structures of its earlier texts by making it explicit in the later ones. The series as a whole operates not only to encapsulate the genre of children's literature but also to offer a metafictional commentary on it.

It may do this in more ways than one. Focusing on the ways in which themes and events in the series reflect the economic field in which the books are marketed, Elizabeth Teare argues that "the stories the books tell . . . enact both our fantasies and our fears of children's literature and publishing in the context of twenty-first-century commercial and technological culture."[176] They might thus encapsulate not just the genre but also the field of children's literature.

The Harry Potter books also encapsulate the genre in another way: by packing into one story the concerns and characteristics of a surprising range of kinds of literature, particularly children's literature. To begin with, a number of commentators have offered readings of the series that reveal the ways in which it clings to basic story patterns they assume to be at the heart of stories generally or stories for children in particular. Some commentators read it as a characteristic fairy tale, offering the symbolic Freudian resonances described by Bruno Bettelheim, or as a characteristic myth, following the Jungian patterns of what Joseph Campbell identifies as the story of the hero with a thousand faces.[177] Jan Lacoss focuses on the "functions" that Vladimir Propp identifies as universal in fairy tales: "In fact, each book follows the sequence, and the overall plot of the series also appears to do so"; and M. Katherine Grimes finds Otto Rank's "ten basic elements" of hero myths in it.[178] That these different commentators can so easily find evidence of these different and supposedly more universal elements in the series might suggest that the story is more universal than the elements. Perhaps Rowling has devised a narrative so succinctly complete in its expression of essential human (or perhaps just Euro-American?) narrative that it can be successfully accessed and interpreted by a range of theoretically different but avowedly universal patterns and archetypes.

According to Giselle Liza Anatol, the novels are "reminiscent of Judeo-Christian, ancient Greek and Roman, and Celtic myths; quest narratives, particularly Arthurian legend; European fairy tales; Victorian novels and orphan stories; adventure stories; contemporary popular culture narratives like Superman and Spiderman comic books, with the mild-mannered 'nerd' saving the day, as well as *Star Wars* . . . and children's detective fiction."[179] Anatol also speaks of "the incredible range of genres woven together in the novels—fairy tale, bildungsroman, boarding school narrative, detective novel, adventure story, fantasy quest tale" (x). Other types of children's fiction can be added to this list: high fantasy in the tradition of Tolkien, comic fantasy in the tradition of Roald Dahl, "Bad Boy" stories in the tradition of Thomas Aldrich's original *Bad Boy* and Richmal Crompton's "Just William" series, ghost stories, horror stories, stories about pets and other animals, sports stories focusing on descriptions of games, contemporary young-adult realistic fiction. Texts for children in other genres can also be added to the list. Peter Applebaum reads Harry as a version of the "gundam child" of *anime*, fighting a battle he inherited from a previous generation and using magic as anime uses technology.[180] In terms of the six characteristic texts I discussed in chapter 1, the Harry Potter books offer the same basic plot pattern and encounter with "wildness" of "The Purple Jar" and *The Snowy Day;* the whimsically imaginative fantasy of *Alice's Adventures in Wonderland* (not to mention an unsettlingly shifty setting) and *Dr. Doolittle* (not to mention a lover of animals); the homey utopianism and focus on the pleasurable badness of sometimes bad boys reminiscent of *Henry Huggins;* and a view of contemporary reality and a discourse on power and learning the truth about one's parents similar to that in *Plain City.* Perhaps the most distinctive quality of the series is the way in which it enlists so many kinds of fiction found separately in other books for children. It is less like any other individual children's book than it is like children's literature generally, as a genre.

But as I suggested earlier about the depiction of magic in the series, its wild abundance of connections to varying kinds of literature is not merely anarchic. Ann Alton reads the series as a combination of many types of children's literature: "Genres traditionally dismissed as 'despised' genres—including pulp fiction, mystery, gothic and horror stories, detective fiction, the school story and the closely related sports story, and series books—appear throughout the *Harry Potter* books, along with more 'mainstream' genres (at least in children's literature) such as fantasy, adventure, quest romance, and myth."[181] But, Alton argues, "Rather than creating a hodgepodge with no recognizable or specific pattern, Rowling has fused these genres into a larger mosaic, which not only connects readers' generic expectations with the tremendous success and popularity of the *Harry Potter* series but also leads to the ways in which the series conveys literary meaning" (141). In reading the novels as a mosaic combining many genres, Alton suggests another way in which the series sums up the genre of children's literature as a whole.

Meanwhile, many commentators suggest that the differing genres at work in Harry Potter operate to balance each other in what becomes an orderly and meaningful way that sustains the complicating ambiguities I discussed earlier. Mary Pharr says, "Just as it is both a children's and an adult's series, it is also both solemn and quite funny," and Pat Pinsent talks about how Rowling combines "stock material from the genre of magic fantasy . . . with equally stereotypical elements from the boarding school story such as the trio of friends foiling the unpleasant teacher."[182] Speaking of the same combination, Amanda Cockrell says, "The juxtaposition of schoolboy humor with the battle against the darkness is a disturbing notion in itself, arguing an ambiguity that is rare in children's fantasy."[183] Meanwhile, Karin Westman suggests that "the series partakes in a tradition of narrative realism as much as fantasy," and Terry Doughty agrees: "Rowling addresses many of the same problems treated in contemporary realistic fiction for boys. The one major distinction is that of genre."[184] Similarly, Maria Nikolajeva speaks of "the fortunate blend of the romantic and the ironic, the straightforward and the reasonably intricate, the heroic and the everyday in Harry Potter"; Roni Natov argues, "As Harry embodies both the ordinary and the extraordinary, his narratives contain realistic and romantic elements"; Katherine Grimes asserts, "The true joy of the Harry Potter series is that the books' protagonist is both a bigger-than-life hero and a true-to-life boy, just as the books are both magical and realistic"; and Philip Nel offers a similar pairing: "Rowling's frequent juxtaposition of ordinary and extraordinary creates a fantasy that has a deliberately everyday quality. Indeed, Rowling's secondary world gains credibility from the ways in which her characters accept the magical as normal."[185]

The ambivalence implied by these combinations of differing genres is most clearly highlighted by the range of ways in which commentators read its defining binaries. As with *Peter Rabbit,* critics tend to agree on what binaries are in play and to identify ones found often if not always in literature for children, but they disagree about what position the novels take in relation to these binaries. For instance, many commentators, focusing on the ways in which the books combine the anarchy of magic with the usual order of normal reality, consider the position the books take in regard to the subversion or preservation of order. For some, the series is inherently subversive, inherently radical. According to Susan Hall, "The wizard world depicted by Rowling is (as yet) neither an anarchy nor a dictatorship and appears at first glance considerably more attractive than the Muggle world. However, one finds it does not recognize the rule of law . . . at all."[186] Rebecca Stephens reads a similar objection in the fundamentalist Christian dislike of the series: "What is truly troubling to *Potter* detractors seems to be the lack of a single controlling authority in the books. . . . In Rowling's books, traditional power structures are actively subverted, as are paradigms of hierarchy and rule-centered behavior."[187] Reading the series as a version of the fairy tale "Cinderella," in which the protagonist is a male who follows the original by behaving in ways and experiencing "symbols and actions that are *gendered feminine,*" Ximena Galardo-C. and C. Jason Smith say, "All these elements in sum work to interrogate simplistic dichotomous propositions such as masculine and feminine, good and evil, friend and enemy, self and other. On these grounds, then, the Harry Potter series is radical."[188] A little less definitively, Noel Chevalier speaks of Harry as a "heroic resistance figure, on the side of moral right, but not necessarily on the side of order and conformity."[189]

Many commentators, however, read the series as subversive of its own apparent subversion. Farah Mendlesohn speaks of Rowling's "rejection of the subversive opportunities available to the fantasist."[190] For her, "Rowling . . . has created a hero and a moral structure in which the rights of birth, while simultaneously denied, underpin the structures of heroism that are the basis of her ideological universe. . . . Rowling is playing a double game: niceness will, eventually, be rewarded, and thus we are persuaded that we, too, should try to be nice, but the hidden message is that niceness is a function of inner royalty and one is either born with it, or one is not" (162–163). She concludes that the series is anything but subversive, that "the moral conflict within the Potter books is between different structures of authority and differing ideologies of conservatism" (167).

Like Mendlesohn's, a number of readings identify ideological slippages in the series' binaries—ways in which they actually support values opposite to those they at first seem to espouse. Roberta Trites reads the magic and regulations of Hogwarts as representative of the blend of the watchful control suggested by the image of the panopticon—which works to ensure that those under its authoritarian gaze act always as if they are under constant observation—and the apparent indulgence in carnivalesque fun that all schools offer: "The carnivalesque has, nevertheless, a constraining function since its ultimate goal is to ensure the status quo. Thus, schools repress with authoritarian measures, such as the panopticon, and they repress with allegedly antiauthoritarian measures, such as carnivals— but in order to endure, the institution must necessarily involve some form of tolerable institutional repression."[191] Noticing that "the postgraduate careers of Bill and Charlie Weasley after they leave Hogwarts seem to echo the British imperial enterprise," Anatol identifies a hierarchizing colonial attitude that contradicts the tolerance of difference the book explicitly espouses: "the school of magic comes to symbolize the imperial center that unenlightened foreigners threaten to infiltrate."[192] Furthermore, while Rowling represents contemporary Britain by giving many of her characters names associated with some of the cultures that make up the country's multicultural mix, she rarely actually names a race: "One possibility for why racial identity *cannot* be mentioned in Rowling's texts is that the works wobble between seeking a way out of the imperialist agenda and experiencing a certain nostalgia for the safety and security attributed to the empire."[193] Julia Park finds a similar lack of coherence between the series' attack on the intolerance of Voldemort and his followers for giants, house elves, Muggles, and others they think of as racially inferior and Rowling's maintenance on classes and hierarchies, school houses and bureaucratic authorities: "Despite halfhearted attempts at social commentary, she is still bound by her middle-class upbringing. Her experience of British class structure and society is reflected in the wizard world she has created, and what a rigid, structured world it truly is."[194] Tammy Turner-Vorbeck agrees, asserting that the Harry Potter books represent "an aggregation of quintessential, hegemonic, hierarchical middle-class social and cultural values."[195] But according to Elizabeth E. Heilman and Anne E. Gregory, "The *Harry Potter* books legitimize numerous forms of social inequality and their related cultural norms, rituals, and traditions. Yet, there are tensions and critiques within the texts as well."[196]

One particular tension or contradiction that interests several commentators emerges from the huge economic success of the series. Ironically, Rowling appears to attack consumerist acquisition, especially in her descriptions of Harry's Muggle relatives, the Dursleys. Is it possible that a text so successful at making money actually looks down on moneymaking? Perhaps not. Anatol points out that readers are invited to view Draco Malfoy's father's gift of good brooms to his quidditch team as cheating but to feel good about Harry's receipt of an even better broom; much of the texts' wish-fulfillment involves desirable objects that Harry is free to consume, and as the series proceeds, he gets progressively richer. As Karin Westman says, "Reading only the Dursley sections of the books, we might expect the focus of Rowling's critique to be the dangers of consumerism and conspicuous consumption, a world Harry would leave behind when he begins his life as a wizard. What are we to make, then, of the rampant consumerism that greets Harry when he enters the wizarding world?"[197] Elizabeth Teare similarly asks, "Are the Harry Potter books a real alternative to children's commodity culture, or are they just the most cleverly packaged part of it?"[198] She concludes that "the novels' uneven, interesting, and compromised depiction of children and commodity culture offers a useful arena in which such concerns can be thought about, though not satisfactorily resolved" (342).

The suggestion that there is no resolution adds another possible view of the series' politics: it is neither subversive nor subversive of subversion but remains consistently ambivalent. What the commentaries I have been describing see as ideological slippage might be the same kind of eternally balanced presentation of binaries I ascribed to *Peter Rabbit*. Elaine Ostry suggests that it is and attributes it to the series' appropriation of the traditional patterns of the fairy tale: "This ideological doubleness mirrors the fairy tale, which is simultaneously radical and traditional. Because of Rowling's faithfulness to the fairy tale, she often contradicts herself. Just as the fairy tale's radical qualities are matched by traditional inflexibility, so is Rowling's antimaterialism matched by an awe of wealth, her antiracism foiled both by a reliance on 'color blindness' and stock types, and her hero simultaneously ordinary and princely."[199] Ostry goes on to interpret this "ambivalence as part of the innate tensions of children's literature" (90) based on her conviction that "the double nature of the fairy tale—traditional and radical—is echoed in children's literature at large" (98). In other words, the ideological ambivalence of the Harry Potter books is merely the ideological ambivalence of children's literature as a whole. The series is not only a type of the genre; it represents a tradition going back even beyond children's literature to the tales that precede it.

And finally, also, there is one more balance of binary opposites: the books not only represent that tradition, but they do so in a way that rings significant changes on previous versions of it. As Nicholas Tucker suggests, they cleverly combine the fairy tale with aspects of contemporary culture: "The author successfully incorporates the fizz and excitement of the modern video game into the prose page. . . . The suspension of time, and the way that Harry and his friends can chart everyone's current movements on their special Marauder's Map are both familiar devices from video games. Pages of description in a Potter book can be as active as any of those screen games where clicking on to a particular feature reveals some unexpected, hidden secret within. The game of quidditch could come straight from any video arcade."[200] In offering a variation that blends fairy tale characteristics with current aspects of contemporary culture, the Potter series represents a particularly shrewd position taken in the field of children's literature.

Conclusion: Children's Literature as Nonadult?

The Harry Potter series has attracted a wide audience of adult readers—a fact that might undermine the case I am trying to make in this book that texts written for children have distinctive characteristics. If adults can read and enjoy Harry Potter as they read and enjoy novels written specifically for adults, then are the Potter books really so different? And if the Potter books typify children's literature as a genre, is children's literature really so different?

The obvious answer would be no, if not for one other significant factor: I don't believe that most of the adults who read the Harry Potter books do read them as they read and enjoy adult fiction. Instead, the series enters adult reading experiences specifically *as* children's literature. Many of the adult readers with whom I have discussed the series suggest that the widespread media discussion of the phenomenon of adults reading the series has given them permission not only to read but also to reveal publicly that they read books that would otherwise be unacceptable or embarrassing exactly because they *are* children's literature and therefore not considered suitable reading for mature adults. I have rarely been able to persuade these adults to try reading other, less socially acceptable, children's books. Furthermore, these adult readers also often tell me of their awareness of the Potter books as being intended for children in the course of reading them—an awareness that has given a special slant to their reading, often involving some form of utopianism about how Rowling appeals to the wonderfully free imaginations of children or some nostalgia for their memories of their own childhood and childhood reading. These adults read the Potter books not because they are not children's literature but because they are—perhaps the only children's literature adults can read without shame. That makes them unlike other children's books—but also unlike other adult books.

And it makes them unlike other children's books merely by being, for these readers, the unique representatives of the genre of children's literature as a whole. For these adult readers, in a very real sense, the Potter series typifies the genre. If my arguments earlier have any credence, the series typifies the genre quite accurately. I might argue, then, that the Potter series is appropriate reading for adults exactly because its distinctively inclusive representation of the genre of children's literature as a whole gives it the complexity that theoretically distinguishes adult texts from ones written for children. In typifying the genre, it transcends the simplicity assumed to be characteristic of texts in the genre.

But then this one set of texts of children's literature does, at least in this one paradoxical way, share the complexity that theoretically distinguishes adult texts from ones written for children. I am also aware of other aspects of the characteristics of children's literature as I have described them in this book that might suggest that the distinctions I am making between the two kinds of texts are less clear-cut than I am arguing. I will conclude the book by confronting them.

The first is inherent in the idea of binaries that looms so large in my descriptions of children's literature. As I have suggested, the structuralist theory that focuses on the relationships of binary oppositions claims that thinking in this way is basic to human thought—and it is certainly characteristic of the great canonical tradition of Western literature. If that is so, then operating in terms of binaries merely makes texts of children's literature like all other texts produced in the Western world in its lengthy binary period, now possibly coming to an end. I could, presumably, apply the strategies I have been using here to read other kinds of fiction and reach similar conclusions about them.

Because the binaries do operate at least in my own thinking about texts as an inheritor of and participant in that Western binary tradition, I believe I could reach similar conclusions—indeed, when I read texts of adult literature, I often do. But they are not in fact the *same* ones. The difference emerges both from the specific binaries the texts engage and in the ways in which they engage them.

If, as I have argued, the binarism of children's literature emerges from the primal scene of children's literature—an adult with the mission of writing specifically for an audience of children—then the binaries of children's literature will differ from those of other texts by always relating significantly to the cultural ideas of childhood as different from adulthood that engendered and still support that primal scene. Other texts might oppose child or adult, or home and away, or wildness and civilization but rarely with the clear-cut insistence on their difference from each other and dogged insistence on reinforcing that difference that texts of children's literature typically do.

Just as our ideas of childhood imply the ideas of adulthood they oppose and differ from, children's literature also implies its other: adult literature. But when children's literature is not the subject of discussion, there is no such thing as "adult literature." Scholars who study literature written primarily for adults do not announce themselves as Adult Literature scholars. What they study, is, simply, literature, and they rarely if ever understand it *as* adult literature—i.e., as literature that is unlike children's literature. Understood simply as literature, literature for adults exists and is discussed primarily as itself, not in terms of an opposite that it is not. But the reverse is almost never true. Like this book, discourse about children's literature almost always centers on how it differs from its other—the literature it then does identify as adult literature. Consider for instance, an invitation I received some years ago to speak at a symposium. Listing the questions to be discussed, the invitation began, "What is children's literature? Is it different from literature for adults?" That these two questions were related was implied simply by the fact that they were listed together, on one line, two halves of an implied whole, as if answering the first question would be impossible without immediately asking the second.

I believe that it would in fact be impossible, simply because, as the question and as discourse about children's literature generally imply, children's literature differs from literature for adults simply in *being* different from literature for adults—in existing exactly because it is unlike literature for adults. It exists as half of a binary it always implies. Its very existence and character depends on the other that it insists it is not. Texts for adults contain binaries, but they rarely imply their own existence as half of a larger binary, a different kind of text they succeed in not being.

But if children's literature exists most fundamentally in terms of not being something else outside it, then it cannot exist in people's thinking about it without reference to that which it is not. Can the literature itself be untainted by elements of the adult? If people like me cannot think about children's literature except in terms of the adult literature that it is not, can children's literature itself think childhood without inherent adult content? Can there be such a thing as a children's literature that is not permeated by the unchildlike that it claims to be eliminating and opposing? As I have been suggesting throughout, I believe that such a literature is impossible. Children's literature is literature that claims to be devoid of adult content that nevertheless lurks within it.

This suggests another important way in which the boundaries between children's literature and other literature might be less firm than I have implied. Paradoxically, however, that also makes clear exactly how children's literature is different from adult literature. Not only does it conceal the adult material with which adult literature explicitly deals, but also it tends to clearly mark that material *as* adult—as what implied child readers ought not to be or know or admit to being or knowing. In working to construct childhood as a smaller and more protected version of being human, a safe home separate from the more dangerous world around it, children's literature paradoxically closets its adulthood, keeps it a safely hidden secret that allows the supposed safety and innocence of the protective structure that surrounds it. Curiously, the closeting of adult content within texts for children mirrors but strangely undermines the way in which children's literature itself acts to closet childhood within the larger adult world.

As I have been describing it here, children's literature is a project whose very foundational considerations engender its inevitable failure. It always tries above all else to be nonadult, and it always, inevitably, fails. Yet it always tries again, and fails again, in terms of the patterns of variation I have described and the rich ambiguities they can engender. This means that texts of children's literature can be and often are as complex as texts for adults—but the complexity is of a very specific and quite different sort.

1. Six Texts

1. Myers, "Socializing Rosamond," 52.

2. H. Lofting, *The Story of Doctor Dolittle*. All references are to the 1978 Dell Yearling edition. A new version of this edition, published in 1988 and including an afterword by Lofting's son Christopher, deletes some parts of the book and rewrites others. According to Daphne Kutzer, "The editing by Dell in the 1980's removes much that is relevant to a discussion of Lofting's imperialism" (Kutzer, *Empire's Children*, 80)—including much that might strike more recent audiences as racist. Because I am discussing *Dr. Dolittle* here as part of an effort to identify the similarities of texts of children's literature written in different times, I work with the text as it existed in its own original time, before the changes made in the 1980s.

3. Bourdieu, *The Field of Cultural Production*, 125.

4. Jameson, *The Political Unconscious*, 9.

5. Edgeworth, "The Purple Jar," in Demers and Moyles, *From Instruction to Delight*, 141. All subsequent references are to this edition.

6. Lewis, "On Three Ways of Writing for Children," 236.

7. See Iser, *The Act of Reading*, 69.

8. Cleary, *Henry Huggins*, 7. All references are to the 1979 Dell Yearling edition.

9. Keats, *The Snowy Day*, not paginated.

10. Ruskin, *The Art Criticism of John Ruskin*, 2.

11. Mitchell, *Iconology*, 118.

12. Danto, "The Artworld," 431.

13. Hamilton, *Plain City*, 7.

14. Carroll, *Alice's Adventures in Wonderland*, 9.

15. The early editions of "The Purple Jar" housed in the Osborne Collection of Early Children's Books at Toronto Public Library contain no illustrations. A late nineteenth-century edition of *Early Lessons* available on the Internet Archive does contain one image for "The Purple Jar," of Rosamond admiring the jar in the shop window.

16. Nodelman, "Some Presumptuous Generalizations," 177.

17. Rabkin, *The Fantastic in Literature*, 41.

18. Darton, *Children's Books in England*, 141.

19. Avery, *Nineteenth Century Children*, 25.

20. Wyile, "First-Person Engaging Narration in the Picture Book," 194.

21. Wordsworth, "Ode: Intimations of Immortality from Recollections of Early Childhood," lines 67, 64.

22. Nodelman, "Progressive Utopia," 74.

23. Myers, "Socializing Rosamond," 55.

24. Watts, "Against Idleness and Mischief," lines 1–2.

25. Empson, *Some Versions of Pastoral*, 216.

26. Freud, *A General Introduction to Psychoanalysis*, 320.

27. Krips, *The Presence of the Past*, 16.

28. See, e.g., Nodelman and Reimer, *The Pleasures of Children's Literature*, 197–203, where Mavis Reimer and I provide an extensive discussion of this narrative pattern. See also Clausen, "Home and Away in Children's Fiction"; Reimer and Rusnak, "The Representation of Home in Canadian Children's Literature"; Stott, "Pseudo-sublimity and Inarticulate Mumblings in Violent Juxtaposition"; Stott and Francis, "'Home' and 'Not Home' in Children's Stories"; and Waddey, "Home in Children's Fiction."

29. Lefebvre, *The Production of Space*, 26.

30. Ibid.

31. *Oxford English Dictionary*, 2nd ed., s.v. "variation."

32. See, e.g., Nodelman, "John Fowles's Variations in *The Collector*." An MLA International Bibliography search of "variation AND fiction" reveals work on James Joyce, Wallace Stevens, and many others.

2. Exploring Assumptions

1. De Lauretis, *The Practice of Love*, xiv.

2. Fish, *Is There a Text in This Class?* 161.

3. Jameson, *The Political Unconscious*, 9.

4. Zipes, *Sticks and Stones*, 70.

5. P. Hunt, *Criticism, Theory, and Children's Literature*, 16.

6. I discuss these critiques in more detail in chapter 4.

7. Stainton Rogers and Stainton Rogers, "Word Children," 180–183.

8. John Stephens, *Language and Ideology in Children's Fiction*, 3–4.

9. Lesnik-Oberstein, introduction to *Children's Literature: New Approaches*, 4, 20.

10. Nodelman, "The Hidden Meaning and the Inner Tale," 147.

11. Cocks, "The Implied Reader," 116n83.

12. Walsh, "Child/Animal," 160.

13. Walsh, "Author and Authorship," 43.

14. Walsh, "Child/Animal," 162.

15. Jones, "Getting Rid of Children's Literature," 294.

16. Ibid, 298. Jones is quoting Galbraith, "Hear My Cry," 199.

17. Bourdieu, *The Field of Cultural Production*, 139.

18. Ibid., 133.

19. McGillis, "Learning to Read," 130.

20. Chambers, *Tell Me*, 43.

21. O'Sullivan, *Comparative Children's Literature*, 11.

22. Jameson, *The Political Unconscious*, 98.

23. Lévi-Strauss, *The Savage Mind*, 17.

24. Stevenson, "My Shadow," lines 9–12.

25. C. Hunt, "Young Adult Literature," 4.

26. Trites, *Disturbing the Universe*, 2, 3.

27. Cooperative Children's Book Center, "Children's Books by and about People of Color Published in the United States."

28. Farquhar, *Children's Literature in China*, 138.

29. P. Hunt, *International Companion Encyclopedia of Children's Literature*, 2nd ed., 1, xix.

30. P. Hunt, preface to *Children's Literature*, xiii.

31. P. Hunt, *International Companion Encyclopedia of Children's Literature*, 2nd ed., 1:xix.

32. Nikolajeva, *Children's Literature Comes of Age*, 43.

33. Nodelman and Reimer, "Teaching Canadian Children's Literature," 22.

34. Weinreich, *Children's Literature*, 34.

35. Fishelov, *Metaphors of Genre*, 10.

36. Feuer, "Genre Study and Television," 144.

37. Derrida, "The Law of Genre," 243.

38. Bartlett, *Remembering*, 201.

39. Fowler, *Kinds of Literature*, 20. On Saussure's theory of *langue* and *parole* see Saussure, *Course in General Linguistics*, esp. chap. 3.

40. Shannon, "A Mathematical Theory of Communication," 14.

41. Derrida, "The Law of Genre," 224–225.

42. Bakhtin, "The Problem of Speech Genres," 64, 69.

43. I am making use here of Pierre Bourdieu's ideas about how fields of cultural production operate in terms of position-takings. The next section of this chapter, "Genre and Field," specifically addresses the relationships between genre and the field of children's literature production.

44. Juvan, "Generic Identity and Intertextuality."

45. Todorov, "The Origin of Genres," 162.

46. Miller, "Genre as Social Action," 37.

47. Freedman and Medway, introduction to *Learning and Teaching Genre*, 2.

48. Beebee, *The Ideology of Genre*, 7, 13.

49. Coe, "Teaching Genre as Process," 158, 159.

50. Freedman and Medway, introduction, 4.

51. Juvan, "Generic Identity and Intertextuality."

52. Derrida, "The Law of Genre," 225, 227–228.

53. Beebee, *The Ideology of Genre*, 28.

54. Fowler, *Kinds of Literature*, 20.

55. Jameson, *The Political Unconscious*, 99.

56. Bourdieu, *The Field of Cultural Production*, 30.

57. See Hade, "Storyselling"; and Rosen, ""Raising the Issues.""

58. Bourdieu, *Distinction*, 170.

59. Johnson, "Editor's Introduction," 6, 9–10.

60. Zipes, *Sticks and Stones*, 71–72.

61. Bourdieu, *The Field of Cultural Production*, 132.

62. Ibid., 118.

63. Johnson, "Editor's Introduction," 9.

64. Ibid., 10.

65. Frye, "The Archetypes of Literature," 11.

66. Nikolajeva, *Children's Literature Comes of Age*, 48.

67. Sobol, *Encyclopedia Brown, Boy Detective*, 2.

68. Sobol, *Encyclopedia Brown Keeps the Peace*, 8.

69. Ibid., 8.

70. Sobol, *Encyclopedia Brown, Boy Detective*, 2, 3.

71. Sobol, *Encyclopedia Brown and the Case of the Secret Pitch*, 17.

72. Sobol, *Encyclopedia Brown, Boy Detective*, 1.

73. Sobol, *Encyclopedia Brown and the Case of the Secret Pitch*, 8.

74. Ibid.

75. Nodelman, "Out There in Children's Science Fiction," 294.

76. Beebee, *The Ideology of Genre*, 263.

3. Children's Literature as a Genre

1. PABBIS, "What to Do."

2. Trimmer, "On the Care Which Is Requisite in the Choice of Books for Children," 4.

3. Nodelman, "Editor's Comments," 162.

4. Lesnik-Oberstein, *Children's Literature: Criticism and the Fictional Child*, 164.

5. Nodelman, "Hatchet Job," 43.

6. Lesnik-Oberstein, introduction to *Children's Literature: New Approaches*, 3.

7. "Madonna Plans 'Morality Tale.'"

8. Weinreich, "What Is So Special about Children's Literature?"

9. Jones, "Getting Rid of Children's Literature," 288, 300.

10. Bator, *Signposts to Criticism of Children's Literature*, 5.

11. Sale, *Fairy Tales and After*, 1.

12. Althusser, "Ideology and Ideological State Apparatuses," 245.

13. Sale, *Fairy Tales and After*, 4.

14. Townsend, "Standards for Criticism for Children's Literature," 196–197.

15. Bator, *Signposts to Criticism of Children's Literature*, 6.

16. Shavit, *Poetics of Children's Literature*, 59.

17. Quoted in ibid., 21.

18. Quoted in Townsend, *A Sense of Story*, 160.

19. Quoted in ibid., 36.

20. Gardam, "Some Wasps in Her Marmalade," 489.

21. Lewis, "On Three Ways of Writing for Children," 233.

22. Steig, "Never Going Home," 38.

23. As I discuss in chapter 4, Julia Dusinberre speculates in *Alice to the Lighthouse* about the origins of some qualities of twentieth-century modernist texts in the work of nine-teenth-century writers of children's literature.

24. Heins, "Out on a Limb with the Critics," 404.

25. J. Stephens, *Language and Ideology in Children's Fiction*, 86.

26. Lukens, *A Critical Handbook of Children's Literature*, 9.

27. Weinreich, *Children's Literature*, 39, 49.

28. Ibid., 34.

29. O'Sullivan, *Comparative Children's Literature*, 14.

30. Steig, "Never Going Home," 36.

31. Townsend, "A Sense of Story," 10.

32. Stewig, *Children and Literature*, 2.

33. McGillis, *The Nimble Reader*, viii–ix.

34. P. Hunt, "Criticism and Children's Literature," 117.

35. Pelorus (pseud.), "Graduate to Grown-Up Books?" 60.

36. Fadiman, "The Case for a Children's Literature," 7.

37. P. Hunt, "Criticism and Children's Literature," 118.

38. Tomlinson and Lynch-Brown, *Essentials of Children's Literature*, 2.

39. Hillman, *Discovering Children's Literature*, 2.

40. Steig, "Never Going Home," 38.

41. Hillman, *Discovering Children's Literature*, 3.

42. Glazer and Williams, *Introduction to Children's Literature*, 10.

43. Smith, *The Unreluctant Years*, 12, 11.

44. "Our meddling intellect / Mis-shapes the beauteous forms of things / We murder to dissect" (Wordsworth, "The Tables Turned," lines 26–28).

45. "Delight and liberty, the simple creed / Of Childhood, whether busy or at rest, / With new-fledged hope still fluttering in his breast" (Wordsworth, "Ode: Intimations," lines 136–138).

46. Hancock, *A Celebration of Literature and Response*, 5.

47. Bakhtin, "The Problem of Speech Genres," 95.

48. Rudd, "Theorising and Theories," 33.

49. McGillis, "And the Celt Knew the Indian," 225.

50. Reynolds, *Radical Children's Literature*, 182.

51. Rudd, "Theorising and Theories," 33.

52. McMaster, "'Adults' Literature,' by Children," 281.

53. See Ellis, *One Fairy Story Too Many*; and Zipes, *The Brothers Grimm*.

54. Hollindale, *Signs of Childness in Children's Books*, 28.

55. Rudd, "Theorising and Theories," 38.

56. Lesnik-Oberstein, *Children's Literature: Criticism and the Fictional Child*, 2.

57. In *Centuries of Childhood* Philippe Ariès identifies "towards the end of the sixteenth century" as the time when "the idea originated of providing expurgated editions of the classics for the use of children" (109).

58. Bator, *Signposts to Criticism of Children's Literature*, 6.

59. Darton, *Children's Books in England*, 1.

60. All six books have been popular enough to remain in print since their original publication. *The Voyages of Dr. Dolittle,* a sequel to *The Story of Dr. Dolittle,* won one of the earliest of the Newbery Medals, in 1923. *The Snowy Day* won the Caldecott Medal as the best illustrated children's book in the United States in 1963, and although *Henry Huggins* went awardless, two books about Henry Huggins's friend Beezus's sister Ramona, *Ramona and Her Father* and *Ramona Quimby, Age 8,* were named 1978 and 1982 Newbery Honor Books. While *Plain City* itself won no awards, similar young-adult novels by Virginia Hamilton won the Newbery and two *Boston Globe-Horn Book* awards as the best children's fiction of their year, and the American Library Association granted Hamilton its Laura Ingalls Wilder Award for Lifetime Achievement just two years after the publication of *Plain City.* "The Purple Jar" and *Alice's Adventures in Wonderland* predate children's book awards.

61. P. Hunt, *Criticism, Theory, and Children's Literature,* 61–62.

62. Ibid., 192, 198.

63. Ibid., 87.

64. Nikolajeva, *The Rhetoric of Character in Children's Literature,* x.

65. Inglis, *The Promise of Happiness,* 311. Inglis works especially with views Leavis puts forward in *The Great Tradition.*

66. Temple et al., *Children's Literature in Children's Hands,* 9–10.

67. Weinreich, *Children's Literature,* 56.

68. Townsend, "Standards for Criticism for Children's Literature," 199.

69. Lesnik-Oberstein, *Children's Literature: Criticism and the Fictional Child,* 102.

70. Blum, *Hide and Seek,* 6.

71. Lesnik-Oberstein, *Children's Literature: Criticism and the Fictional Child,* 159.

72. Rose, *The Case of Peter Pan,* 2.

73. Ibid., 4.

74. The Web magazine *Nerve* introduces a series of interviews of experts on child sexuality in this way: "These words, 'child' and 'sexuality,' when uttered in the same breath, invariably frighten upstanding citizens who naturally want to protect children from abuse and exploitation. If the result isn't silence, it's the same-old uninspired, paranoid rhetoric that begets more of the same. It's no wonder we can't speak pointedly about kids, culture and sex—we don't know how" ("Politicizing Puberty").

75. Or allows. In the "Politicizing Puberty" interviews in *Nerve,* James Kincaid invites readers to ponder "what our culture does with ideas of 'innocence,' how 'innocence' gives us something to sanitize and pant after, something we can pretend to protect while exploiting it to the hilt."

76. J. Stephens, *Language and Ideology in Children's Fiction,* 3.

77. McGillis, *The Nimble Reader,* 79.

78. Rose, *The Case of Peter Pan,* 50.

79. Richardson, "Romanticism and the End of Childhood," 31. He is referring to my "The Other: Orientalism, Colonialism, and Children's Literature" and Valerie Polakow Suransky's *The Erosion of Childhood.*

80. Reimer, "Making Princesses," 111. I discuss the literature of empire further in the next chapter.

81. Said, *Orientalism,* 21.

82. Smith, *The Unreluctant Years*, 12.

83. Kincaid, *Child-Loving*, 70.

84. Said, *Orientalism*, 208.

85. Hollindale, "Ideology and the Children's Book," 20.

86. Quoted in Said, *Orientalism*, 39.

87. Ibid., 40.

88. Hazard, *Books, Children & Men*, 1.

89. Reimer, "Power and Powerlessness," 10.

90. Hazard, *Books, Children & Men*, 166.

91. Kincaid, *Child-Loving*, 7.

92. Said, *Orientalism*, 79.

93. Clark, *Kiddie Lit*, 7.

94. Spitz, *Inside Picture Books*, xiv.

95. Blum, *Hide and Seek*, 23.

96. Kidd, "Psychoanalysis and Children's Literature," 110.

97. Ibid., 122.

98. Coats, *Looking Glasses and Neverlands*, 1.

99. Reynolds, *Children's Literature in the 1890s and 1990s*, 33.

100. Clark, *Kiddie Lit*, 5.

101. Nodelman, "Children's Literature as Women's Writing."

102. Reimer, "These Two Irreconcilable Things," 51.

103. Paul, *Reading Otherways*, 71.

104. Wilkie-Stibbs, *The Feminine Subject in Children's Literature*, xi.

105. Reynolds, *Children's Literature in the 1890s and 1990s*, 33.

106. Coats, *Looking Glasses and Neverlands*, 162.

107. J. Stephens, "Editor's Introduction," ix.

108. Ibid.

109. Griswold, *Feeling like a Kid*, 5, 13, 14.

110. Hollindale, *Signs of Childness in Children's Books*, 46, 47.

111. Carpenter, *Secret Gardens*, 1.

112. P. Hunt, *Criticism, Theory, and Children's Literature*, 11.

113. Reynolds, *Radical Children's Literature*, 15.

114. Lurie, *Don't Tell the Grown-Ups*, x, xi.

115. Ibid., xiv–xv.

116. Ibid., 95.

117. Reynolds, *Radical Children's Literature*, 62.

118. Clark, *Kiddie Lit*, 175.

119. McGillis, *The Nimble Reader*, 112.

120. May, *Children's Literature and Critical Theory*, 56.

121. Kohl, *Should We Burn Babar?* 60.

122. Shavit, *Poetics of Children's Literature*, 66.

123. Nikolajeva, " 'A Dream of Complete Idleness,' " 313.

124. Montgomery, *Anne of Green Gables*, 276.

125. Natov, *The Poetics of Childhood*, 101.

126. Bhabha, "Of Mimicry and Man," 86.

127. Ibid., 88.

128. Cadden, *Ursula K. Le Guin beyond Genre*, 137.

129. Fadiman, "The Case for a Children's Literature," 13.

130. Hillman, *Discovering Children's Literature*, 3.

131. Inglis, *The Promise of Happiness*, 101.

132. McDowell, "Fiction for Children and Adults," 51.

133. Bator, *Signposts to Criticism of Children's Literature*, 6. Bator seems to be referring to my comment in "Interpretation and the Apparent Sameness of Children's Novels" that "children's fiction is indeed significantly different from other kinds of fiction" (19) and to Isabelle Jan's statement in *On Children's Literature* that her purpose is "to discover the characteristic features of the genre and what constitutes its unvarying core" (15). In "Interpretation and the Apparent Sameness of Children's Novels" I suggest that children's literature is different because of its "fascination with the same basic sets of opposite ideas, and a propensity for bringing them into balance, so that both can be included in a vision of what life is" (126), but I don't develop the idea any further. Jan suggests that the core of children's literature is that "it should evoke the world of childhood" (143) but says little about exactly how it does so.

134. Tomlinson and Lynch-Brown, *Essentials of Children's Literature*, 2; Temple et al., *Children's Literature in Children's Hands*, 9.

135. Bawden, "A Dead Pig and My Father," 13.

136. Chambers, "The Reader in the Book," 131.

137. Lewis, "On Three Ways of Writing for Children," 239.

138. Pearce, "The Writer's View of Childhood," 51.

139. Quoted in Bator, *Signposts to Criticism of Children's Literature*, 21.

140. Southall, "Sources and Responses," 88, 89.

141. De Jong, "Acceptance Paper," 434.

142. Griswold, *Feeling like a Kid*, 4.

143. Cameron, *The Green and Burning Tree*, 14, 232, 233.

144. Inglis, *The Promise of Happiness*, 7.

145. Dusinberre, *Alice to the Lighthouse*, 76.

146. Krips, *The Presence of the Past*, 16.

147. Inglis, *The Promise of Happiness*, 121.

148. Hazard, *Books, Children & Men*, 42.

149. J. Butler, *Gender Trouble*, 33.

150. Hollindale, *Signs of Childness in Children's Books*, 14.

151. J. Butler, *Gender Trouble*, 137.

152. Natov, *The Poetics of Childhood*, 2.

153. Inglis, *The Promise of Happiness*, 8.

154. Natov, *The Poetics of Childhood*, 3, 4.

155. Inglis, *The Promise of Happiness*, 69.

156. Ibid., 61.

157. Natov, *The Poetics of Childhood*, 129.

158. Tomlinson and Lynch-Brown, *Essentials of Children's Literature*, 2.

159. Wyile, "Expanding the View of First-Person Narration," 190.

160. Lundin, *Constructing the Canon of Children's Literature*, 116.

161. Lewis, "On Three Ways of Writing for Children," 236.

162. Nina Bawden, "A Dead Pig and My Father," 9.

163. Nikolajeva, *The Rhetoric of Character in Children's Literature*, 205.

164. Peter Brooks, "Toward Supreme Fictions," 8.

165. Freud, "Leonardo da Vinci and a Memory of His Childhood," 452.

166. Freud, *A General Introduction to Psychoanalysis*, 221.

167. Brooks, "Toward Supreme Fictions," 10. Although Brooks uses the term *unheimisch*, I have used the more common *unheimlich* in discussing his ideas.

168. Trites, "The Uncanny in Literature," 162.

169. See Rollin, *Cradle and All*; and Rollin and West, *Psychoanalytic Responses to Children's Literature*.

170. Kincaid, *Child-Loving*, 71.

171. According to Charlotte Huck, when *In the Night Kitchen* first came out, librarians in Caldwell Parish, Louisiana, painted diapers to cover the offensive parts. See Huck, *Children's Literature in the Elementary School*, 42.

172. Reynolds, *Children's Literature in the 1890s and 1990s*, 23.

173. McGillis, *The Nimble Reader*, 52.

174. Brooks, "Toward Supreme Fictions," 11.

175. Gose, *Mere Creatures*, 84.

176. Frye, *Anatomy of Criticism*, 97.

177. Rudd, "Beatrix Potter and Jacques Derrida," 14.

178. F. Butler, "Children's Literature: The Bad Seed," 40.

179. Clark, *Kiddie Lit*, 96.

180. Shavit, *Poetics of Children's Literature*, 37.

181. Reimer, "The Masculine Reader in *Tom Brown's Schooldays*," 9.

182. Richardson, "Nineteenth Century Children's Satire and the Ambivalent Reader," 123.

183. Shavit, *Poetics of Children's Literature*, 15.

184. Many of Philippe Ariès's much-disputed claims about adults generally treating children like adults in the past are based on descriptions specifically of children at court, who seem to have had more knowledge at an earlier age than most children did or do.

185. Reimer, "The Masculine Reader in *Tom Brown's Schooldays*," 10.

186. Richardson, "Nineteenth Century Children's Satire and the Ambivalent Reader," 125.

187. Chambers, "The Reader in the Book," 131.

188. Rose, *The Case of Peter Pan*, 59.

189. Wall, *The Narrator's Voice*, 30.

190. Rose, *The Case of Peter Pan*, 60.

191. J. Stephens, *Language and Ideology in Children's Fiction*, 57.

192. Rose, *The Case of Peter Pan*, 62.

193. J. Stephens, *Language and Ideology in Children's Fiction*, 63.

194. Lewis, "On Three Ways of Writing for Children," 236.

195. Temple et al., *Children's Literature in Children's Hands,* 9.

196. Brooks, "Toward Supreme Fictions," 12.

197. Crago, "Children's Literature," 62.

198. Hughes, "Children's Literature," 32.

199. Crago, "Children's Literature,"62.

200. Nikolajeva, *The Rhetoric of Character in Children's Literature,* 206.

201. Babbitt, "Happy Endings?" 158.

202. Nikolajeva, *The Rhetoric of Character in Children's Literature,* 26.

203. McGillis, *The Nimble Reader,* 52.

204. Smedman, "Springs of Hope," 91–92.

205. Tomlinson and Lynch-Brown, *Essentials of Children's Literature,* 2.

206. Carpenter, *Secret Gardens,* 1.

207. Nikolajeva, " 'A Dream of Complete Idleness,' " 306.

208. Rose, *The Case of Peter Pan,* 9.

209. P. Hunt, *Criticism, Theory, and Children's Literature,* 76.

210. Ong, *Orality and Literacy,* 42.

211. Weinreich, "What Is So Special about Children's Literature?"

212. Moss, "The Spear and the Piccolo," 138; Poss, "An Epic in Arcadia," 84.

213. Nikolajeva, " 'A Dream of Complete Idleness,' " 306.

214. Fadiman, "The Case for a Children's Literature," 12–13.

215. Greg, "Pastoral," 10.

216. Natov, *The Poetics of Childhood,* 91.

217. Gilead, "The Undoing of Idyll in *The Wind in the Willows,*" 146.

218. Empson, *Some Versions of Pastoral,* 17.

219. Natov, *The Poetics of Childhood,* 92.

220. Empson, *Some Versions of Pastoral,* 19.

221. Ibid., 203.

222. Clausen, "Home and Away in Children's Fiction," 143.

223. Nodelman and Reimer, *The Pleasures of Children's Literature,* 155.

224. Moss and Stott, *The Family of Stories,* 18.

225. Hourihan, *Deconstructing the Hero,* 10.

226. J. Stephens, *Language and Ideology in Children's Fiction,* 101.

227. Blum, *Hide and Seek,* 125.

228. Clark, *Kiddie Lit,* 143.

229. Nodelman, "Interpretation and the Apparent Sameness of Children's Novels," 19–20.

230. See Nodelman and Reimer, *The Pleasures of Children's Literature,* 155.

231. McGillis, *The Nimble Reader,* 138.

232. Hourihan, *Deconstructing the Hero,* 15.

233. Jones, "Getting Rid of Children's Literature," 298. Jones quotes from Prout, *The Future of Childhood,* 143.

234. Rose, *The Case of Peter Pan,* 50.

235. McGillis, *The Nimble Reader,* 148.

236. Nikolajeva, *Children's Literature Comes of Age,* 50.

237. Ewers, "The Limits of Literary Criticism of Children's and Young Adult Literature," 87.

238. Nodelman, "Interpretation and the Apparent Sameness of Children's Novels," 5.

239. Nikolajeva, *Children's Literature Comes of Age*, 50–51.

240. Ibid., 54.

241. Freud,. *Beyond the Pleasure Principle*, 601.

242. Stott, "Pseudo-sublimity and Inarticulate Mumblings in Violent Juxtaposition," 10.

243. See Nodelman, "Text as Teacher."

244. Williams, *Marxism and Literature*, 188.

245. Kundera, *The Book of Laughter and Forgetting*, 164–165.

246. Attali, *Noise*, 6.

247. Kundera, *The Book of Laughter and Forgetting*, 165 (italics mine).

248. McGillis, *The Nimble Reader*, 173.

4. The Genre in the Field

1. Adams, "The First Children's Literature," 19.

2. Adams, "Medieval Children's Literature," 4.

3. Ibid., 16.

4. Shavit, *Poetics of Children's Literature*, 31.

5. O'Sullivan, *Comparative Children's Literature*, 21.

6. Morganstern, "The Fall into Literacy and the Rise of the Bourgeois Child," 136.

7. Krips, *The Presence of the Past*, 24.

8. Morganstern, "The Rise of Children's Literature Reconsidered," 64–65.

9. Ibid., 71.

10. Hardt and Negri, *Empire*, 224.

11. Darton, *Children's Books in England*, 1.

12. Ibid., 2.

13. P. Hunt, *Children's Literature*, 35.

14. Summerfield, *Fantasy and Reason*, 83, 86.

15. O'Malley, "The Coach and Six," 26. In "The Power of Public Opinion" Jackie C. Horne critiques O'Malley and others who view children's literature as originating in the needs of the middle class by suggesting that understandings of class in this time were more complex than people tend now to assume and are not necessarily accounted for by more recent views of how class operates: "If values that contemporary literary critics tend to associate with an ideological middle class were in fact also present in the gentry and laboring classes, then a separate class distinguished by its ideology alone fails to cohere" (3). But that doesn't call into question the significance of the ideology itself in shaping children's literature; and while Horne's strong arguments for a more complex view of the variations in these early texts reveal the dangers of generalization, they might tend to draw attention away from the kinds of shared and ongoing samenesses in texts for children that I am focusing on in this book.

16. Quoted in Darton, *Children's Books in England*, 4.

17. Hardt and Negri, *Empire*, xii.

18. Jameson, *The Political Unconscious*, 63.

19. Kristeva, *Desire in Language*, 221.

20. McLuhan, *Understanding Media*, 172.

21. See Ong, *Orality and Literacy*.

22. See Berger, *Ways of Seeing*.

23. See, e.g., Mulvey, "Visual Pleasure and Narrative Cinema"; and Olin, "Gaze." In *Notes on "The Gaze"* Daniel Chandler offers a useful commentary on Mulvey's views and responses to them.

24. Lacan, "Agressivity in Psychoanalysis," 10.

25. Lacan, "The Mirror Stage," 4, 6.

26. See Barthes, *S/Z*.

27. See Nikolajeva, *Children's Literature Comes of Age*, 50.

28. Kuznets, "Family as Formula," 148.

29. Weber, *The Protestant Ethic and the Spirit of Capitalism*.

30. Darton, *Children's Books in England*, 53.

31. Janeway, "Of a notorious wicked child," in "From *A Token for Children*," 50.

32. O'Malley, "The Coach and Six," 25.

33. Ibid., 18.

34. Richardson, "Romanticism and the End of Childhood," 25.

35. Dusinberre, *Alice to the Lighthouse*, 14; Garlitz, "The Immortality Ode," 639.

36. Knoepflmacher, "The Balancing of Child and Adult," 499.

37. Knoepflmacher, *Ventures into Childland*, xiv.

38. Richardson, "Romanticism and the End of Childhood," 28.

39. Kutzer, *Empire's Children*, xiv.

40. Hunt and Sands, "The View from the Center," 40.

41. Ibid., 42.

42. Wallace, "De-scribing *The Water-Babies*," 176.

43. Jameson, *The Political Unconscious*, 98.

44. Said, *Orientalism*, 15; Reimer, "Making Princesses," 112.

45. Carpenter, *Secret Gardens*, x.

46. Reynolds, *Children's Literature in the 1890s and 1990s*, 21.

47. Carpenter, *Secret Gardens*, x.

48. Showalter, *Sexual Anarchy*, 3.

49. Ibid., 8. Showalter is quoting from Toril Moi's *Sexual/Textual Politics*, 167.

50. Dusinberre, *Alice to the Lighthouse*, 33–34.

51. Sedgwick, *Epistemology of the Closet*, 195.

52. Reynolds, *Children's Literature in the 1890s and 1990s*, 23.

53. Dresang, *Radical Change*, 4.

54. Ibid., 243.

55. McGillis, *The Nimble Reader*, 112.

56. Walter, *Making Up Megaboy*, 17.

57. Bakhtin, "Discourse in the Novel," 677.

58. Bakhtin, *Problems of Dostoevsky's Poetics*, 18.

59. McCallum, *Ideologies of Identity in Adolescent Fiction*, 17.

60. Walter, *Making Up Megaboy*, 59.

61. Kaplan, "Read All Over," 38.

62. Bakhtin, *Rabelais and His World*, 15.

63. Frye, *Anatomy of Criticism*.

64. Kundera, *The Book of Laughter and Forgetting*, 164.

65. Nikolajeva, *Children's Literature Comes of Age*, 65.

66. Nikolajeva, "Exit Children's Literature," 222.

67. O'Sullivan, *Comparative Children's Literature*, 27.

68. Bourdieu, *Masculine Domination*, 1.

69. Jameson, *The Political Unconscious*, 99.

70. O'Sullivan, "Alice in Different Wonderlands," 20. O'Sullivan refers to Hazard's phrase from *Books, Children & Men*, 145.

71. Nikolajeva, *Children's Literature Comes of Age*, 43.

72. Ibid.

73. O'Sullivan, *Comparative Children's Literature*, 59.

74. Ibid., 67.

75. J. Stephens, "Editor's Introduction," v.

76. Nikolajeva, *Children's Literature Comes of Age*, 14.

77. O'Sullivan, *Comparative Children's Literature*, 12.

78. Fishelov, *Metaphors of Genre*, 17.

79. Toye, "Preface," xii.

80. Egoff, *The Republic of Childhood*, 11.

81. Egoff and Saltman, *The New Republic of Childhood*, 306.

82. Lecker, "Would You Publish This Book?" 16. The Massey Commission was a government report on the state of Canadian culture released in 1951 that led to initiatives in later decades.

83. Meek, "The Englishness of English Children's Books," 98.

84. Lorimer, review of *Hip and Trivial*, by Robert Wright.

85. " 'I wasn't trying to, quote, "Americanize" them,' Arthur Levine, the books' United States editor, said. 'What I was trying to do is translate, which I think is different. I wanted to make sure that an American child reading the books would have the same literary experience that a British kid would have. A kid should be confused or challenged when the author wants the kid to be confused or challenged and not because of a difference of language' " (Levine is quoted in Radosh, "Why American Kids Don't Consider Harry Potter an Insufferable Prig," 56).

86. My friend Canadian novelist Carol Matas has recently set children's novels in New York, Chicago, Los Angeles, and Palm Springs.

87. E. Mackey, *The House of Difference*, 145.

88. Anderson, *Imagined Communities*, 6.

89. Allor, Juteau, and Shepherd, "Contingencies of Culture."

90. Bennett, Turner, and Volkerling, "Introduction: Post-Colonial Formations."

91. Webb, "Text, Culture, and Postcolonial Children's Literature," 72.

92. J. Stephens, "Representation of Place in Australian Children's Picture Books," 99.

93. Frye, *The Bush Garden*, 217.

94. E. Mackey, *The House of Difference*, 47.

95. Frye, *The Bush Garden*, 225.

96. Reimer and Rusnak, "The Representation of Home," 28.

97. Webb, "Text, Culture, and Postcolonial Children's Literature," 72.

98. Birney, "Canada: Case History." In a later poem, "Canada: Case History: 1973," Birney rejected the metaphor of adolescence and said Canada was "No more the high school land" (175).

99. Dorscht, "Decolonizing Canadian Writing," 138–139.

100. Metcalf, *What Is a Canadian Literature?* 13.

101. Ang and Stratton, "Asianing Australia," 17.

102. New, *Borderlands,* 43.

103. Blodgett, "Is a History of the Literature of Canada Possible?" 3.

104. As I suggested in chapter 2, a statistical survey titled "Children's Books by and about People of Color Published in the United States," conducted by the Cooperative Children's Book Center of the University of Wisconsin, reveals that a very small proportion of books for children published in the United States are about or by Africans or African Americans.

105. New, *Borderlands,* 5.

106. See Reimer, *Home Words.*

107. I offer more detailed discussions of many of the novels mentioned in this paragraph in three related articles: "A Monochromatic Mosaic"; "Of Solitudes and Borders"; and "At Home on Native Land."

108. Zipes, *Sticks and Stones,* 43.

109. Lundin, *Constructing the Canon of Children's Literature,* 3.

110. Kessen, "Rumble or Revolution," 278.

111. Burman, *Deconstructing Developmental Psychology,* 50.

112. Stainton Rogers and Stainton Rogers, *Stories of Childhood,* 39–40.

113. May, *Children's Literature and Critical Theory,* 139.

114. Zipes, *Sticks and Stones,* 50.

115. Bourdieu, *Language and Symbolic Power,* 58.

116. Association for Library Service to Children, "Terms and Criteria: John Newbery Medal."

117. Parravano, " 'Alive and Vigorous,' " 436.

118. Kidd, "Prizing Children's Literature," 170.

119. Zipes, *Sticks and Stones,* 8.

120. "The 25 Most Intriguing People '95."

121. I discuss the Goosebumps books in more detail in "Ordinary Monstrosity."

122. Griffith and Frey, *Classics of Children's Literature.*

123. Eliot, *What Is a Classic?* 10, 27.

124. Ibid., 29.

125. Kermode, *The Classic,* 44.

126. Bourdieu, *The Field of Cultural Production,* 111.

127. Frank, "When Less Is Not More."

128. Kermode, *The Classic,* 140.

129. Kermode, *The Genesis of Secrecy,* 64.

130. Kermode, *Forms of Attention,* 90.

131. Interview in *Life.After.Theory,* ed. Payne and Schad, 127.

132. Taplin, "A Surplus of Signifiers," 344.

133. Kermode, *The Classic,* 136.

134. Ibid., 133.

135. Norton, *Through the Eyes of a Child,* 273–274.

136. Pollard and Keeling, "In Search of His Father's Garden," 118, 120, 122.

137. Lukens, *A Critical Handbook of Children's Literature,* 55.

138. Moynihan, introduction to *Masterworks of Children's Literature,* 15.

139. May, "Beatrix Potter in the Year 2000," 28.

140. Potter, *The Tale of Peter Rabbit,* 9.

141. Pollard and Keeling, "In Search of His Father's Garden," 121; Carpenter, "Excessively Impertinent Bunnies," 279.

142. Lurie, *Don't Tell the Grown-Ups,* 95.

143. MacDonald, "Why This Is Still 1893," 186.

144. Cummins, " 'You Should Not Loiter Longer,' " 94.

145. Sale, *Fairy Tales and After,* 142.

146. Ibid., 83.

147. Scott, "Between Me and the World," 192; Scott, "An Unusual Hero," 23; Scott, "Between Me and the World," 198; Scott, "Clothed in Nature," 81.

148. Frey, "Victors and Victims in the Tales of *Peter Rabbit* and *Squirrel Nutkin,*" 106.

149. Kutzer, "A Wildness Inside," 204.

150. Hourihan, *Deconstructing the Hero,* 218.

151. Inglis, *The Promise of Happiness,* 109.

152. Nikola-Lisa, "The Cult of Peter Rabbit," 65, 64.

153. Frey, "Victors and Victims in the Tales of *Peter Rabbit* and *Squirrel Nutkin,*" 11.

154. Pollard and Keeling, "In Search of His Father's Garden," 128.

155. Hollindale, "Humans Are So Rabbit," 163; Byrnes, "A Jungian Perspective on the Enduring Appeal of Peter Rabbit," 138, 139.

156. Rahn, "Tailpiece," 79.

157. Eastman, "Beatrix Potter's *The Tale of Peter Rabbit,*" 104, 105.

158. M. Mackey, *The Case of Peter Rabbit,* 6, 12.

159. Dresang, "Radical Qualities of *The Tale of Peter Rabbit,*" 109.

160. Hollindale, "Humans Are So Rabbit," 167.

161. Frey, "Victors and Victims in the Tales of *Peter Rabbit* and *Squirrel Nutkin,*" 107.

162. Kermode, *The Classic,* 95n2.

163. Fishelov, *Metaphors of Genre,* 12.

164. May, "Beatrix Potter in the Year 2000," 28; Sendak, *Caldecott & Co.,* 76.

165. Carpenter, "Excessively Impertinent Bunnies," 286.

166. Avery, "Beatrix Potter and Social Comedy," 198; MacDonald, "Why This Is Still 1893," 197.

167. The discussion of the Harry Potter novels that follows was written prior to the publication of the seventh volume of the series in 2007—but, perhaps blindly, I find nothing in *Harry Potter and the Deathly Hallows* that might contradict the conclusions I reach here.

168. Dresang, "Radical Qualities of *The Tale of Peter Rabbit*," 112.

169. Cockrell, "Harry Potter and the Secret Password," 18.

170. Mills, "Archetypes and the Unconscious in *Harry Potter* and Diana Wynne Jones's *Fire and Hemlock* and *Dogsbody*," 8.

171. Nikolajeva, "*Harry Potter*—A Return to the Romantic Hero," 131.

172. Tucker, "The Rise and Rise of Harry Potter," 230.

173. Behr, " 'Same-as-Difference,' " 123.

174. Ibid., 113.

175. Trites, "The Harry Potter Novels as a Test Case for Adolescent Literature," 472.

176. Teare, "Harry Potter and the Technology of Magic," 329.

177. See Bettelheim, *The Uses of Enchantment*; and Campbell, *The Hero with a Thousand Faces*.

178. Lacoss, "Of Magic and Muggles," 85; Grimes, "Harry Potter," 107.

179. Anatol, introduction to *Reading Harry Potter*, xx.

180. Applebaum, "Harry Potter's World," 28.

181. Alton, "Generic Fusion and the Mosaic of *Harry Potter*," 141.

182. Pharr, "In Medias Res," 65; Pinsent, "The Education of a Wizard," 49.

183. Cockrell, "Harry Potter and the Secret Password," 17.

184. Westman, "Specters of Thatcherism," 328; Doughty, "Locating Harry Potter in the 'Boys' Book' Market," 246.

185. Nikolajeva, "*Harry Potter*—A Return to the Romantic Hero," 140; Natov, "Harry Potter and the Extraordinariness of the Ordinary," 130; Grimes, "Harry Potter," 90; Nel, "Is There a Text in This Advertising Campaign?" 251.

186. Hall, "Harry Potter and the Rule of Law," 147.

187. R. Stephens, "Harry and Hierarchy," 56, 58.

188. Gallardo-C. and Smith, "Cinderfella," 200, 203.

189. Chevalier, "The Liberty Tree and the Whomping Willow," 398.

190. Mendlesohn, "Crowning the King," 160.

191. Trites, "The Harry Potter Novels as a Test Case for Adolescent Literature," 475.

192. Anatol, "The Fallen Empire," 164, 171.

193. Ibid., 174.

194. Park, "Class and Socioeconomic Identity in Harry Potter's England," 180.

195. Turner-Vorbeck, "Pottermania," 20.

196. Heilman and Gregory, "Images of the Privileged Insider and Outcast Outsider," 242.

197. Westman, "Specters of Thatcherism," 310.

198. Teare, "Harry Potter and the Technology of Magic," 333.

199. Ostry, "Accepting Mudbloods," 90.

200. Tucker, "The Rise and Rise of Harry Potter," 231.

Adams, Gillian. "The First Children's Literature: The Case for Sumer." *Children's Literature* 14 (1986): 1–30.

———. "Medieval Children's Literature: Its Possibility and Actuality." *Children's Literature* 26 (1998): 1–24.

Adams, Hazard, and Leroy Searle, eds. *Critical Theory since 1965.* Tallahassee: Florida State University Press, 1986.

Alcott, Louisa May. *Little Women.* 1868. Edited by Anne Hiebert Alton. Peterborough, ON: Broadview Press, 2001.

Aldrich, Thomas Bailey. *The Story of a Bad Boy.* Boston: Fields, Osgood, 1870.

Allor, Martin, Danielle Juteau, and John Shepherd. "Contingencies of Culture: The Space of Culture in Canada and Québec." *Culture and Policy* 6, no. 1: www.gu.edu.au/centre/cmp/kcpubs.html (accessed June 23, 2002).

Althusser, Louis. "Ideology and Ideological State Apparatuses." Translated by Ben Brewster. In Adams and Searle, *Critical Theory since 1965,* 239–250.

Alton, Anne Hiebert. "Generic Fusion and the Mosaic of *Harry Potter.*" In Heilman, *Harry Potter's World,* 141–162.

Anatol, Giselle Liza. "The Fallen Empire: Exploring Ethnic Otherness in the World of Harry Potter." In Anatol, *Reading Harry Potter,* 163–178.

———. Introduction to Anatol, *Reading Harry Potter,* ix–xxv.

———, ed. *Reading Harry Potter: Critical Essays.* Westport, CT: Praeger, 2003.

Anderson, Benedict. *Imagined Communities: Reflections on the Origin and Spread of Nationalism.* Rev. ed. London: Verso, 1991.

Ang, Ien, and Jon Stratton. "Asianing Australia: Notes Toward a Critical Transnationalism in Cultural Studies." *Cultural Studies* 10, no. 1 (1996): 16–36.

Applebaum, Peter. "Harry Potter's World: Magic, Technoculture, and Becoming Human." In Heilman, *Harry Potter's World,* 25–51.

Applegate, K. A. *Animorphs 1: The Invasion.* New York: Scholastic, 1996.

Ariès, Philippe. *Centuries of Childhood: A Social History of Family Life.* New York: Vintage, 1962.

Association for Library Service to Children. "Terms and Criteria: John Newbery Medal." www.ala.org/ala/alsc/awardsscholarships/literaryawds/newberymedal/newberyterms/newberyterms.htm (accessed June 19, 2007).

Attali, Jacques. *Noise: The Political Economy of Music.* Translated by Brian Massumi. Minneapolis: University of Minnesota Press, 1985.

Atwood, Margaret. *Cat's Eye.* Toronto: McClelland-Bantam, 1988.

——. *Survival: A Thematic Guide to Canadian Literature.* Toronto: Anansi, 1972.

Avery, Gillian. "Beatrix Potter and Social Comedy." *Bulletin of the John Rylands University Library of Manchester* 76, no. 3 (Sept. 1994): 185–200.

——. *Nineteenth Century Children: Heroes and Heroines in English Children's Stories, 1780–1900.* London: Hodder, 1965.

Babbitt, Natalie. "Happy Endings? Of Course, and Also Joy." In Haviland, *Children and Literature,* 155–159.

Bakhtin, Mikhail M. "Discourse in the Novel." In Adams and Searle, *Critical Theory since 1965,* 665–678.

——. "The Problem of Speech Genres." In *Speech Genres and Other Late Essays.* Translated by Vern W. McGee. 60–102. Austin: University of Texas Press, 1986.

——. *Problems of Dostoevsky's Poetics.* Edited and translated by Caryl Emerson. Minneapolis: University of Minnesota Press, 1984.

——. *Rabelais and His World.* Translated by Hélène Iswolsky. Bloomington: Indiana University Press, 1984.

Barrie, J. M. *Peter Pan.* 1911. Edited by Jack Zipes. New York: Penguin, 2004.

——. *Sentimental Tommy.* 1896. New York: Scribner, 1913.

Barthes, Roland. *S/Z.* Translated by Richard Miller. New York: Hill and Wang/Farrar, Straus and Giroux, 1974.

Bartlett, Frederick. *Remembering: A Study in Experimental and Social Psychology.* 1932. Cambridge, UK: Cambridge University Press, 1967.

Bator, Robert, comp. *Signposts to Criticism of Children's Literature.* Chicago: American Library Association, 1983.

Baum, L. Frank. *The Wonderful Wizard of Oz.* 1900. New York: Dover, 1996.

Bawden, Nina. "A Dead Pig and My Father." *Children's Literature in Education* 5 (1974): 3–13.

Beebee, Thomas O. *The Ideology of Genre: A Comparative Study of Generic Instability.* University Park: Pennsylvania State University Press, 1994.

Behr, Kate. " 'Same-as-Difference': Narrative Transformations and Intersecting Cultures in Harry Potter ." *JNT: Journal of Narrative Theory* 35, no. 1 (winter 2005): 112–132.

Bennett, Tony, Graeme Turner, and Michael Volkerling. "Introduction: Post-Colonial Formations." *Culture and Policy* 6, no. 1: www.gu.edu.au/centre/cmp/kcpubs.html (accessed June 23, 2002).

Berger, John. *Ways of Seeing.* London: British Broadcasting Corporation; Harmondsworth: Penguin, 1972.

Bettelheim, Bruno. *The Uses of Enchantment: The Meaning and Importance of Fairy Tales.* New York: Knopf, 1976.

Bhabha, Homi. "Of Mimicry and Man." In *The Location of Culture,* 85–92. London: Routledge, 1994.

Birney, Earle. "Canada: Case History." WTS. http://home.golden.net/wts/words/otherw ords/wts-canadacasehistory.html (accessed June 18, 2007).

——. "Canada: Case History: 1973." In *The Collected Poems of Earle Birney.* Vol. 2. Toronto: McClelland and Stewart, 1975.

Blake, William. *Songs of Innocence and Experience.* 1789. The William Blake Archive.www
.blake archive.org/exist/blake/indexworks.htm (accessed June 9, 2007).

Blodgett, E. D. "Is a History of the Literature of Canada Possible?" *Essays on Canadian Writing* 50 (fall 1993): 1–18.

Blum, Virginia. *Hide and Seek: The Child between Psychoanalysis and Fiction.* Urbana: University of Illinois Press, 1995.

Blume, Judy. *Are You There, God? It's Me, Margaret.* New York: Yearling, 1986.

Bourdieu, Pierre. *Distinction: A Social Critique of the Judgment of Taste.* Cambridge, MA: Harvard University Press, 1984.

——. *The Field of Cultural Production.* Edited by Randal Johnson. New York: Columbia University Press, 1993.

——. *Language and Symbolic Power.* Translated by John B. Thompson. Cambridge, MA: Harvard University Press, 1991.

——. *Masculine Domination.* Translated by Richard Nice. Stanford: Stanford University Press, 2001.

Bradford, Clare. *Reading Race: Aboriginality in Australian Children's Literature.* Carlton, Vic.: Melbourne University Press, 2001.

Brainerd, Charles J., ed. *Recent Advances in Cognitive Developmental Research.* New York: Springer-Verlag, 1983.

Brooks, Martha. *Bone Dance.* Toronto: Groundwood, 1997.

Brooks, Peter. "Toward Supreme Fictions." In *The Child's Part,* edited by Peter Brooks, 5–14. Boston: Beacon, 1969.

Burman, Erica. *Deconstructing Developmental Psychology.* London: Routledge, 1994.

Burnett, Frances Hodgson. *The Secret Garden.* 1888. New York: Penguin, 1999.

Butler, Francelia. "Children's Literature: The Bad Seed." In Bator, *Signposts to Criticism of Children's Literature,* 37–49.

Butler, Judith. *Gender Trouble: Feminism and the Subversion of Identity.* New York: Routledge, 1990.

Byrnes, Alice. "A Jungian Perspective on the Enduring Appeal of Peter Rabbit." In Mackey, *Beatrix Potter's Peter Rabbit,* 130–143.

Cadden, Mike. *Ursula K. Le Guin beyond Genre: Fiction for Children and Adults.* New York: Routledge, 2005.

Cameron, Eleanor. *The Green and Burning Tree: On the Writing and Enjoyment of Children's Books.* Boston: Atlantic/Little, Brown, 1969.

Campbell, Joseph. *The Hero with a Thousand Faces.* New York: Pantheon, 1949.

Carpenter, Humphrey. "Excessively Impertinent Bunnies: The Subversive Element in Beatrix Potter." In *Children and Their Books: A Celebration of the Work of Iona and Peter Opie,* edited by Gillian Avery and Julia Briggs, 271–298. Oxford: Clarendon Press, 1989.

——. *Secret Gardens: A Study of the Golden Age of Children's Literature.* London: Unwin Paperbacks, 1987.

Carroll, Lewis. *Alice's Adventures in Wonderland; and, Through the Looking Glass and What Alice Found There.* Edited by Roger Lancelyn Green. Oxford: Oxford University Press, 1982.

Cawelti, John. *Adventure, Mystery, and Romance.* Chicago: University of Chicago Press, 1976.

Chambers, Aidan. "The Reader in the Book: Notes from a Work in Progress." In Bator, *Signposts to Criticism of Children's Literature,* 127–135.

——. *Tell Me: Children, Reading, and Talk.* Stroud, Gloucestershire: Thimble, 1993.

Chandler, Daniel. "Laura Mulvey on Film Spectatorship." In *Notes on "The Gaze."* www .aber.ac.uk/media/Documents/gaze/gaze09.html (accessed June 17, 2007).

Chevalier, Noel. "The Liberty Tree and the Whomping Willow: Political Justice, Magical Science, and Harry Potter." *Lion and the Unicorn* 29, no. 3 (Sept. 2005): 397–415.

Clark, Beverly Lyon. *Kiddie Lit: The Cultural Construction of Children's Literature in America.* Baltimore: Johns Hopkins University Press, 2003.

Clark, Joan. *The Dream Carvers.* Toronto: Viking, 1995.

——. *The Hand of Robin Squires.* Toronto: Clarke, Irwin, 1977.

Clausen, Christopher. "Home and Away in Children's Fiction." *Children's Literature* 10 (1982): 141–152.

Cleary, Beverly. *Henry Huggins.* 1950. New York: Dell Yearling, 1979.

——. *Ramona and Her Father.* New York: Morrow, 1977.

——. *Ramona Quimby, Age 8.* New York: Morrow, 1981.

Coats, Karen. *Looking Glasses and Neverlands: Lacan, Desire, and Subjectivity in Children's Literature.* Iowa City: University of Iowa Press, 2004.

Cockrell, Amanda. "Harry Potter and the Secret Password: Finding Our Way in the Magical Genre.'" In Whited, *The Ivory Tower and Harry Potter,* 15–26.

Cocks, Neil. "The Implied Reader: Response and Responsibility: Theories of the Implied Reader in Children's Literature Criticism." In Lesnik-Oberstein, *Children's Literature: New Approaches,* 93–117.

Coe, Richard M. "Teaching Genre as Process." In Freedman and Medway, *Learning and Teaching Genre,* 157–169.

Cooperative Children's Book Center, School of Education, University of Wisconsin–Madison. "Children's Books by and about People of Color Published in the United States." www.education.wisc.edu/ccbc/books/pcstats.htm (accessed Aug. 8, 2006).

Crago, Hugh. "Children's Literature: On the Cultural Periphery." In Bator, *Signposts to Criticism of Children's Literature,* 61–65.

Crompton, Richmal. *Just William.* 1922. London: Macmillan Children's, 1983.

Culleton, Beatrice. *In Search of April Raintree.* Winnipeg: Pemmican, 1983.

Cummins, June. "'You Should Not Loiter Longer': Beatrix Potter, Christina Rossetti, and Progressive Intertextual Revision." In Mackey, *Beatrix Potter's Peter Rabbit,* 79–98.

Curtis, Christopher. *Bud Not Buddy.* New York: Delacorte, 1999.

Danto, Arthur. "The Artworld." In *The Philosophy of the Visual Arts,* edited by Philip Alperson, 426–433. New York: Oxford University Press, 1992.

Darton, F. J. Harvey. *Children's Books in England: Five Centuries of Social Life.* 3rd ed. Revised by Brian Alderson. Cambridge, UK: Cambridge University Press, 1982.

De Jong, Meindert. "Acceptance Paper." *Newbery Medal Books: 1922–1955,* edited by Bertha Mahoney Miller and Elinor Whitney Field, 434–439. Boston: Horn Book, 1955.

De Lauretis, Theresa. *The Practice of Love: Lesbian Sexuality and Perverse Desire.* Bloomington: Indiana University Press, 1994.

Demers, Patricia, and Gordon Moyles, eds. *From Instruction to Delight: An Anthology of Children's Literature to 1850.* Toronto: Oxford University Press, 1982.

Derrida, Jacques. "The Law of Genre." In *Acts of Literature*, edited by Derek Attridge, 221–252. New York: Routledge, 1992.

Dorscht, Susan Rudy. "Decolonizing Canadian Writing: Why Gender? Whose English? When Canada?" *Essays on Canadian Writing* 54 (winter 1994): 124–152.

Doughty, Terri. "Locating Harry Potter in the 'Boys' Book' Market." In Whited, *The Ivory Tower and Harry Potter*, 243–257.

Doyle, Brian. *Mary Ann Alice*. Toronto: Douglas and McIntyre, 2001.

Doyle, Roddy. *Paddy Clarke, Ha-Ha-Ha*. New York: Viking, 1994.

Dresang, Eliza. *Radical Change: Books for Youth in a Digital Age*. New York: H. Wilson, 1999.

———. "Radical Qualities of *The Tale of Peter Rabbit*." In Mackey, *Beatrix Potter's Peter Rabbit*, 99–116.

Dusinberre, Julia. *Alice to the Lighthouse: Children's Books and Radical Experiments in Art*. New York: St. Martin's, 1987.

Eastman, Jackie F. "Beatrix Potter's *The Tale of Peter Rabbit*: A Small Masterpiece." In *Touchstones: Reflections on the Best in Children's Literature*. Vol. 3, *Picture Books*, edited by Perry Nodelman, 100–107. West Lafayette, IN: ChLA Publishers, 1989.

Edgeworth, Maria. *Early Lessons*. Internet Archive. www.archive.org/details/earlylessonsw ithooedgeuoft (accessed May 19, 2007).

———."The Purple Jar." 1801. In Demers and Moyles, *From Instruction to Delight*, 141–145.

Egoff, Sheila. *The Republic of Childhood: A Critical Guide to Canadian Children's Literature in English*. 2nd ed. Toronto: Oxford University Press, 1975.

Egoff, Sheila, and Judith Saltman. *The New Republic of Childhood: A Critical Guide to Canadian Children's Literature in English*. Toronto: Oxford University Press, 1990.

Egoff, Sheila, Gordon Stubbs, Ralph Ashley, and Wendy Sutton, eds. *Only Connect: Readings on Children's Literature*. 3rd ed. Toronto: Oxford University Press, 1996.

Eliot, T. S. *What Is a Classic? An Address Delivered before the Virgil Society on the 16th of October 1944*. London: Faber and Faber, 1945.

Ellis, John M. *One Fairy Story Too Many: The Brothers Grimm and Their Tales*. Chicago: University of Chicago Press, 1983.

Empson, William. *Some Versions of Pastoral*. 1935. Harmondsworth, Middlesex: Penguin, 1966.

Ewers, Hans-Heino. "The Limits of Literary Criticism of Children's and Young Adult Literature." Translated by J. D. Stahl. *Lion and the Unicorn* 19, no. 1 (Jan. 1995): 77–94.

Fadiman, Clifton. "The Case for a Children's Literature." In Bator, *Signposts to Criticism of Children's Literature*, 7–18.

Farquhar, Mary Ann. *Children's Literature in China: From Lu Xun to Mao Zedong*. London: M. E. Sharpe, 1999.

Feuer, Jane. "Genre Study and Television." In *Channels of Discourse, Reassembled: Television and Contemporary Criticism*, edited by Robert C. Allen, 138–159. London: Routledge, 1992.

Fish, Stanley. *Is There a Text in This Class? The Authority of Interpretive Communities*. Cambridge, MA: Harvard University Press, 1980.

Fishelov, David. *Metaphors of Genre: The Role of Analogies in Genre Theory*. University Park: University of Pennsylvania Press, 1993.

Fowler, Alistair. *Kinds of Literature: An Introduction to the Theory of Genres and Modes.* Cambridge, MA: Harvard University Press, 1982.

Frank, Robert H. "When Less Is Not More." *New York Times,* July, 17, 2000, Final edition, A19.

Freedman, Aviva, and Peter Medway. "Introduction: New Views of Genre and Their Implications for Education." In Freedman and Medway, *Learning and Teaching Genre,* 1–22.

——, eds. *Learning and Teaching Genre.* Portsmouth, NH: Boynton/Cook, 1994.

Freud, Sigmund. *Beyond the Pleasure Principle.* In Gay, *The Freud Reader,* 594–626.

——. *A General Introduction to Psychoanalysis.* Translated by Joan Riviere. 1924. New York: Perma Books, 1953.

——. "Leonardo da Vinci and a Memory of His Childhood." In Gay, *The Freud Reader,* 443–480.

Frey, Charles. "Victors and Victims in the Tales of *Peter Rabbit* and *Squirrel Nutkin.*" *Children's Literature in Education* 18, no. 2 (1987): 105–112.

Frye, Northrop. *Anatomy of Criticism: Four Essays.* Princeton, NJ: Princeton University Press, 1957.

——. "The Archetypes of Literature." In *Fables of Identity: Studies in Poetic Mythology,* 7–20. New York: Harcourt, Brace and World, 1963.

——. *The Bush Garden: Essays on the Canadian Imagination.* Toronto: Anansi, 1971.

Galbraith, Mary. "Hear My Cry: A Manifesto for an Emancipatory Childhood Studies Approach to Children's Literature." *Lion and the Unicorn* 25, no. 2 (April 2001): 187–205.

Gallardo-C., Ximena, and C. Jason Smith. "Cinderfella: J. K. Rowling's Wily Web of Gender." In Anatol, *Reading Harry Potter,* 191–205.

Gardam, Jane. "Some Wasps in Her Marmalade." Part 1. *Horn Book* 60 (1978): 489–496.

Garlitz, Barbara. "The Immortality Ode: Its Cultural Progeny." *Studies in English Literature* 6 (1966): 639–649.

Garner, Alan. *Red Shift.* 1973. London: Collins Lions, 1975.

Gay, Peter, ed. *The Freud Reader.* New York: Norton, 1989.

Genette, Gérard. *Narrative Discourse: An Essay in Method.* Translated by Jane E. Lewin. Ithaca, NY: Cornell University Press, 1980.

Gilead, Sarah. "The Undoing of Idyll in *The Wind in the Willows.*" *Children's Literature* 16 (1988): 145–158.

Gilligan, Carol. *In a Different Voice: Psychological Theory and Women's Development.* Cambridge, MA: Harvard University Press, 1982.

Glazer, Joan, and Gurney Williams III. *Introduction to Children's Literature.* New York: McGraw-Hill, 1979.

Gose, Elliot. *Mere Creatures: A Study of Modern Fantasy Tales for Children.* Toronto: University of Toronto Press, 1988.

Grahame, Kenneth. *The Wind in the Willows.* 1908. New York: Aladdin Books, 1989.

Greg, W. W. "Pastoral: A Literary Inquiry." In *Pastoral and Romance: Modern Essays in Criticism,* edited by Eleanor Terry Lincoln, 7–11. Englewood Cliffs, NJ: Prentice-Hall, 1969.

Griffith, John W., and Charles H. Frey. *Classics of Children's Literature.* 6th ed. Prentice Hall, 2005.

Grimes, M. Katharine. "Harry Potter: Fairy Tale Prince, Real Boy, and Archetypal Hero." In Whited, *The Ivory Tower and Harry Potter*, 89–122.

Griswold, Jerry. *Feeling like a Kid: Childhood and Children's Literature*. Baltimore: Johns Hopkins University Press, 2006.

Hade, Daniel. "Storyselling: Are Publishers Changing the Way Children Read?" *Horn Book* 78 (Sept./Oct. 2002): 509–517.

Hall, Susan. "Harry Potter and the Rule of Law: The Central Weakness of Legal Concepts in the Wizard World." In Anatol, *Reading Harry Potter*, 147–162.

Hamilton, Virginia. *Plain City*. New York: Scholastic, 1993.

Hancher, Michael. *The Tenniel Illustrations to the "Alice" Books*. Columbus: Ohio State University Press, 1985.

Hancock, Marjorie R. *A Celebration of Literature and Response: Children, Books, and Teachers in K–8 Classrooms*. Upper Saddle River, NJ: Merrill, 2000.

Hardt, Michael, and Antonio Negri. *Empire*. London: Harvard University Press, 2000.

Haviland, Virginia, ed. *Children and Literature: Views and Reviews*. Glenview, IL: Scott, Foresman, 1973.

——, ed. *The Open-Hearted Audience: Ten Authors Talk about Writing for Children*. Washington: Library of Congress, 1980.

Hazard, Paul. *Books, Children & Men*. Boston: Horn Book, 1944.

Heilman, Elizabeth E., ed. *Harry Potter's World: Multidisciplinary Critical Perspectives*. New York: RoutledgeFalmer, 2003.

Heilman, Elizabeth E., and Anne E. Gregory. "Images of the Privileged Insider and Outcast Outsider." In Heilman, *Harry Potter's World*, 241–257.

Heinlein, Robert A. *Rocket Ship Galileo*. New York: Scribner, 1947.

Heins, Paul. "Out on a Limb with the Critics." In Haviland, *Children and Literature*, 400–407.

Heneghan, James. *Promises to Come*. Toronto: Overlea House, 1988.

Hillman, Judith. *Discovering Children's Literature*. 2nd ed. Upper Saddle River, NJ: Merrill, 1999.

Hoffman, Heinrich. *Struwwelpeter: Fearful Stories and Vile Pictures to Instruct Good Little Folks*. 1845. Reprinted with an introduction by Jack Zipes. Venice, CA: Feral House, 1999.

Hollindale, Peter. "Humans Are So Rabbit." In Mackey, *Beatrix Potter's Peter Rabbit*, 161–172.

——. "Ideology and the Children's Book." *Signal* 55 (Jan. 1988): 3–32.

——. *Signs of Childness in Children's Books*. Stroud, Glos: Thimble Press, 1997.

Horne, Jackie C. "The Power of Public Opinion: Constructing Class in Agnes Strickland's *The Rival Crusoes*." *Children's Literature* 35 (2007): 1–26.

Hourihan, Margery. *Deconstructing the Hero: Literary Theory and Children's Literature*. London: Routledge, 1997.

Huck, Charlotte S. *Children's Literature in the Elementary School*. 3rd ed., updated. New York: Holt, Rinehart and Winston, 1979.

Hughes, Felicity. "Children's Literature: Theory and Practice." In Bator, *Signposts to Criticism of Children's Literature*, 26–36, 242–248.

Hughes, Monica. *Hunter in the Dark*. New York: Atheneum, 1984.

———. *Log Jam*. Toronto: Irwin, 1987.

Hunt, Caroline. "Young Adult Literature Evades the Theorists." *Children's Literature Association Quarterly* 21, no. 1 (spring 1996): 4–11.

Hunt, Peter, ed. *Children's Literature: An Illustrated History*. Oxford: Oxford University Press, 1995.

———. "Criticism and Children's Literature." In Bator, *Signposts to Criticism of Children's Literature*, 114–125.

———. *Criticism, Theory, and Children's Literature*. Oxford: Basil Blackwell, 1991.

———, ed. *International Companion Encyclopedia of Children's Literature*. London: Routledge, 1996.

———, ed. *International Companion Encyclopedia of Children's Literature*. 2nd ed. 2 vols. London: Routledge, 2004.

Hunt, Peter, and Karen Sands. "The View from the Center: British Empire and Post-Empire Children's Literature." In McGillis, *Voices of the Other*, 39–54.

Inglis, Fred. *The Promise of Happiness: Value and Meaning in Children's Fiction*. Cambridge, UK: Cambridge University Press, 1981.

Iser, Wolfgang. *The Act of Reading: A Theory of Aesthetic Response*. Baltimore: Johns Hopkins University Press, 1978.

Jameson, Fredric. *The Political Unconscious: Narrative as a Socially Symbolic Act*. Ithaca, NY: Cornell University Press, 1981.

Jan, Isabelle. *On Children's Literature*. Edited by Catharine Storr. New York: Schocken, 1974.

Janeway, James. "From *A Token for Children*." In Demers and Moyles, *From Instruction to Delight*, 45–53.

Johnson, Randal. "Editor's Introduction: Pierre Bourdieu on Art, Literature, and Culture." In Bourdieu, *Field of Cultural Production*, 1–25.

Jones, Diana Wynne. *Chronicles of Chrestomanci*. 2 vols. New York: HarperCollins, 2001.

Jones, Katharine. "Getting Rid of Children's Literature." *Lion and the Unicorn* 30, no. 3 (Sept. 2006): 287–315.

Joyce, James. *A Portrait of the Artist as a Young Man*. 1916. New York: Penguin, 1976.

Juvan, Marko. "Generic Identity and Intertextuality." *CLCWeb: Comparative Literature and Culture* 7, no. 4 (Dec. 2005). http://clcwebjournal.lib.purdue.edu/clcweb05-1/juvan05.html (accessed May 26, 2007).

Kaplan, Deborah. "Read All Over: Postmodern Resolution in Macaulay's *Black and White*." *Children's Literature Association Quarterly* 28, no. 1 (spring 2003): 37–41.

Katz, Welwyn. *Come like Shadows*. Toronto: Viking, 1993.

———. *False Face*. Toronto: Groundwood, 1987.

———. *Out of the Dark*. Toronto: Groundwood, 1995.

———. *Time Ghost*. Toronto: Groundwood, 1994.

Keats, Ezra Jack. *The Snowy Day*. New York: Viking, 1962.

Keene, Carolyn. *The Secret of the Old Clock*. New York: Grosset and Dunlap, 1930.

Kermode, Frank. *The Classic: Literary Images of Permanence and Change*. Cambridge, MA: Harvard University Press, 1975.

———. *Forms of Attention*. Chicago: University of Chicago Press, 1985.

——. *The Genesis of Secrecy: On the Interpretation of Narrative.* Cambridge, MA: Harvard University Press, 1979.

Kessen, William. "Rumble or Revolution: A Commentary." In *Development in Context: Acting and Thinking in Specific Environments,* edited by Robert H. Wozniak and Kurt W. Fischer, 269–279. Hillsdale, NJ: Laurence Erlbaum, 1993.

Kidd, Kenneth. "Prizing Children's Literature: The Case of Newbery Gold." *Children's Literature* 35 (2007): 166–190.

——. "Psychoanalysis and Children's Literature: The Case for Complementarity." *Lion and the Unicorn* 28, no. 1 (Jan. 2004): 109–130.

Kincaid, James. *Child-Loving: The Erotic Child and Victorian Culture.* New York: Routledge, 1992.

King, Thomas. *A Coyote Columbus Story.* Illustrated by W. K. Monkman. Toronto: Groundwood/Douglas and McIntyre, 1992.

Kinnell, Margaret. "Early Texts Used by Children." In Hunt, *International Companion Encyclopedia of Children's Literature,* 141–151.

Kipling, Rudyard. *The Complete Stalky and Co.* 1899. Oxford: Oxford University Press, 1987.

——. *Kim.* 1901. Edited by Zohreh T. Sullivan. New York: Norton, 2002.

Kirkpatrick, D. L., ed. *Twentieth Century Children's Writers.* New York: St. Martin's, 1978.

Knoepflmacher, U. C. "The Balancing of Child and Adult: An Approach to Victorian Fantasies for Children." *Nineteenth Century Fiction* 37, no. 4 (1983): 497–530.

——. *Ventures into Childland: Victorians, Fairy Tales, and Femininity.* Chicago: University of Chicago Press, 1998.

Kohl, Herbert. *Should We Burn Babar? Essays on Children's Literature and the Power of Stories.* New York: New Press, 1995.

Krips, Valerie. *The Presence of the Past: Memory, Heritage, and Childhood in Postwar Britain.* New York: Garland, 2000.

Kristeva, Julia. *Desire in Language: A Semiotic Approach to Literature and Art.* Edited by Leon S. Roudiez. New York: Columbia University Press, 1980.

Kropp, Paul. *Moonkid and Liberty.* Don Mills: Stoddart, 1988.

Kundera, Milan. *The Book of Laughter and Forgetting.* Translated by Michael Henry Heim. Harmondsworth, Middlesex: Penguin, 1981.

Kutzer, Daphne. *Empire's Children: Empire and Imperialism in Classic British Children's Books.* New York: Garland, 2000.

——. "A Wildness Inside: Domestic Space in the Work of Beatrix Potter." *Lion and the Unicorn* 21, no. 2 (April 1997): 204–214.

Kuznets, Lois. "Family as Formula: Cawelti's Formulaic Theory and Streatfeild's 'Shoe' Books." *Children's Literature Association Quarterly* 9, no. 4 (winter 1984–1985): 147–149, 201.

Lacan, Jacques. "Agressivity in Psychoanalysis." In *Écrits,* 8–29.

——. *Écrits: A Selection.* Translated by Alan Sheridan. New York: Norton, 1977.

——. "The Mirror Stage as Formative of the Function of the I as Revealed in Psychoanalytic Experience." In *Écrits,* 1–7.

Lacoss, Jan. "Of Magic and Muggles: Reversal and Revolutions at Hogwarts." In Whited, *The Ivory Tower and Harry Potter,* 67–88.

Landow, George P. *Hypertext: The Convergence of Contemporary Theory and Technology*. Baltimore: Johns Hopkins University Press, 1991.

Leavis, F. R. *The Great Tradition: George Eliot, Henry James, Joseph Conrad*. London: Chatto and Windus, 1948.

Lecker, Robert. "Would You Publish This Book? Material Production, Canadian Criticism, and *The Theatre of Form*." *Studies in Canadian Literature* 25, no. 1 (2000): 15–36.

Lefebvre, Henri. *The Production of Space*. Translated by Donald Nicholson-Smith. Oxford: Blackwell, 1991.

Le Guin, Ursula K. *Tehanu: The Last Book of Earthsea*. New York: Atheneum, 1990.

———. *The Wizard of Earthsea*. Harmondsworth, Middlesex: Penguin, 1971.

L'Engle, Madeleine. *A Wrinkle in Time*. 1962. New York: Dell, 1976.

Lenski, Lois. *Cotton in My Sack*. Philadelphia: Lippincott, 1949.

Lesnik-Oberstein, Karín. *Children's Literature: Criticism and the Fictional Child*. Oxford: Clarendon Press, 1994.

———, ed. *Children's Literature: New Approaches*. Basingstoke, Hampshire: Palgrave Macmillan, 2004.

———. Introduction. In Lesnik-Oberstein, *Children's Literature: New Approaches*, 1–24.

Lévi-Strauss, Claude. *The Savage Mind*. Chicago: University of Chicago Press, 1966.

Lewis, C. S. "On Three Ways of Writing for Children." In Haviland, *Children and Literature*, 231–240.

Lofting, Christopher. "Afterword." In *The Story of Dr. Dolittle*, by Hugh Lofting. New York: Dell Yearling, 1988.

Lofting, Hugh. *The Story of Dr. Dolittle*. 1920. New York: Dell Yearling, 1978.

Lorimer, Rowland. Review of *Hip and Trivial: Youth Culture, Book Publishing, and the Greying of Canadian Nationalism*, by Robert Wright. Reviews/Comptes Rendus. *Labour/Le Travail* 52. The History Cooperative. www.historycooperative.org/journals/llt/52/br_10.html. (accessed June 18, 2007).

Lukens, Rebecca J. *A Critical Handbook of Children's Literature*. 7th ed. Boston: Allyn and Bacon, 2003.

Lundin, Anne. *Constructing the Canon of Children's Literature: Beyond Library Walls and Ivory Towers*. New York: Routledge, 2004.

Lunn, Janet. *The Root Cellar*. Toronto: Lester and Orpen Dennys, 1981.

———. *Shadow in Hawthorn Bay*. New York: Scribner, 1986.

Lurie, Alison. *Don't Tell the Grown-Ups: The Subversive Power of Children's Literature*. Boston: Little, Brown, 1998.

Macaulay, David. *Black and White*. Boston: Houghton Mifflin, 1990.

MacDonald, Ruth K. "Why This Is Still 1893: *The Tale of Peter Rabbit* and Beatrix Potter's Manipulations of Time into Timelessness." *Children's Literature Association Quarterly* 10, no. 4 (winter 1986): 185–187.

Mackey, Eva. *The House of Difference: Cultural Politics and National Identity in Canada*. London: Routledge, 1999.

Mackey, Margaret, ed. *Beatrix Potter's Peter Rabbit: A Children's Classic at 100*. Lanham, MD: Children's Literature Association and Scarecrow Press, 2002.

———. *The Case of Peter Rabbit: Changing Conditions of Literature for Children*. New York: Garland, 1998.

"Madonna Plans 'Morality Tale.'" *BBC News World Edition.* April 17, 2003. http://news
.bbc.co.uk/2/hi/entertainment/2955837.stm (accessed May 29, 2007).

Major, Kevin. *Blood Red Ochre.* New York: Delacorte, 1989.

———. *Hold Fast.* Toronto: Clarke, Irwin, 1978.

Matas, Carol. *Daniel's Story.* New York: Scholastic, 1993.

May, Jill P. "Beatrix Potter in the Year 2000." *Journal of Children's Literature* 26, no. 2 (fall
2000): 28–34.

———. *Children's Literature and Critical Theory: Reading and Writing for Understanding.* New
York: Oxford University Press, 1995.

McCallum, Robyn. *Ideologies of Identity in Adolescent Fiction: The Dialogic Construction of
Subjectivity.* New York: Garland, 1999.

McDowell, Malcolm. "Fiction for Children and Adults: Some Essential Differences." *Children's Literature in Education* 4, no. 1 (March 1973): 50–63.

McFarlane, Sheryl. *Waiting for the Whales.* Illustrated by Ron Lightburn. Victoria, BC: Orca,
1991.

McGillis, Roderick. "And the Celt Knew the Indian." In McGillis, *Voices of the Other,* 223–
236.

———. "Learning to Read, Reading to Learn; or Engaging in Critical Pedagogy." *Children's
Literature Association Quarterly* 22, no. 3 (fall 1997): 126–132.

———. *The Nimble Reader: Literary Theory and Children's Literature.* New York: Twayne, 1996.

———, ed. *Voices of the Other: Children's Literature and the Postcolonial Context.* New York:
Garland, 1999.

McLuhan, Marshall. *Understanding Media: The Extensions of Man.* New York: McGraw Hill,
1965.

McMaster, Juliet. "'Adults' Literature,' by Children." *Lion and the Unicorn* 25, no. 2 (April
2001): 277–296.

Meek, Margaret, ed. *Children's Literature and National Identity.* Stoke on Trent and Sterling:
Trentham, 2001.

———. "The Englishness of English Children's Books." In Meek, *Children's Literature and
National Identity,* 89–100.

Mendlesohn, Farah. "Crowning the King: Harry Potter and the Construction of Authority."
In Whited, *The Ivory Tower and Harry Potter,* 159–181.

Metcalf, John. *What Is a Canadian Literature?* Guelph, ON: Red Kite Press, 1988.

Miller, Carolyn R. "Genre as Social Action." In *Genre and the New Rhetoric,* edited by Aviva
Freeman and Peter Medway, 23–42. London: Taylor and Francis, 1994.

Mills, Alice. "Archetypes and the Unconscious in *Harry Potter* and Diana Wynne Jones's
Fire and Hemlock and *Dogsbody.*" In Anatol, *Reading Harry Potter,* 3–13.

Milne, A. A. *Winnie the Pooh.* New York: E. P. Dutton, 1926.

Mitchell, W. J. T. *Iconology: Image, Text, Ideology.* Chicago: University of Chicago Press,
1986.

Modleski, Tania. *Loving with a Vengeance: Mass-Produced Fantasies for Women.* 1982. New
York: Methuen, 1984.

Moi, Toril. *Sexual/Textual Politics.* London: Methuen, 1985.

Montgomery, L. M. *Anne of Green Gables.* 1908. Toronto: Seal Books, 1981.

Morganstern, John. "The Fall into Literacy and the Rise of the Bourgeois Child." *Children's Literature Association Quarterly* 27, no. 3 (fall 2002): 136–145.

———. "The Rise of Children's Literature Reconsidered." *Children's Literature Association Quarterly* 26, no. 2 (summer 2001): 64–73.

Morss, John R. *Growing Critical: Alternatives to Developmental Psychology.* London: Routledge, 1996.

Moss, Anita. "The Spear and the Piccolo: Heroic and Pastoral Dimensions of William Steig's *Dominic* and *Abel's Island.*" *Children's Literature* 10 (1982): 124–140.

Moss, Anita, and Jon Stott. *The Family of Stories: An Anthology of Children's Literature.* New York: Holt, Rinehart and Winston, 1986.

Moynihan, William T. Introduction to *Masterworks of Children's Literature.* Vol. 8, *The Twentieth Century.* Edited by William T. Moynihan and Mary E. Shaner, 1–34. New York: Stonehill/Chelsea House, 1986.

Mulvey, Laura. "Visual Pleasure and Narrative Cinema." *Screen* 16, no. 3 (1975): 6–18.

Munsch, Robert. *Smelly Socks.* Illustrated by Michael Martchenko. Markham, ON: Scholastic, 2004.

Myers, Mitzi. "Socializing Rosamond: Educational Ideology and Fictional Form." *Children's Literature Association Quarterly* 14, no. 2 (summer 1989): 52–58.

Natov, Roni. "Harry Potter and the Extraordinariness of the Ordinary." In Whited, *The Ivory Tower and Harry Potter,* 125–139.

———. *The Poetics of Childhood.* New York: Routledge, 2003.

Nel, Philip. "Is There a Text in This Advertising Campaign? Literature, Marketing, and Harry Potter." *Lion and the Unicorn* 29, no. 2 (April 2005): 236–267.

Nesbit, E. *The Story of the Treasure Seekers.* 1899. Harmondsworth, Middlesex: Penguin Puffin, 1995.

New, W. H. *Borderlands: How We Talk about Canada.* Vancouver: UBC Press, 1998.

Newbery, John. *A Little Pretty Pocket Book.* 1744. Worcester MA: Isaiah Thomas, 1787. http://hdl.loc.gov/loc.rbc/juv.05880 (accessed June 16, 2007).

Nikolajeva, Maria. *Children's Literature Comes of Age: Toward a New Aesthetic.* New York: Garland, 1996.

———. " 'A Dream of Complete Idleness': Depiction of Labor in Children's Fiction." *Lion and the Unicorn* 26, no. 3 (Sept. 2002): 305–321.

———. "Exit Children's Literature." *Lion and the Unicorn* 22, no. 2 (April 1998): 221–236.

———. "Harry Potter—A Return to the Romantic Hero." In Heilman, *Harry Potter's World,* 125–140.

———. *The Rhetoric of Character in Children's Literature.* Lanham, MD: Scarecrow, 2002.

Nikola-Lisa, W. "The Cult of Peter Rabbit: A Barthesian Analysis." *Lion and the Unicorn* 15, no. 2 (April 1991): 61–66.

Nodelman, Perry. "At Home on Native Land: A Non-Aboriginal Canadian Scholar Discusses Aboriginality and Property in Canadian Double-Focalized Novels for Young Adults." In *Home Words: Discourses of Children's Literature in Canada,* edited by Mavis Reimer. Waterloo, ON: Wilfred Laurier University Press, 2008.

———. "Children's Literature as Women's Writing." Column on Critical Theory and Children's Literature. *Children's Literature Association Quarterly* 13, no. 1 (spring 1988): 31–34.

———. "Editor's Comments: Signs of Confusion." *Children's Literature Association Quarterly* 11, no. 4 (winter 1986–1987): 162–164.

———. "Hatchet Job." Review of *Children's Literature: Criticism and the Fictional Child*, by Karín Lesnik-Oberstein. *Children's Literature Association Quarterly* 21 no. 1 (spring 1996): 42–45.

———. "The Hidden Meaning and the Inner Tale: Deconstruction and the Interpretation of Fairy Tales." *Children's Literature Association Quarterly* 15, no. 3 (fall 1990): 143–148.

———. "Interpretation and the Apparent Sameness of Children's Novels." *Studies in the Literary Imagination* 18, no. 2 (fall 1985): 5–20.

———. "John Fowles's Variations in *The Collector*." *Contemporary Literature* 28, no. 3 (autumn 1987): 332–346.

———. "A Monochromatic Mosaic: Class, Race, and Culture in Double-Focalized Canadian Novels for Young People." *CCL/LCJ: Canadian Children's Literature / Littérature canadienne pour la jeunesse* 115–116 (fall-winter 2004): 32–60.

———. "Of Solitudes and Borders: Double-Focalized Canadian Books for Children." *CCL/ LCJ: Canadian Children's Literature / Littérature canadienne pour la jeunesse* 109–110 (spring-summer 2003): 58–86.

———. "Ordinary Monstrosity: R. L. Stine's Goosebumps Books." *Children's Literature Association Quarterly* 22, no. 3 (fall 1997): 118–125.

———. "The Other: Orientalism, Colonialism, and Children's Literature." *Children's Literature Association Quarterly* 17, no. 1 (spring 1992): 29–35.

———. "Out There in Children's Science Fiction: Forward into the Past." *Science-Fiction Studies* 12, no. 3 (Nov. 1985): 285–296.

———. "Pleasure and Genre: Speculations on the Characteristics of Children's Fiction." *Children's Literature* 28 (2000): 1–14.

———. "Progressive Utopia: Or How to Grow Up without Growing Up." In Egoff et al., *Only Connect*, 74–82.

———. "Some Presumptuous Generalizations about Fantasy." In Egoff et al., *Only Connect*, 175–178.

———. "Text as Teacher: The Beginning of *Charlotte's Web*." *Children's Literature* 13 (1985): 109–127.

———. *Words about Pictures: The Narrative Art of Children's Picture Books*. Athens: University of Georgia Press, 1988.

Nodelman, Perry, and Mavis Reimer. *The Pleasures of Children's Literature*. 3rd ed. Boston: Allyn and Bacon, 2003.

———. "Teaching Canadian Children's Literature: Learning to Know More." *CCL/LCJ: Canadian Children's Literature / Littérature canadienne pour la jeunesse* 98 (summer 2000): 15–35.

Norton, Donna. *Through the Eyes of a Child: An Introduction to Children's Literature*. Columbus, OH: Charles E. Merrill, 1983.

Olin, Margaret. "Gaze." In *Critical Terms for Art History*, edited by Robert Nelson and Richard Shiff, 208–218. Chicago: University of Chicago Press, 1996.

O'Malley, Andrew. "The Coach and Six: Chapbook Residue in Late Eighteenth Century Children's Literature." *Lion and the Unicorn* 24, no. 1 (Jan. 2000): 18–44.

——. *The Making of the Modern Child: Children's Literature and Childhood in the Late Eighteenth Century.* New York: Routledge, 2003.

Ong, Walter J. *Orality and Literacy: The Technologizing of the Word.* London: Methuen, 1982.

Ostry, Elaine. "Accepting Mudbloods: The Ambivalent Social vision of J. K. Rowling's Fairy Tales." In Anatol, *Reading Harry Potter,* 89–101.

O'Sullivan, Emer. "Alice in Different Wonderlands: Varying Approaches in the German Translations of an English Children's Classic." In Meek, *Children's Literature and National Identity,* 11–21.

——. *Comparative Children's Literature.* London: Routledge, 2005.

PABBIS (Parents Against Bad Books in Schools). "What to Do." www.pabbis.com/ what todo.html (accessed May 29, 2007).

Park, Julia. "Class and Socioeconomic Identity in Harry Potter's England." In Anatol, *Reading Harry Potter,* 179–189.

Park, Linda Sue. *A Single Shard.* New York: Clarion Books, 2001.

Parravano, Martha V. " 'Alive and Vigorous': Questioning the Newbery." *Horn Book* 75, no. 4 (July/Aug. 1999): 434–444.

Paul, Lissa. *Reading Otherways.* Portland, ME: Calendar Islands Publishers, 1998.

Payne, Michael, and John Schad, eds. *Life.After.Theory.* London: Continuum, 2003.

Pearce, Phillipa. "The Writer's View of Childhood." In *Horn Book Reflections on Children's Books and Reading,* edited by Elinor Whitney Field, 49–53. Boston: Horn Book, 1960.

Pelorus (pseud.). "Graduate to Grown-Up Books?" In Bator, *Signposts to Criticism of Children's Literature,* 59–60.

Perkins, Lynne Rae. *Criss Cross.* New York: Greenwillow Books, 2005.

Pharr, Mary. "In Medias Res: Harry Potter as Hero-in-Progress." In Whited, *The Ivory Tower and Harry Potter,* 53–66.

Pinsent, Pat. "The Education of a Wizard: Harry Potter and His Predecessors." In Whited, *The Ivory Tower and Harry Potter,* 27–50.

Plumwood, Val. *Feminism and the Mastery of Nature.* London: Routledge, 1993.

"Politicizing Puberty: The Zoning of Child Sexuality in Art, Advertising, and the American Household." *Nerve,* Oct. 2, 1998. www.nerve.com/dispatches/voicebox/puberty/ (accessed June 3, 2007).

Pollard, Scott, and Kara Keeling. "In Search of His Father's Garden." In Mackey, *Beatrix Potter's Peter Rabbit,* 117–130.

Poss, Geraldine D. "An Epic in Arcadia: The Pastoral World of *The Wind in the Willows.*" *Children's Literature* 4 (1975): 80–90.

Potter, Beatrix. *The Tale of Peter Rabbit.* 1900. London: Frederick Warne, 1964.

Prout, Alan. *The Future of Childhood.* London: RoutledgeFalmer, 2005.

Rabkin, Eric S. *The Fantastic in Literature.* Princeton, NJ: Princeton University Press, 1976.

Radosh, Daniel. "Why American Kids Don't Consider Harry Potter an Insufferable Prig." *New Yorker,* Sept. 20, 1999, 54, 56. www.radosh.net/writing/potter.html (accessed June 18, 2007).

Rahn, Suzanne. "Tailpiece: *The Tale of Two Bad Mice.*" *Children's Literature* 12 (1984): 178–191.

Raschka, Chris. *Arlene Sardine.* New York: Orchard, 1998.

Raskin, Ellen. *Nothing Ever Happens on My Block*. New York: Atheneum, 1966.

Reimer, Mavis, ed. *Home Words: Discourses of Children's Literature in Canada*. Waterloo, ON: Wilfrid Laurier University Press, 2008.

——. "Making Princesses, Re-making *A Little Princess*." In McGillis, *Voices of the Other*, 111–134.

——. "The Masculine Reader in *Tom Brown's Schooldays*." *Masculinities* 3, no. 1 (spring 1995): 1–16.

——. "Power and Powerlessness: Reading the Controversy over *The Mighty Morphin Power Rangers*." *CCL/LCJ: Canadian Children's Literature / Littérature canadienne pour la jeunesse* 90 (1998): 6–16.

——. " 'These Two Irreconcilable Things—Art and Young Girls': The Case of the Girls' School Story." In *Girls, Boys, Books, Toys: Gender in Children's Literature and Culture*, edited by Beverly Lyon Clark and Margaret. R. Higgonet, 40–52. Baltimore: Johns Hopkins University Press, 1999.

Reimer, Mavis, and Anne Rusnak. "The Representation of Home in Canadian Children's Literature / La représentation du *chez-soi* dans la littérature de jeunesse canadienne." *CCL/LCJ: Canadian Children's Literature / Littérature canadienne pour la jeunesse* 100–101 (winter 2000-spring 2001): 9–33.

Rey, H. A. *Curious George*. 1941. Boston: Houghton Mifflin, 1973.

Reynolds, Kimberley. *Children's Literature in the 1890s and 1990s*. Plymouth: Northcote House, 1994.

——. *Radical Children's Literature: Future Visions and Aesthetic Transformations in Juvenile Fiction*. New York: Palgrave Macmillan, 2007.

Richardson, Alan. "Nineteenth Century Children's Satire and the Ambivalent Reader." *Children's Literature Association Quarterly* 15, no. 3 (fall 1990): 122–126.

——. "Romanticism and the End of Childhood." In *Literature and the Child: Romantic Continuations, Postmodern Contestations*, edited by James Holt McGavran, 23–43. Iowa City: University of Iowa Press, 1999.

Richler, Mordecai. *Jacob Two-Two Meets the Hooded Fang*. New York: Knopf, 1975.

Rivers, Karen. *Dream Water*. Victoria: Orca, 1999.

Rollin, Lucy. *Cradle and All: A Cultural and Psychoanalytic Reading of Nursery Rhymes*. Jackson: University Press of Mississippi, 1992.

Rollin, Lucy, and Mark West. *Psychoanalytic Responses to Children's Literature*. Jefferson, NC: McFarland, 1999.

Rose, Jacqueline. *The Case of Peter Pan; or, The Impossibility of Children's Fiction*. London: Macmillan, 1984.

Rosen, Michael. "Raising the Issues." *Signal* 76 (Jan. 1995): 26–44.

Rowling, J. K. *Harry Potter and the Chamber of Secrets*. New York: Arthur A. Levine, 1999.

——. *Harry Potter and the Deathly Hallows*. New York: Arthur A. Levine, 2007.

——. *Harry Potter and the Goblet of Fire*. New York: Arthur A. Levine, 2000.

——. *Harry Potter and the Half-Blood Prince*. New York: Arthur A. Levine, 2005.

——. *Harry Potter and the Order of the Phoenix*. New York: Arthur A. Levine, 2003.

——. *Harry Potter and the Prisoner of Azkaban*. New York: Arthur A. Levine, 1999.

——. *Harry Potter and the Sorcerer's Stone*. New York: Arthur A. Levine, 1998.

Rudd, David. "Beatrix Potter and Jacques Derrida—Problematic Bedfellows in the Teaching of Children's Literature?" *English in Education* 30, no. 1 (1996): 8–17.

———. "Theorising and Theories: The Conditions of Possibility of Children's Literature." In Hunt, *Encyclopedia*, 2nd ed., 29–43.

Ruskin, John. *The Art Criticism of John Ruskin*. Edited by Robert L. Hiebert. Garden City, NY: Doubleday Anchor, 1964.

Said, Edward. *Orientalism*. New York: Pantheon, 1978.

Sale, Roger. *Fairy Tales and After: From Snow White to E. B. White*. Cambridge, MA: Harvard University Press, 1978.

Saussure, Ferdinand de. *Course in General Linguistics*. New York: McGraw-Hill, 1966.

Scieszka, John. *The Stinky Cheese Man and Other Fairly Stupid Tales*. New York: Viking, 1992.

Scott, Carole. "Between Me and the World: Clothes as Mediator between Self and Society in the Work of Beatrix Potter." *Lion and the Unicorn* 16, no. 2 (Dec. 1992): 192–198.

———. "Clothed in Nature or Nature Clothed: Dress as Metaphor in the Illustrations of Beatrix Potter and C. M. Barker." *Children's Literature* 22 (1994): 70–89.

———. "An Unusual Hero: Perspective and Point of View in *The Tale of Peter Rabbit*." In Mackey, *Beatrix Potter's Peter Rabbit*, 19–30.

Sedgwick, Eve Kosofsky. *Epistemology of the Closet*. Berkeley: University of California Press, 1990.

Sendak, Maurice. *Caldecott & Co.: Notes on Books & Pictures*. New York: Noonday, 1990.

———. *In the Night Kitchen*. New York: Harper, 1970.

———. *Outside over There*. New York: Harper, 1981.

———. *Where the Wild Things Are*. New York: Harper, 1963.

Shannon, C. E. "A Mathematical Theory of Communication." *Bell System Technical Journal* 27 (July, Oct., 1948): 379–423, 623–656. http://cm.bell-labs.com/cm/ms/what/shannonday/paper.html (accessed May 26, 2007).

Shavit, Zohar. *Poetics of Children's Literature*. Athens: University of Georgia Press, 1986.

Showalter, Elaine. *Sexual Anarchy: Gender and Culture at the Fin de Siècle*. New York: Viking, 1990.

Silvey, Anita. *Children's Books and Their Creators*. Boston: Houghton Mifflin, 1995.

Siskin, Clifford L. *The Historicity of Romantic Discourse*. New York: Oxford University Press, 1988.

Smedman, Sarah M. "Springs of Hope: Recovery of Primordial Time in 'Mythic' Novels for Young Readers." *Children's Literature in Education* 16 (1988): 91–108.

Smith, Lillian. *The Unreluctant Years: A Critical Approach to Children's Literature*. Harmondsworth, Middlesex: Penguin, 1976.

Sobol, Donald. *Encyclopedia Brown, Boy Detective*. 1963. Nashville: Thomas Nelson, 1973.

———. *Encyclopedia Brown and the Case of the Secret Pitch*. New York: Lodestar-Dutton, 1965.

———. *Encyclopedia Brown Keeps the Peace*. New York: Lodestar-Dutton, 1969.

Southall, Ivan. "Sources and Responses." In Haviland, *The Open-Hearted Audience*, 83–99.

Spiegelman, Art. "In the Dumps." *New Yorker*, Sept. 27, 1993, 80–81.

Spitz, Ellen Handler. *Inside Picture Books*. New Haven, CT: Yale University Press, 1999.

Stacey, Cherilyn. *How Do You Spell Abducted?* Calgary, AB: Red Deer Press, 2002.

Stainton Rogers, Rex, and Wendy Stainton Rogers. *Stories of Childhood: Shifting Agendas of Child Concern.* Toronto: University of Toronto Press, 1992.

———. "Word Children." In *Children in Culture: Approaches to Childhood,* edited by Karín Lesnik-Oberstein, 178–203. New York: St. Martin's, 1998.

Steig, Michael. "Never Going Home: Reflections on Reading, Adulthood, and the Possibility of Children's Literature." *Children's Literature Association Quarterly* 18, no. 1 (spring 1993): 36–39.

Steig, William. *Dominic.* New York: Farrar, Straus, Giroux, 1972.

Stephens, John. "Editor's Introduction: Always Facing the Issues—Preoccupations in Australian Children's Literature." *Lion and the Unicorn* 27, no. 2 (April 2003): v–xvii.

———. *Language and Ideology in Children's Fiction.* London: Longman, 1992.

———. "Representation of Place in Australian Children's Picture Books." In *Voices from Far Away: Current Trends in International Children's Literature Research,* edited by Maria Nikolajeva, 97–118. Stockholm: Centrum för Barnkulturfoskning vid Stockholm Universitet, 1995.

Stephens, Rebecca. "Harry and Hierarchy: Book Banning as a Reaction to the Subversion of Authority." In Anatol, *Reading Harry Potter,* 51–65.

Stevenson, Robert Louis. "My Shadow." In *A Child's Garden of Verses and Underwoods.* New York: Current Literature, 1906. Bartleby.com, 2000: www.bartleby.com/188/119.html (accessed June 7, 2007).

———. *Treasure Island.* 1883. New York: Signet, 1998.

Stewig, John Warren. *Children and Literature.* Chicago: Rand McNally, 1980.

Stine, R. L. *Monster Blood.* New York: Scholastic, 1992.

Stott, Jon C. "Pseudo-sublimity and Inarticulate Mumblings in Violent Juxtaposition: The World of Comic Books." *Children's Literature Association Quarterly* 7, no. 1 (spring 1982): 10–12.

Stott, Jon C., and Christine Doyle Francis. "'Home' and 'Not Home' in Children's Stories: Getting There—and Being Worth It." *Children's Literature in Education* 24, no. 3 (1993): 223–233.

Streatfeild, Noel. *Ballet Shoes.* London: Dent, 1936.

Summerfield, Geoffrey. *Fantasy and Reason: Children's Literature in the Eighteenth Century.* Athens: University of Georgia Press, 1984.

Suransky, Valerie Polakow. *The Erosion of Childhood.* Chicago: University of Chicago Press, 1982.

Tan, Shaun. *The Lost Thing.* Sydney: Lothian, 2001.

Taplin, Oliver. "A Surplus of Signifiers." *Essays in Criticism* 26 (1976): 339–345.

Teare, Elizabeth. "Harry Potter and the Technology of Magic." In Whited, *The Ivory Tower and Harry Potter,* 329–342.

Temple, Charles, Miriam Martinez, Junko Yokota, and Alice Naylor. *Children's Literature in Children's Hands: An Introduction to Their Literature.* Boston: Allyn and Bacon, 1998.

Todorov, Tzvetan. "The Origin of Genres." *New Literary History* 8, no. 1 (autumn 1976): 159–170.

Tomlinson, Carl M., and Carol Lynch-Brown. *Essentials of Children's Literature.* Rev. ed. Boston: Allyn and Bacon, 1996.

Townsend, John Rowe. *A Sense of Story.* London: Longman, 1971.

———. "Standards for Criticism for Children's Literature." In *The Signal Approach to Children's Books,* edited by Nancy Chambers, 193–207. Metuchen, NJ: Scarecrow, 1980.

———. "Under Two Hats." In Haviland, *The Open-Hearted Audience,* 133–151.

Toye, William. "Preface." In Egoff, *The New Republic of Childhood,* xi–xiv.

Travers, Pamela. *Mary Poppins.* 1934. San Diego: Harcourt Brace, 1997.

Trimmer, Sarah. "On the Care Which Is Requisite in the Choice of Books for Children." 1803. In Haviland, *Children and Literature,* 4–7.

Trites, Roberta. *Disturbing the Universe: Power and Repression in Adolescent Literature.* Iowa City: University of Iowa Press, 2000.

———. "The Harry Potter Novels as a Test Case for Adolescent Literature." *Style* 35, no. 3 (fall 2001): 472–485.

———. "The Uncanny in Literature." *Children's Literature Association Quarterly* 26, no. 4 (winter 2001–2002): 162.

Tucker, Nicholas. "The Rise and Rise of Harry Potter." *Children's Literature in Education* 30, no. 4 (1999): 221–234.

Turner-Vorbeck, Tammy. "Pottermania: Good Clean Fun or Cultural Hegemony?" In Heilman, *Harry Potter's World,* 13–24.

"The 25 Most Intriguing People '95." *People Weekly,* Dec. 25, 1995, 102–103.

Vygotsky, L. S. *The Vygotsky Reader.* Edited by René van der Veer and Jaan Valsiner. Oxford: Blackwell, 1996.

Waddey, Lucy. "Home in Children's Fiction: Three Patterns. " *Children's Literature Association Quarterly* 8, no. 1 (spring 1983): 13–15.

Wall, Barbara. *The Narrator's Voice: The Dilemma of Children's Fiction.* New York: St. Martin's, 1991.

Wallace, Jo-Ann. "De-scribing *The Water-Babies:* 'The Child' in Post-colonial Theory." In *De-scribing Empire: Post-colonialism and Textuality,* edited by Chris Tiffin and Alan Lawson, 171–184. London: Routledge, 1994.

Walsh, Sue. "Author and Authorship. Effigies of Effie: On Kipling's Biographies." In Lesnik-Oberstein, *Children's Literature: New Approaches,* 25–50.

———. "Child/Animal: It's the 'Real' Thing." In "Children in Literature." Special issue, *Yearbook of English Studies* 32 (2002): 151–162.

Walter, Virginia. *Making Up Megaboy.* Illustrated by Katrina Roeckelein. New York: DK Ink, 1998.

Watts, Isaac. "Against Idleness and Mischief." 1715. In Demers and Moyles, *From Instruction to Delight,* 68.

Webb, Jean. "Text, Culture, and Postcolonial Children's Literature: A Comparative Perspective." In McGillis, *Voices of the Other,* 71–88.

Weber, Max. *The Protestant Ethic and the Spirit of Capitalism.* 1905. *Weberian Sociology of Religion.* www.ne.jp/asahi/moriyuki/abukuma/weber/world/ethic/pro_eth_frame.html (accessed June 17, 2006).

Weinreich, Torben. *Children's Literature: Art or Pedagogy?* Frederiksberg, Denmark: Roskilde University Press, 2000.

———. "What Is So Special about Children's Literature?" Articles and Papers. Danish Centre for Children's Literature. www.cfb.dk/site.aspx?p=738 (accessed May 29, 2007).

Westman, Karin E. "Specters of Thatcherism: Contemporary British Culture in J. K. Rowling's Harry Potter Series." In Whited, *The Ivory Tower and Harry Potter*, 305–328.

White, E. B. *Charlotte's Web*. New York: Harper, 1952.

Whited, Lana A., ed. *The Ivory Tower and Harry Potter: Perspectives on a Literary Phenomenon*. Columbia: University of Missouri Press, 2002.

Whiteley, Opal. *The Diary of Opal Whiteley*. 1920. *Intersect Digital Library*. http://intersect .uoregon.edu/opal/ (accessed June 9, 2007).

Wieler, Diana. *Bad Boy*. Toronto: Groundwood-Douglas and McIntyre, 1989.

Wilkie-Stibbs, Christine. *The Feminine Subject in Children's Literature*. New York: Routledge, 2002.

Williams, Raymond. *Marxism and Literature*. Oxford: Oxford University Press, 1977.

Wordsworth, William. "Ode: Intimations of Immortality from Recollections of Early Childhood." Representative Poetry Online. http://rpo.library.utoronto.ca/poem/2352.html (accessed May 21, 2007).

——. "The Tables Turned." Representative Poetry Online. http://rpo.library.utoronto.ca/ poem/ 2373.html (accessed May 21, 2007).

Wyile, Andrea Schwenke. "Expanding the View of First-Person Narration." *Children's Literature in Education* 30, no. 3 (1999): 185–202.

——. "First-Person Engaging Narration in the Picture Book: Verbal and Pictorial Variations." *Children's Literature in Education* 32, no. 3 (2001): 191–202.

Wynne-Jones, Tim. *The Maestro*. Vancouver: Groundwood-Douglas and McIntyre, 1995.

——. *Zoom at Sea*. Toronto: Douglas and McIntyre, 1983.

Zipes, Jack. *The Brothers Grimm: From Enchanted Forests to the Modern World*. New York: Routledge, 1988.

——. *Sticks and Stones: The Troublesome Success of Children's Literature from Slovenly Peter to Harry Potter*. New York: Routledge, 2001.

Zipes, Jack, Lissa Paul, Lynne Vallone, Peter Hunt, and Gillian Avery, eds. *The Norton Anthology of Children's Literature: The Traditions in English*. New York: Norton, 2005.

actions, focus on, 14–15, 65–67, 77, 214–16

Adams, Gillian, 126, 246–47, 248

adaptation theories, 128, 142

addressee, 148

adults: as audience, 218; children as different from, 63, 99–100, 167, 264–65; hidden, 130, 206–10, 265, 279, 340–41; as producers of children's literature, 85–86, 156, 212; protection of children by, 53, 63–64, 78, 121, 158, 163; as purchasers of children's books, 4–5; as readers of children's books, 140–41, 206–8, 338–39; reading as, 82–90; right to wield power of, 34, 35, 78; views of childhood by, 67–68, 78, 84–85, 147–48, 149, 151–53, 159–61, 188. *See also* writers

Aeneid (Virgil), 316

Aesop's fables, 218, 270, 320

"Against Idleness and Mischief" (Watts), 37

Agassiz, Louis, 325

Alcott, Louisa May, 174, 277–78

Aldrich, Thomas, 333

Alice's Adventures in Wonderland (Carroll): ambivalence in, 271; as canonical, 277–78; child readers of, 210; as children's literature, 2; compared to *Plain City,* 54; desire and knowledge in, 37–43; ending of, 41, 60; home/away/home pattern in, 59; interpretive attention to, 15; literary systems and, 208; as metafiction, 17–18, 315; narrative of, 266; narrator of, 21–22; pastoral idyll and, 221; plot of, 1, 236–37; selection of, 94, 98–100; shadow text of, 14–18; variation in, 72–73

Allor, Martin, 296

Althusser, Louis, 139

Alton, Ann, 334

ambivalence: in *Alice,* 271; in *Anne of Green Gables,* 226–27; audience and, 185; centrality of, 80, 181–85, 249–50, 337–38; change and stasis, 81; home/away/home pattern and, 67–68; hybridity and, 256; implied readers and, 208–10; mimicry and, 186–87; Orientalism and, 166–67. *See also* binaries

American books: in Australia, 105; in Canada, 89, 106, 293–94

Anatol, Giselle Liza, 333, 336, 337

Anderson, Benedict, 295

Ang, Ien, 301

animals: in *Dr. Dolittle,* 43, 71, 72; in *Henry Huggins,* 50–51; in *Peter Rabbit,* 321–24; stories about, 19, 191; sublimation and, 202

Animorphs books (Applegate), 146, 180

Anne of Green Gables (Montgomery): ambivalence in, 226–27; as Canadian, 290, 291; gender and, 173, 174; on growing up, 186; interpretations of, 93–94; repetition in, 232

Applebaum, Peter, 333

Applegate, K. A., Animorphs books of, 146, 180

archetypes, 126–27

Are You There, God? It's Me, Margaret (Blume), 20

Ariès, Philippe, 247

assumptions: of adults, 67–68, 78, 84–85, 147–48, 149, 151–53, 159–61, 188; about adult writers, 151; of change, 31, 78; about child readers, 224–25; about children's literature, 81, 248–49; choice of six texts and, 92–106; of gender, 173–76, 178–79; about genre, 106–16; reading as adult, 82–90; of representativeness, 90–92, 102–6; of right of adults to wield power, 34, 35, 78